ICONS
OF THE
AMERICAN MARKETPLACE

CONSUMER BRAND EXCELLENCE

AMERICAN
BENCHMARK
PRESS
New York

 Published in the United States by Random House Custom Media, a member of The Crown Publishing Group, a division of Random House, Inc., New York.

For all inquiries regarding Random House Custom Media products and services, please write to custommedia@randomhouse.com.

Printed in the United States of America

Book design by Blue Cup Creative

This book may be purchased for business or promotional use for special sales. For information, write to: Special Markets Department, Random House, Inc., 1745 Broadway, New York, NY 10019 or specialmarkets@randomhouse.com.

10 9 8 7 6 5 4 3 2 1
Library of Congress Cataloging in Publication Data:
Icons of the American marketplace : consumer brand excellence. – 1st ed.
p. cm.
Includes index.
ISBN 978-0-307-38345-7 (alk. Paper)
1. Brand name products—United States.
HD69.B713 2007
658.8'27--dc22
2007002625

Contents

Introduction:

William J. McEwen, PhD

Building a Great Brand … and Keeping it Great

We're in awe of the brands in this book, brands that truly stand apart from all others. We wonder just how they got there, and we seek to follow their lead because we want to capture some of their magic. But greatness is not about mimicking the success of others.

At a fundamental level, there's really not that much of a mystery. A great brand is simply a powerful promise. This promise creates a very personal, emotional connection with consumers. But it's not enough to have a big idea and it's not enough to make a big promise. The promise must be *kept* … not just once, but at each and every consumer encounter. A great brand is much like a great marriage. It takes work, time, mutual respect, and evidence of real commitment.

And so, great brands don't just happen. Great brand relationships aren't random events. They can't be built with a single Super Bowl commercial, however memorable it might be. There is much more to greatness than a distinctive logo, a stunning package design, and a high-profile ad campaign. Brands touch customers in many more important ways. And, since promises must be kept, the brand promise must be shared not just with consumers, but with every person in the organization who touches a customer. That's because it's the promise-keepers who ultimately make the difference between a promise with potential and one with real brand-building power.

The hallmarks of greatness are easy to see, but difficult to achieve. Great brands instill confidence but, even more, they breed passion. They create passionate customers. And they enkindle passionate employees, as proud of the products and services they provide as are the customers who buy and use them. It is upon this platform of passion that a brand's real equity depends.

William J. McEwen, PhD, is a global practice leader at The Gallup Organization, where he consults with major clients on brand communications and brand equity management. Before joining Gallup, he spent 25 years in senior planning and account management positions with leading advertising agencies, including McCann-Erickson, FCB, and D'Arcy. Dr. McEwen's brand experience ranges from snack foods and beer to computers and business banking. He received a doctorate from Michigan State University and was a tenured faculty member at the University of Connecticut. Dr. McEwen lives in Newport Beach, California.

The American Benchmark Press

Advisory Board

Lee Abrams

Lee Abrams

XM's senior vice president and chief creative officer, Lee Abrams, has been shaping the American radio industry for over three decades. During the past 40 years he has brought unparalleled ratings and economic success to radio stations in over 200 markets, including 97 of the top 100. In the radio ring, he has won 318 programming battles, while losing only 11. In 1993 Newsweek listed Abrams as one of America's "100 Cultural Elite" for his contributions to creating modern-day radio; *Radio Ink* listed Abrams as one of the 75 most important radio figures of all time.

Abrams joined XM in June 1998 to help create the next generation of radio: satellite radio. With 100+ stations to develop and program, Abrams is once again challenged to reinvigorate the radio landscape.

As a founding partner of Burkhart/Abrams, the Atlanta-based consulting giant, Abrams invented and built the first successful FM format, "Album Rock." He also designed numerous other highly successful radio formats including the first "Classic Rock" format at San Francisco's KFOG; the first FM "Urban/Dance" format at New York's WKTU, and the first "New Age/Jazz" format. In addition, he created the original blueprint for the NBC Radio Network. His corporate clients have included every major broadcast group as well as Coca-Cola, TNT, Sony, and Walt Disney.

In 1989, Abrams joined ABC Networks as an internal consultant and oversaw the revolutionary "Z-Rock" format, which was the first satellite-delivered "Superstation," as well as being the first "Active Rock" format, and was instrumental in the launch of many top morning radio shows including *The Howard Stern Show.*

While at XM, Abrams has invited artists ranging from Bob Dylan to Snoop Dogg to create original radio shows.

Musically, Abrams produced the Grammy Award–winning CD *Ah Via Musicom* by Eric Johnson, has appeared on several Alan Parsons Project CDs, and has worked with major labels and recording artists as a consultant and label head. His clients have included such industry leaders as the Moody Blues, Yes, Steve Winwood, Iron Maiden, Bob Seger, and Robert Palmer.

Abrams' other media projects have included the redesign of *Rolling Stone* magazine and the launch of the cable networks TNT and MTV. He has served as an advisor to dozens of entertainment companies. In addition, Abrams has been the subject of feature articles in thousands of consumer publications, including *Playboy, Esquire,* the *New York Times, GQ, People,* the *Wall Street Journal,* the *Los Angeles Times,* the *Washington Post,* and *Wired.*

Gay Bryant

Gay Bryant

Success magazine editor-in-chief Gay Bryant, a veteran of national women's magazines, has spent more than 25 years in the consumer publishing industry in senior editorial roles. She served as vice president and editor of *Family Circle* and editor-in-chief of *Mirabella,* where she won the National Magazine Award for General Excellence. Bryant has also held top editorial positions at *Working Woman, Executive Female, and Corporate Board Member.* For four years Bryant served as editorial director of Sydney-based Murdoch Media, where she was responsible for six publications *(Family Circle, Marie Claire, Marie Claire Lifestyle, New Woman, Better Homes & Gardens and Men's Health),* plus magazine development and masthead television programming. Acknowledged for her ability to launch, develop, and turn around national magazines, Bryant also excels at the hands-on aspects of editing, from budget management to cover selection and caption writing.

Cathy Gudis

Cathy Gudis

Cathy Gudis is a professor of history at the University of California, Riverside, where she teaches courses in the history of advertising and mass media, consumer culture, and urban studies. She received a BA in philosophy from Smith College and a PhD in American studies from Yale University, and has held fellowships at the Smithsonian Institution's National Museum of American History and the Graham Foundation for the Advanced Study in the Fine Arts, among others. Dr. Gudis is the author of *Buyways: Billboards, Automobiles, and the American Landscape* (Routledge, 2004), a book about the history of the outdoor advertising industry. She is a coeditor of *Cultures of Commerce: Representation and American Business Culture, 1877–1960* (Palgrave/Macmillan, 2006), a book of essays on how American commerce has been depicted in fiction, film, advertising, and architecture. Gudis has worked for many years as an editor and curator for art and history museums nationwide, recently completing a multimedia, citywide public history project in Los Angeles entitled *Curating the City.* She is currently working on a book entitled *To Market, To Market,* a history of the logo, the big box store, and the cargo container.

G. Kelly O'Dea

G. Kelly O'Dea

Described in a 2005 Harvard Business School case as "a global marketing pioneer, business builder, and change leader," Kelly is a recognized strategy and marketing expert with a 25-year track record that crosses virtually all market categories. His experience runs deep in building profitable brands, global networks, and clients' businesses across channels, borders, and change cycles. He is an outspoken advocate of the need to evolve business models in today's dramatically changing marketplace—what he calls the next economy. In 2004 he brought these beliefs to market with the launch of AllianceHPL Worldwide, a global strategic innovation firm, organized as a unique cooperative of leading edge resources focused on helping clients to raise the game with innovative solutions that optimize profitable growth, value, and market leadership.

Kelly has worked with many of the world's blue-chip accounts including IBM, Compaq, Samsung, Microsoft, Fujitsu, AT&T, Boeing, McDonald's, Ford, Shell, PepsiCo, Kraft, and Unilever. He also spent 12 years living and working overseas.

In mid-2002 Kelly moved within Interpublic Group (IPG) from FCB to the Advanced Marketing Services division as vice chairman to focus on leveraging the firm's strategic assets and advisory capabilities. This included the successful repositioning and re-launch of MCA (Marketing Corporation of America) in 2003. His work at IPG served as the strategic foundation for AllianceHPL.

Kelly spent many years with Ogilvy & Mather Worldwide, where he was president of Worldwide Client Services and a member of the Worldwide Board and Executive Committee. He designed and led Ogilvy's successful global account restructuring based on networking and transnational brand management, a subject that was highlighted in a popular Harvard Business School case study on change leadership. He won the David Ogilvy Annual Award three times for outstanding client results and also played a lead role in winning several major global accounts, including IBM, TWA, AT&T, Ford, and Jaguar, all of which he managed worldwide. During his five-year tenure as president of Worldwide Client Services, total global client revenue grew 52%, and operating profits nearly tripled.

He has served on various corporate, industry, and non-profit boards throughout his career and devotes much of his public service time to the field of education. He is chairman of Outward Bound International, the global leader in experiential education, and Operation Tone Up, an organization devoted to getting children into the early habit of healthy living. He lectures at leading graduate schools and is a regular speaker and media commentator on subjects of global marketing, the technology market, next economy issues and change leadership.

Educated in the United States and Europe, Kelly graduated first in his class with an International MBA from Thunderbird Graduate School of International Management. He holds a BA in political science and economics from the University of Portland (Oregon). He serves as a trustee and board director of both institutions.

In his free time, Kelly is an active sportsman who enjoys competitive skiing, racquet sports, golf and offshore yacht racing (where he has logged several thousand miles around the world and has been part of the winning crews on the Fastnet and South China Sea Challenge.) He has also hosted / led several Outward Bound expeditions in various parts of the world.

Bernd Schmitt

Bernd Schmitt

Bernd Schmitt is the Robert D. Calkins Professor of International Business at Columbia Business School in New York, where he directs the Center on Global Brand Leadership, the leading global forum on branding issues for researchers and executives. He is co-founder and CEO of The EX Group.

He is widely recognized for his major contribution to branding, marketing, and management through his unique focus on the customer experience. His frameworks and tools are used worldwide by companies committed to delivering value and a great experience to their customers.

Schmitt has authored or co-authored more than 50 articles in marketing and psychology journals and six books which have been translated into 16 languages. In his acclaimed book *Experiential Marketing,* he provided a framework for an integrated marketing approach that moves beyond the functional features and benefits of a brand. His book *Customer Experience Management* provides a five-step process for connecting with customers at every touchpoint.

Schmitt has consulted and developed brand and experience strategies for clients in consumer package goods, automobiles, electronics, software, financial services, pharmaceuticals, beauty and cosmetics, hospitality, and media. His consulting and seminar clients have included more than 50 companies in both consumer and B2B markets including Ericsson, Estée Lauder, Henkel, Hilton Hotels, LVMH, McKinsey & Co., Microsoft, Motorola, Philip Morris, Pfizer, Procter & Gamble, SAP, Siemens, Sony, Telefónica, Unilever, Vodafone, and Volkswagen.

He is a frequent keynote speaker at conferences worldwide. He has been profiled on CNNfn's *Business Unusual* show and in several articles in business journals around the world. He appeared on BBC, CNBC, CNBC-Asia, CNN, NHK and on the *Daily Show with Jon Stewart.* He has contributed articles on business issues to the *New York Times,* the Asian *Wall Street Journal,* and the *Financial Times.*

Rod Shade

Roderick N. Shade

Roderick Shade, who founded the renowned design firm by the same name over ten years ago, has designed residences and commercial properties throughout the United States and internationally. His work has been published in *Architectural Digest, House and Garden, House Beautiful,* and a host of newspapers and other fine shelter and lifestyle magazines. Mr. Shade's designs have appeared in several important national show houses, benefiting a variety of charities, including New York's prestigious Kips Bay Decorator Show House, the Traditional Home Show House and the Hamptons Designers Show House. In 2003, shortly after being named to *Architectural Digest*'s list of the world's top 100 designers and architects, he was asked to install a room at the magazine's first and only design exhibit, held at New York's One Central Park in the newly constructed Time Warner Center. In addition, Mr. Shade is currently on the top designer list of *House Beautiful, New York, Gotham,* and *Quest* magazines. Earlier in his career, he founded the acclaimed Harlem United Designer Show House, where his room "Urban Oasis" won accolades from numerous international design pundits.

A visionary in the interior design field, Mr. Shade is a prolific designer of both furniture and fabric. His signature line of residential furniture debuted in 2000 and now includes both traditional and contemporary forms. Mr. Shade's fabric collection for Decorators Walk is available in F. Schumacher & Co. showrooms nationwide. His first book, *Harlem Style,* was published in 2002 and another is planned for late 2006. Located in New York City, Roderick N. Shade Inc. Interior Design specializes in significant and unique "new traditional" interiors infused with glamour, edginess and unexpected surprises, for the traditional or contemporary aesthetic.

Originally from San Diego, Mr. Shade grew up in a construction family and apprenticed at several high-end design firms in Los Angeles and New York. He is passionate about design and enjoys working with clients who "have great ideas, work with me, and trust me to add my own magic and to surpass their expectations." In 2005, Mr. Shade was appointed honorary chair of the San Diego Historical Society Show House and project designer for the *Better Homes and Gardens* "America's Home," to be built in Atlanta. He is also the newest elected Trustee for DIFFA. Shade has appeared on numerous national television shows, including *Trading Spaces, CBS This Morning, Entertainment Tonight,* and *Fox News.*

Brett Shevack

Brett Shevack

Brett Shevack is one of the best known and most highly regarded creative thinkers and entrepreneurs in the advertising and communications industry.

Brett Shevack joined BBDO New York in 2002 in the newly created position of Vice Chairman, Brand Initiatives. This is a unique role to which Brett is ideally suited and a position that is unprecedented in the industry, giving BBDO a tremendous competitive advantage.

In this role, Brett focuses on generating business-building ideas that offer tremendous upside to clients and that complement the work BBDO does. These include new product ideas, programs that strengthen core retailer relationships, strategies to gain competitive leverage against branded and non-branded products, and more. It is a "360-degree perspective" which Brett brings to the business following years as a creative director and, later, as founder of his own agency, Partners & Shevack, an agency that grew to over $300 million in annualized billings, with major clients in a broad range of categories, before it was acquired in 1998.

At BBDO, Brett is the architect of a proprietary BBDO program called "BIG" (Brand Initiatives Generation™)—a new discipline designed to develop an ongoing stream of business-building thinking and ideas for every brand. The program also encourages the agency—in particular account management—to contribute to a client's business as if it was the "owner" of the brand.

He has also been a frequent contributor to industry publications; just recently writing on "open source innovation" and the changing way companies are sourcing new ideas.

Joel Stein

Joel Stein

Joel Stein is desperate for attention. He grew up in Edison, N.J., went to Stanford, and then worked for Martha Stewart for a year. After two years of fact-checking at various publications, he got hired as a sports editor at *Time Out New York.* Two years later he lucked into a job as a staff writer for *Time* magazine, where he has written a dozen cover stories on subjects such as Michael Jordan, Las Vegas, the Internet bubble and—it being *Time* and he being a warm body in the office—low-carb diets. Since 1995, he has been writing a Tuesday op-ed column at the *Los Angeles Times.*

Being desperate for attention, he has appeared on any TV show that asks him: VH1's *I Love the Decade You Tell Me I Love,* HBO's *Phoning It In,* Comedy Central's *Reel Comedy* and E! Entertainment's *101 Hottest Hot Hotties' Hotness.*

He's also written lots of failed network sitcoms, which have paid him very well. This has made ABC his favorite brand in the world.

Abby Terkuhle

Abby Terkuhle

Abby Terkuhle has over 20 years of commercial television promotion, production, and series experience. He is the founder and president of Aboriginal Entertainment, a New York firm that produces original programming for film and television, as well as digital content across multiple media platforms. At Aboriginal, Abby developed and currently serves as executive producer for *Artstar,* an eight-part unscripted high definition series set in the New York art world with Deitch Projects for Gallery HD.

Most recently Abby was founder and president of MTV Animation, the network's full-service production studio. MTV Animation produced such critically acclaimed and commercially successful TV hits as *Aeon Flux, Beavis and Butt-head, Daria, Celebrity Deathmatch* and the theatrical hit *Beavis and Butt-head Do America* which Abby also produced.

As Creative Director at MTV: Music Television, he spearheaded MTV's award-winning, in-house advertising and on-air promotions, establishing MTV as one of the most recognized global brands in entertainment. His interest in new forms of animation changed the look of MTV with groundbreaking station identification and art breaks, shorts, and full-length animated programming, beginning with the Emmy Award–winning *Liquid Television.*

Earlier in his career, Abby was a film segment producer for NBC's *Saturday Night Live* and a producer for Showtime/The Movie Channel. He is the recipient of numerous prestigious television programming, marketing, and promotion accolades including the Emmy, Clio, Cable Ace, Broadcast Design, and Promax Awards. He holds a BA in communications from Loyola University and lives in New York City with his wife and daughter.

Jean Hoehn Zimmerman

Jean Hoehn Zimmerman

Jean Hoehn Zimmerman recently retired as executive vice president of Chanel, Inc. after 27 years of increasing responsibilities culminating in direct responsibility for long-range divisional planning, marketing, sales, advertising, and product development for the cosmetic and fragrance division in the United States. Prior to that, she was at Estée Lauder, Bristol-Myers Squibb, and YSL-Charles of the Ritz. After graduating with honors from the University of Florida in 1968, Jean came to New York and never left.

In addition to being a working mother, Jean is a past president and chairman and a current board member of Cosmetic Executive Women. She has also served on the Fragrance Foundation board of directors and has raised funds for The New York Committee for Cerebral Palsy and the March of Dimes. She currently serves on the advisory board for FIT Graduate School, where she is also an adjunct faculty member. She has received many awards for her philanthropic efforts, including the Cartier Scholarship Recognition Award, the Cosmetic Executive Woman Achiever Award, the University of Florida Alumni of Distinction Award and the Leah Harrison Humanitarian Award for Montefiore Medical Center after donating her kidney to her father several years ago. Since retiring, she spends her time consulting, traveling, spending time with her family, and tuning up her golf and tennis skills. She lives in New York City with her husband, Arne. She has three grown children, two step-children and a dog, Sadie.

Essays
by the American Benchmark Press
Advisory Board

Great brands have souls. In this data-driven era, it's not hard to successfully market garbage. All you have to do is discover a hot button and create an effective campaign to convince people you have what they want or need.... and that is the problem with life in the 21st Century.

Brands that have succeeded over the span of time all have certain integrity and quality that resonates beyond the ad and marketing blitz. Drill into that integrity and you will find a soul. It can be a person or a united group with a vision and a mission, and that mission reaches beyond the commercial implications. It is a spiritual commitment to delivering a product with passion and purpose that breathes humanity more than business plan.

It is all about the balance of art and business. An organic idea executed with imagination and expertise. One that doesn't *need* the *ubiquitous* hype that's engulfed our lives.

America's marketers have shot themselves in the foot with dated campaigns that "market revolution" but in fact offer nothing new or needed. There is an inevitable backlash to the hype ... the over-sell without substance that's about to occur. The lies and exaggerations that worked for so long are being discounted, and the survivors will be the brands with ... a soul.

–Lee Abrams

As Editor-in-Chief of *Success* magazine, I have come to realize that with a word like "success," branding becomes a huge challenge. The complexity of such an emotive and significant idea is impossible to capture with font and color alone. Thus, we knew that a simple logo would never be sufficient; it would take an entire magazine. We are attempting to create a community of like-minded businesspeople who want success to be the central characteristic of their lives, and that requires a willingness to allow our readers to define what that means for themselves—we do not represent our version of success; we represent theirs. Our brand must be constantly reinvented, an idea that evolves with the current iterations of what success means, as varied and individual as each of our readers. We feature people who have identified the life they want and worked hard to achieve it. In the end, they are our brand. They are a greater symbol of "success" than the word on our cover could ever be.

–Gay Bryant

It is difficult to imagine a time when brands weren't part of the American lexicon and global cultural identity. Yet they are actually a recent phenomenon, and the history of their emergence narrates huge shifts over the last 100 years or so in business, culture, and the expression of modern selfhood. Brands were crucial elements in transforming America from a nation of villages to a mass urban culture, unified around the mass-produced stuff that after industrialization people increasingly bought, wore, and used on a daily basis. By wrapping a product with nifty new packaging (including the high-tech marvels of the early 1900s, such as cellophane), giving it a name, and protecting it by trademark, manufacturers could seek out national, and even international markets for their mass-produced goods. Without brands, consumption could never have kept up with efficient production, and advertising would not have emerged as a respectable and lucrative profession capable of knitting small and big towns and cities together through a common language of images, slogans, and desire.

Brands therefore marked a critical transformation of American culture: from a nation focused on industrial production, thrift, and a Protestant work ethic, to a nation organized around consumption and immediate self-gratification. Shopping and spending replaced prudence and saving. Brands also conferred personality, meaning, and emotional significance to goods that had previously been merely stuff (think of the myriad meanings attached to products as indistinguishable as soap, or water). With this transformation, the objective estimation of value based on materials and cost of production became moot; subjective exchange value offered far more, and was far more inscrutable, unstable, and (advertisers hoped) expansive. Brands helped products transcend their material roots.

Today, brands are part of a universal language that signifies who we are and what we want to be as individuals, communities, and nations. Yet their meanings are always in flux, open to revision, changing continuously. Brand meanings change not just at the hands of image-makers and brand managers but moreso by the people who ultimately buy, use, and thus confer value on products. Brands, then, are the ultimate markers of cultural values and historical change, beyond the ken or control of critics and historians, no matter how we try to understand their meanings. That job is up to the consumer market itself.

–Cathy Gudis

Brands 2.0—Designed by YOU

Time magazine's designation of "you" as the 2006 Person of the Year served as timely recognition of the fundamental changes being driven by the rapid rise of the World Wide Web. According to *Time*, "It's a story about community and collaboration on a scale never seen before...about the cosmic compendium of knowledge... and about the many wresting power from the few..."

It's also about the next generation of branding and "you" are right in the center of it.

The Revolution Becomes Reality

The implications and challenges for brands and branding in a digital world are huge. While successful brands will still be those that build superior relationships based on performance, value, and trust, the dynamics of reaching and interacting with potential customers will continue to dramatically change.

Armed with mountains of internet-generated information and thousands of channels available for communication on all levels, the balance of power between company and customer has flip-flopped—the customer is now informed, in charge, and ever more discriminating. Non-performing products and services die fast because people know more and share more in their various digital communities. Good products and services proliferate, from both large and small companies. This levels the competitive playing field and provides significantly more choice (but produces headaches for those trying to sell their brands).

Out with Old ... Fast!

It's therefore no surprise that traditional branding approaches of yesteryear are fast becoming extinct as the landscape changes. Brands must now compete for customers' attention in an increasingly fragmented, complex web of connections. Customers' use of media is changing—from few to many different channels (most of which are now delivered via the Internet)—and the nature of communicating is evolving from passive to interactive.

Mass marketing is dead. It's no longer one-to-millions, it's millions-one-by-one. Simply finding the right people to see the brand's message is only part of the challenge. It must now also be the right message at the right time in the right form. You can't simply intrude with print, banner, or TV messages on the Internet. The Web requires its own form of communication and conversation that grabs the attention of potential customers in relevant ways. Otherwise, "you" will reject them.

The Future is Now

We are only now beginning to see the successive waves of change that will progressively transform the face of branding worldwide. It is entirely conceivable that future brand relationships will be largely digital as technologies converge and the World Wide Web environment develops into an everyday community destination for people. Increasingly, "you" will directly affect the future design of products as marketers learn how to listen to the rich feedback customers give through their channel choices, community forums, chat rooms and blogs.

Brands will become increasingly more important and valuable in this new world. Those brands that adapt will be rewarded and prosper. Those that don't will suffer quickly. In all cases, "you" will be the judge.

–G. Kelly O'Dea

1. Brand experiences don't just happen; they need to be planned. In that planning process, be creative; use surprise, intrigue and, at times, provocation. Shake things up.

2. Think about the customer's brand experience first—and then about the functional features and benefits of your brand.

3. Be obsessive about the details of the experience. Traditional satisfaction models are missing the sensory, gut-feel, brain blasting, all-body, all-feeling, all-mind "EJ" experience. (EJ=Exultate Jubilate.) Let the customer delight in exultant jubilation!

4. Find the "duck" for your brand. Several years ago, I stayed for the first time in the Conrad Hotel in Hong Kong. In the bathroom on the rim of the bathtub they had placed a bright yellow rubber duck with a red mouth. I fell in love with the idea (and the duck) immediately. This little duck has become part of my life; I mention it in my speeches. They have really struck a chord with this little duck. It's the one thing that I always remember when I think about the hotel—and it becomes the starting point of remembering the entire hotel experience. The lesson here? Every company needs to have a duck for its brand. That is, a little element that triggers, frames, summarizes, stylizes the experience.

5. Think consumption situation, not product. That is, "grooming in the bathroom," not "razor." "Casual meal," not "hot dog." "Travel," not "transportation." Move along the socio-cultural.

6. Strive for "holistic brand experiences" that dazzle the senses, appeal to the heart, challenge the intellect, are relevant to people's lifestyles and provide relational, i.e., social identity appeal.

7. Profile and track experiential impact with the Experiential Grid. Profile different types of experiences (SENSE, FEEL, THINK, ACT, and RELATE) across experience providers (logos, ads, packaging, advertising, web sites etc.)

8. Use methodologies eclectically. Some methods may be quantitative (questionnaire analyses or logic); others qualitative (a day in the life of the customer). Some may be verbal (focus group); others visual (digital camera techniques). Some may be conducted in artificial lab settings; others in pubs or cafes. Anything goes! Be explorative and creative, and worry about reliability, validity and methodological sophistication later.

9. Consider how the brand experience changes when extending the brand—into new categories, onto the web, around the globe. Ask yourself how the brand be leveraged in a new category, in an electronic medium, in a different culture through experiential strategies.

10. Add dynamism and "Dionysianism" to your company and brand. Most organization and brand owners are too timid, too slow, and too bureaucratic. The term "Dionysian" is associated with the ecstatic, the passionate, the creative. Let this spirit breathe in your organization, and watch how things change.

—Bernd Schmitt

Building great brands is easy.

All it takes are people who bring clear vision, instinctive feel, and relentless creativity to everything they do. Who encourage the flow of new ideas, love what they do and motivate others with their enthusiasm. People who are competitive and want to win. Who are entrepreneurial whether they are working in a startup or within a huge global company. People who think and act like brand owners, whether they are in management, marketing, sales, or on the factory floor. People who are by nature inquisitive and know the importance of gaining a deep understanding of the consumer. People who are passionate evangelists for their brand and make it an important part of their life, whether they eat it, wear it, drive it, or use it.

All it takes is a company that recognizes that strong brands need smart, continuous investment. A company that makes innovation its most important product and recognizes that sacrificing quality for the sake of short term goals is suicide. A company that knows bureaucracy kills innovation blood flow. And creates an open environment that stimulates new thinking. A company that deeply respects its customers.

All it takes is an advertising agency that feels and acts like a stakeholder of the brand and gets deeply involved in every aspect of a client's business. An agency that always recommends what is best for the brand, not just best for the relationship. An agency that aspires to groundbreaking creative work, not just good meetings. An agency that attracts great people in all disciplines and encourages their thinking. An agency that is always out in front of a client, not just reacting.

Yup, building great brands is easy.

–Brett Shevack

During its 25 years on the air, MTV has achieved a greater brand identity than any other television channel. That is, more people are aware of what MTV is and what it stands for than they are with any other network. They may not all want their MTV, but at least they know why.

MTV worked, I think, because it had a simple vision. It took two things the baby boom generation loved—rock and roll and television and put them together in a new kind of visual playground.

As Creative Director of MTV, I ran the On-Air Creative Department. Our challenge in the early days was to create a totally unique environment that would give the network a look, feel, style, pace, intensity and attitude—an identity like nothing else seen before on television. We created this brand recognition through a radical new kind of self-promotion that rejected the irritating marketeering gimmicks—bugs, buzzwords, pontificating new fall slogans—practiced by other networks. Instead, the writers and artists chose to use their promo time, on-air and off-air and on-line to basically screw around, experiment, and have fun.

We resorted to animated IDs, off-center testimonials, funny image promos, and edgy print campaigns that seemed to have no purpose other than to dazzle and entertain. Our door was always open to new ideas; ideas that were done both in-house and out-of-house. Ideas both solicited and unsolicited. We encouraged our people to take risks even if they failed, because failure itself can be an important creative tool. What worked best for us was avoiding two extremes: taking ourselves for granted and taking ourselves too seriously.

We referred to what we did as shameless self promotion, but really one could call it aimless self-promotion. And its unstated message was clear: MTV is a place that likes to screw around, experiment, and have fun. In the process, we got a generation to think of MTV as their channel.

—Abby Terkuhle

Strong Brands are icons and beacons for consumers globally. Whatever the product category, they provide a mental measurement, a status, and a strong positioning against which other competing brands are measured. A brand recognized as being the "best of class" is a language universally understood and acknowledged by consumers all over the world and it offers immediate recognition for what the brand stands for in any language. Interestingly enough, there are specific words and thoughts consumers associate with strong brands, whether they love them or not. If one can keep the brand recognition factors close to the pulse of the consumer and thriving there, the shot for longevity is excellent…as long as the point of differences and the brand strengths remain on top of the marketing pyramid. Every brand has core values that make it what it is…and just as importantly, make it what it isn't.

—Jean Hoehn Zimmerman

ICONS

OF THE AMERICAN MARKETPLACE

CONSUMER BRAND EXCELLENCE

7-Eleven, Inc.

The Slurpee is an American classic—and most people know precisely where to find it—at their local branch of 7-Eleven. 7-Eleven, Inc. is the premier name and largest chain in the convenience retailing industry. Additionally, 7-Eleven was the first convenience store to operate 24 hours a day, sell fresh-brewed coffee in to-go cups, have a self-serve soda fountain, and offer super-size drinks such as the Big Gulp.

7-Eleven began in 1927 when Texan Joe Thompson and his partners formed the Southland Ice Company in Dallas in response to an urgent need for ice in the area. Thompson bought up Texas ice plant operations, adding a few food items at one store on the advice of one of his dock managers, then—because of surprising success—adding food at all locations. Thompson began promoting the grocery operations by calling them Tote'm Stores and erecting totem poles by the docks. He also added gas stations to some locations. By 1936, the company was the largest dairy retailer in the Dallas/Fort Worth area. Ten years later, the company name was changed to The Southland Corporation and the stores were named 7-Eleven, for the hours of store operation at the time. When Thompson died in 1961, his eldest son, John, became president, opening stores in Colorado, New Jersey, and Arizona in 1962 and in Utah, California, and Missouri in 1963.

The Slurpee's origins can be traced to 1959, when a soda machine at a Kansas drive-in stopped working and its owner, Omar Knedlik, resorted to serving bottled soda from a freezer. Customers loved the ultracold, slushy drinks. This led Knedlik to seek out the Dallas machinery manufacturer John E. Mitchell and develop a system for soft-serve soda. Early machines, however did not yield immediate success.

In 1965, one of these machines caught the interest a 7-Eleven zone manager while he was on a visit to a competitor. He persuaded 7-Eleven to test the machines, the success of which led 7-Eleven to add Slurpees to all stores by 1967. Today Slurpees are 7-Eleven's best-selling product—enough of the drinks are sold each year to fill up 12 Olympic-size swimming pools. Slurpees are available in dozens of flavors, depending on the store branch and time of year. 7-Eleven recently launched a Slurpee Web site.

In the early 1970s, Southland franchised the 7-Eleven format in England and Japan. In 1998, Southland acquired the Christy's chain in New England and Red-D-marts in Indiana, among other stores. Finally, in 1999, Southland changed its name to 7-Eleven to reflect the core of its business; in 2000, the company opened its 20,000th store. For its 75th anniversary in 2002, 7-Eleven launched its most extensive advertising campaign ever.

Headquartered in Dallas, Texas, 7-Eleven, Inc. operates or franchises approximately 7,000 7-Eleven stores in the United States and Canada and licenses approximately 23,600 7-Eleven stores in 18 other countries and U.S. territories throughout the world.

Vital Statistics
Established 1927
Founder Joe Thompson
Annual Sales $43 billion (2005)

ATM HERE!
NUMB IN PUBLIC
SLURPEE
GET YOUR COOL ON
SLURPEE
$1.19
$1.35
$1.55
$1.65
$1.19
Coca-Cola
Fanta blue raspberry
Fanta Pina Colada
BLUE blunder BERRy
Darth Dew

Ace Hardware

In 1924, a group of Chicago-area hardware store owners—Richard Hesse, E. Gunnard Lindquist, Frank Burke, and Oscar Fisher—realized that they could reduce costs and optimize their buying power by joining their ventures. In 1928, they incorporated as Ace Stores Inc., named after the World War I "ace" fighter pilots. Hesse was elected president, and by 1949, the company spanned seven states with a total of 133 individual retailers. Hesse converted the company to a cooperative in 1973, the same year he stepped down.

The cooperative was a new form of American business that makes retailers into owners and shareholders of a company. Ace Hardware retailers benefit from a nationwide brand, economies of scale, and centralized warehouses, but they operate independently. Unlike a franchise, each store looks different and may offer a different assortment of items. Retailers pay a fee to use the Ace brand and participate in the network, and they earn dividends on Ace's profits.

Ace thrived from the boom in home improvement that began in the 1970s. Realizing that most customers wanted to repaint their houses, Ace decided it could offer them better paint prices if it opened its own manufacturing facility. In 1984, Ace introduced Ace Paint, which became the 12th-largest paint manufacturer in the United States. Produced in two high-tech manufacturing facilities, the paint is popular with consumers for its value pricing and array of colors—including trendy options such as Peace River, Magic Spell, and Her Majesty. Ace Paint is the company's most popular product around the world.

In 1988, Ace hired a spokesman: John Madden, the former NFL coach who led the Oakland Raiders to victory in Super Bowl XI and had since become a sports commentator. The Emmy Award-winning sportscaster of *Monday Night Football* has appeared in Ace Hardware commercials ever since, broadcasting that "Ace is the home of the helpful hardware folks," a slogan that later became "Ace . . . the helpful place." In 2002, Ace signed on an additional spokesman, home improvement expert Lou Manfredini, known as the Ace Helpful Hardware Man. Manfredini, who owns his own Ace store, dispenses advice on local TV and radio shows on behalf of the company.

Today, Ace is the country's leading hardware cooperative, with 4,700 stores across the United States and in 70 other countries. The company encourages owner-dealers to customize their stores for the local markets, cultivate customer loyalty, and promote the Ace "helpful" promise. In the age of big-box home improvement stores, Ace competes by emphasizing the quality of its customer service and the fact that Ace stores tend to be in neighborhoods where people live rather than in remote malls. Ace Hardware plans to strengthen its supply chain to further lower prices and add 150–200 new stores each year by attracting new entrepreneurs with a toolbox of incentives and financing options.

Vital Statistics
Founders Richard Hesse, E. Gunnard Lindquist, Fran Burke, and Oscar Fisher
Established 1924
Headquarters Oak Brook, Illinois
Annual Sales $3.5 billion (2005)

ACE ACE ACE ACE ACE ACE
ACE ACE ACE ACE ACE ACE
ACE ACE ACE ACE ACE ACE
ACE ACE ACE ACE ACE ACE ACE
ACE ACE ACE ACE ACE ACE
ACE ACE ACE ACE ACE ACE
ACE ACE ACE ACE ACE ACE
ACE ACE ACE ACE ACE ACE ACE
ACE ACE ACE ACE ACE ACE
ACE ACE ACE ACE ACE ACE
ACE ACE ACE ACE ACE ACE
ACE ACE ACE ACE ACE ACE ACE
ACE ACE ACE ACE ACE ACE
ACE ACE ACE ACE ACE ACE
ACE ACE ACE ACE ACE ACE
ACE ACE ACE ACE ACE ACE ACE
ACE ACE ACE ACE ACE ACE
ACE ACE ACE ACE ACE ACE
ACE ACE ACE ACE ACE ACE
ACE ACE ACE ACE ACE ACE ACE

Adobe

If you are even semi-computer literate, you have come across Adobe, the company that sparked the desktop publishing revolution. In 2007, Adobe will celebrate its 25th anniversary and its strong history of creating award-winning software that has redefined business, entertainment, and personal communications. Adobe is widely recognized as an icon of innovation and creativity.

Adobe's impact on modern design and publishing has been compared to Gutenberg's invention of moveable type. Like Gutenberg, Adobe's influence is deep and widespread. Virtually every visual image you see today in all mediums—from magazines, newspapers, and Web sites to packaged goods, billboards, advertisements, movies, TV, and mobile devices—has likely been touched by Adobe software. With a reputation for excellence and a portfolio of many of the most respected and recognizable software brands, Adobe has had a sweeping impact on the way that businesses engage their customers and on the design experiences that consumers have every day.

Adobe founders Chuck Geschke and John Warnock shared a vision for publishing and graphic arts that would forever change how people create and engage with information. The two men met in the late 1970s while working at the renowned Xerox Palo Alto Research Center (PARC), where they researched device-independent graphic systems and printing. Geschke and Warnock eventually realized that the only way to take their ideas from the lab to the burgeoning technology market would be to create their own company.

In 1982, they founded Adobe Systems Incorporated (named after a creek behind Warnock's home in Los Altos, California) on a simple premise: how could text and images on a computer screen translate beautifully and accurately into print? A year later, they helped launch the desktop publishing revolution by introducing Adobe PostScript technology, providing a radical new approach to printing text and images on paper. For the first time, a computer file could be printed exactly as it appeared on screen. Building on its success with PostScript, Adobe expanded into desktop software applications with Adobe Illustrator and Adobe Photoshop software—and the design industry was never the same. These groundbreaking applications redefined the quality and complexity of images that could be created for print, and later extended those benefits to content created for video, film, Web, and alternative computing devices. Today, Adobe's Creative Suite software dominates the market for creative professional tools.

Furthering its vision to reinvent and improve computing, Adobe released Adobe Acrobat software and the Adobe Portable Document Format (PDF), combining its expertise in desktop software with its roots in PostScript printing. The appointment of Bruce Chizen as Adobe's CEO in 2000 further strengthened the company's market position, as Adobe delivered on growth strategies to provide platforms for enterprises while maintaining a leadership position as a desktop software company. With its acquisition of Macromedia, Inc. in 2005—developer of the ubiquitous Flash technology and a pioneer in multimedia and Web development—Adobe further expanded its strong technology foundation and portfolio of customer solutions.

Vital Statistics
Parent Company Adobe Systems Incorporated
Headquarters San Jose, California
Employees Approximately 6,000 worldwide
Annual Sales $2.575 billion (2006)

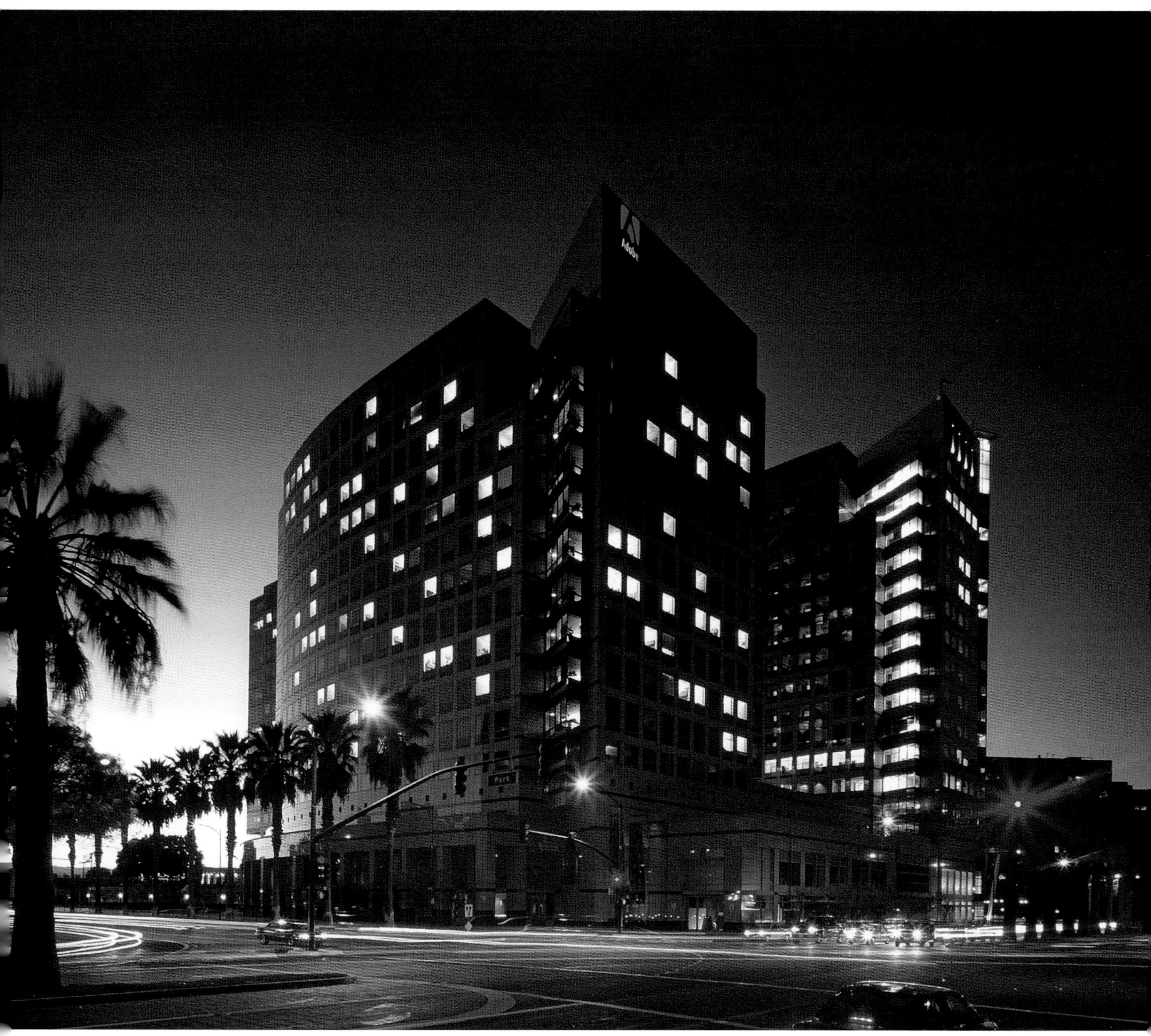

Photo by William A. Porter

Advil

Throughout the 1950s, researchers at the Boots Pure Drug Company in Nottingham, United Kingdom, were on a mission to develop a drug to treat rheumatoid arthritis. Under the leadership of chemist Stuart Adams, the group synthesized hundreds of compounds before hitting upon one, a carboxylic acid that appeared to have twice the anti-inflammatory properties of aspirin. Boots named the drug ibuprofen and patented it in 1961. Ibuprofen was originally sold as a prescription pain medicine under the brand name Brufen in the United Kingdom and Motrin in the United States.

Ibuprofen works by inhibiting the body's ability to produce prostaglandins, chemicals that cause inflammation pain. A nonsteroidal anti-inflammatory (NSAID), ibuprofen reduces fever and relieves the minor aches and pains of headaches, backaches, arthritis, and muscle and menstrual cramps.

In 1984, the USFDA approved ibuprofen for use as an over-the-counter pain reliever. Whitehall Laboratories, a division of American Home Products (AHP), was the first American company to license nonprescription-strength ibuprofen from Boots, which held the patent until 1985. American Home Products marketed the pain reliever tablets under the brand name Advil. In fewer than 10 years, sales of Advil surpassed aspirin and went head to head with Tylenol, the leading acetominophin product in the USA.

The Advil bottle quickly became a fixture in the household medicine cabinet, alongside AHP's other brands such as Centrum, Dimetapp, and Robitussin. The pain reliever just as easily found its way into popular culture. The alternative rock group They Might Be Giants wrote a song called "Till My Head Falls Off" in which a man counts the number of pills in his bottle of Advil. Advil hired celebrities to represent the drug in TV commercials. In one, retired celebrity pitcher Nolan Ryan, free of aches and pains, plays baseball with his wife. "I feel ready to go another nine innings!" he says.

In 2002, American Home Products changed its name to Wyeth. The pharmaceutical company markets Advil to a wide demographic—including grandparents with arthritis, athletes and laborers with muscle pain, office workers with backache, and women with menstrual cramps. Wyeth has also launched Children's and Infants' Advil and spun off several varieties of adult products, including Advil for Flu & Cold, Advil PM as a sleep aid, and Advil Migraine in a liquid capsule. Advil remains the leading nonprescription ibuprofen pain reliever and among the top five best-selling over-the-counter brands in the United States.

Vital Statistics
CompanyName Wyeth
Product Launch Date 1961
Founder Stuart Adams/Boots Pure Drug Company
Headquarters Madison, New Jersey

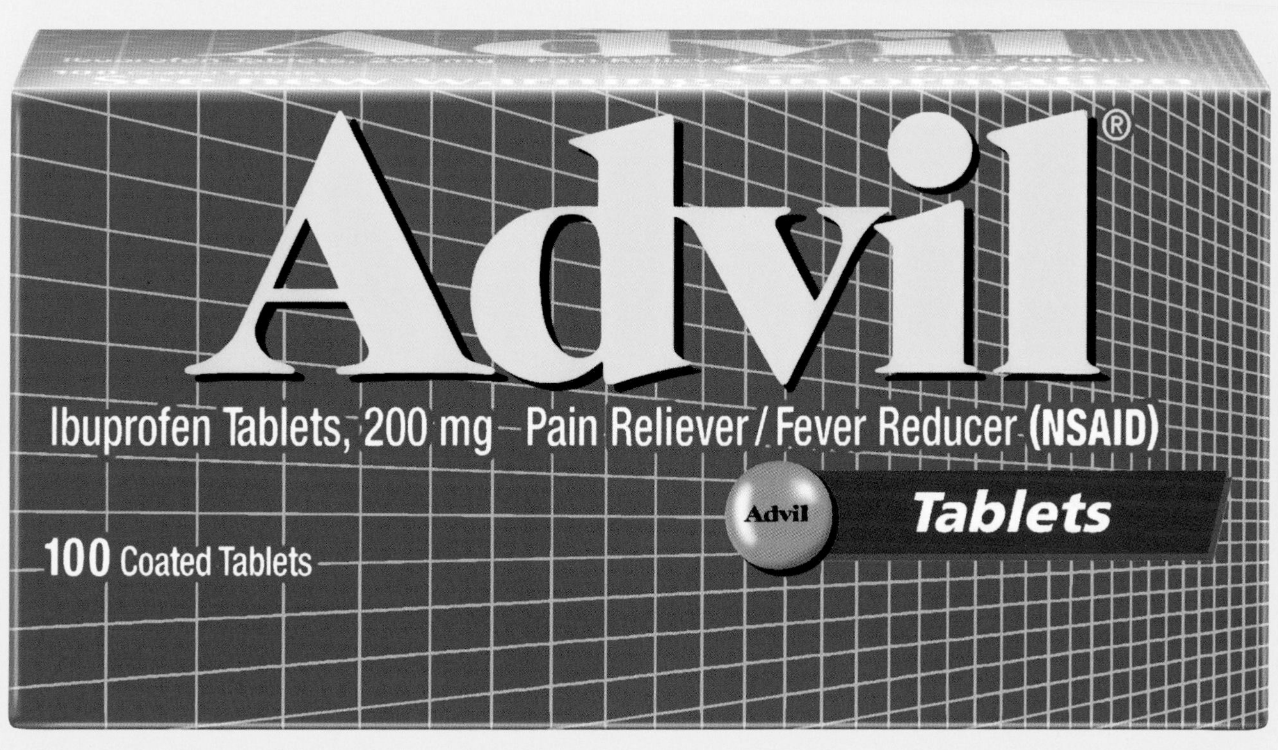
Advil®
Ibuprofen Tablets, 200 mg Pain Reliever / Fever Reducer (NSAID)
Advil
Tablets
100 Coated Tablets

Airstream

In Episode 305 of *The Apprentice,* Donald Trump's reality TV show, contestants were presented with a difficult and unusual task. The two teams were told that they must come up with a profitable business that could be run out of a custom-fit Airstream trailer. The team that dreamed up the business with the highest daily revenue would win the contest. The contestants brainstormed. One team converted their Airstream into a mobile massage and manicure parlor. The other made it into a mobile casting studio. The team with the casting studio won by a slim margin, but the greater recognition went to Airstream, one of America's longest-lasting brands.

AIRSTREAM

Wallace "Wally" Merle Byam created the Airstream trailer in 1931 as a way to make travel mainstream. He wanted Americans to have the freedom to drive anywhere on the open road, and to do it with comfort and style. Inspired by the fledgling aerospace industry, Byam designed it to have an aerodynamic aluminum shell and be light enough to be towed by a car. Unlike other trailers on the market, many of which tend to look boxy, the Airstream distinctively resembles a plane. In fact, the shape of the Airstream is so unique that models are displayed in the Smithsonian Institution and the Henry Ford Museum.

The Airstream trailer is different in at least one other way: it lasts for generations. Astonishingly, 65 percent of all Airstreams built since 1931 are still in use today. Airstream owners are fiercely loyal; approximately one in eight belong to the Wally Byam Caravan Club International (WBCCI), founded in 1956. The WBCCI promotes the spirit of the Airstream as a vehicle for adventure, freedom, serendipity, and friendship. Members pride themselves on "going where others only dream of going." The Airstream isn't just a trailer, it's a lifestyle.

More than 65,000 Airstreams are in use today. In recent years, Airstream has upgraded its floor plans, upgraded its amenities, and expanded its product line. Of Airstream's current lineup, a WBCCI member is likely to buy the Classic, a trailer that looks very similar to the original model with its oak or hickory interior and retails at a base of approximately $60,000. The International CCD, targeted to design aficionados, is Airstream's sleekest model, with a matte metal interior, strong accent colors, and lower price point. The best-selling trailer is the Safari, which is lightweight and value priced at an entry-level cost half that of the Classic. One of Airstream's newest and most innovative offerings is the tiny Basecamp, which is targeted to new, younger customers. The Basecamp is a sport utility travel trailer (SURV) that has Airstream's distinctive aluminum shell but expands in the back to double its living space.

Airstream continues to be on the leading edge of innovation, planning for lighter and cheaper models on the entry-level end and new designer models on the high end. The company has recently entered the Canadian, British, and European markets, and expects to continue to make deep inroads. If there's one lesson from Wally Byam and Airstream—and even *The Apprentice*—it's that the American Dream is refreshingly mobile.

Vital Statistics
Company Name Thor Industries, Inc.
Founder Wallace "Wally" Merle Byam
Employees 351
Main Production Site Jackson Center, Ohio
Annual sales $43.9 million (2005)

AIRSTREAM

Alka-Seltzer

Plop, plop, fizz, fizz—Alka-Seltzer is one of Bayer's most successfully advertised products and has helped countless Americans manage pain, and—most famously—indigestion.

Alka-Seltzer

Alka-Seltzer was introduced to combat indigestion in 1931 by Miles Laboratories, a company purchased by Bayer in 1979. Alka-Seltzer is a line of medications sold over the counter and taken as rapidly dissolving tablets that form an effervescent solution in water. The original Alka-Seltzer was touted as a remedy for headaches, indigestion, and hangovers, containing 1,916 milligrams of sodium bicarbonate, 1,000 milligrams of citric acid, and 325 milligrams of aspirin. The product was designed to treat pain and neutralize excess stomach acid, thus the Alka, which was derived from the word alkali. It is sold in the form of large effervescent tablets, about 1 inch in diameter, that are dissolved in four ounces of water. As the tablets dissolve, the acid and bicarbonate react, producing carbon dioxide gas and the characteristic fizz. In early years, it was marketed as a cure-all; one notable ad suggested taking it for "the blahs." It was also sold in glass bottles until 1984, when they were discontinued because of expense and breakage problems, and Alka-Seltzer was confined to its current foil packaging.

Alka-Seltzer rode to fame on the coattails of its clever advertisements. From 1954 to 1964, its commercials featured the animated character Speedy Alka-Seltzer, whose voice was supplied by voice-over actor Dick Beals. Speedy was shelved in the late 1960s and early 1970s, but returned for the American Bicentennial and the 1980 Winter Olympics. The aforementioned "Plop, plop, fizz, fizz, oh, what a relief it is" was composed by Tom Dawes of Twin Star Music and became one of the most well-known commercial jingles in advertising history. During the 1970s, another commercial that created a splash depicted a heartburn victim bedside in pajamas moaning, "I can't believe I ate the whole thing!" In the 1976 Columbia Pictures movie *Taxi Driver,* Travis Bickle, played by Robert De Niro, puts Alka-Seltzer in his water during a scene in a luncheonette.

Today, Bayer manufactures a range of variations on its basic product, available in original and lemon-lime flavors, and Alka-Seltzer PM for nighttime relief. The Alka-Seltzer Plus line of cold medicines has brought effervescent treatment to a new generation of consumers. On March 28, 2006, Alka-Seltzer celebrated its 75th anniversary with the world's largest buffet (as noted by *Guiness*) at the Las Vegas Hilton. The event was hosted by Kathy Griffin and benefited America's Second Harvest–the Nation's Food Bank Network, the nation's largest charitable hunger-relief organization.

Vital Statistics
Company Name Bayer
Established 1863

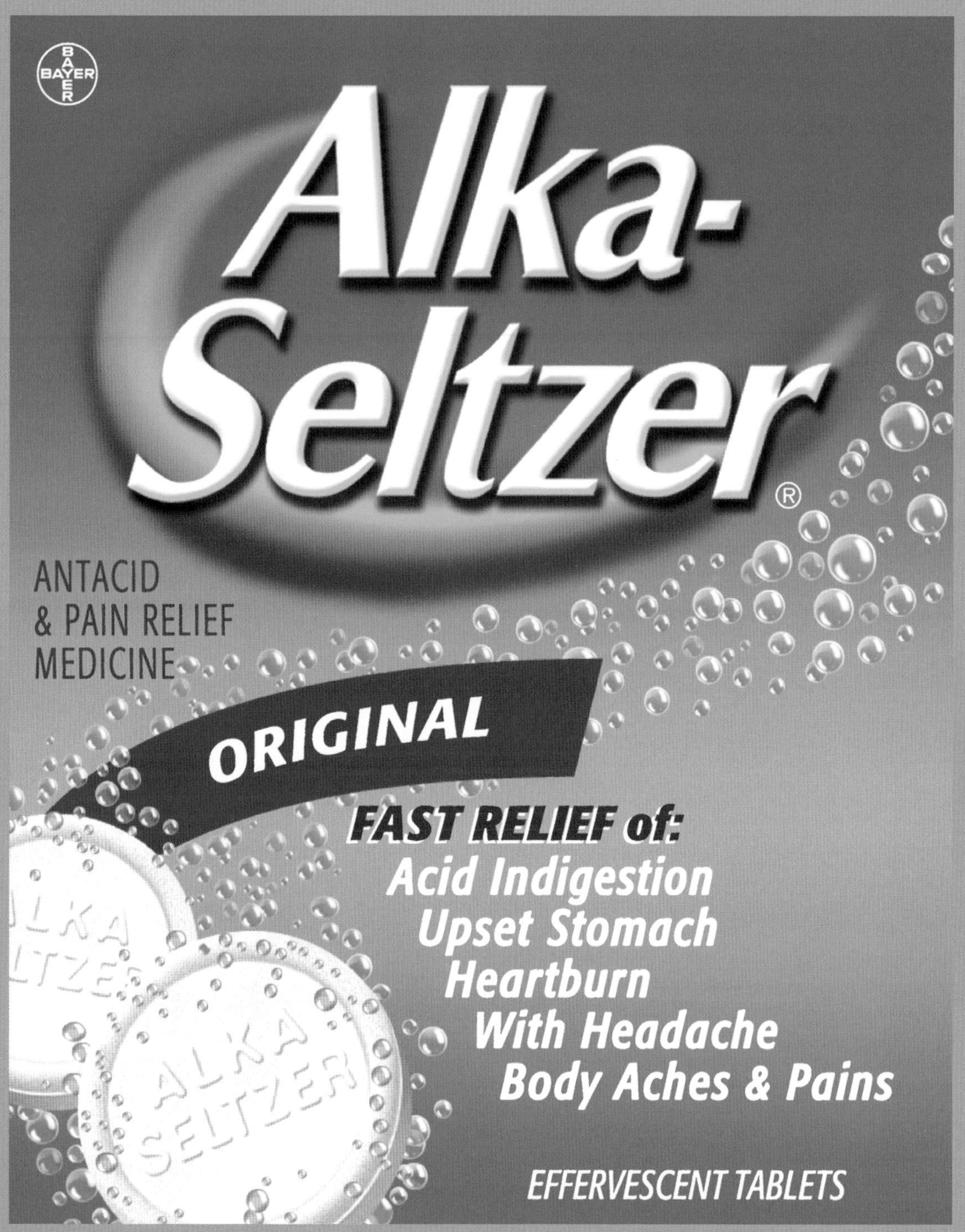
BAYER
Alka-Seltzer®
ANTACID
& PAIN RELIEF
MEDICINE
ORIGINAL
FAST RELIEF of:
Acid Indigestion
Upset Stomach
Heartburn
With Headache
Body Aches & Pains
EFFERVESCENT TABLETS
ALKA SELTZER

American Express Co.

American Express is perhaps best known as the credit card you "don't leave home without," but the company also runs one of the biggest travel agencies in the world, issues traveler's checks, publishes magazines such as *Travel & Leisure* and *Food & Wine,* and serves as a financial planner for millions. Founded more than 150 years ago by a man who started with a New York-based delivery service, American Express is now a multibillion-dollar success story and one of the most recognizable brands in the world.

In 1841, Henry Wells founded an express delivery service in New York, with no idea what his business was to become in subsequent years. Nine years later, he joined forces with his two largest competitors to found a company called American Express. Wells had dreams of expansion, and when his board didn't share his vision, he formed another company with his vice president, William Fargo: Wells Fargo. The men remained in their positions at American Express, however, and merged American Express with Merchants Union Express in 1868 to help devise a money order to compete with the existing government offering. In 1891, because of the trouble Wells Fargo was having cashing checks in Europe, American Express introduced what was to become a company cornerstone: Travelers Cheques.

The World Wars presented challenges for American Express, as the government decided to consolidate all express delivery services in an effort to cut costs, but company owners were compensated for their losses, allowing the company to stay strong. At the end of World War II, American Express solidified its position as an international force to be reckoned with—combining branches focused on money exchange, overseas freight, and financial services. The most significant moment in the company's history, however, came in 1958 with the introduction of the American Express charge card. James Robinson, who became CEO in 1977, decided he wanted to transform American Express into the nation's leading financial services provider. He focused on providing money orders, traveler's checks, travel services, credit card services, and financial planning. In the 1990s, because of increasing competition, American Express decided to divest itself from many of the businesses it had acquired in previous decades, as the "financial services supermarket" had never realized its potential. Harvey Golub became the CEO in 1993. Six years later, the company made a significant investment in what is now Ticketmaster and launched its online banking service. In 2000, in a move to expand to new frontiers, the company opened a headquarters in China. It also purchased more than 4,500 ATMs from Electronic Data Systems. In 2001, American Express, with headquarters across the street from the World Trade Center towers, was hard hit on September 11. More than 4,000 American Express employees were in the Manhattan offices that morning, and 11 died. The offices themselves suffered major damage, and employees worked off-site for almost a year.

Today, American Express is a major player on the world stage. It is one of the leading credit card providers to individuals, small businesses, and huge corporations. Its clever advertisements, featuring serious artists such as Kate Winslet writing about their dreams, as well as popular entertainers such as Ellen DeGeneres touting their personal AmEx cards, have drawn in new generations of fans. The company has retained its reputation for reliable services in an ever-changing world.

Vital Statistics

Classic Product credit card

Established 1850

Founder Henry Wells

Employees 65,800

Annual Sales $24,267 million (2005)

© AMEX

American Girl, Inc.

One of the most respected brands in the children's toy and book industries, American Girl focuses on the well-being and positive growth of young girls. With the simple mission of "celebrating girls," American Girl has created a sensation among girls and parents alike.

A trip to Colonial Williamsburg in 1985 inspired Pleasant Rowland to create the popular historical collection of 18-inch dolls and books. Rowland, a former teacher and publisher of educational books, was looking for the right gifts for her young nieces. Disillusioned by her options, she developed the American Girl concept, targeting 8–12-year-old girls, which aimed to combine important history lessons with creative play to encourage a child's development. This vision of integrating learning and play while emphasizing traditional American values materialized in the stories of three different nine-year-old heroines living out adventures at momentous times in American history.

Rowland's idea for historical dolls did not get the hoped-for response when she explained it to a focus group of mothers. But once she had prototype dolls, accessories, and books, the mothers were enthusiastic. Each doll came with an introductory novel about the character's life and an additional five books featuring tales of her adventures and challenges. Rowland's idea to provide a high-quality product while encouraging young girls not to grow up too fast was the start of Pleasant Company now called American Girl.

The original line started with three historical characters: Kirsten (1854), Samantha (1904), and Molly (1940). The beautifully-crafted dolls came to life in accompanying books bringing their stories, and history, alive for millions of young girls. One of the original three historical dolls, Kirsten Larson, is a Swedish immigrant living in the Minnesota Territory in 1854. Her story is about a pioneer adjusting to life in a new and unfamiliar land. Rowland's dolls were a huge success, and during the first Christmas season, the company sold $1.7 million worth of products through its mail-order catalogue.

The historical line of characters expanded, and sales soared. In 1992, the company launched *American Girl* magazine, an advertising-free publication designed to celebrate achievements and foster creativity in young girls in an age-appropriate manner. With more than 700,000 subscribers, *American Girl* has been ranked among the top 10 children's magazines in the country and is the largest magazine dedicated exclusively to girls. As a result of the magazine's success, American Girl, Inc. introduced a line of contemporary 18-inch dolls and accessories called Just Like You. Designed to represent the diversity of today's American girls, the line includes books, toys, and clothing to showcase their wide array of lifestyles and interests. Additionally, Bitty Baby, a line of soft baby dolls and related toys, was created for young girls ages three to six to encourage nurturing behavior.

Since its first catalogue in 1986, American Girl has expanded to provide products for each stage of a girl's development. The American Girl products are marketed through the American Girl catalogue, Web site, and proprietary retail stores. Books published by American Girl are also distributed through bookstores across the country. Since 1998, American Girl, Inc. has been a wholly owned subsidiary of Mattel, the world's leading toymaker.

Vital Statistics
Parent Company Mattel, Inc.
Established 1986
Founder Pleasant T. Rowland
Annual Sales $436 million
Headquarters Middleton, Wisconsin

1854
MEET
KIRSTEN
An American Girl
THE AMERICAN GIRLS COLLECTION
1904
Book 1
MEET
SAMANTHA
An American Girl
THE AMERICAN GIRLS COLLECTION
1944
Book 1
MEET
MOLLY
An American Girl
THE AMERICAN GIRLS COLLECTION

Andersen Windows

Once upon a time, if a window was needed, it was either hastily built by carpenters at the construction site or slapped together beforehand at the lumberyard. As a result, windows were usually too big or too small, and almost never just right. To the rescue came Hans Andersen, a Danish immigrant who owned Andersen Lumber Company in Hudson, Wisconsin. In 1903, Andersen pledged to construct uniform, high-quality window frame units that would become a market standard. These state-of-the-art windows would bring an end to wicked leaks and drafts, and homeowners would live happily ever after.

Andersen's business thrived, benefiting from the young nation's construction boom and the owner's good head for business. Unlike other entrepreneurs at the time, Hans Andersen believed strongly in profit sharing and paying high wages to his employees. After Andersen's death in 1914, his sons, Fred and Herbert, carried on their father's legacy of treating employees generously. They set up incentive and retirement programs, and even kept their workers employed during the Great Depression by planting trees. Andersen remains renowned for its employee stewardship and community involvement.

Andersen distinguished its windows from others not only by building them as high-quality, ready-made units, but also by making them big. The company coined the term *Windowalls* to describe their large windows that are so weather-tight they could be walls. A popular ad for Andersen Windowalls depicted two brown houses in a snowy setting, one with Andersen windows and one without any windows at all, with the tagline below the latter reading, "The way to insulate with a view." The insulating glass used in Andersen windows is so effective that it eliminates the need for storm windows.

Over the decades, Andersen has lived up to its reputation as the "beautiful way to save fuel." The company has been a leading innovator in new technologies in windows, including the Perma-Shield-clad window, a tough vinyl exterior for wood windows. In 1991, Andersen also launched Fibrex, an insulating composite made of rot-resistant, low-maintenance wood fiber. In 1999, Andersen became the first window and patio door company to earn the Environmental Protection Agency's Energy Star Outstanding Homes Manufacturer Ally award.

In an era when people are fearful of the effects of global warming, energy-efficient windows and doors have become essential to home buyers. Andersen continues to introduce new energy-saving features with the recent introduction of High-Performance Low-E window line, which features argon filters in double-glazed windowpanes that keep homes warm in winter and cool in the summer. The glass used in Andersen windows also reduces the transmission of cancer-causing ultraviolet light to 17 percent from 62 percent in regular glass.

Today, Andersen is the world's best-known window brand, manufacturing more than six million wood windows, patio doors, and storm doors annually. Available in more than 600,000 shapes, sizes, and colors, Andersen opens windows of opportunity to architects, builders, and home buyers seeking the right fit.

Vital Statistics

Classic Product windows

Established 1903

Founder Hans Andersen

Main Production Site Bayport, Minnesota

Employees 8,500

Annual Sales $2.5 billion (2005.)

Annie's Homegrown

Annie Withey was in her early twenties in 1982 when she created Smartfood Cheddar Popcorn. The cheese-flavored popcorn made with natural ingredients was an instant success with snackers looking for healthful alternatives. So it's no wonder that in 1989 she started Annie's Homegrown to make all-natural macaroni and cheese. Her goal was to make a good-tasting, healthful mac 'n' cheese mix in a box. It was a smart strategy, particularly for a food item usually purchased by parents who wanted something easy but wholesome for their kids. The distinctive purple box, with a picture of Bernie the Bunny and the word ***homegrown,*** sends a message that Annie's is better for you than competing products.

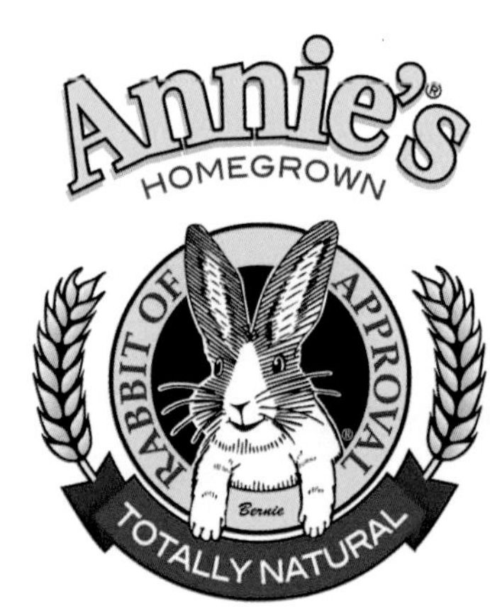

Annie's used to be confined to natural foods stores or in the natural foods section of the supermarket, but the products are now so popular that they're shelved in supermarkets nationwide. Annie's is the second-largest brand of macaroni and cheese in the country. Annie's popularity has been helped by the growth of the natural and organic foods market, the fastest-growing segment of the food retailing industry. Since its inception, Annie's has grown from one product to 50 products, including: Natural Mac & Cheese; Certified-Organic Mac & Cheese; Cheddar Bunnies; Bunny Grahams; Simple Organic Skillet Meals; Totally Natural Pasta Meals; and Certified Organic Canned Meals. The organic farmers with whom Annie's does business don't use synthetic fertilizers, herbicides, or pesticides, nor do they use genetically modified organisms or irradiation. Company materials profile many of the organic farmers and show pictures of sweeping grain fields.

But for Withey, natural and organic aren't just marketing strategies; they are intertwined with her company's public mission. The company slogan, "Eat Responsibly. Act Responsibly," underscores Withey's commitment to giving back to the community. Bearing out the motto, Annie's Homegrown offers scholarships to environmental studies students and runs a program called Cases for Causes, where cases of Annie's products are donated to nonprofit organizations focused on organic gardening and environmental education efforts. The company Web site offers "free stuff," including bumper stickers and pins with slogans such as "Be Green," "Think Organic," and "Stand for Peace." Withey works from her 100-acre organic farm in Hampton, Connecticut, and sells her produce at a local farmers' market.

Although the company founder has given up involvement in day-to-day operations and is now dubbed "inspirational leader," she stays in close touch with her customers via phone, e-mail, and letters. Annie's unique packaging, which lists an 800 number and the company address, and offers coupons, actively encourages customer feedback and word-of-mouth marketing. Withey's phone number is printed on the back of the box because she wants her customers to realize that there is a real Annie. Thousands of customers write in every month, and Annie speaks to as many as 50 callers a day, receiving feedback about the products and getting input for new ideas.

Vital Statistics
Parent Company Homegrown Naturals, Inc.
Product Launch 1989
Headquarters Napa, California
Employees 65
Annual Sales $70 million (2006)

Annie's
Shells & White Cheddar
MADE WITH ORGANIC PASTA
Annie's
HOMEGROWN
RABBIT OF APPROVAL
Bernie
TOTALLY NATURAL
Shells &
White Cheddar
Macaroni & Cheese
100% REAL CHEESE
No Artificial Anything!™
0g Trans Fat
Naturally Good Source of Calcium and Protein
SEE NUTRITION INFORMATION FOR SODIUM CONTENT NET WT 6 OZ (170g)

Arm & Hammer Baking Soda

The orange-yellow box of Arm & Hammer Baking Soda is a staple in homes across America. For more than 150 years, Arm & Hammer has been used as a natural deodorizer, cooking agent, and toothpaste. It started back in 1846 when Dr. Austin Church and his brother-in-law John Dwight began manufacturing sodium bicarbonate for commercial use. The first factory was in Dwight's kitchen, with the baking soda, (then called *saleratus* from Latin for aerated salt), being put, by hand, into paper bags. In 1847, John Dwight & Company started selling one-pound packages of Dwight's Saleratus under the trademark Cow Brand. The cow was used as the trademark because sour milk was often used with saleratus in baking.

Sodium bicarbonate, or baking soda, is a mineral that helps regulate pH balance—keeping a substance neither too acidic nor too alkaline—in all living things. Baking soda is made when sodium bicarbonate is mined in the form of soda ash and then dissolved into a solution. Carbon dioxide bubbles through the solution, and sodium bicarbonate is the result.

Because of the product's popularity, Church thought there was a large market for *saleratus,* or baking soda, and developed larger production facilities. He formed a partnership named Church & Co. with his sons James A. Church and E. Dwight Church and used the Arm & Hammer brand as the company trademark. In 1896, the descendants of the founders of both companies consolidated to form Church & Dwight Co., Inc.

Arm & Hammer Baking Soda has a multitude of uses in the home. An essential ingredient in baking for centuries, baking soda is used as a leavening agent. When batter or dough with baking soda is combined with acidic ingredients and heated, it gives off carbon dioxide and causes the dough to rise. Arm & Hammer Baking Soda is also well known for its deodorizing capabilities. Using it in the refrigerator and freezer balances pH by neutralizing acidic, or sour, smells, thereby helping food retain its freshness. Arm & Hammer Baking Soda sprinkled on carpets and upholstery neutralizes odor and keeps your home smelling fresh. It has also proven effective as an antacid, toothpaste, and laundry booster, and as a surface cleaner for the kitchen and bathroom.

Church & Dwight has always been environmentally conscious and was the sole sponsor of the first Earth Day in 1970. As a natural and gentle cleaner, Arm & Hammer Baking Soda was used by the National Trust for Historic Preservation to clean away 99 years of coal tar from the inner walls of the Statue of Liberty for its 100th anniversary.

Arm & Hammer is widely used throughout the home, and over the years, Church & Dwight has focused on its core product yet expanded its line to include laundry detergent, toothpaste, and cat litter deodorizer as well as its famed baking soda in the form of the Fridge-n-Freezer Odor Absorber, Baking Soda Shaker, and Baking Soda Resealable Pouch.

Vital Statistics

Company Name	Church & Dwight Co.
Classic Product	Arm & Hammer Baking Soda
Established	1846
Founders	Austin Church and John Dwight
Annual Sales	$1.7 billion (2005)

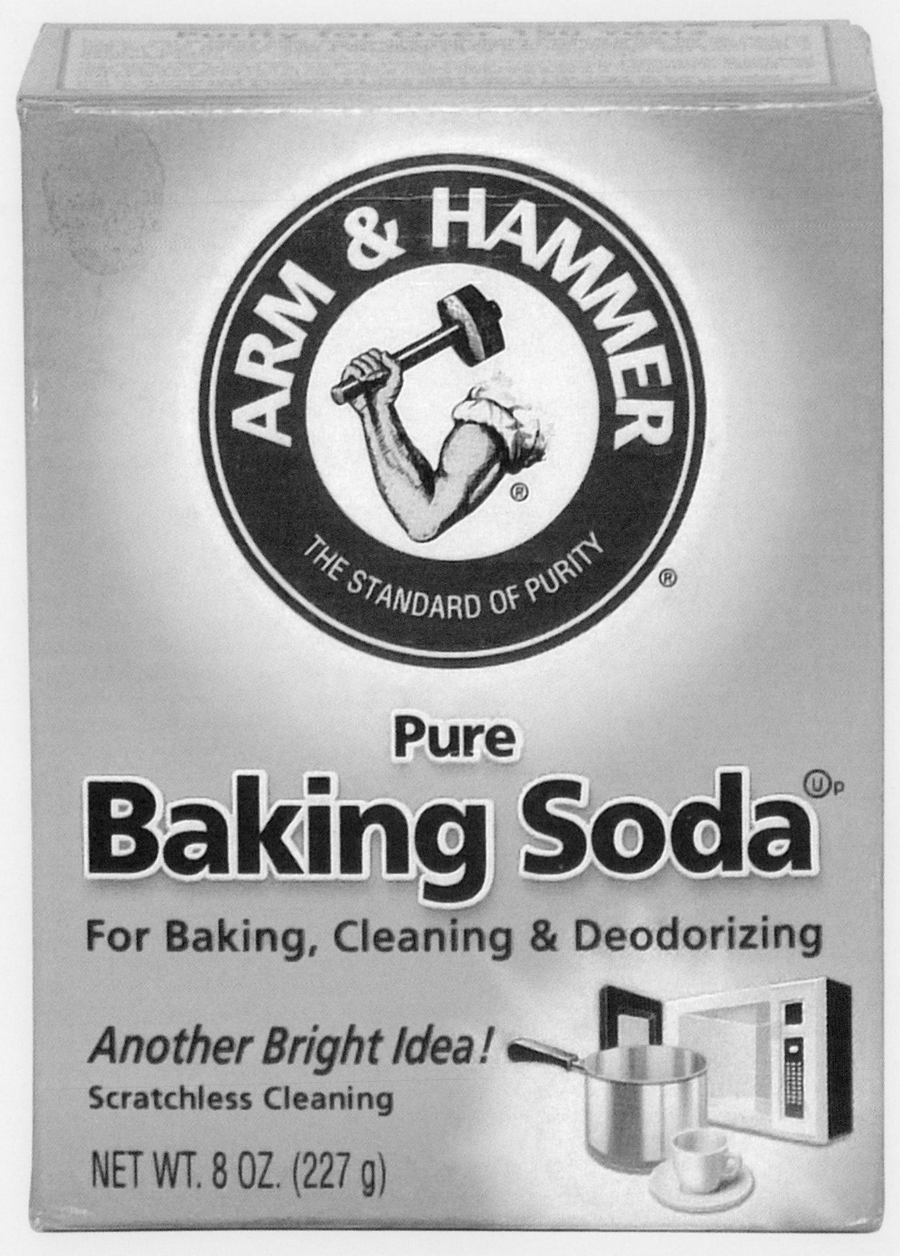

Aveda

Environmentally conscientious consumers love Aveda cosmetics, perfumes, and skin and hair products for their natural, organic ingredients and focus on smart packaging, but the line's clean, elegant look and top-notch quality have ensured a much wider market. Started by a hairstylist in Minneapolis, Aveda was eventually purchased by Estée Lauder, who took its unique approach to the masses. Today, Aveda is one of Estée Lauder's most successful brands, and its products, such as the unforgettable Rosemary Mint Shampoo, are coveted all over the world.

Aveda inventor Horst Rechelbacher (Horst) began his career styling hair at a beauty salon in his Austrian hometown at the age of 14. By 19, he was working in the United States and well on his way to achieving fame. After a near-fatal car accident and the opening of his own Midwestern salon, Horst headed to India for a spiritual retreat. He returned inspired to make his own line of plant-based beauty products with the help of his herbalist mother, to be sold at his salons under the label Horst. The first product was a brown Clove Shampoo designed to enhance the color of brown hair; the shampoo remains a best seller. After another trip to India, in 1978, he founded Aveda.

The word *Aveda* means "all knowledge" or "knowledge of nature" in Sanskrit. Aveda took off, and soon its products could be found in hundreds of thousands of salons and stores throughout the world. In 1997, partly because of a desire for international expansion, Horst sold Aveda to Estée Lauder for $300 million. Today, Horst is a benefactor to the world of complementary and alternative medical research, a collector and dealer of art and antiques, and an important adviser to Aveda. Aveda distinguishes itself from other cosmetics companies with its commitment to naturally derived, usually organic sources in its products, which can make their creation a challenge—to which Aveda is always willing to rise. One example is the fragrance Love, which contains sandalwood oil. When Aveda discovered that gangs were poaching from and destroying sandalwood forests in India to obtain the oil, it stopped making the product altogether. The company did not reintroduce Love until it found an alternate source of the oil in Australia.

Today, Aveda's commitment to the world is stronger than ever. The company is involved with projects all over the globe such as promoting sustainable community-based business for Australia's aboriginal Kutkabubba community and returning post-apartheid farmers to their ancestral lands in South Africa. Products such as Rosemary Mint Shampoo have spawned the new unisex Rosemary Mint Body Care Collection, and Aveda is generally considered the jewel in the crown that is Estée Lauder.

Vital Statistics
Classic Product Shampoo
Founder Horst Rechelbacher
Brand Established 1978

AVEDA
THE ART AND SCIENCE OF PURE
FLOWER AND PLANT ESSENCES
shampure™
SHAMPOO
SHAMPOOING

above and beyond shampoo
with morikue™ protein
au-dessus et au-delà du shampooing
à la protéine morikue™
8.5 fl oz/oz liq/250 ml ℮

Avery Dennison

Avery Dennison has made life a lot easier and more efficient, and no household or business is unaware of the labels that have made this company world renowned. Through product and technology innovation spanning several decades, Avery Dennison has become a global leader in self-adhesive base materials and self-adhesive consumer and office products. Its self-adhesive technology and applications touch every major market around the world, from brand identification for the retail industry to reflective materials for the U.S. Department of Transportation.

A business and industry were created in 1935 when entrepreneur R. Stanton Avery manufactured the world's first self-adhesive labels under the name Kum Kleen Products in a 100-square-foot rented space in Los Angeles. A fire destroyed the plant's equipment in 1938, but through drive and innovation, Avery renamed the company Avery Adhesives and set out to develop improved machinery. As a result, Avery developed the first die-cutting method, in-line machinery, and rotary die for the manufacture of self-adhesive labels. He also developed the first synthetic-based pressure-sensitive adhesive and quick-release coated backing for self-adhesive products, the first systematic approach to label identification and pricing, and the first manual dispenser for self-adhesive labels. These innovations, which vastly improved the making of labels, propelled the company's success, and by 1945, the company's sales were near half a million dollars.

World War II brought new industrial uses for self-adhesive labels, which continued to fuel the company's growth, and with its first license holder in England, Avery Adhesives established new customers abroad. With the loss of its patent rights in 1952, Avery Adhesives created a new business to produce and market self-adhesive base materials (later called Fasson) and constructed its first base materials plant in Ohio.

Avery continued to expand with the innovation of new self-adhesive products as well as revolutionary technology and environmentally safe coating methods that helped the company forge new markets, firmly establishing it as a leader in the industry. Avery Dennison is at the forefront of the growing and competitive industry, and its label business, providing products that are staples in the home and office, continues to be a strong asset. The company has diversified and grown over several decades, manufacturing and marketing office products, specialty chemicals, and research and development advances in adhesive technology.

Avery Dennison is a global leader in the making of adhesive labels used for packaging, mailers, and other items, with pressure-sensitive adhesives and materials accounting for more than half the company's sales. The company's most widely used products are the self-adhesive stamps used by the U.S. Postal Service.

Vital Statistics
Classic Product labels
Established 1935
Founder R. Stanton Avery
Employees 22,000
Annual Sales $5.5 billion (2005)

Great For
Internet
Shipping
8126™
2
labels
per sheet
50
Labels
Avery®
TEMPLATES
Just Click & Create™
Easy to use templates for
Microsoft® Word
Works with:
US Postal Service®
Click-N-Ship®
· Pitney Bowes
shipstream™ manager
deluxe
· eBay® & PayPal®
Online Postage
and other popular shipping
software
FGL
Enterprises
SHIP TO:
KAREN TAPLEY
12525 SAINT GETTINGER ST
SAN FRANCISCO CA 94111
Tracking Number
8H 385 578 3939 KL90
A-05977
A-05977
CER
actual label size not shown
AVERY®
5½" x 8½" (actual size)
for printing of 4" x 6" shipping labels
White
Shipping Labels
Ink Jet
Perforated label sheet provides easy
separation into label and receipt part
8126™

Band-Aid

Contrary to popular belief, a healing wound does not need to "breathe." In fact, medical experts say that warm, moist environments speed up the healing process, which means wounds should be covered until they're fully healed. Bandaging a wound also decreases the risks of scarring, scabbing, reinjury, and reinfection. This is good news for Johnson & Johnson, which owns the Band-Aid brand of adhesive bandages. Band-Aid, the world's best-selling adhesive bandage, is so well established that it has become a genericized trademark like Kleenex and Xerox. When people need adhesive bandages, they ask for Band-Aids.

Humans have always made bandages to cover wounds. The ancient Egyptians used papyrus. Early Europeans used soft, absorbent leaves. And in 1920, Earle Dickson of Brunswick, New Jersey, used cotton gauze and adhesive tape. Dickson invented the Band-Aid for his accident-prone wife, Josephine. When Dickson came home from his job as a cotton buyer at Johnson & Johnson, he would help Josephine bandage the cuts and scrapes she got from cooking and cleaning. Realizing it would be a good idea to have a supply of ready-made bandages, he took a roll of adhesive tape, placed squares of cotton gauze at intervals along the strip, and covered the adhesive with crinoline. When Josephine needed a bandage, she could simply cut herself a strip. Dickson told his boss at Johnson & Johnson about his invention. The company decided to mass-produce the ready-made bandages, which they called Band-Aids, and promote Dickson to vice president.

Band-Aids have since had a role in American history and popular culture. Millions of Band-Aids were shipped overseas to military hospitals during World War II. Band-Aids were sent into space with the Mercury astronauts in 1963 and shipped to Russia when the Iron Curtain fell in 1988. Brooke Shields, John Travolta, Chris Evert, and many other American icons have made Band-Aid commercials. Snoopy, Spider-Man, Batman, Care Bears, SpongeBob SquarePants, and Dora the Explorer have all appeared as Band-Aid designs.

Johnson & Johnson Band-Aids remain on the cutting edge of first-aid technology. In 1997, the company launched Antibiotic Adhesive bandages, the first bandages to come with a built-in ointment. Advanced Healing Strips, launched in 2001, form an airtight seal and moisture lock. For friction blisters, hangnails, paper cuts, and other minor wounds, Band-Aid recommends Liquid Bandage, which adds healing moisture to a dry wound. Scar Healing, the newest Band-Aid line, is designed to fade existing scars. Band-Aid products come in a variety of shapes and sizes suitable for elbows, shins, feet, knees, fingers, and other commonly abraded body parts. They also come in various adhesive strengths, including Active Flex, which allow better fexibility, and waterproof Tough Strips, with a stronger adhesive.

Johnson & Johnson has sold more than a hundred billion Band-Aids since Earle Dickson invented the product in 1920. Undoubtedly, this iconic brand has real sticking power.

Vital Statistics
Inventor Earle Dickson
Headquarters New Brunswick, New Jersey

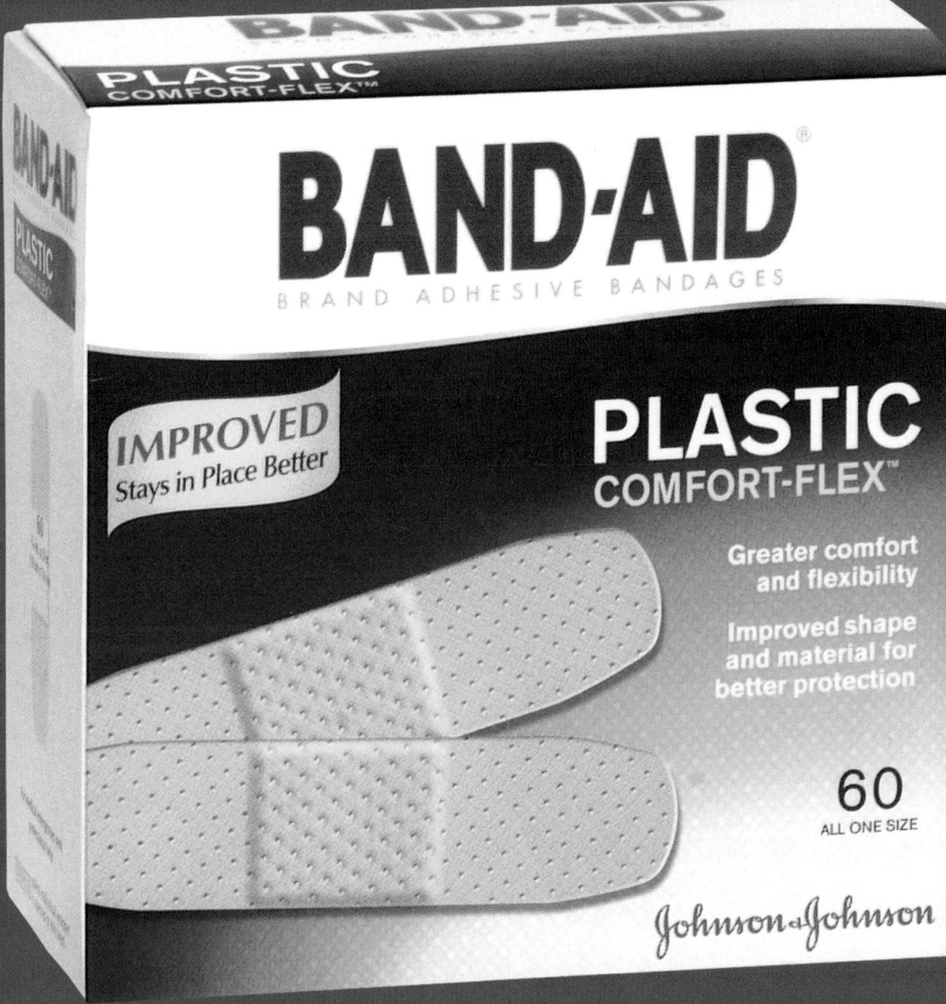
PLASTIC
COMFORT-FLEX™
BAND-AID®
BRAND ADHESIVE BANDAGES
IMPROVED
Stays in Place Better
PLASTIC
COMFORT-FLEX™
Greater comfort
and flexibility
Improved shape
and material for
better protection
60
ALL ONE SIZE
Johnson & Johnson

Ben & Jerry's Homemade

In 1963, Ben Cohen and Jerry Greenfield met in gym class at their junior high school in Merrick, New York. A few years later, Ben took on a summer job driving a musical ice cream truck and selling ice cream pops and cones to kids. Meanwhile, Jerry went on to college, where he got a job scooping ice cream at the school cafeteria. Several years and many odd jobs later, Ben and Jerry met again and decided to open an ice cream business. They took a five-dollar correspondence course in ice cream making and concocted several gourmet flavors using fresh cream, fruit, nuts, chocolate, and their imaginations. In 1978, the friends opened Ben & Jerry's Homemade ice cream parlor in Burlington, Vermont. In 1981, *Time* magazine deemed it "the best ice cream in the world." In 1984, Ben & Jerry's went public.

BEN&JERRY'S.

From the very beginning, a commitment to social responsibility has distinguished the Ben & Jerry's brand. Cohen and Greenfield first set a salary cap for company executives. In 1985, they established the Ben & Jerry's Foundation to fund community-oriented projects across the United States and pledged 7.5 percent of the company's pre-tax profits to the charity. Their packaged ice cream and frozen yogurt comes in recycled, unbleached cardboard containers, and they use cream from local dairies that pledge not to use bovine growth hormone. Some Ben & Jerry's flavors have had a social mission, such as Rainforest Crunch made with nuts from the rain forest and Chocolate Fudge Brownie made with brownies from a bakery that employs former homeless people.

In 1987, Ben & Jerry's introduced Cherry Garcia, its most popular flavor to date. Named in tribute to the Grateful Dead lead guitarist and songwriter, Jerry Garcia, Cherry Garcia is cherry ice cream with chocolate flakes and bits of Bing cherries. Ben & Jerry's offers its customers the opportunity to request flavors and name them, and Cherry Garcia was one recommended by two anonymous Deadheads in Portland, Maine. The company printed bumper stickers in psychedelic neon that read, "What a long, strange dip it's been." When Jerry Garcia passed away in 1995, Ben & Jerry's produced a limited run of Cherry Garcia ice cream with black cherries as an expression of mourning.

In 2000, Cohen and Greenfield sold Ben & Jerry's Homemade to Unilever, the British-Dutch food conglomerate, for $326 million. Today, Ben & Jerry's owns or franchises more than 430 ice cream parlors in North America and approximately 150 throughout Mexico, Canada, and Asia. It continues to introduce new flavors each year and establish new franchises in Europe. The foundation contributes at least $1.1 million to social causes annually. Ben Cohen and Jerry Greenfield are still involved after the buyout and strive to maintain the progressive principles on which their company was founded. Their efforts include a "One Sweet Whirled" campaign against global warming and the "American Pie" campaign, designed to persuade Americans to demand a change in spending priorities from war to education and other programs for kids.

Vital Statistics
Founders Bennett Cohen and Jerry Greenfield
Classic Product Ice cream
Established 1978
Headquarters Burlington, Vermont
Annual Sales $272 million

BEN&JERRY'S
Chunky
Monkey
ICE CREAM
Banana Ice Cream with
Chocolatey Chunks & Walnuts
BEN&JERRY'S
Chunky
Monkey
ICE CREAM
Banana Ice Cream with
Chocolatey Chunks & Walnuts

Benjamin Moore & Co.

What began more than a century ago as a small paint business in Brooklyn, started by an Irish immigrant and his brother, has become an industry leader with annual sales topping a billion dollars. Benjamin Moore & Co. has produced high-quality paint since 1883. Calsom Finish, a calsomine coating for walls and ceilings, turned a profit in its very first year. Shortly thereafter, the company moved its headquarters into New York City and then west into New Jersey, where it continues to reside today.

Benjamin Moore is committed to providing its customers—homeowners, professional painting contractors, interior designers, architects, and facility specifiers—with premium products. The company continues its founder's unwavering commitment to excellence along with a keen sense of responsibility to both community and the environment. Research and development is a crucial part of Benjamin Moore's business, whereby all products are subject to rigorous, ongoing scientific testing. More than 100 chemists, chemical engineers, technicians, and support staff maintain the stringent Benjamin Moore standards as well as develop new products. This staff operates out of eight team-based laboratories, each equipped with state-of-the-art instruments to focus on a specific area of coating expertise. Together, these laboratories develop all of Benjamin Moore's proprietary paint formulations and color standards.

This commitment to research and innovation has led Benjamin Moore to a number of industry firsts: the introduction of the first eggshell interior finish in 1972; the first Computer Color Matching System in 1982, now an industry standard; the first pearl interior finish in 1988; and Eco Spec in 1994, a low-VOC/low odor latex paint which carries the seal of approval from both the Greenguard Environmental Institute and Green Seal. Environmental responsibility has always played a key role in the company's focus and success. Benjamin Moore enhances its commitment to develop products that minimize their impact on the environment with the introduction of Aura, an extremely environmentally responsible interior paint. This super premium product, dubbed by the company as "simply the finest paint we've ever made," meets the most stringent air quality regulations while excelling in its performance characteristics. The technology coup accompanying Aura is the company's introduction of ColorLock, a patent-pending innovation that literally locks color pigment into the paint film. It is this platform on which the company will build its future products.

Benjamin Moore & Co. was honored by the North American Hazardous Materials Management Association with its Leadership Award for Product Stewardship as a result of a pilot program to collect and rework latex paint waste from municipal paint collection depots. Systems for paint disposal and recycling programs like the pilot program emphasize the company's commitment to environmental health and safety. Another strong point of differentiation for the Benjamin Moore brand is its distribution through a network of independent paint and decorating retailers—borne of its founder's original business commitment to independent merchants.

Although the Benjamin Moore product line has expanded and changed dramatically since its humble beginnings in 1883, Mr. Moore's original philosophy—honesty, integrity, providing value, and maintaining the highest of standards for all products—keeps the company one of the nation's leading paint manufacturers.

Vital Statistics

Parent Company	Berkshire Hathaway
Established	1883
Founder	Benjamin Moore
Headquarters	Montvale, New Jersey
Sales	$1 billion

Benjamin Moore
Aura
Waterborne Interior Paint
SATIN FINISH
PINTURA AL AGUA PARA EL INTERIOR
ACABADO SATINADO
BASE 1 526 1X

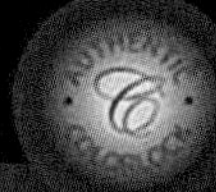

AUTHENTIC COLORLOCK
Proprietary technology results in exceptional beauty, remarkable coverage & superior durability.

Best Buy

Best Buy is well named—it is the biggest consumer electronics outlet in the United States, operating a chain of almost 800 stores in the United States and Canada selling electronic gadgets, movies, music, computers, and appliances. The stores also offer installation and maintenance services, technical support, and subscriptions for cell phone and Internet services.

Covering an average of about 42,000 square feet, the so-called "big box" stores are in 49 states and five Canadian provinces. In addition to the Best Buy brand, the company operates under the names Magnolia Audio Video and Future Shop. When Minnesotan Dick Schulze lost patience with his father's lack of interest in his ideas to improve the family electronics distribution business, he quit. In 1966, he and a partner founded a home/car stereo store called Sound of Music. In 1971, Schulze bought out his partner and began to expand. In the early 1980s, he broadened his product line and targeted older, more affluent customers by offering appliances and VCRs, not just the music that attracted the dwindling teen market. In 1983, Schulze changed the company's name to Best Buy and began to open the superstores that would become a company trademark. The firm went public two years later, and Best Buy began a rapid expansion. Between 1984 and 1987, it expanded from 8 stores to 24, and sales jumped from $29 million to $240 million. The next year another 16 stores opened and sales jumped by 84 percent. To counteract growing competition, in 1989 Schulze introduced the Concept II warehouse-like store format, which left shopping largely in the hands of the shopper and entailed taking sales staff off commission and reducing the number of employees per store by about a third. The strategy proved successful.

In the 1990s, Best Buy scaled back on expansion and introduced its Concept IV stores, which highlighted digital products and featured stations for computer software and DVD demonstrations. In 1999, the company launched BestBuy.com, Inc. and a year later agreed to pay $88 million for Seattle-based Magnolia Hi-Fi, a privately held chain of 13 high-end audio and video stores. The company began its international expansion in November 2002 with its $377 million acquisition of Future Shop, Canada's leading consumer electronics retailer. Over the next year, Best Buy opened eight of its own Best Buy stores in Ontario, Canada. In June 2002, Schulze turned over his CEO responsibilities to vice chairman Brad Anderson, remaining chairman of the board of the company he'd founded almost 40 years earlier. Best Buy acquired Geek Squad, a computer support provider, for $3 million the same year—this quirky feature sends trained professionals into homes to fix, install, and reorganize home electronics systems and has proved insanely popular with technophobes everywhere.

Schulze's dream came true when, in 2004, *Forbes* magazine named Best Buy Company of the Year. In 2006, the company announced its plans to enter China with a four-story flagship site in the Jiang Shan Building in Shanghai's Xu Jia Hui commercial district. That same year, Best Buy secured majority ownership in Five Star Appliance, China's fourth-largest retailer, for $180 million, securing a base of 136 retail stores. Today, Best Buy is the preferred destination of millions of electronics-savvy consumers all over the world.

Vital Statistics
Classic Product home electronics
Established 1966
Founder Dick Schulze
Annual Sales $30,848 million

BEST
BUY
Geek
Squad

Betty Crocker

In 1921, the Washburn Crosby Company offered a flour-sack-shaped pincushion to customers who correctly completed a puzzle. Along with thousands of submissions were hundreds of inquiries about baking. Seizing the opportunity to connect with customers, the flour milling company created a persona in whose name they could answer the questions. They called her Betty Crocker because the first name *Betty* sounded friendly and the surname *Crocker* was that of recently retired director William Crocker.

In 1924, the company created a radio program featuring Betty Crocker. Soon called "The Betty Crocker Cooking School of the Air," the show became one of the longest running shows in radio history. Betty Crocker, meanwhile, became America's most trusted name in baking.

The Washburn Crosby Company consolidated with several smaller mills in 1928 to become General Mills. The food conglomerate, which would grow to become a Fortune 500 company, developed the Betty Crocker product line to include cake and cookie mixes, Hamburger Helper, instant mashed potatoes, and more.

The first cookbook using the name Betty Crocker was published in 1933. In 1942, "The Betty Crocker Cook Book of All-Purpose Baking" was published, containing 220 of Betty's own recipes. Betty's portrait, created in 1936, is that of a sensible homemaker, an image that has been updated nearly once per decade to reflect the changing styles and faces of American women.

In the late 1940s, the brand's most famous product–cake mix–was created in the Betty Crocker test kitchens. In the 1950s, General Mills made changes to the cake mixes, including eliminating powdered eggs. It turned out that home cooks preferred adding a few of their own ingredients to help the cake feel more "genuine." Cooks also asked for a layer cake, which came out in 1949 in two varieties: Devils Food and Party Layer Cake Mix. Throughout the 1960s, softer and more refined flour and sugar were used, as well as a new homogenized shortening.

In 1978, Betty Crocker created her most successful cake mix recipe. In response to the demand for a maximally moist cake, pudding was added to the mix. The winning combination debuted as Betty Crocker SuperMoist cake mixes. SuperMoist mixes were softer, richer, spongier and tastier than ever before. In 2003, the Betty Crocker Kitchens added even more pudding mix to the best-selling SuperMoist layer cake to further enhance its texture. SuperMoist cakes are still available in more than 20 flavors, including Butter Pecan, Cherry Chip, French Vanilla, and chocolate varieties made with Hershey's cocoa.

In 1996, General Mills created a new Betty Crocker portrait from a computer-generated composite of 75 winners of a nationwide "Spirit of Betty Crocker" contest. Today's customers still seek advice and recipes from "America's First Lady of Food" via the Betty Crocker Web site, e-mail newsletters, magazines and cookbooks.

The brand remains strong for the 21st century, encompassing dozens of products, from the SuperMoist cake mix and frosting lines to Hamburger and Tuna Helper mixes to a licensed line of small kitchen appliances.

U.S. retail sales for Betty Crocker dessert mixes are growing–7 percent in 2006–and the brand has gained ground in the overall $1.5 billion U.S. dessert mix category. Internationally, Betty Crocker is a popular baking mix brand in Australia and the United Kingdom.

Betty Crocker Kitchens

Vital Statistics

Parent Company	General Mills
Classic Product	SuperMoist cake mix
Established	1921
Main Production Site	Minneapolis, Minnesota

Birdhouse Skateboards

Without a doubt, Tony Hawk is the most recognizable skateboarder in the world. A 12-time World Champion and 16-time ESPN X-Games medalist, Hawk is famous for inventing dozens of skateboarding maneuvers, including the frontside 540 rodeo flip, the backside varial, and the 720. His most legendary trick is the 900—two and a half rotations, or 900 degrees—a stunt performed midair above a vertical ramp. Executed for the first time at the X Games in 1999, this trick landed Hawk a ranking in ESPN's Greatest Moments in Sport History.

Tony Hawk is also an accomplished businessman. In 1992, he and his friend Per Welinder founded Birdhouse Skateboards. The company makes and sells skateboards, wheels and accessories. The skateboard decks are made of 7-ply hard rock Canadian maple and emblazoned with the Birdhouse logo. Many designs play on the avian theme, featuring stylized skeletons of bats, vultures, baby birds, falcons, and dragons. Also on offer are longboard cruisers and classic decks in 1970s and 1980s styles. There's even a Rasta deck in green, red, and yellow.

Tony Hawk is not the only legend in Birdhouse's professional team. In 2006, the company announced the addition of US Gold Medalist snowboarder Shaun White to the Birdhouse lineup. Bringing his snowboarding skills to the arena of vertical skateboarding, White, like Hawk, seeks to push the envelope of maneuvers performed on a skateboard. Where Hawk set the bar at the 900, White has been busy working on the 1080—three complete revolutions in the air.

In addition to its celebrity vertical skaters, Birdhouse also has a well-rounded team of street skaters—professionals that perform kickflips, heelflips, lipslides, bluntslides and other tricks on handrails, ledges, and down sets of stairs. The brand sells vivid, comic book–inspired signature decks of popular skateboarders such as Matt Ball, Brian Sumner, Steve Nesser, Willy Santos, Jeremy Klein, and Ragdoll. Birdhouse skateboards are priced so that almost anyone can afford them.

Now retired from competition, Tony Hawk has enjoyed the same stunning success in business as he did in sports. Birdhouse is now a division of Blitz Distribution, which Hawk and Welinder set up several years after they founded Birdhouse. Blitz has grown to include other skateboard brands such as Flip, Baker, Fury, Hook-Ups, and SK8 Mafia.

Hawk's other businesses include 900 Films, a film and video production company, and Boom Boom Huck Jam, an arena tour featuring virtuoso skateboarders performing in large spaces. He has licensed his name and likeness to Activision's best-selling Tony Hawk's Pro Skater video game series, which has generated more than $1 billion in retail sales. Hawk also runs a foundation that helps build skate parks across America, especially in low-income neighborhoods.

Hawk and Welinder see Birdhouse Skateboards as a vehicle for bringing skateboarding to the world. The more people who can buy a great board and go skateboarding, the better it is for the sport. Hawk plans to help keep skateboarding hip and innovative, and he's likely to succeed. Most skateboarders would agree that if Hawk can do a 900, he can do just about anything.

Vital Statistics

Classic Product skateboards

Established 1992

Founders Tony Hawk and Per Welinder

Parent Company Blitz Distribution

Headquarters Huntington Beach, California

Annual Sales $25 million (2006)

Black & Decker

S. Duncan Black and Alonzo G. Decker, Sr., started their company back in 1910 by manufacturing candy dippers and milk-bottle-cap machines. Rather than manufacturing industrial products that were invented and sold by others, Black & Decker started designing and manufacturing its own line of electric-powered tools in 1916. Among these tools was the world's first portable half-inch electric drill with a pistol grip, trigger switch, and universal motor. Tipping the scales at more than 21 pounds and costing $230, the drill was considered lightweight and inexpensive.

In 1917, Black & Decker received a patent for the pistol grip and trigger switch on its drill, and in that same year it built its first plant in Towson, Maryland. Sales exceeded the $1 million mark in 1918, and the company grew with sales representation in the USSR, Japan, and Australia. In 1922, the company formed its first foreign subsidiary in Canada—the start of rapid international expansion that helped propel Black & Decker to the front of the international market.

During World War II, Black & Decker continued to produce power tools within legislated limits, and the Towson plant manufactured fuses, gun shells, and other products for the Allies. The company's contribution toward the war effort earned them four WWII citations, including the prestigious Army-Navy "E" award for production.

While Black & Decker was adding plants and manufacturing facilities in the United States and abroad to accommodate demand, products of the highest caliber were constantly being developed and introduced. Home Utility electric tools were launched in 1946, the first line aimed at the do-it-yourself market. The eponymous Black & Decker power drill was offered in a variety of styles, including the first cordless electric drill powered by nickel-cadmium in 1961. The following year also saw the introduction of the world's first cordless outdoor product, a hedge trimmer.

The year 1964 was one of several accomplishments for Black & Decker. Sales passed the $100 million mark, and the company tuned in to television advertising. Black & Decker supplied NASA with a cordless minimum-torque-reaction space tool, and a few years later, it was responsible for the development of a power head for use on the Apollo Lunar Surface Drill to remove core samples of the moon. More recently, innovations such as Dustbuster handheld cordless vacuum (1979) and Auto Wrench handheld power adjustable wrench (2006) continue to make housekeeping and home repairs easier and faster to accomplish.

The company has continuously moved into new markets, leaving its mark in indelible orange and black—making Black & Decker a leader as a global manufacturer and marketer of high-quality power tools and accessories, hardware and home improvement products, and technology-based fastening systems. With products and services marketed in more than 100 countries, Black & Decker is recognized worldwide as a brand of excellence known for its dedication to product innovation, design, and quality.

Vital Statistics
Established 1910
Founder S. Duncan Black and Alonzo G. Decker, Sr.
Classic Product cordless high-performance drill
Sales $6.4 billion (2006)

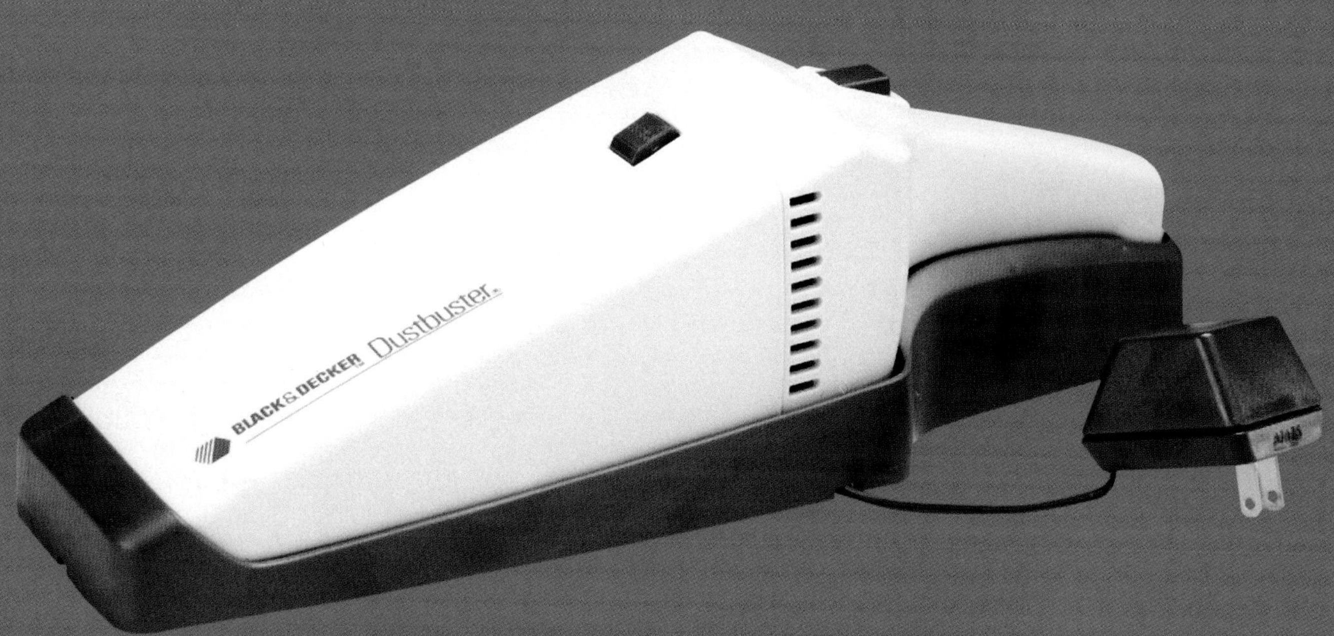
BLACK & DECKER
Dustbuster

Bounce

Bounce dryer sheets are a technological marvel—fabric softener in the form of a whisper-light sheet that can breathe its fresh scent into almost anything. Over the past 35 years, Bounce has become a staple in laundry rooms because of its convenience, ease of use, dramatic ability to reduce static cling, and the soft, fresh scent it imparts to clothes right out of the dryer. Bounce is one of the choice products offered by American industry giant Procter & Gamble, which has been helping Americans maintain their homes for nearly two centuries.

Since 1837, Procter & Gamble has made doing the laundry more convenient and effective for Americans. More recently, the company has also spread these benefits to consumers around the world. The company continues to develop products and improve formulas with the most up-to-date technology. Bounce made its first appearance in 1972, as part of the company's desire to keep pace with changing laundry needs in the 1970s, a major growth period for Procter & Gamble. Bounce was the first dryer sheet on the market and is currently offered in a variety of scents including Fresh Linen Scent, Outdoor Fresh Scent, Spring Awakening, and Summer Orchard. Bounce dryer sheets are also available in an unscented version, Bounce Free. Bounce's latest offering is its line of Bounce with Febreze Fresh Scent products, which allow consumers to get the fresh scent of Febreze in their fabrics.

Bounce quickly became the country's most popular dryer sheet for reducing static, and over the years consumers have developed new and innovative uses for the product outside of the laundry room. Bounce sheets can be placed under a mattress pad for a lingering freshness throughout the night, inside shoes for a clean, fresh scent, in a wastebasket for freshening, and in drawers or linen closets to help keep clothes smelling newly washed. Consumers also claim that Bounce dryer sheets can freshen suitcases, cars, books and photo albums that are not opened frequently. Bounce has developed additional means of communicating with consumers, eager for these ideas and to share their own. An online magazine allows readers to discover innovative products and find tips, samples, and offers to help simplify life with Bounce dryer sheets. The Fresh Ideas Message Board is where suggestions can be posted and picked up.

Today, Bounce is a modern, evolving product line, with its own Web site: www.BounceEverywhere.com.

The Procter & Gamble Company is one of the world's largest and most successful makers of household products. P&G has 18 billion-dollar brands, and Bounce is one of the company's recognizable, reliable offerings.

Vital Statistics
Parent Company The Procter & Gamble Company
Product Launch 1972

Helps Repel Lint and Hair
Ayuda a repeler pelusas y pelo
Aide à tenir peluches, cheveux et poils à distance
See Back
Vea atrás
Détalls au dos
Bounce®
Outdoor Fresh Scent™
Aroma de Frescura Natural
Fraîche senteur de grand air
0 1 2 3 4
SCENT LEVEL · NIVEL DE FRAGANCIA · INTENSITÉ DU PARFUM
80 162 x 228 mm 6.4 x 9 INCHES/PULGADAS/POUCES
SHEETS/HOJAS/FEUILLES
Fabric Softener • Suavizador de Telas • Assouplissant textile

Brooks Brothers

Established in 1818, Brooks Brothers is the oldest clothing retailer in the United States and known for its classic style and superior quality. Henry Sands Brooks opened his first store on the northeast corner of Catherine and Cherry streets in New York City, calling it H. & D.H. Brooks & Co. Brooks's guiding principle for the company: "To make and deal only in merchandise of the finest quality, to sell it at a fair profit and to deal with people who seek and appreciate such merchandise." From the start, Brooks distinguished itself through the excellent workmanship found in both its custom- and ready-made clothing.

In 1845, Brooks introduced the first ready-to-wear suits in America, causing pioneers of the 1849 gold rush, unable to wait on tailors' schedules, to flock to the store for ready-made clothing. This was the first of many firsts that Brooks Brothers introduced to America. The company's trademark Golden Fleece symbol was adopted in 1850. The Golden Fleece, a sheep suspended in a ribbon, had long been a symbol of British wool merchants. Dating back to the 15th century, it had been an emblem of the Knights of the Golden Fleece, founded by Philip the Good, Duke of Burgundy. According to Greek mythology, the Golden Fleece (a magical flying ram) was sought by Jason and the Argonauts.

Brooks Brothers introduced many items to America that came to epitomize classic American style. In 1890, a Brooks Brothers senior partner returned from a trip to England with the silk foulard necktie, which quickly became part of American wardrobes. The button-down, polo collar shirt was conceived by John Brooks, grandson of the founder, after he attended an English polo match in 1896. It was an instant hit and soon became one of the company's best-selling items. Other firsts include the English polo coat in 1919, the repp tie in 1920, argyle socks in 1949, and fabrics such as Indian madras in 1920 and seersucker in 1930.

In the summer of 1915, Brooks Brothers relocated to its present 10-story flagship store at 346 Madison Avenue. This placed it in the neighborhood that had recently become the preferred location for many of New York's most prominent social organizations, including the Harvard and Yale clubs. Brooks Brothers found its home among the Ivy League preppy set that embraced its style. Notable others who wore Brooks Brothers were Ulysses S. Grant's Union officers, who wore tailored Brooks Brothers uniforms; John F. Kennedy, who popularized the two-button suit worn at his inauguration; several of Hollywood's best-dressed men, such as Cary Grant, Clark Gable, and Gary Cooper; and the trouser-wearing Katharine Hepburn, an icon of classic American style.

Over the years, Brooks Brothers has successfully expanded to include factory stores, an online shop, stores in Japan and Italy, and, in 1999, a second flagship store at Fifth Avenue and 53rd Street. More recently, Brooks Brothers opened two stores in London, where many of the classic Brooks Brothers styles originated.

Vital Statistics
Established 1818
Founder Henry Sands Brooks
Owner Retail Brand Alliance
Headquarters New York, New York

Brooks Brothers
15½-34
Est 1818
THE ORIGINAL POLO SHIRT
TRADITIONAL FIT
ALL SUPIMA COTTON
MADE IN USA
OF IMPORTED FABRIC

W. Atlee Burpee & Company

The oldest and largest supplier of seeds to home gardeners in the United States, W. Atlee Burpee & Company started in Philadelphia in 1876 with a young man named Washington Atlee Burpee, who had an interest in poultry breeding. This interest eventually expanded to include breeding of livestock, dogs, and plants. The science of genetics, at the time in its infancy, also fascinated young Burpee. His fascination in these areas led to what became the largest mail-order seed company in the world—mailing a million catalogues a year to American gardeners by 1915.

Pursuing his interests, Burpee read all he could about breeding, and by his midteens, he was corresponding with breeders in England. They exchanged information, and Burpee even conducted his own experiments, gaining recognition when he published papers on his research in England. But Burpee's father had other plans, and young Burpee honored his father's wishes by enrolling in the University of Pennsylvania Medical School. Realizing that he had no interest in following in his father's footsteps, he dropped out. His mother, a bit more understanding of her son's desires, lent him $1,000 to set up a company to breed poultry.

Burpee had reasonable success in the first two years but realized he needed to diversify to solve his business problems: sustaining business from year to year and providing products that could survive shipping. He began to breed dogs, hogs, sheep, and goats. The addition of plants and flowers to the catalogue came when some customers, farmers who had emigrated to America, praised his livestock but lamented the poor quality of the seeds they were getting locally for their vegetable crops. The farmers asked whether Burpee could provide seed or refer them to someone who could. Another story claims that Burpee's hogs were very particular about their feed and that Burpee realized that shipping feed and seed would be easier and more cost-effective than shipping livestock. This business development would appease the livestock as well as the homesick farmers looking for familiar crops.

The Burpee catalogue was a result of an annual trip to Europe each spring. Burpee set out in the south and made his way north, collecting seeds along the way. His compiled observations and notes in a field book would later become that year's catalogue. By the 1880s, Burpee was supplying the northeastern United States as well as the flourishing Great Plains states with livestock and seed through its growing mail-order company. The Burpee secret: it guaranteed satisfaction for one year from the purchase date or the company would replace the seeds. This guarantee of success fueled the company's popularity and growth.

In 1888, Burpee bought Fordhook, his farm in Doylestown, Pennsylvania, which became the world-famous plant-development facility that enabled Burpee to adapt European plants and flowers to the American climate. By the 1890s, Burpee & Company was the largest seed company in the world.

W. Atlee Burpee & Company continues to expand by constant innovation in the world of agriculture and horticulture. From the Surehead, a new variety of cabbage Burpee created just one year after starting his business in 1876, to the first yellow sweet corn, offered in the Burpee catalogue of 1902, to a variety of marigolds—Burpee's best selling flower—W. Atlee Burpee & Company taught America and the world how to grow.

Vital Statistics

Classic Product	seeds
Established	1876
Founder	Washington Atlee Burpee
Sales	$32 million

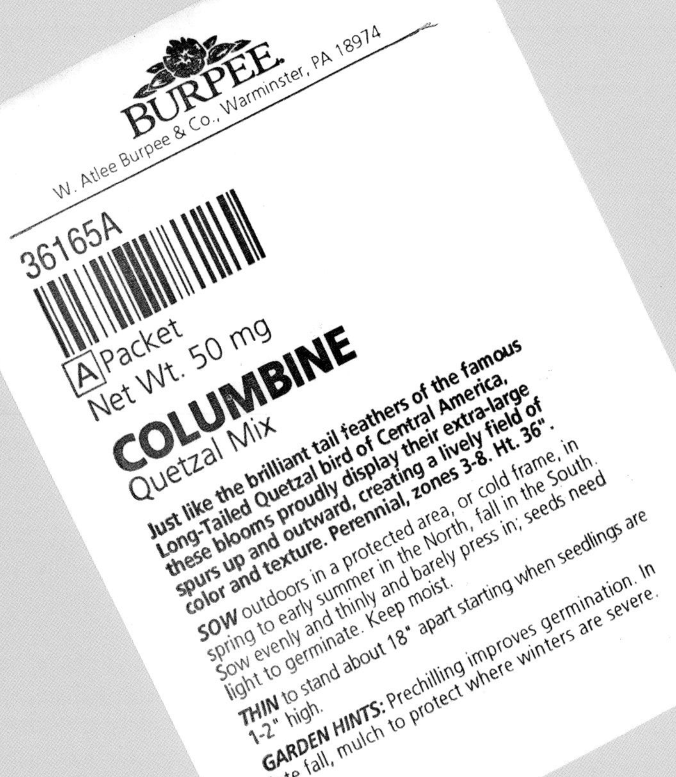

BURPEE.
W. Atlee Burpee & Co., Warminster, PA 18974
36165A
A Packet
Net Wt. 50 mg
COLUMBINE
Quetzal Mix
Just like the brilliant tail feathers of the famous Long-Tailed Quetzal bird of Central America, these blooms proudly display their extra-large spurs up and outward, creating a lively field of color and texture. Perennial, zones 3-8. Ht. 36".
SOW outdoors in a protected area, or cold frame, in spring to early summer in the North, fall in the South. Sow evenly and thinly and barely press in; seeds need light to germinate. Keep moist.
THIN to stand about 18" apart starting when seedlings are 1-2" high.
GARDEN HINTS: Prechilling improves germination. In late fall, mulch to protect where winters are severe.

Butterball

There is scarcely a more iconic American dish than Thanksgiving turkey, which is almost always a Butterball. Butterball, owned by Butterball LLC, today includes fresh and frozen whole turkeys, boneless turkey roasts, seasoned turkey roasts, turkey cuts, premium cold cuts and sausage products, bacon, and chicken and turkey strips. The company's Butterball Turkey Talk-Line experts answer calls nonstop throughout the holiday season. Butterball has been the top selling brand of turkey in the United States for more than 50 years.

Butterball was born when, in 1954, young entrepreneur Frank Swift set out to create an especially plump, juicy turkey that would also be easy to prepare. Swift & Company, his Downer's Grove, Illinois-based meat producer, began researching turkey breeds and ultimately pursued one with a larger-than-typical breast. Swift decided to call the turkeys Butterballs, not—as many consumers believed—because the turkeys were injected with butter but because the word connoted plumpness and tenderness, the hallmarks of a Butterball turkey. In perfecting his product, Swift made several innovations based on major research to determine what factors were most appealing to American cooks. One advance was the removal of the leg tendons from Butterball drumsticks. Another was the Swift way of shaping turkeys, by looping the tails and tucking in the legs, making the birds easier to pack and store and reducing exposed surface area to potential freezer burn. Liquid freezing was introduced in 1959, and all Butterball plants were equipped with the technology by 1965. Although Butterball turkey breasts had long been basted with a vegetable oil mixture, in 1985 the company perfected the technique of needle injection, making for moister-than-ever white meat. Initially, Butterball turkeys were produced in 36 factories; today they are shipped from three modern, state-of-the-art plants.

Taste was key, but Butterball reached the top by paying attention to convenience as well. In 1972, turkey lifters made their first appearance, eliminating the battle between unwieldy turkey and home cook. Butterball began separating the giblets and neck into plastic bags that were easy to remove from the defrosted bird. And in 1976, the launch of the size selector allowed consumers to see at a glance the weight of the turkeys in a freezer case and then made the turkey easy to lift and handle once it was back in the kitchen. And, since 1981, Butterball's toll-free Turkey Talk-Line (1-800-BUTTERBALL) has helped millions of people solve their cooking problems. Through the next 26 years Butterball and the Turkey Talk-Line changed with the times. In 1991, the Turkey Talk-Line went bi-lingual, adding a Spanish option for callers. Butterball.com launched in 1995 (now available in Spanish too) full of information and delicious recipes that can be accessed year-round. Finally, 2006 brought a podcast featuring cooking tips and stories straight from the Turkey Talk-Line.

The experts at the Butterball Turkey Talk-Line continue to answer questions, from the basic to the ludicrous, including one customer who asked if he could thaw his Butterball in an electric blanket. The answer is no, but the message imparted by the friendly voice on the line is the same as it always will be: "The best of all is Butterball."

Vital Statistics
Parent Company Butterball LLC
Founder/Inventor Frank Swift
Employees 38,000
Annual Sales $14,600 million

Cadillac

Famous for its tail fins of the 1950s as well as its technical innovations, including V8 engines and electric starters, Cadillac has long been a titan of American automakers. Because of Cadillac's styling and quality, it became the car of choice for many celebrities. Joan Crawford drove a 1933 Caddy, boxer Sugar Ray Robinson cruised in a pink one, and the Escalade is the favorite of today's hip-hop artists. The phrase "This is the Cadillac of [fill in the blank]" is often used by salespeople to make the point that their product is top of the line.

Bought by General Motors in 1909, Cadillac was formed in 1902 when Henry Ford's original backers became disillusioned with Ford's focus on race cars. They called in engineer Henry M. Leland to advise them in selling off the plant, but instead Leland persuaded them to continue in the car business. They chose the name *Cadillac* after the French explorer of the same name, who founded Detroit in 1701.

The first Cadillac, introduced at the 1903 New York auto show, was an immediate success, with 2,286 orders taken in the first week, a huge number in that era. In 1907, Leland developed a way to manufacture parts that were so precise they could easily be interchanged. To prove it, three Cadillacs were completely disassembled, with their 721 component parts scrambled into one huge pile. Using only wrenches and screwdrivers, the cars were reassembled and driven 50 miles. As a result, Cadillac won the prestigious Dewar Trophy for the most important advancement of the year in the auto industry. Cadillac proved itself again in 1912 when it offered the first successful electric starter. Developed by Charles F. Kettering and marketed as more convenient for ladies than the hand crank, the starter used a combined generator and electric motor that cranked the engine flywheel. The breakthrough earned another Dewar Trophy. Other innovations include the first V8 engine in 1915, shatter-resistant safety glass in 1926, and the first fully synchronized transmission (which prevented crunching gears when shifting) in 1928.

Technical prowess aside, Cadillac became known for building large, powerful luxury cars. General Motors style chief Harley J. Earl was instrumental in developing Cadillac's signature tail fins and wraparound windshield. The tail fins were originally inspired in 1948 by the twin rudders of the Lockheed P-38 Lightning, and by 1959, Cadillac's exaggerated profile was being copied in everything from other automobiles to cat-eye eyeglasses.

The gas crises of 1973 and 1979 forced Cadillac, along with other U.S. car manufacturers, to downsize their offerings. Gone were the big Fleetwoods and DeVilles and in their place came the Cimarron and Seville. The Seville hit the big time in 1992, when it was restyled as the Seville STS. It was larger than in previous years, with an aggressive outer styling but a comfortable, distinctive interior. Between 2001 and 2004, Cadillac sales rose sharply. The STS underwent another transformation in 2005 when the crisp lines, hard creases, and sharp corners of the company's Art and Science styling were incorporated.

Vital Statistics
Company Name General Motors
Established 1908
Headquarters Detroit, Michigan
Annual Sales $192,604 million

Callaway Golf Company

It all began with a three-man golf-equipment company in Temecula, California, called Hickory Stick USA. Ely Callaway, a successful businessman in textiles and wine, took notice of the tiny company after he saw a pitching wedge in a golf shop that reminded him of the hickory-shafted clubs he had used as a kid. The difference was that the core was hollowed and filled with steel for consistency and strength. Callaway bought half the company the following year and changed the name to Callaway Hickory Stick USA. Adhering to a proven business model of thinking big and hiring the smartest people, he brought in a pool cue maker named Richard C. Helmstetter as chief club designer. Callaway began carving out a niche as a small manufacturer of unique, high-performance golf equipment.

By 1998, Ely Callaway had bought out his partners and renamed the company Callaway Golf. Its primary focus shifted from re-creating classic clubs to pioneering original and innovative designs. The year 1991 changed everything for Callaway Golf when the Big Bertha Stainless Steel Driver was introduced. Helmstetter and his team designed a stainless steel driver with a larger, more forgiving head than anything previously designed. It was named, by Ely Callaway, after the World War I "Big Bertha" cannon, famed for its distance and accuracy. This revolutionary new golf club propelled Callaway Golf on its path to incredible success and has forever changed the way people play golf.

Noted for bringing a new level of innovation to the game and more fun to the average golfer, Callaway Golf clubs were also noticed by the pros. By the end of the 1992 golf season, the Big Bertha Driver was ranked number one on the Senior Professional Golfers' Association, the Ladies Professional Golfers' Association and the Hogan (now Nationwide) tours. The second generation of Big Bertha clubs, the Great Big Bertha Driver, came out in 1995. It had a larger head–now made of titanium–and longer shaft yet was lighter than its steel predecessor. The Biggest Big Bertha Titanium Driver followed in 1997.

At the dawn of the new millennium, Callaway Golf branched out by deciding to design, manufacture and sell superior golf balls. The Rule 35 ball was introduced in 2000, and its superior performance quickly made it the number two ball in top 10 finishes and wins across the five major professional tours in their first year in play.

Callaway Golf continues its winning tradition of combining advanced technology, high-quality construction, and innovative design to make superior golf equipment that enhances performance and enjoyment for all golfers. Ely Callaway's business philosophy–to make superior products that are different from anything else on the market–has been pivotal in making Callaway Golf one of the largest makers of golf clubs in the world. Simply put, Callaway Golf offers products and services to make every golfer a better golfer.

Vital Statistics
Company Name Callaway Golf Company
Classic Product Big Bertha driver
Established 1982
Founder Ely Callaway
Annual Sales Net sales of $1.018 billion

BIG BERTHA
460
10
Callaway
GOLF
1
Callaway
GOLF
1
Callaway
GOLF
1
Callaway
GOLF
BIG BERTHA
THU 6

Calphalon

In 1963, entrepreneur and food enthusiast Ron Kasperzak established Commercial Aluminum Cookware after purchasing a general-purpose metal spinning and stamping facility in Toledo, Ohio. He then set out to expand and upgrade the facility's limited line of aluminum cookware for the food service industry. The Calphalon brand has its roots in the commercial kitchen, but the growth of the Calphalon brand parallels a larger cultural movement—the birth and subsequent growth of the gourmet cooking movement in the United States.

It was right around the time Ron established his company that many Americans got their first taste of classic French cooking, watching Julia Child on public TV. In California, Chuck Williams was busy creating a chain of stores dedicated to gourmet cooking called Williams-Sonoma. Back in Toledo, Ron's enhanced line of cookware was enthusiastically embraced by professional chefs. Within ten years, Commercial Aluminum was the second leading supplier of cookware to the food service industry.

In the late 1960s, Commercial Aluminum adapted an electrochemical method of treating raw aluminum, called hard anodizing. This process altered the surface of the metal and made it harder than stainless steel. It made the cooking surface stick-resistant and non-reactive. It also changed the color of the aluminum to the Calphalon signature matte gray. Though many cookware companies eventually followed his lead, Ron Kasperzak is credited with creating the original hard anodized aluminum cookware. He named his invention Calphalon and continued to sell it to the restaurant trade.

By the 1970s, there was considerable momentum behind the gourmet cooking movement, and Ron Kasperzak's Calphalon was beginning to develop an almost cult-like following among the savviest at-home gourmets. By the 1980s, the gourmet lifestyle, once the domain of an elite, dedicated few, had reached the masses. The Calphalon brand grew more widely known and consumer demand for the company's cookware increased. By 1993, consumer sales so outpaced trade sales that Commercial Aluminum Cookware closed its commercial division.

In the early 1990s, home chefs were placing greater value on convenience than ever before. In response, Calphalon introduced a premium quality nonstick cookware in 1993 and launched another decade of design and technological innovation. The late 1990s saw an increased focus on home improvement and home décor, and the kitchen, in particular, emerged as the center of social life. Consumer interest in cooking surged, and home chefs looked to their kitchens as an opportunity to make a statement about themselves. They wanted beautifully designed kitchenware to complement their beautifully designed kitchens.

Consequently, over the past decade Calphalon products have begun to reflect a greater emphasis on aesthetics and the diverse needs of individual cooks. Only Calphalon offers home chefs all three essential cooking surfaces: anodized aluminum, nonstick, and stainless steel. The Calphalon assortment now spans a wider range of price points, and is accessible to a wider range of consumers. Today, the Calphalon kitchenware collection includes premium quality bakeware, cutlery, textiles, barware, and kitchen accessories, along with its wide assortment of gourmet cookware. In 2001, Calphalon opened the doors of its first cooking school—the Calphalon Culinary Center—in Chicago. A second Culinary Center in Toronto, Ontario, opened in 2003. The opening of the Calphalon Kitchen Outlet stores in 2006 continues to strengthen the bond between Calphalon and the consumer.

Vital Statistics
Classic Product Kitchenwares
Established 1963 (as Commercial Aluminum Cookware)
Founder Ronald Kasperzak
Parent Company Newell Rubbermaid
Headquarters Toledo, Ohio

Campbell Soup Company

It was 1869 and Ulysses S. Grant was president when a fruit merchant named Joseph Campbell and an icebox manufacturer named Abraham Anderson formed a business in New Jersey that would become an American classic. Originally called the Joseph A. Campbell Preserve Company, their business produced canned tomatoes, vegetables, jellies, soups, condiments, and minced meats. The moment that altered Campbell's history, however, occurred in 1897, when the company's general manager hired his 24-year-old nephew Dr. John T. Dorrance, a European-trained chemist who invented the world's first condensed soup.

Dorrance's invention lowered the costs for packaging, shipping, and storage, making it possible to sell a 10-ounce can of Campbell's condensed soup for a dime, compared with more than 30 cents for regular soup. In 1898, a company executive attended a football game between rivals Cornell University and the University of Pennsylvania and was so struck by Cornell's new red-and-white uniforms that he persuaded the company to use the colors on cans of Campbell's soups. In 1900, Joseph Campbell died, but his soup won the Gold Medallion for Excellence at the Paris Exposition, a medal that has been featured on its label ever since. There were five original varieties—Tomato, Consommé, Vegetable, Chicken, and Oxtail—and by 1904, Campbell's was selling 16 million cans of soup a year. In 1922, the company adopted its current name, having dropped all other products because of the soup's overwhelming popularity.

Advertising has always been a major part of Campbell's success. In 1904, for example, the appealing Campbell Kids, created by artist Gebbie Drayton, made their first appearance in advertisements on New York City trolley cars—a clever attempt to appeal to working mothers and to market the company's by-then 21 soup varieties. In the 1930s, the now-familiar "M'm! M'm! Good!" jingle was first heard on radio spots; in the 1950s, both the Campbell Kids and the slogan made their way into American homes via television. Another significant factor in Campbell Soup's stratospheric rise was the inspiration to use the product in recipes. A cookbook published in 1916 titled *Helps for the Hostess* introduced American housewives to dishes with Campbell's; later cookbooks featured now-iconic recipes such as Green Bean Casserole and Glorified Chicken. Americans now use more than 440 million cans each year for this purpose alone. In fact, Campbell's Soup ranks behind only meat/poultry, pasta, and seasonings/spices as the ingredient most often used in dinner preparations. In 1954, Campbell's went public with one class of common stock and was admitted for trading on the New York Stock Exchange. Eight years later, pop artist Andy Warhol immortalized the brand by creating his famous Campbell's Soup cans, claiming he had eaten the soup for lunch for 20 years. Campbell's has always adapted to fit the times, introducing its line of Healthy Request Soups, with less sodium, cholesterol, fat, and calories, to please the modern palate. The company has also acquired other significant brand names, from Pepperidge Farm to Franco-American, V8, Swanson, and Godiva Chocolates, all under the Campbell's umbrella. In 1990, Campbell's produced its 20 billionth can of condensed tomato soup.

Today, Campbell's products are available in practically every country in the world. Regional varieties such as Watercress and Duck-Gizzard Soup in China and a Cream of Chili Poblano soup in Mexico have appeared in response to cultural differences, but the classics—Tomato and Chicken Noodle—have never gone out of style. In 2004, the Campbell Soup Company celebrated its 50th year of listing on the New York Stock Exchange, and the Campbell Kids turned 100 years old. The company is the world's biggest provider of soup.

Vital Statistics

Established	1869
Founders	Joseph Campbell and Abraham Anderson
Employees	24,000
Annual Sales	$7,548 million

Cannondale Bicycle Corp.

Cannondale founder Joe Montgomery was inspired to start his business upon seeing a cyclist weighted down with a heavy backpack struggling to ride uphill. Montgomery reasoned that it would be easier to tow the load behind the bicycle on an extra set of wheels. Hence, he launched the world's first bicycle-towed trailer, "The Bugger." The original company had just three employees, and for its first three weeks of existence, did not have its own telephone. When Peter Myers, an employee, was dispatched to establish phone service for the company, he did so from a pay phone across the street. When asked how the company should be listed in the phone directory, he looked up and saw the sign for the train station, "Cannondale Crossing," named for a valley where actual cannons were transported across a river during the Revolutionary War. Peter blurted out, "Call it Cannondale."

After naming the company after a train station in Cannondale, Connecticut, the modestly financed business started by making biking accessories. The corporate line of bags and clothing was included in the L.L. Bean catalogue, providing the capital needed to start manufacturing bicycles. As production demand grew, Cannondale eventually opened a manufacturing facility in Bedford, PA with seven employees. That facility is still the heartbeat of Cannondale. The average tenure of people working at the factory today is over 10 years.

Cannondale focused on developing strong relationships with its dealers. By going directly to them to provide training and support, Cannondale staff could stand behind its products and ascertain customer needs and desires. By cutting out the distributors, the company also cut 25 percent of the costs, which are passed down to the consumers. The result is high-quality, high-performance bicycles at affordable prices. Cannondale also cosponsors bike racing teams to help promote its products.

Working on the idea that a bicycle made of aluminum, instead of steel, would be lighter and therefore faster, Cannondale introduced its first bicycle in 1983. Combining design and technology, the bicycle was made of handcrafted aluminum, making it lighter and more flex-resistant. Sales quickly shot up to $7 million, and the following year, Cannondale introduced its first mountain bike. The company continued to expand with an innovative line of products, including racing, hybrid, touring, and specialty bikes.

Cannondale is the leading manufacturer of high-end aluminum bicycles, selling more than 80 models in more than 70 countries around the world. The company also makes and sells bicycle parts and accessories, including clothing, packs, bags, and bike trailers. For more than 30 years, Cannnondale has led the way in bicycle design and technology innovation. In July 2005, Cannondale acquired Sugoi Performance Apparel, based in Vancouver, Canada.

Vital Statistics

Founder Joe Montgomery

Established 1971

Headquarters Bethel, Connecticut

Employees over 900

Carnival Cruise Lines

Carnival is synonymous with cruise vacations, from fun in the sun in the Caribbean to high-seas elegance on the *Queen Mary II.* With a wide variety of cruise lines to cater to a wide range of markets, Carnival, the world's number-one cruise operator, has something to offer everyone.

Ted Arison, an Israeli immigrant and cruise industry pioneer, started Carnival Cruise Lines in 1972. Arison started in the business in the 1960s, forming Norwegian Caribbean Lines with shipping magnate Knut Kloster. In 1971, he persuaded his longtime friend Meshulam Riklis, who owned American International Travel Service (AITS), to bankroll his $6.5 million purchase of the *Empress of Canada* in 1972. Arison set up Carnival Cruise Lines as a subsidiary of AITS and renamed the ship *Mardi Gras*. The *Mardi Gras* ran aground on its maiden voyage and put Carnival in the red for three years. In 1974, Arison bought out Riklis for $1 and assumed the $5 million debt.

Arison sought to bring affordable vacation packages to young middle-class consumers and to create a new type of cruise ship that featured live music, gambling, and other kinds of entertainment on board. His vision proved successful: Carnival was profitable within a month, and by the end of the following year, Arison had paid off Carnival's debt and bought its second ship. Carnival continued to expand and build ships, creating a global cruise line and one of the largest vacation companies in the world. The corporation consists of 12 leading cruise brands: Carnival Cruise Lines, Holland America Line, Princess Cruises, and Seabourn Cruise Line in North America; P&O Cruises, Cunard Line, and Ocean Village in the United Kingdom; AIDA in Germany; Costa Cruises in southern Europe; and P&O Cruises in Australia.

Because of the many cruise lines that Carnival has in its portfolio, the company is able to offer a wide variety of holiday and vacation packages to a very large customer base with diverse cultural and leisure-time interests. Carnival is noted for its wide array of offerings and exceptional value, which has made it the most profitable company in the leisure-travel industry.

Carnival Cruise Lines, the flagship brand of Carnival Corporation, is the most popular and most profitable cruise line in the world, operating 22 ships that cruise to destinations in the Bahamas, Canada, the Caribbean, the Mexican Riviera, New England, Alaska, Hawaii, Bermuda, Europe, and the Greek Isles.

Carnival Corporation operates a fleet of 82 ships, with several more scheduled for delivery, and has approximately 175,000 passengers at sea on a Carnival Corporation cruise at any given time. Its fleet also boasts the *Queen Mary 2,* the largest ocean liner in the world.

Vital Statistics
Parent Company Carnival Corporation
Established 1972
Founder Ted Arison
Annual Sales $11 billion

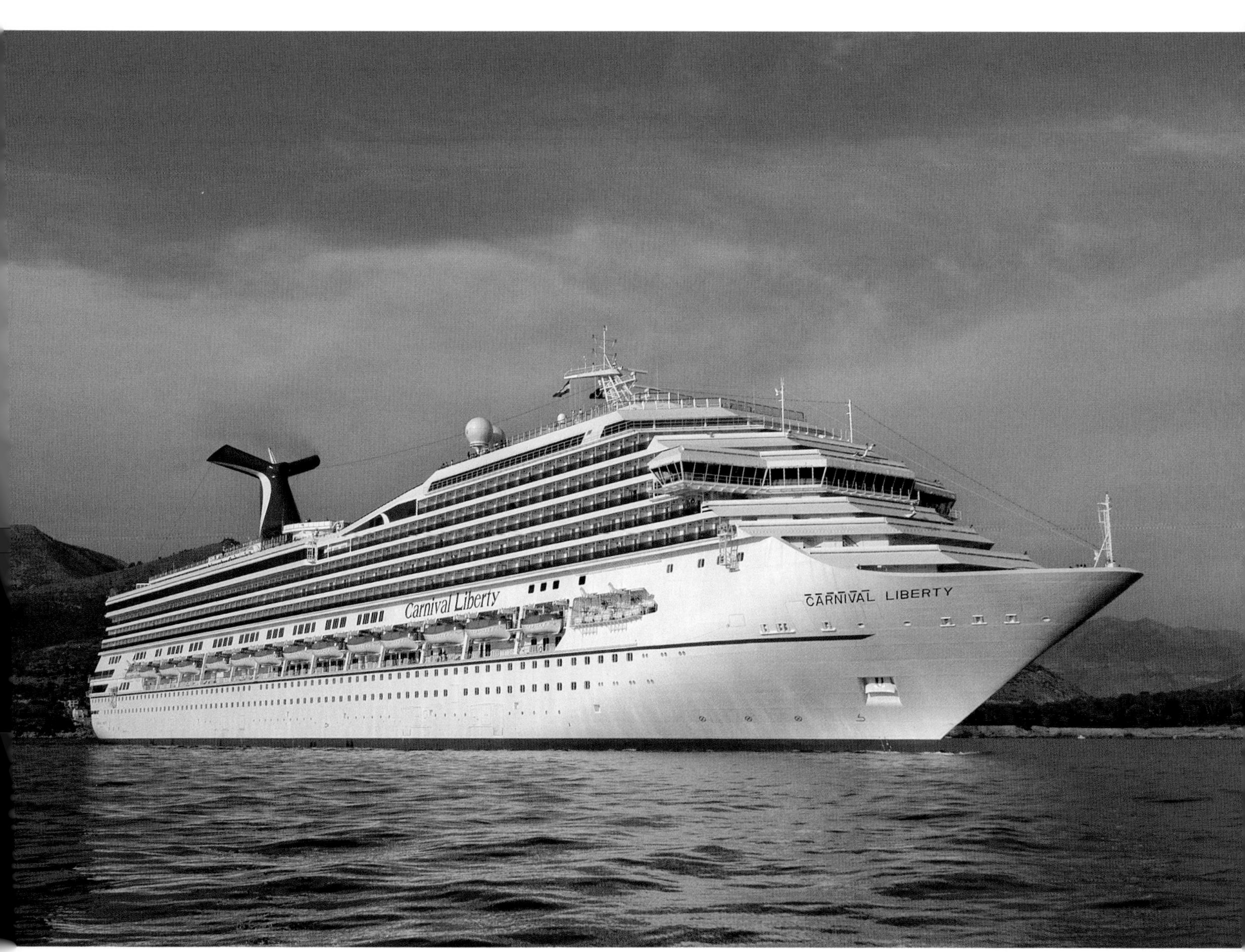
Carnival Liberty
CARNIVAL LIBERTY

Carrier

The Sistine Chapel, George Washington's Mount Vernon Estate, the Great Hall of the People in Beijing, and the XXVIII Olympics in Athens all have at least one thing in common: they're climate-controlled by Carrier systems. Carrier, a division of United Technologies, is the world's largest manufacturer of air-conditioning, ventilating, refrigerating, and heating systems and products. One of America's most recognized brands, a Carrier unit is shipped every three seconds of every day, somewhere around the world.

Carrier is named after Willis Haviland Carrier, inventor of the air conditioner, a man so dedicated to his work that he had to be reminded to eat and get a haircut. In 1902, he invented the first air conditioner. In 1906, he filed a patent for "The Apparatus for Treating Air," the first of his many inventions to control temperature and humidity. In 1915, Carrier and six other engineers formed the Carrier Engineering Corporation. The company's first best-selling product was a "centrifugal chiller" designed to cool large industrial spaces. The air conditioner helped these early American businesses flourish. Many industries—from film to tobacco to textiles—experienced tremendous growth because they achieved much better and more consistent results in a climate-controlled environment.

Enthusiasm for "manufactured weather" quickly spread among the American public. Soon enough, people were flocking to department stores and movie theaters equipped with Carrier air conditioners. In 1928, Carrier introduced the "weathermaker," the first successful consumer air conditioner. By the time Carrier passed away in 1950, he had been credited with helping industrialize the American Southwest and saw his systems installed in everything from atomic submarines to planes.

Carrier remains the industry leader in air-conditioning and ozone protection. Its current focus is on designing machines with maximum energy efficiency. The improved technologies will, by 2030, result in a reduction in U.S. carbon dioxide emissions equivalent to removing one million cars from the road each year. Moreover, the new units decrease energy consumption, and offer better environmental preservation. Carrier utilizes Puron, a high-tech refrigerant that contains no hydrofluorocarbons or other ozone-depleting substances. The company leads the charge on new technologies that allow consumers to set climate-controlled zones and control their home system via the Internet or telephone. The Infinity air conditioner by Carrier provides reliable, ultra-high efficiency cooling for long-lasting comfort and energy savings. Carrier also prides itself on its silencing system—a combination of mufflers, sound hoods, and vibration isolators and insulators—that makes its products among the quietest on the market.

Carrier systems are now sold in 172 countries on six continents around the world. Every three seconds a Carrier system is installed somewhere, from the smallest studio apartment in Tokyo to landmarks such as the Great Library of Alexandrina in Egypt—a vision that Willis Carrier would undoubtedly think is very cool.

Vital Statistics
Established 1915
Headquarters Farmington, Connecticut
Founder Willis Carrier
Employees 41,300
Annual Sales $13.5 billion (2006)

Carrier
Carrier

Century 21 Real Estate LLC

Decades before the 21st century, Century 21 Real Estate LLC established itself as the world's most recognized brand in real estate. With more than 8,400 independently owned offices in more than 46 countries, the franchise organization has thrived as the market for real estate intensifies. Brokering sales of homes and vacation and commercial properties in more than 40 countries and territories, the Century 21 system has broken significant new ground in global markets.

Century 21 Real Estate LLC was founded in 1971 by Orange County, California, real estate brokers Art Bartlett and Marsh Fisher. Throughout the 1970s, Bartlett and Fisher converted dozens of existing real estate companies into franchises, effectively creating an instant brand. Before Fisher and Bartlett, real estate was a localized business with hundreds of regional offices. By pooling advertising funds and creating a network, each franchise benefited from greater name recognition and property information. In 1977, the company went public. Soon afterward, it started to create "master franchises" by acquiring real estate offices in broad regions of the United States and by opening offices in Canada, the United Kingdom, Mexico, the Philippines, and many other countries. In 1980, the company merged with TransWorld Corp. In 1984, it was bought out by Metropolitan Life Insurance, which sold the company to Hospitality Franchise Systems (HFS) in 1995. In 1997, HFS became Cendant, which separated in 2006. The real estate divisions became Realogy Corporation of which Century 21 is now a subsidiary.

The Century 21 system's success is built on superior customer service—and the company continues to emphasize the importance of the sales associate in a real estate transaction. As a franchise, Century 21 has been able to empower its team of more than 140,000 sales associates with the tools to offer better client support: training, skills, and access to a wealth of real estate information within the company's global network. The company emphasizes how its agents provide clients with "peace of mind" as many of them undergo the most important transactions—and transitions—of their lives. In 2006, the company launched a series of commercials called "Agents of Change" in which people grapple with the emotional realities of buying or selling a home for the first time or in a new country. One commercial features an elderly couple sitting in a car looking at the family house they're about to sell. The husband gets upset as he reminisces about the house and all the memories of their years living there. Suddenly, a Century 21 sales associate shows up at the window and soothes him by saying that the memories are something he can take with him anywhere he goes.

Realizing that the virtual worlds of TV and Internet are important to selling real estate, the Century 21 system developed a relationship with CNN, which airs Century 21 ads and programming segments on TV and on the CNN Web site. Furthermore, Century21.com has more than 2.5 million visitors each month. To help accomplish its mission to help people everywhere become homeowners, the Century 21 system plans to continue to expand internationally, especially in China, and target the growing Hispanic market in the United States.

Vital Statistics

Company Name Century 21 Real Estate LLC
Classic Product Real estate
Established 1971
Founders Art Bartlett and Marsh Fisher
Sales Associates 140,000

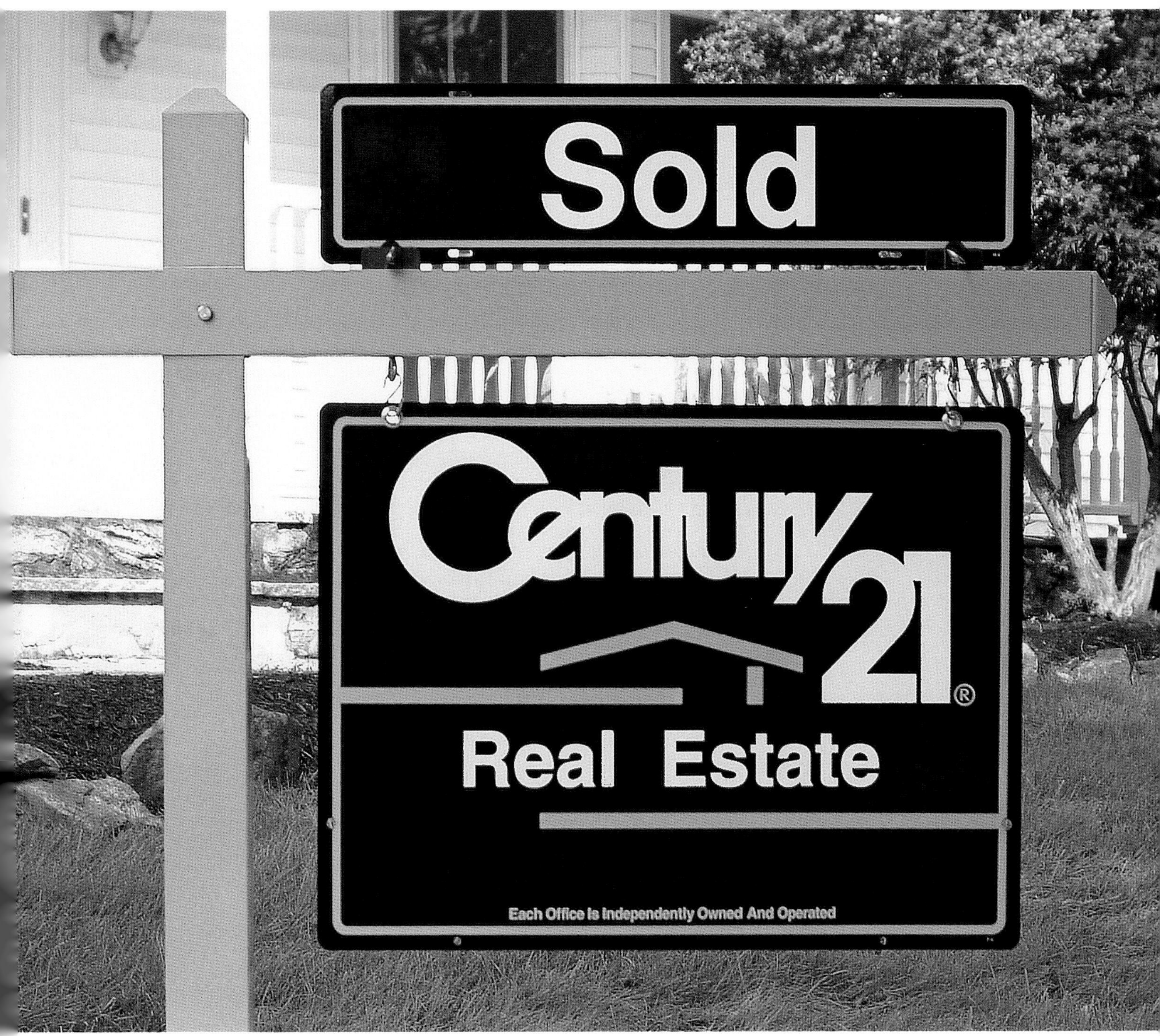
Sold
Century 21®
Real Estate
Each Office Is Independently Owned And Operated

Champion

Champion is the world's top producer of spark plugs for all types of combustion engines and has been for more than a century. Champion's now-famous Performance Driven approach to helping engines has been trademarked, and the company provides both resistor and nonresistor plugs. Champions can be found in power equipment, nearly all automotive applications, and even Dale Earnhardt Jr.'s Number 8 NEXTEL Cup Chevrolet.

In 1970, Champion introduced the use of iridium, which helps stabilize ignition voltage, in aviation and industrial spark plugs. Champion iridium sparkplugs provide unprecedented performance, a fine-wire iridium center electrode, and a ground electrode that grants longevity and resistance to erosion. The plugs feature an alloy, trademarked as Heat-Active, that ensures the plugs reach and maintain operating temperatures regardless of engine load. The Heat-Active alloy makes for maximum heat dissipation and conductivity. For decades, Champion has offered a variety of types of sparkplugs for consumers. The Champion Double-Platinum Power sparkplugs use platinum on the center and ground electrodes, a combination that allows the plugs to provide little wear and tear and longer life. This particular design is used primarily for a distributorless ignition showcasing a Waste Spark design. Champion Platinum Power sparkplugs have a platinum pad that is welded to a nickel alloy center electrode, allowing for consistent voltage to fire the plugs, and are known for their durability. Other types of Champion sparkplugs include the Truck Plug Spark Plugs and the Copper Plus Spark Plugs. The Truck Plug sparkplugs are used in pickups and sport utility vehicles. They have extra-large center and ground electrodes—20 percent larger than ordinary sparkplug and with a zirconia-enhanced insulator that is 40 percent stronger than ordinary sparkplugs. The Copper Plus sparkplugs are used primarily in equipment such as lawnmowers and power and garden tools. Champion also manufactures sparkplugs for marine equipment, such as inboards with diesel engines, outboards, jet boats, and personal watercraft. These plugs are specifically tailored for saltwater environments because of their stainless steel, rustproof threads. And finally, Champion produces sparkplugs for power sport vehicles, from motorcycles and all-terrain vehicles to snowmobiles and jet-skis. Today, Champion is produced under the auspices of parent Federal-Mogul Corporation, a company that makes its business acquiring and keeping the finest engineers and metallurgists to keep Champion sparkplugs at the top.

Champion has developed a strong relationship with professional sports car racing over the past hundred years that is stronger than ever. Champion has formed partnerships with NASCAR, National Hot Rod Association (NHRA), and Formula 1 racing teams. The company motto—Performance Driven—means drivers everywhere are proud of their Champion connection. Four out of the last five NASCAR champions, the last six NHRA Top Fuel champions, and 400 Formula 1 race winners have all used Champion sparkplugs in their victorious cars. Most recently, Dale Earnhardt Jr. has signed on as Champion's spokesman, promoting Champion sparkplugs in magazines and store promotional campaigns. Champion hopes to continue its unparalleled relationship with racing, which it considers an ideal proving ground for its product. But Champion also prides itself on creating spark plugs for everyday drivers, who have come to depend on the company's reliability and excellence.

Vital Statistics

Parent Company Federal-Mogul Corporation

Classic Product Spark plugs

Product Launch 1899

Employees 41,700

Annual Sales $6,286.0 million (2005)

ChapStick

It is the rare American who has not tucked a ChapStick tube into a pocket, purse, or glove compartment. As a 125-plus year old product, ChapStick has truly withstood the test of time with consumers. Like so many American originals, ChapStick was born in a home kitchen with a dose of ingenuity and a dream.

In the early 1880s, Dr. C. B. Fleet—a Lynchburg, Virginia, physician—invented ChapStick as a lip balm. He took his handmade product, which resembled wickless candles wrapped in tinfoil, to area stores, but the product never quite took off. In 1912, however, another Lynchburg resident, John Morton, bought the rights to the ChapStick product from Fleet for five dollars. His wife melted the pink mixture on her kitchen stove and poured the liquid through a small funnel into brass tubes, placing the racks of tubes on her porch to cool. She then cut the pieces into sticks and placed them in containers for shipping. In this form, ChapStick found a customer base, and the Mortons were soon able to found the Morton Manufacturing Corporation. ChapStick is a cleverly designed, diminutive lip balm in a tube that helps prevent and temporarily protect chafed, chapped, cracked, or windburned lips. ChapStick functions as both a sunscreen to prevent sunburn and as a skin moisturizer and lubricant. Some varieties contain topical analgesics to relieve sore lips, and many contain flavorings. In 1963, the AH Robins Company acquired ChapStick from the Morton Manufacturing Corporation. Then, ChapStick Lip Balm regular stick was the only variety; ChapStick flavored sticks appeared in 1969, ChapStick Sunblock 15 in 1981, ChapStick Petroleum Jelly Plus (in Regular, Sunblock 15, and Cherry-flavored varieties, all in squeezable tubes) in 1985, and ChapStick Medicated (in sticks, squeezable tubes, and jars) in 1992. Coincidentally, ChapStick played a role in one of the 20th century's great dramas when E. Howard Hunt and G. Gordon Liddy used "ChapStick" microphones during the Watergate burglary, and U.S. Olympic skier Suzy Chaffee gave the product a lovable face when she starred in ChapStick commercials as "Suzy Chapstick."

In 1989, AH Robins was acquired by American Home Products Corporation, which is today known as Wyeth. The ChapStick product has undergone a number of changes in formula, form, and packaging throughout the years, including producing it on a modern production line.

ChapStick has become a leading lip balm and is available in many varieties, each with its own flavors and applicators. Various formulations include the Classics, Moisturizers, Medicated, Flava-Craze, and Overnight, with SPFs from 0 to 30, depending on the variety. Chapstick often creates marketing partnerships such as with Disney and the Susan G. Komen Foundation.

Vital Statistics
Parent Company Wyeth Corporation
Classic Product Lip balm
Inventor Dr. C. B. Fleet

ChapStick®
Skin Protectant/Sunscreen SPF 4
CLASSIC
Original
Protects to Help Heal
for Softer, Healthier Lips
Every Day
NET WT 0.15 OZ. (4 g)
ChapStick®
Skin Protectant/Sunscreen SPF 4
CLASSIC
ORIGINAL

Charmin

At the turn of the millennium, Charmin launched a new ad campaign for its new extra-soft bathroom tissue. Titled "Call of Nature," the ads feature cuddly bear cubs dancing in the woods while singing "Hey little fella, got to change your touch, what you thought was enough might be too much; see, it's more cushionny than ever before, with Charmin-Ultra, Less is More, Cha-cha-cha-Charmin." The cubs are delighted by the softer toilet paper, and the ad definitively answers the question, "Does a bear poo in the woods?"

Equally certain is Charmin's presence in the toilet paper market. The Charmin brand was introduced in 1928 by the Hoberg Paper Company in Green Bay, Wisconsin. The company had modeled the design of the bathroom tissue on women's fashions of the 1920s. Legend has it that a Hoberg employee who sampled the toilet paper described it as "charmin," and the name stuck. Pronounced "SHAR-men," the toilet paper was so popular that in 1957 Hoberg changed its name to the Charmin Paper Company.

Further developments occurred after Procter & Gamble bought the Charmin brand in 1957. To address consumers' desire for softer bathroom tissue, in 1965 P&G patented a new manufacturing process for superior softness without sacrificing absorbency, strength, and economy. P&G also launched a decades-long ad campaign starring an old-fashioned grocer they named Mr. Whipple. Mr. Whipple would catch various customers squeezing the Charmin and would reprimand them, saying "Please don't squeeze the Charmin!" In 1978, Mr. Whipple was named the best-known American after former President Richard Nixon and Billy Graham.

Charmin bathroom tissue is now available in a variety of sizes and thicknesses, from Charmin Basic, an unscented value option, to the cushier two-ply Charmin Ultra, Charmin Scents, and Charmin Plus with Lotion. In 2001, Charmin launched freshMates, a line of flushable premoistened wipes. In 2005, Charmin introduced the Mega Roll, the equivalent of four regular rolls of toilet tissue, and the Charmin Extender that customers can put in their toilet paper holders to accommodate the gigantic new roll. Charmin is sold across the United States and Canada.

Charmin enhances its brand presence by offering the "Potty Palooza" at festivals and family-oriented events across the country. A relief from portable toilets, Charmin's facilities are outfitted with hardwood floors, skylights, televisions, and, of course, Charmin toilet paper. Outside, children have their pictures taken with the Charmin cubs. Charmin's message is clear: it aims to make the whole bathroom experience better than bearable.

Vital Statistics
Classic Product toilet paper
Parent Company Procter & Gamble
Founded 1928 (as Hoberg Paper Company)
Headquarters Cincinnati, Ohio
Annual Sales $1 billion (2005)

6 MEGA Rolls! = 24 REGULAR ROLLS*
Rollos Regulares*
Charmin
Ultra
Our Softest Touch & Most Absorbent
Nuestro Charmin más suave y absorbente
1 Mega Roll = 4 Regular Rolls*
For use with the Charmin Extender
Para uso con el adaptador Charmin

Chef Boyardee

Contrary to all rumors, Chef Boyardee was not a fictional character created to sell canned ravioli. Hector Boiardi was, in fact, an Italian-born chef who opened a restaurant in Cleveland, Ohio, in the 1920s. The restaurant, Il Giardino d'Italia, was so popular that patrons asked him to put extra sauce in milk bottles so they could take it home to eat during the week. The demand for his pasta sauce was so great that Boiardi opened a large plant in Milton, Pennsylvania, in 1937. He distributed the sauce nationwide, along with dry pasta and grated cheese. Boiardi sold his products under the name Chef Boyardee because it sounded more American.

Chef Boyardee merged with food conglomerate American Home Foods in 1946. Boiardi remained an adviser until his death in 1985. The Chef Boyardee brand expanded to include a whole line of canned pastas, including ravioli and spaghetti and meatballs. Boiardi's face was printed on the packaging of Chef Boyardee products, and he starred in his own television commercials. Chef Boyardee became the nation's best-selling canned pasta.

Chef Boyardee ads in recent years have been pitched to kids, the brand's biggest fans. In one award-winning commercial, an animated can of Chef Boyardee ravioli follows a little girl home from the grocery store, braving an obstacle course of doors, cars, and stairs. In another, the Tin Man wears the Chef Boyardee label around his middle and is chased by a group of hungry Chef Boyardee-loving kids. Hector Boiardi is immortalized in a MasterCard Priceless commercial that features Chef Boyardee as an animated cartoon figure. Kids who join the online Chef's Club can play online games such as Cross the Sauce and Chef Can Chase.

The Chef Boyardee brand was bought by ConAgra Foods in 2000. The line now consists of oveer 30 varieties of canned and microwavable pastas, including tongue-twisting favorites such as Beefaroni, Twistaroni, and Pizzazaroli. Pastas are offered in kid-friendly shapes such as ABCs 'n 123's and dinosaurs. Spider-Man, the X-Men, and Teenage Mutant Ninja Turtles have even made guest appearances as pasta shapes. The brand also carries parent-friendly pizza and pasta kits, sauces, and low-fat pastas.

ConAgra has tweaked the recipes for a number of Chef Boyardee products, including the meatballs and pizza sauce. "Boy, this stuff is good" is the brand's new catchphrase, and, judging from Chef Boyardee's steady sales, many generations agree.

Vital Statistics
Company Name ConAgra Foods
Classic Product canned pastas
Established 1937
Founder Hector Boiardi
Headquarters Omaha, Nebraska

LOOK!
EASY OPEN
TOP
Chef
BOYARDEE®
MINI
Ravioli®
Beef Ravioli In
Tomato & Meat Sauce
NET WT.
15 OZ
425g

Chevrolet Impala

Is there anything more American than a Chevy? For almost a century, Chevrolet has been providing durable, stylish automobiles to discerning drivers who covet American aesthetic and ingenuity. Chevrolet is one of parent company General Motors' most popular brands, and has survived a wide range of incarnations—no pun intended—since its auspicious debut as a challenge to the Model T Ford. In 2005, Chevrolet actually eclipsed Ford, still its number-one rival, for the first time in 19 years. In fact, Chevrolet is the country's best-selling brand of car.

Who better to found a car company than a race-car driver? In 1911, Swiss race-car driver Louis Chevrolet and William C. Durant, the founder of General Motors, joined forces with the shared goal of taking the auto industry by storm. The first Chevrolet was designed specifically to compete with the Model T, but a year later, a more original design—the Classic Six—was introduced and garnered immediate praise. The Classic Six was a five-passenger touring sedan equipped with a 6-cylinder engine. It could achieve speeds of up to 65 miles per hour, an impressive feat for the time. In 1916, Chevrolet had made enough money to enable Durant to purchase a majority of General Motors shares; a year later he was GM president, and Chevrolet was merged into the larger company as a distinct division, which it has remained ever since. One of the most famous Chevrolet cars appeared in 1958: the imposing Impala. By 1963, 1 out of every 10 cars sold in America was a Chevrolet, and many of those were Impalas.

The Impala was intended to be a luxury car that average Americans could afford. Ed Cole, Chevrolet's chief engineer in the late 1950s, described it as a "prestige car within the reach of the average American citizen." The first Impalas were sports coupes, painted metallic green with white interiors. The cars had hardtops, six taillights, and the distinction of being named after an African antelope. By 1965, the Impala was America's best-selling car. In 1959, Chevrolet started selling two- and four-door versions of the Impala. Six years later, the Impala Caprice debuted with wood-grained accents on the dashboard and innovative interior door handles. The Impala was perpetually redesigned: made larger in 1971, and then taller and narrower in 1977 to meet the design demands of the times and provide more headroom, legroom, and trunk space. In 1992, Impala made another statement, as a concept car designed by John Moss, a General Motors designer.

Today, Impalas—and many other Chevrolet designs—are beloved all over the world. In 2004, the Impala was the third-best-selling car in the United States. They were popular with recreational drivers and used as taxis and police cars. The 2006 version, with its totally revised interior featuring wood and chrome accents, was named Fleet Car of the Year by *Automotive Fleet* and *Business Fleet* magazines. Chevrolet has announced that in 2007, the Impala will be available in new colors, and that it will likely be redesigned in 2009. From Chevy's top-of-the-line luxury model to serious muscle car to reliable performance vehicle, the Impala, like the company that created it, is a true American classic.

Opposite: Chevrolet Impala accessorized with a one-piece, custom-molded Spoiler Kit, stainless steel exhaust tips and 18-inch chrome wheels. Available from Chevrolet Accessories. X07SP_CH009 (United States)

Vital Statistics

Company Name	Chevrolet
Classic Product	Impala
Established	1911
Founder	Louis Chevrolet and William C. Durant
Employees	1,911
Annual Sales	$3,034 million

Chicken of the Sea

When Jessica Simpson asked her then-husband, Nick Lachey, on their MTV show *Newlyweds* if Chicken of the Sea was chicken or tuna, she proved herself one of the only Americans unfamiliar with this household staple of almost a century. In 1914, Gilbert Van Camp, a descendant of Dutch seafaring immigrants, established Van Camp Seafood Co. in California. He decided to call his primary product–canned albacore tuna–Chicken of the Sea because of its white meat and mild flavor. The initial product also featured yellowfin and skipjack tuna varieties, because albacore was not yet available year-round.

Chicken of the Sea took off in 1917 because of food shortages both domestically and abroad caused by World War I. Beef and pork in particular were hard to come by and canned tuna was deemed a healthful, high-protein alternative. By the time the war ended two years later, tuna was the most popular fish in America, and Van Camp Seafood was booming. Although the postwar recession hurt sales temporarily, the company kept growing, introducing other canned fish varieties, such as salmon. World War II also saw canned tuna sales skyrocket, and in the late 1940s, television advertising helped make Chicken of the Sea one of the nation's leading seafood brands. In 1952, the lovable Mermaid was introduced as the company's symbol, and in the 1960s, the Chicken of the Sea jingle, "Ask any Mermaid you happen to see . . . What's the best tuna? Chicken of the Sea," was developed and continues to be used in today's advertising. Ralston Purina purchased Van Camp Seafood Co. in 1963.

In 1988, the P. T. Mantrust Co. bought Van Camp Seafood for $260 million and maintained American leadership. Van Camp implemented "The Mermaid Cares" dolphin-safe policy in April 1990 and was among the industry's leaders in implementing programs to prevent accidental dolphin mortality. The company refused to buy tuna caught by drift nets or any other means harmful to dolphins, forcing the fishing boats of the Eastern Pacific to find new fishing areas or turn to skipjack tuna, which doesn't school with dolphins. Van Camp also began using recycled materials for its cans, continuing to build public trust and respect. The Chicken of the Sea brand continued to grow, and Van Camp expanded its offerings with products such as crabmeat, shrimp and oysters. In 1997, Tri-Union Seafoods bought Van Camp for $97 million, and Van Camp Seafood Company changed its name to Chicken of the Sea International. Since 2000, Chicken of the Sea has continued to innovate the shelf-stable seafood market with the introduction of a complete line of pouched seafood, including tuna, salmon, oysters, crab, imitation crab, shrimp and clam varieties. In 2003, Chicken of the Sea introduced a chunkier chunk light tuna and in 2005 introduced a complete line of restaurant-quality seafood steaks in pouches. In 2007, Chicken of the Sea introduced a completely new packaging concept–"peel and eat" cups, which come in chunk light tuna, chunk white tuna and salmon, and a line of all-natural tuna and salmon under the Genova brand.

Chicken of the Sea achieved pop culture notoriety with the aforementioned Jessica Simpson incident, which received so much press coverage that the company invited her to its sales conference for promotional purposes. The story of Simpson's appearance was picked up by close to 750 prime-time affiliates, 10 national television shows, including E! and Inside Edition, and more than 22 cable shows. The company's public relations firm estimated that this promotional event reached an audience of more than 38 million television viewers, surely reintroducing some to the company that has reliably provided top-notch seafood products to Americans for almost 100 years. While the company has changed over the years, its products have always been healthful and trusted for great taste and high quality.

Vital Statistics

Parent Company Tri-Union Seafoods LLC/Chicken of the Sea International

Classic Product canned tuna

Established 1914

Founder/Inventor Gilbert Van Camp

Annual Sales $450.5 million

Citigroup

Citigroup, the first financial services company in the United States to house banking, insurance, and investments under one corporate roof, became the giant that it is through a series of bold moves. Citigroup is the largest financial services company in the world, with assets of more than $1 trillion. Citigroup manages 200 million customer accounts in more than 100 countries, and is also a powerhouse in corporate and investment banking, insurance, and credit cards.

Citibank began in 1812, when Colonel Samuel Osgood, the first U.S. postmaster general and treasury commissioner, took over the failing New York City branch of the First Bank of the United States. He reorganized it as the City Bank of New York. The bank converted from a state bank to a national one in 1865 at the end of the Civil War and distributed the new national currency and sold government bonds. Taking the new name of National City Bank of New York (NCB), the bank adopted the eight-letter wire code address "Citibank," which in 1976 became its legal name.

By the early 20th century, senior management was already introducing many innovations in banking. NCB President Frank A. Vanderlip was instrumental in pressing for the passage of the Federal Reserve Act in 1913, which allowed federally chartered banks to conduct business in foreign branches for the first time. Soon thereafter NCB purchased the International Banking Corporation, which included an entire international banking network spanning London to Singapore. Setting its sights on the untapped potential in personal banking, NCB became the first major bank to offer interest on savings accounts and to offer personal consumer loans.

Another innovation that the entire industry soon copied was the negotiable certificate of deposit. Introduced in 1961 by Walter Wriston, the CD gave large depositors higher returns on their savings in exchange for reduced liquidity. Wriston, who was promoted to president in 1967 and chairman in 1970, also led the entry into the credit card business. Another pioneering move was a $500 million investment in the late 1970s in automated teller machines, which by virtue of their convenience attracted many new customers.

By the early 1990s, Citicorp (the holding company for Citibank and its other businesses) faced serious challenges brought on by a weak economy and unprofitable loans in commercial real estate. Chairman John S. Reed faced the difficulties by announcing a two-year plan that emphasized cost cutting, growth constraint, and tighter control over expenses.

The tide had turned by 1998, when Citicorp joined Travelers Group Inc. to create Citigroup, Inc., the largest financial services firm in the world. Citicorp's John Reed and Travelers chairman Sanford Weill agreed to run the new company together. In 2000, Reed left the company, leaving Sandy Weill as sole CEO.

Weill oversaw several major acquisitions in the early 2000s, targeting midlevel banking and finance markets abroad as well as in the United States. In 2003 Citigroup reported a record net income of $15.28 billion for the year, increased its dividend by 75 percent, and acquired the huge credit card business of Sears, Roebuck and Co. In 2005, William R. Rhodes was named CEO, and in 2006, the company launched Citibank Direct, an Internet bank.

Vital Statistics

Headquarters New York, New York

Established 1998

Employees 307,000

Annual Sales $1.494 trillion (2005)

Claritin

Claritin allergy products have made it possible for millions of allergy sufferers to live life "CLARITIN Clear." This groundbreaking second generation antihistamine redefined what allergy relief can be by delivering non-drowsy, 24 hour relief from a sufferer's worst allergy symptoms all in a single pill. Claritin came to the OTC market at a time when most OTC allergy medicines were only short acting 4-6 hour medicines that came with the potential unwanted side effect of drowsiness.

The active ingredient in Claritin, loratadine, is an antihistamine. This ingredient works by blocking the release of histamine, one of the chemicals the immune system produces when an allergic reaction occurs. Earlier prescription non-drowsy antihistamines faltered after the FDA warned about possible links to heart problems.

Non-drowsy Claritin was introduced as a prescription allergy medication in 1993. A year later, long-lasting Claritin-D was introduced—combining the relief of loratadine with the power of a nasal decongestant, pseudoephedrine. Claritin RediTabs followed in 1997 and utilizes a proprietary formulation that dissolves up to three times faster than any other tablet. Claritin allergy products quickly became the most-prescribed antihistamine.

When Claritin tablets moved from prescription to over-the-counter status in 2002, it was the largest Rx-to-OTC switch ever—and the first for a non-sedating antihistamine. In its first full year on store shelves, Claritin racked up $415 million in sales. It's no wonder that before long, "Claritin became synonymous with allergy relief much like Tide is to laundry detergent". As the brand's advertisements promise, Claritin lets people "Live Claritin Clear" all year long. In fact, Claritin is the only allergy medication clinically proven to make people as alert and focused as someone without allergies so they can think more clearly. Claritin provides relief from both outdoor allergens such as pollen and ragweed and from indoor allergens such as mold, dust, and pet dander.

Today, Claritin is the number-one pharmacist recommended allergy brand and Claritin-D is the number-one pharmacist recommended multi-symptom allergy product! Claritin remains the number-one-selling OTC allergy brand, available in six effective formulations—including once-daily CLARITIN Tablets, orally dissolving Claritin RediTabs, Claritin-D in both 12- and 24-hour versions, Children's Claritin Grape Syrup and Chewables, and Claritin Hives Relief Tablets.

Vital Statistics
Company Name Schering-Plough
Classic Product Claritin allergy medication
Established 1971
Employees 32,600

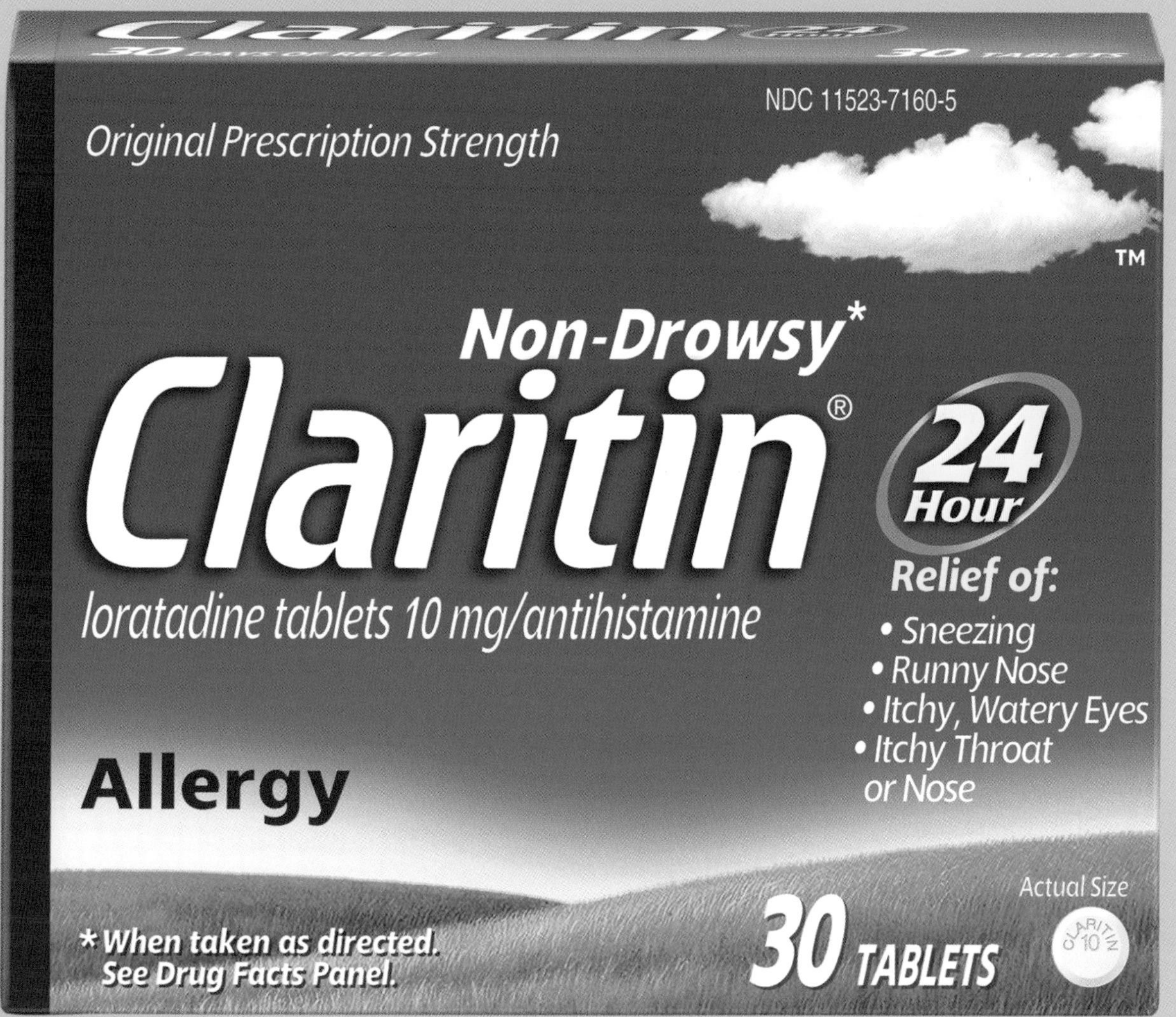
NDC 11523-7160-5
Original Prescription Strength
Non-Drowsy*
Claritin®
24 Hour
loratadine tablets 10 mg/antihistamine
Relief of:
• Sneezing
• Runny Nose
• Itchy, Watery Eyes
• Itchy Throat or Nose
Allergy
Actual Size
* When taken as directed. See Drug Facts Panel.
30 TABLETS

Claussen

Americans eat more than 2.5 billion pickles a year, and the number is rising thanks to the pickle's new status as a crunchy low-carb snack food. A Claussen pickle has only five calories, one gram of carbohydrates, and zero grams of fat. "Choose Claussen. Crunch Smart" is Claussen's ad campaign, which reminds consumers that pickles are as bold and crunchy as other snack foods, and much more healthful.

"Crunchy" is key to the Claussen brand. Pickle connoisseurs are known to have "crunch-off" contests to determine a pickle's crunchiness. A good pickle is characterized by crunch that is audible from 10 paces away. Limp, warm pickles are known as "denture dills." To be crunchy, a pickle must be cool, crisp, and uncooked. Whereas most other pickle brands are sold warm in the condiment aisle, Claussen pickles are found only in the refrigerated deli section of the supermarket. Claussen is the top-selling refrigerated pickle brand in the world.

The Claussen Pickle Co. was founded in 1870 in Chicago. Claussen pickles had been processed in Chicago for more than 100 years when in 1970, Oscar Meyer Foods, best known for its deli meats, bought the Claussen brand. In 1981, Kraft Foods bought Oscar Meyer. Claussen pickle products are now manufactured primarily in Woodstock, Illinois, which processes more than 100 million pounds of pickles annually, the equivalent of more than 20,000 miles of cucumbers. Because Claussen jars fresh pickles year-round, cucumbers are flown in from as far away as Honduras in the cold months. Claussen's signature blend of pickle spices come from around the world.

Although Claussen Kosher Dills are the brand's best-selling pickle, Kraft has introduced a variety of new flavors, including Bread N' Butter (a sweet-and-sour old-fashioned variety), Deli Style Hearty Garlic, New York Deli Half Sours, and Sweet Gherkins. Claussens also come in a variety of shapes and sizes, from snack-friendly wholes, spears, and mini dills, to sandwich-ready chips and even a burger-sized pickle. The Claussen brand also includes relish, sauerkraut, and pickled tomato halves.

Kraft continues to promote Claussen pickles as a way to "put the crunch on carbs and calories." No longer relegated to the side of a pastrami sandwich, the pickle has a new status as the snack food of choice for people who want flavor without the fat, and crunch without the carbs.

Vital Statistics
Classic Product pickles
Company Name Kraft Foods
Established 1870
Employees 400
Headquarters Northfield, Illinois
Annual Sales $130 million (2005)

ALWAYS KEEP REFRIGERATED
Claussen
Great with sandwiches!
COLD · CRISP · DELICIOUS
Claussen
KOSHER DILL
WHOLES
1g Carb
5 Calories
32 FL OZ
(1 QT)
946 mL
ALWAYS KEEP REFRIGERATED
SEE NUTRITION INFORMATION FOR SODIUM CONTENT.
Nutrition Facts
Serving Size
about 1/2 pickle (28g)
Servings Per Container 20

Coach Inc.

In recent years, Coach has exploded onto the fashion scene with footwear, sunglasses, watches, and even perfume. However, many years ago, when the company first introduced its initial line of twelve handbags, it established a reputation for quality that can withstand any trend. Today, Coach offers a broad assortment of fine accessories and gifts for women and men, from handbags to outerwear, scarves, jewelry, and even pet accessories. The freestanding Coach stores have become destination locations for fashion shoppers all over the world, and Coach products are also sold in department stores, the Coach catalogue, and Coach.com.

COACH

In 1941, Coach was founded in a Manhattan loft by a family with generations of leather-making experience in its history. The founder of Coach was first inspired by a baseball glove, particularly its distinctive markings and how it burnished beautifully with age. After refining the leather, making it softer and stronger, he created Coach's first handbag. It became an instant classic. Early on, Coach made a decision to use only the top ten percent of the leather selection for its products. Leather was chosen based on its character, grain, strength and tactile quality. Tanned for days in huge drums, the natural markings rose to the surface to ensure that no two leathers would be the same. Since then, Coach has added a full assortment of new leathers, fabrics and materials, yet this glove-tanned leather remains a Coach tradition. And it still burnishes as beautifully as it did back when Babe Ruth played baseball.

In 1985, the Sara Lee Corporation acquired Coach with the intention of growing the company. Coach flourished, and in 2000 became a publicly traded company on the New York Stock Exchange under the symbol COH. Coach began its forays into the world of fashion, transforming itself from a purveyor of classic handbags into a modern, cutting-edge marketer of must-have designs. Today, Coach is at the forefront of fashion and style, offering accessible luxury lifestyle collections to consumers across the globe. There are a number of lifestyle collections that have become icons of American style, including the Coach Hamptons Weekend Collection, Soho, and Legacy. The Travel Collection offers luggage and travel accessories in lightweight, durable materials. The Business Collection features functional sophisticated briefcases, organizers, planners, notepads, computer cases, and cell phone cases. Quality, durability, and function remain paramount. Coach also sells leather-care products that enable its classic leather products to last for decades—there are many Coach customers who report back that they are still using their original bags from the early years. In fact, Coach allows customers to ship any Coach product to the home offices to be repaired at any point after purchase throughout the life of the product. There are now more than 300 Coach stores in North America and nearly 200 locations in nineteen countries worldwide. On the horizon is a fragrance line, to appear in Spring 2007.

Vital Statistics
Classic Product luxury leather handbags and accessories
Product Launch 1941
Employees 5,700
Annual Sales $2,111.50 million (2006)

Coca-Cola

Probably the most recognized brand name anywhere in the world, Coca-Cola was invented in 1886 by Dr. John S. Pemberton, a Confederate Army veteran trying to make a remedy for headaches. He boiled down a mixture of coca leaves, kola nut extracts, and sugar and took it to a pharmacy where the soda jerk inadvertently mixed it with seltzer instead of water. Now, more than 120 years later, Coke and Diet Coke are the world's pre-eminent soft drinks. A Landor research study showed that *Coca-Cola* is the most recognized phrase in the world after *OK,* and the Coke logo is second only to the cross as the most recognizable symbol in the world.

Coke was popular right from the start, served exclusively from soda fountains for five cents a glass. But it was in 1899 that two young attorneys from Chattanooga, Tennessee, paid one dollar to buy exclusive bottling rights to the drink that Coca-Cola started developing into the best seller that it is today. The entrepreneurs fanned out across the country, selling bottling rights to local individuals. Company owner Asa Griggs Candler supported the bottlers by supplying them with durable metal signs sporting the white Coca-Cola name in Spenserian script. Candler also gave away coupons for free glasses of Coca-Cola and promoted the beverage with calendars, posters, serving trays, and other paraphernalia. Candler succeeded early on in associating Coca-Cola with a happy, sociable lifestyle.

Worried that their Coca-Cola bottles weren't distinctive enough from those of their competitors, the company asked glass manufacturers to submit ideas for a new bottle. In 1916, a new, curved bottle was introduced. Based on the shape of a cacao pod and with a 6.5-ounce capacity, the new Contour Bottle became one of the few packages ever to receive trademark status by the U.S. Patent Office. Six-pack cartons were introduced in 1923, open-top red metal coolers were soon to follow, and by the end of the 1920s, bottle sales of Coke were greater than fountain sales.

In the meantime, with Prohibition on, Coke was being promoted as "The Great National Temperance Beverage." This campaign persisted despite the legend that the drink contained cocaine, a derivative of one of its ingredients, the coca leaf. Neither Coca-Cola nor any other product of The Coca-Cola Company has ever used cocaine as an added ingredient.

Other memorable slogans included "The Pause that Refreshes," "It's the Real Thing," and "Things Go Better with Coke." Norman Rockwell painted some memorable Coca-Cola ads, and the classic Haddon Sundblom Santa Claus still appears on Coke Christmas cartons and bottles. The 1971 TV commercial "I'd like to teach the world to sing ..." was famous for bringing an upbeat message to troubled Americans during the Vietnam War.

Coca-Cola's international presence took off during World War II, when General Dwight D. Eisenhower ordered 10 bottling plants built in North Africa because Coke raised soldier morale, and by war's end there were 54 more plants throughout Europe. The company entered the Soviet Union in 1979 and re-entered the China market in 1980, and performance has continued to be very strong in both countries.

Vital Statistics
Established 1886
Headquarters Atlanta, Georgia
Inventor Dr. John S. Pemberton
Employees 55,000
Annual Sales $23,104.million (2005)

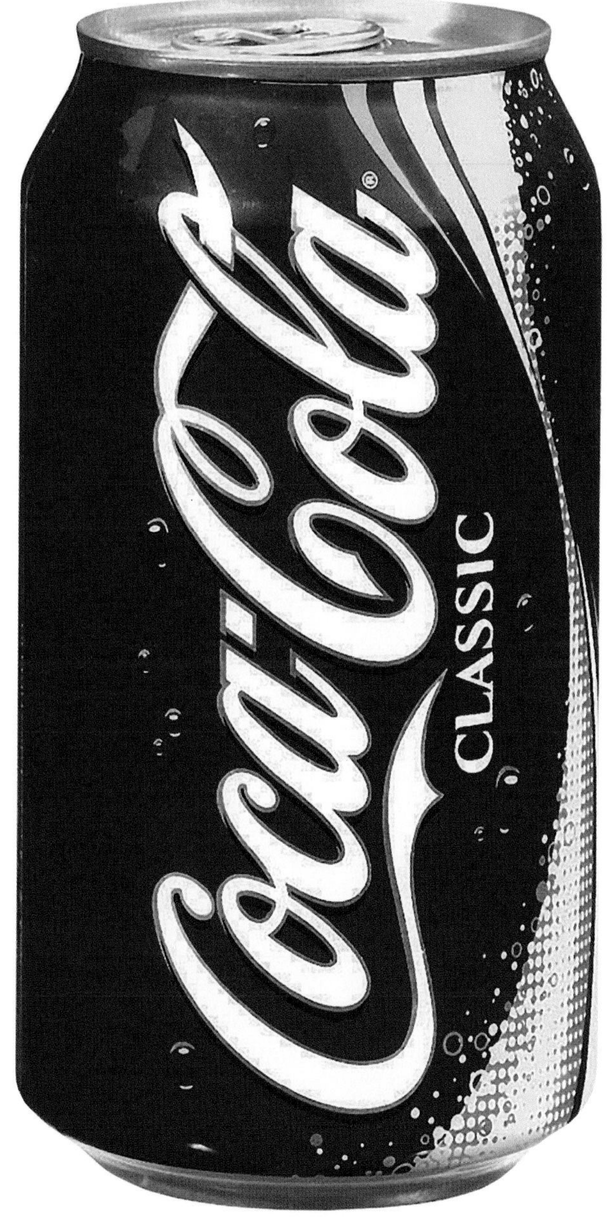

Coleman

The Coleman lantern has long been a comfort to campers who want a reliable source of bright light in what can sometimes seem like very dark woods. Originally invented in 1914 for outdoor use by farmers in inclement weather, the lantern became a staple in American culture during World War I, when the U.S. government declared it essential for farmers working from before dawn until after nightfall to provide wheat and corn for the Allies. Since then more than 60 million lanterns have been sold, and Coleman has become the leading manufacturer of lanterns and stoves for outdoor recreational use.

Company founder William Coffin Coleman (known as W. C.) started out around 1900 by selling a gasoline lamp in Kingfisher, Oklahoma, to the town's shopkeepers. When shopkeepers complained that the lamps got clogged with carbon deposits that then snuffed out the light, Coleman began leasing the lamps instead and servicing them himself. Sales soared, and soon Coleman had moved the company to Wichita, Kansas, bought the rights to the Efficient Lamp, improved its design, and begun selling it as the Coleman Arc Lamp. Ever the entrepreneur, he arranged in 1905 for Arc Lamps to provide the lighting for one of the first known nighttime football games. In 1909, Coleman invented a portable table lamp, and the 1914 invention of the Coleman lantern cemented the company's reputation. It was reported that Admiral Byrd used the lantern at the South Pole, that the descendants of British mutineers from the *Bounty* used it as a lighting source in their Pitcairn Island homes, and that Coleman lanterns lighted air runways in the Andes mountains.

As more and more rural areas got electricity and the market for lanterns began to shrink, Coleman diversified into other products, including oil space heaters, gas floor heaters, and fold-up camp stoves. The stove was immediately popular with those who enjoyed the newly discovered diversion of camping. When World War II began, Coleman was asked to manufacture products for the armed services, including, among other things, ammo boxes for the army and parts for air force bombers.

But the real challenge came in 1942 when the Army Quartermaster Corps asked the company to make a small stove for field troops that was smaller than a quart bottle of milk, could use any type of fuel, and could operate in both icy arctic and extreme heat conditions. The corps requested 5,000 stoves in two months. Coleman came up with the GI Pocket Stove, which met and exceeded Army specifications, and delivered the stoves in November 1942 to troops invading North Africa. The stoves burned for two hours on a cup of fuel from a military jeep or plane. Journalist Ernie Pyle, who wrote extensively about soldiers' wartime experiences, reported that soldiers considered the GI Pocket Stove and the jeep the two most important pieces of noncombatant equipment in World War II.

By the mid-1970s, taking advantage of Americans' growing interest in the great outdoors, Coleman had capitalized on its early success with the lantern and stove by introducing an extensive product line of camping equipment, including ice chests, jugs, tents, sleeping bags, and adjustable backpack frames. New York financier Ronald Perelman bought Coleman in 1989 in a leveraged buyout and during the next decade aggressively set about streamlining operations and acquiring companies in related businesses. Jarden Corporation acquired the Coleman Company, Inc. in 2005.

Vital Statistics

Parent Company The Coleman Company, Inc.

Headquarters Wichita, Kansas

Established 1900

Employees 2,023

Colgate

Colgate-Palmolive is a world leader in oral care products such as mouthwashes, toothpaste, and toothbrushes, and America's number-one seller of toothpaste. The company also makes personal care items and household cleaners; its Hill's Pet Nutrition subsidiary makes Science Diet and Prescription Diet pet food, and the company acquired Tom's of Maine in 2006. In spite of Colgate-Palmolive's wide reach, the name *Colgate* still means one thing to most consumers today: toothpaste.

In 1806, when the Colgate company was founded by 23-year-old New Yorker William Colgate, it sold starch, soap, and candles from its factory and shop. Colgate achieved its true destiny in 1873, when it introduced toothpaste in a jar, followed in 1896 by Colgate Ribbon Dental Cream, in the now-familiar collapsible tube. By 1906, Colgate was making 160 kinds of soap, 625 perfumes, and 2,000 other products, enabling it to go public in 1908. Meanwhile, Milwaukee's B. J. Johnson Soap Company, founded in 1864, had introduced Palmolive, a soap made of palm and olive oils rather than animal fats, which became so popular that the firm changed its name to The Palmolive Company in 1916. Ten years later, Palmolive merged with Peet Brothers, a Kansas City-based soap maker founded in 1872, and Palmolive-Peet merged with Colgate in 1928, forming Colgate-Palmolive-Peet, which was shortened to Colgate-Palmolive in 1953.

In 1981, Colgate celebrated its 175th anniversary and introduced Colgate Winterfresh Gel toothpaste. Three years later, the revolutionary Colgate Pump appeared, and the groundbreaking Colgate Tartar Control toothpaste was introduced in 1986. But the product that was to change Colgate's history forever was Total. Beginning in the late 1980s, Colgate had begun development of a toothpaste that contained a gingivitis-fighting antimicrobial agent, triclosan, which could bind to teeth for up to 14 hours, allowing users to fight bleeding gums and bad breath continuously with only two brushings a day. The company began marketing the product overseas in 1992 under the name *Total,* eventually distributing it to 100 countries. In the United States, however, introduction of Total was held up by the Food and Drug Administration (FDA), which required extensive testing before Colgate could make gingivitis-fighting claims on labels. In 1997, Colgate finally received approval, and Total hit the shelves, accompanied by a $100 million marketing campaign, the company's largest in history. Total pushed Colgate ahead of Crest for the first time ever, making it the leader of the U.S. toothpaste market. In December 1998, the FDA also approved a variant of Total, Total Fresh Stripe, which reached stores several months later. In 2002, Colgate introduced a teeth-whitening gel, Simply White, to compete with rival Procter & Gamble's Crest Whitestrips, Colgate Fresh Confidence, a toothpaste with breath-freshening capabilities, and a battery-operated Colgate Motion toothbrush.

Today, with sales surpassing $11 billion, Colgate sells its products in 222 countries and territories worldwide, sending employees around the globe to preach the importance of oral care. Colgate Total is now the number-one toothpaste recommended by dentists, and Colgate accounts for more than one-third of all toothpaste sales in the United States.

Vital Statistics
Parent Company Colgate-Palmolive
Classic Product toothpaste
Established 1806
Founder William Colgate
Employees 35,800

Conair

Conair—the number one name in hairstyling—makes products that are essentials in bathrooms and salons all over the world. Personal products by Conair include curling irons, hair dryers, mirrors, shavers, and salon products, such as Jheri Redding, designed for home and professional use. The company also manufactures fabric steamers, irons, presses, telephones, answering machines, Interplak electric toothbrushes, and Scunci hair accessories. Conair products can be found at discount chains, department stores, and mass merchants throughout the United States.

It took quite some time for today's modern hair dryers to reach their current state of near perfection and ease of use, although related products were introduced in various incarnations. An electric hair dryer invented by Alexandre Godefoy appeared in 1890, and the first perm machines in the early 1900s. Heated hair curlers were first invented by African-American inventor Solomon Harper in 1930, and curling irons weren't patented until 1980, by Theora Stephens. The Flowbee hair-styler was invented in the late 1980s by a San Diego carpenter named Rick Hunt, who was inspired by the way an industrial vacuum could suck sawdust from his hair after a day on the job. But Conair Corporation—the standard bearer for the world of hair-care products—began as a Brooklyn-based supplier of professional hair rollers in 1959.

Conair founder and owner Leandro P. Rizzuto started his company with the help of his parents, an investment of $100, and the certainty that he could change the way American women styled their hair. Forty-one years later, his company had become a worldwide producer of cutting-edge products in personal care, fitness, cooking, communication, and oral care and had reached an astounding $1 billion in sales. Today, Conair's most exciting offering is the ceramic ionic styler, a bright red hair dryer featuring dual heat technology, including a ceramic heater with full-spectrum infrared heat to prevent frizz and minimize drying time. The ionic styler has 1,875 watts of power and sixteen styling settings. Details such as a folding handle, dual ionic ports, two speeds, three heat settings, a cool shot button, and a turbo switch for highest velocity make this the Rolls Royce of hair dryers. Additional features include a slide switch that allows users to choose from three settings: ionic, ceramic, and ionic and ceramic. Conair also recently launched the Conair instant heat hairsetter roller set featuring ceramic and ionic technology, as well as a travel-size set, which holds twelve rollers in two sizes. Conair Corporation owns many key brands, including Cuisinart, Waring, Interplak, Rusk, ConairPro, Jheri Redding, Conair Shine, Forfex, BaByliss, Southwestern Bell Freedom Phone, and Conairphone, making it a major player on the international stage.

Lee Rizzuto is still at the helm of Conair, which has stuck to its roots—pun intended—while expanding into hair accessories, with the acquisition of Scunci, and hairstyling appliances (hair dryers, curling irons, and straightening irons) for teenage girls, marketed under Mary-Kate and Ashley Olsen's eponymous brand. Rizzuto appears periodically at events such as Hair in Motion, where he shows consumers how his number one product, the hair dryer, brings the art of style from salon to home and back again with flair.

Vital Statistics
Company Name Conair
Classic Product hair dryer
Founder Leandro Rizzuto
Date of Founding 1959
Employees 5,000
Annual Sales $1,277.2 million

Converse Inc.

Established by Marquis Mills Converse in 1908, Converse has been inextricably linked with American sports for almost 100 years. The company has sold more than 750 million pairs of its world-famous Chuck Taylor All Star basketball sneakers but also makes cross-training, running, walking, and tennis shoes, licenses its name to sports apparel, and sells a wide variety of sports-themed products at more than 12,000 retailers and licensees in more than 100 countries around the world.

Marquis Converse launched the Converse Rubber Co. in Malden, Massachusetts, with a mere 15 employees and a capital investment of $250,000. In 1917, the company introduced its canvas All Star shoe, which was almost immediately enthusiastically endorsed by "Mr. Basketball": Chuck Taylor, a popular All American high school player who later suited up with the original Celtics, Buffalo Germans, and Akron Firestones. Four years later, when Taylor joined the Converse sales team, he began selling the eponymous shoes at basketball clinics, making him one of the first athletes to become affiliated with a product in this fashion. Shortly thereafter, Taylor's signature was added to the brand, and—amazingly—he worked for Converse until 1968. Converse fell into bankruptcy in 1929 and was subsequently acquired by Hodgman Rubber. The Depression led to another takeover in 1933, but the Stone family of Boston acquired the company and maintained ownership for the next 39 years. Converse supplied footwear to the U.S. military during World War II and was able to expand after the war, acquiring Tyler Rubber Co. and, eventually, the Hodgman line of sporting goods.

In 1962, Converse developed the low-cut version of the All Star, and Wilt Chamberlain scored his record-breaking 100 points in one game wearing the version of what had become a professional staple. The mid-1970s debut of the One Star, a low-cut performance shoe for basketball, was a high point for Converse, as the shoe took hold with surfers, skaters, and all those desirous of a laid-back, retro, West Coast look—setting the stage for the 1990s, when bands such as Green Day and Pearl Jam performed in their well-worn Converse shoes. Converse maintained its appeal for pro athletes, however, and 8 out of 10 college basketball players wore Converse All Stars throughout the decade. When Julius Erving endorsed Converse's revolutionary Pro Leather, which became known as the Dr. J, the shoe became ubiquitous, and in 1984 both Dr. J's championship-winning 76ers and the gold-medal-winning U.S. Olympic men's basketball team rode their victories home in Converse shoes.

Two of the more memorable ad campaigns of recent decades were Converse's "Choose Your Weapons," featuring Larry Bird and Magic Johnson squaring off in Converse shoes, and Larry Johnson, the 1991 NBA Rookie of the Year, as "Grandmama," one of the first of many African American men in old-lady drag to grab hold of the popular culture. Converse executives took the company public in 1983, about the time the classic Chuck Taylor shoe took off with teens, who still weari it today. Nike bought Converse for about $305 million in 2003, and today operates Converse as a separate unit from its competing sports brands, capitalizing on the nostalgia factor and timeless appeal of the classic American brand. Foot Locker, the company's largest customer, accounts for about 20 percent of sales, but the shoes are also sold in Journeys, Champs Sports, and other retailers nationwide, as well as online.

The Chuck Taylor Converse All Star has become a worldwide icon. New colors, patterns, and special features are introduced regularly, each based on the 1917 original. The Converse collection features some of the most legendary basketball shoes of all time, as well as a new generation of performance shoes for today's demanding athletes. Converse was one of the first companies to blend the worlds of sports and fashion, and it retains its panache and reputation in a world gone mad for sneakers.

Vital Statistics
Established 1908
Founder Marquis Mills Converse
Annual Sales $205.3 million in 2005

Coppertone

For more than half a century, Coppertone has been an American standard. Coppertone is the brand name for a line of suncare products owned by Schering-Plough HealthCare Products Inc. The origin of Coppertone dates back to the early 1940s, when Benjamin Green, a pharmacist and World War II airman, helped develop a sun-protective formula for soldiers. In 1944, Green used his formula as the basis for the first official Coppertone product: Coppertone Suntan Cream, a mixture of cocoa butter and jasmine he mixed up on his wife's stove and tested on his own bald head.

In 1953, the makers of Coppertone solicited drawings from prominent commercial artists for a new ad campaign and ended up with the world-famous Coppertone girl. Joyce Ballantyne Brand, using her three-year-old daughter as a model, came up with an illustration of a young girl in pigtails, with a puppy pulling at her bathing suit bottom. The artist received $2,500 for her winning contribution. Soon, the image could be found on billboards, advertisements, and product labels across the country, accompanied by the teasing slogan, "Don't be a paleface!" The image has been frequently parodied over the years; Jim Carrey's ludicrous 1995 *Rolling Stone* cover and Carmen Electra's 2004 *Esquire* cover are two outstanding examples.

When scientists started to raise awareness on the dangerous effects of sun exposure, the makers of Coppertone rose to the challenge. In 1972, the Coppertone Solar Research Center created the Sun Protection Factor (SPF) system for the U.S.A. which is a standardized measurement of a sunscreen's ability to protect the skin and prevent sunburn. In 1980, the makers of Coppertone introduced the first sunscreens to protect against both UVB and UVA rays. In the late 1980's research revealed the most dangerous exposure to the sun occurs during childhood. Little Miss Coppertone—still around and as beloved as ever—then became the icon for a sun protection line. The brand then launched Coppertone Water BABIES, a line of sun protection especially for young children. Later, Coppertone SPORT sunscreens were introduced with an ultra sweatproof formulation specially developed for an active lifestyle.

Over the years, Coppertone Research has been at the forefront of most sun-protection firsts, including the first mass-produced sunscreen in 1944, the first sunless tanner in 1960, the first ultra sweatproof sunscreen for athletes in 1991, and the first PABA-free sunscreen with Avobenzone in 1993. In 2005, the company revolutionized the category by introducing the convenience of Coppertone Continuous Sprays. These clear, no rub, no mess formulas spray at any angle for quick and even coverage. Schering-Plough, the makers of Coppertone then expanded their portfolio in 2007, by introducing Coppertone QuickCover Lotion Sprays, which combine the convenience of a one touch spray with the benefits of lotions.

Today the Coppertone brand is recognized around the world for its high standards for testing sunscreens and developing superior products. Coppertone products offer sun protection for the entire family and are now, more than ever, providing Better Suncare for Better Summers.

Vital Statistics

Parent Company	Schering-Plough Corporation
Classic Product	Coppertone lotion
Invented	1944
Inventor	Benjamin Green

CorningWare

CorningWare has been one of the leading brands in housewares for decades. Today, the brand is licensed by World Kitchen, LLC, which also manufactures or distributes many of the country's most famous housewares brands, including Baker's Secret, Chicago Cutlery, Corelle, PYREX, and Revere, as well as CorningWare.

CorningWare entered American households in the 1950s with bakeware made of a glass ceramic material originally developed for high-tech commercial applications. Exceptional performance, stylish designs, and easy cleanability immediately established the brand as an American favorite. The brand has had two iconic designs through its almost 50-year history, the A-Line design with the enduring blue cornflower pattern and the French White® fluted style. Both designs were the number one bakeware in the U.S.

In 2002, the brand made a move to stoneware for more product innovation flexibility, to satisfy consumers' desires for variety in color, shape, and design. Today, CorningWare offers key attributes craved by consumers: stylish bakeware that looks great for serving family and friends at any occasion, plus real versatility—bakeware crafted of high-performance stoneware that is safe for use in conventional, convection, and microwave ovens, and for storing foods in the refrigerator and freezer. Its smart designs are perfect for serveware and enhance any table, whether casual or formal.

CorningWare stoneware collections range from the classic CorningWare French White line to the contemporary CorningWare Creations assortment and the graceful CorningWare Traditions. The enduring French White collection owes its popularity to the timeless, patented fluted design with elongated edges. Reliable performance and graceful appeal make French White a must-have for brides-to-be as well as for consumers of all ages. The attraction of CorningWare Creations is its sleek, sophisticated styling, fluid contours and glossy finish in a wide range of sparkling jewel tones. CorningWare Traditions offers a vintage-inspired bakeware and serveware collection with polished shabby-chic charm.

Adding to the CorningWare brand's reputation for style and innovation is the striking and elegant CorningWare Scandia White collection. In a departure from customary stoneware, this collection is fashioned of porcelain ceramic, in an unusual egg-shaped silhouette, with supple horizontal ribbing that appeals to style-conscious consumers.

Consumer research shows that CorningWare has almost 90% total brand awareness and almost three fourths of respondents plan to purchase CorningWare (AAU Study, 2006). The team behind CorningWare bakeware is as determined as ever to be the leader in housewares, offering stylish collections with great performance for future generations to come.

Vital Statistics
Parent Company WKI Holding Company Inc.
Classic Product CorningWare dishes
Product Launch 1958

Costco Wholesale Corporation

If you've ever found yourself with enough paper towels to last for the next 20 years, you've probably shopped at Costco—a chain of popular membership warehouses that sell name-brand products as well as the company's own Kirkland Signature brand. The prices are great, the membership fees low. With 506 warehouses and counting in the United States, Canada, Mexico, Japan, Taiwan, Korea, and the United Kingdom, Costco Wholesale Corporation is the largest and most profitable chain of its kind.

The warehouse shopping phenomenon began in 1976, when The Price Company (PC) opened a membership-only, cash-and-carry warehouse store in the San Diego, California, area called Price Club. PC expanded slowly, adding stores throughout the 1970s and 1980s. Meanwhile, competitors joined the fray, including Costco in 1983, with Jim Sinegal and Jeff Brotman at the helm. Originally based in Seattle, Costco lost money in its first few years, but in 1985, Costco became a publicly owned company. It opened stores in Canada, and then, the following year, added fresh foods to the product line. By 1987, things were looking up for Costco, when sales exceeded $1 billion for the first time. In 1990, Costco opened its first two units in the northeastern United States, and added home improvement and green nursery products to selected warehouses. The company then announced a two-for-one stock split and completed a public offering of 3.45 million shares of common stock. Proceeds of approximately $200 million were used to fund expansion and reduce debt, enabling Costco to open 11 food courts, 19 one-hour photo labs, and four print shops. They also restructured into two divisions: West Coast and East Coast operations. By 1993, Costco was among the top four operators of wholesale warehouses in the country, with approximately 4 million members at its 100 stores in 15 states and Canada. Making its most significant decision to date, Costco merged with the Price Club, becoming Price/Costco Inc.; the name became Costco Wholesale Corp. in 1997.

Although today's customers can buy everything from cars, vacations, glasses, bikes, birthday cakes, and laundry detergent at Costco, the consistent number-one best seller is something no home can do without: industrial-sized packages of toilet paper. Since 1984, Costco has been forced to increase the size of its shopping carts four times, while the average amount members spend—$130 per visit—has continued to grow. Costco has three membership levels, ranging from $50 to $100 a year (in the United States): Business, Gold Star (individual), and Executive.

Today, Costco focuses on offering high-quality, brand-name merchandise at prices below those of traditional wholesalers, discount retailers, and supermarkets. Warehouses are almost entirely self-service, and Costco carries roughly four thousand carefully chosen products at a time; the relatively small product line makes for easier inventory and tracking of prices. In 2007, Costco reportedly had 50 million card holders and 500 warehouses, placing it firmly among America's top five retailers.

Vital Statistics
Founders Jeffrey H. Brotman and James D. Sinegal
Employees 124,600
Annual Sales $58.9 billion (2006)

COSTCO
WHOLESALE

Crane & Co.

Known for its superior products, especially fine writing paper and currency, Crane & Co., Inc. got its start in 1801 when Zenas Crane realized his dream. His father, Stephen Crane, was a papermaker who had sold a special security-type paper to engraver Paul Revere that was used to print Massachusetts colonial banknotes. As a teenager, Zenas learned the process of papermaking: how to clean old cotton rags and beat them into pulp. Wanting to have his own mill, Zenas looked for a location that would provide the materials and the employees needed to make paper. In 1799, Zenas Crane found the property on the banks of the Housatonic River in a small agricultural town in western Massachusetts. It took him two years to raise the money, and in 1801, Zenas and his two partners started the business.

CRANE & CO.

Encouraged by a company advertisement, local housewives provided the mill with rags to produce the paper. Many of the rags were made of tough, homemade linen, which was difficult to reduce to pulp but made a very high grade of paper. This, coupled with Zenas Crane's high standards, established the company's tradition of making products of superior quality. Early customers included banks (many printed their own money), publishers, and shopkeepers.

In 1842, Zenas Crane retired and his four sons took over operations. Two years later, they developed a method of embedding silk threads horizontally into the notes to indicate denominations in order to deter counterfeiting. In 1879, Crane won the contract to make currency paper for the U.S. Treasury, beating out the company that had been supplying the paper. Crane developed a new paper, based on the silk-thread security paper, to meet Treasury specifications and bought another mill that was completely devoted to currency paper. Crane still provides the paper on which U.S. currency is printed, as well as the currency of many other countries.

During the depression that followed the Civil War, many paper mills went bankrupt. Crane took a gamble on a fashion trend and starting making a new paper for men's shirt collars. Men changed their collars daily, so there was a great demand. The trend didn't last long, but while making the paper collars, Crane developed paper belts to drive machinery for which Crane was granted patents in 1867 and 1868. Other products made with Crane paper included baskets, washtubs, and even racing boats.

The writing paper for which Crane is so widely recognized today was developed in the 1860s when elegant women's stationery was all the rage in the United States. Zenas Crane Jr. went to Europe to learn the techniques and returned to create fine social papers that became so popular, the mill could not keep up with the orders. Customers included Tiffany & Co., Marshall Field, and Bailey, Banks & Biddle, just to name a few. Crane stationery was used for the invitations to the dedication of the Statue of Liberty as well as thousands of other notable occasions in history.

Crane continues to stay true to its process of making paper from cotton, unlike many paper mills that turned to wood pulp at the end of the 19th century. This not only saves trees, but also does not contribute to landfill by using recycled materials—Crane uses millions of pounds of recovered cotton fibers to make its stationery and banknote papers. The company continues to be owned and managed by members of the sixth and seventh generations of the Crane family.

Vital Statistics

Established	1801
Founder	Zenas Crane
Signature Product	Stationery
Annual Sales	$300 million (2004)

Crock-Pot

Good food takes time to cook, and some of the best dishes, such as stews, bean dishes, and soups, can require simmering all day—a tough proposition for today's busy cooks. Fortunately, Crock-Pots can solve the problem. Crock-Pots first appeared in 1971, the year after The Rival Company bought another company that manufactured a slow cooker called the Beanery. The Beanery was designed specifically for cooking beans and consisted of a basic heating element with a ceramic interior. Renamed the Crock-Pot, the appliance has since become synonymous with slow cooking. Now, with more than 100 million of them sold, an estimated 80 percent of U.S. households have a Crock-Pot.

Crock-Pots are best known for turning cheap, tough cuts of meat into tender morsels. Recipes typically call for 8 to 10 hours of cooking, plenty of time to break down tough fibers. Meats cooked in a Crock-Pot reach an internal temperature of 170 degrees for beef and 190 degrees for poultry, which keeps the food safe from the danger of bacterial growth during cooking. Crock-Pots consist of an outer housing unit that contains the heating element, the inner ceramic pot, and a lid. The inner pot is removable, so it's possible to serve right from the dish, and cleanup is easy. Sizes range from 1 to 6-1/2 quarts, and the shape can be round or oval. Although cooking a meal for 8 to 10 hours might seem excessive, there are many advantages. The timing corresponds well with a typical workday, for one. You don't need to check the meal at all, for another. Stirring is not only unnecessary but not recommended, because removing the lid causes the cooker to lose heat. Crock-Pots use very little electricity, making them environmentally friendly. They can double as chafing dishes at parties for keeping foods warm, and, most important, the one-pot meal cuts down on the number of dishes to do after dinner.

Recent product enhancements include programmable Crock-Pots, which allow the cook to program the temperature and time in advance. When the meal is done, the setting shifts to warm until people are ready to eat. Also new is the Crock-Pot BBQ Pit, an indoor grill made expressly to slow-cook ribs.

Vital Statistics
Parent Company Jarden Corporation
Product Launch 1971
Headquarters Rye, New York
Employees 17,500
Annual Sales $3,189.1 million (2005)

RIVAL
Crock-Pot
Stoneware Slow Cooker

A. T. Cross Company

A popular gift for generations to commemorate milestone achievements, Cross pens have long been renowned the world over for their distinctive style and superior quality. True industry veterans with more than 160 years of experience, Cross is America's oldest manufacturer of fine writing instruments.

CROSS

As a leading fashion-focused writing instrument and accessories brand, blending the timeless appeal of its brand heritage with contemporary design, detailing, and finishes, Cross appeals to young and old, trendy and traditional alike. Cross is responsible for many landmark innovations in the writing instrument industry, a tradition of innovation continues to this day.

In 1879, Cross pioneered the Stylographic Pen, a forerunner of what would later become the modern Ball-Point Pen, and the Propel-Repel Mechanical Pencil, a forerunner of today's Mechanical Pencils. To commemorate 100 years as a maker of fine writing instruments, in 1946, to commemorate its 100th anniversary Cross released the Century line, which quickly became the company's iconic product. The Ball-Point Pen was first introduced in 1953 as part of the Century collection, utilizing Cross's patented "internal" design mechanism. Cross Desk Sets were added to the product line in 1966.

In 1971, Cross became a public company as trading began on the American Stock Exchange. Innovations that followed this include the introduction of the modern Fountain Pen in the US, and in 2004 Cross introduced a proprietary Sublimation technology, showcasing print designs on the bodies of their ballpoint pens. Most recently, in 2006, celebrating the Auto Racing history of its founding family, Cross introduced its luxurious Autocross Leather pen and accessories collection, with design inspiration taken from fine luxury motorcars of the 1930s.

Although Cross is widely identified by its iconic Century silhouette, first introduced in 1946, the company is constantly growing and evolving as a fashion brand, based on the strength of the core values established by Richard Cross himself nearly two centuries ago: quality, service, and style. In addition to offering impeccably-styled pens, brand extensions such as luxurious leather accessories, fashion-forward business bags, and elegant timepieces and eyewear have broadened the company's audience, helping establish a devoted following across more than seven generations of pen and accessory consumers.

Fine craftsmanship, innovative design, and impeccable customer service have long been hallmarks of Cross quality writing instruments. The commitment to these tenets has provided a stability that has allowed Cross to evolve as a brand: transforming from a small family-owned pen company in the mid 1800s into the fashion-focused global pen and accessory brand it is today. All within the confines of the smallest state in the U.S.—in the bucolic New England town of Lincoln, Rhode Island.

Vital Statistics
Classic Product Century Gold-Filled Ballpoint Pen
Established 1846
Founder Richard Cross
Sales $129 million (2005)

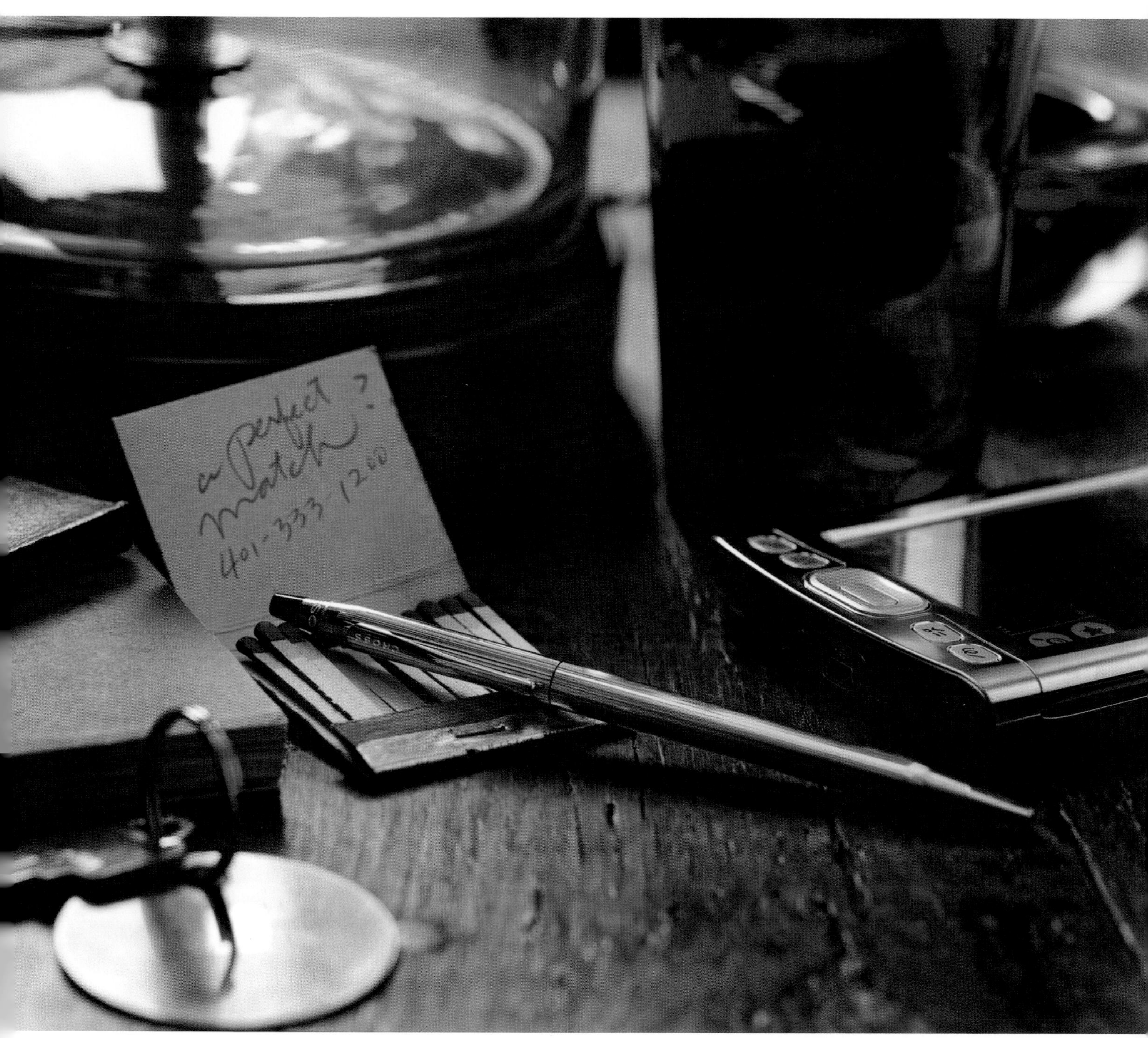
a perfect match?
401-333-1200
CROSS

Dawn Dishwashing Liquid

The world's number-one maker of household products came to be in 1837 when two young men (who were married to sisters) merged their two businesses. Soap factory owner James Gamble and candle factory owner William Procter founded Procter & Gamble in Cincinnati, Ohio, with the advice of their father-in-law and no concept of how far their endeavor was ultimately to reach. During the Civil War, Procter & Gamble really took off by providing much-needed soap and candles to the troops. When they accidentally discovered the formula for floating soap when a workman let a mixture boil too long, Ivory became their name-brand product and remains a defining one to this day. The company also established one of the first employee profit-sharing schemes in the world; today, over 100,000 employees in the group hold 25 percent of the capital.

Dawn was still decades away from joining Procter & Gamble's extensive line, although seeds were sown in the 1920s as Americans became more concerned with convenient products for achieving maximum cleanliness in the home. In 1924, the company set up a market research department to determine what customers most desired, establishing an unbroken chain of communication between consumers and Procter & Gamble. Finally, in 1972, Procter & Gamble introduced original scent Dawn—a translucent blue dish liquid—as a test product. Because of its widespread success, it was expanded to national distribution in 1976, and its popularity has steadily grown since. Dawn's original hallmark was its superior ability to cut grease, and although it is one of the country's top dishwashing liquids, it has gained a reputation for more significant cleanups, including greasy highway messes such as spills of animal fat and baking dough. Dawn dishwashing liquid is also the official grease cutter of the International Chili Society. And, most importantly, Dawn has been used in socially relevant ways. In 1975, the International Bird Rescue Research Center (IBRRC) found that Dawn dishwashing liquid was the most effective product available to remove oil from birds, while being nonirritating to delicate skin and eyes. Since that time, Dawn has been used by animal rescue groups to clean aquatic birds and mammals affected by oil spills. Through its Save-A-Duck program, Dawn has donated thousands of gallons to wildlife rescue efforts and made significant donations to the cause. Since 1979, the IBRRC has used Dawn on all United States oil spills, as well as internationally.

Dawn was used to degrease otters caught in the 1989 Exxon *Valdez* spill in Alaska, at Ashland, Pennsylvania, and the Galapagos Islands, and during the Gulf War. Today, Dawn has a wide range of products that capitalize on modern needs and technology, from the new Power Dissolver and the Power Dish Brush to Dawn with Bleach Alternative, available in popular scents such as Mountain Spring and Fresh Rapids; Ultra Dawn; Dawn Botanicals, in ultramodern Lemongrass & Orange Blossom, Honeysuckle & Rain, and Jasmine & Lavender; Dawn Complete; Dawn Oxi with powerful active oxides; and the latest addition: Dawn Direct Foam, which absorbs two times more grease than ordinary dish liquid. The Procter & Gamble Company is a giant in the area of consumer goods, and Dawn is one of its signature offerings. As the leading maker of household products in the United States, Procter & Gamble has operations in nearly 50 countries around the world and markets its approximately 300 brands in more than 160 countries; more than half the company's revenues are derived overseas.

Vital Statistics

Parent Company The Procter & Gamble Company

Established 1837

Dell Inc.

In April 1984, Michael Dell, a pre-med student at the University of Texas, dropped out of school because his part-time business was doing so well. The college freshman had been making about $80,000 a month from the business he had set up selling overstock computer components. He then expanded his business, selling inexpensive, generic personal computers via direct-mail pieces and ads in hobbyist magazines. In 1985, his first full year of business, Dell sold $34 million worth of computers and became the best-known name in the direct-mail computer market. By 1988, Dell had reached $159 million in sales. That same year, the Dell Computer Corporation (later shortened to Dell Inc.) went public and expanded its distribution worldwide. In 1992, 27-year-old Michael Dell became the youngest CEO to make a ranking in the Fortune 500.

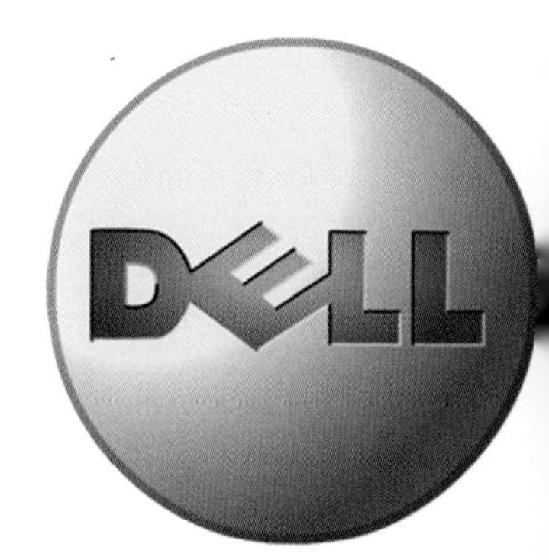

As the information revolution gained steam in the 1990s, Dell made a niche for itself in the market for inexpensive computers. Dell's machines were IBM clones—computer systems (both hardware and software) based on, and compatible with, the brand-name IBM PC. While Dell's competitors—Compaq, Apple, and IBM—suffered during the recession, annual sales at Dell surged to about $1 billion, because its computers simply cost less. In contrast to the other computer companies, Dell kept its operating costs low and focused on marketing to the budget-minded consumer. The goal was to position the personal computer as an appliance rather than an intimidating piece of technology—and to make it affordable to middle-class families. To appeal to the average consumer, Dell invested time and money obtaining information on the buying habits of hundreds of thousands of its customers. By 1996, Dell had hit upon a new marketing gold mine: the Internet. By the late 1990s, Dell was selling $30 million worth of computers and computer equipment each day. Dell Inc., arguably more than any other computer vendor, used the Net to its best advantage as a direct sales tool, an inventory resource, and a means of providing technical support and customer service.

In 2001, Michael Dell put day-to-day operations in the hands of Kevin Rollins, who became president and chief operating officer. As chairman and CEO, Dell was then able to spend more of his time on long-term planning and strategy. In 2004, Dell passed his CEO title to Rollins, but he remains involved as the company's chairman.

Today, Dell Inc is highly regarded as America's most admired company, as reported by *Fortune* magazine. Michael Dell and Kevin Rollins are steering the company toward greater diversification. It plans to maintain its market leadership in computer sales, but, recognizing that the personal computer is morphing into many other forms, Dell has begun to venture into the consumer electronics market with a line of printers, workstations, network servers, storage systems, PDAs, televisions, portable music players, and online music services.

Vital Statistics

Classic Product	personal computer
Established	1984
Founder	Michael S. Dell
Employees	66,100
Annual Sales	$56.74 billion (2006)

Diane von Furstenberg

Diane von Furstenberg arrived in the fashion world in 1972 with her simple knit jersey dresses. By 1976, Diane had sold millions of her signature Wrap dress and came to symbolize female power and freedom to an entire generation by encouraging women to "feel like a woman, wear a dress." After over a decade of a hiatus from fashion that included travel, writing several books, and pioneering into the world of home shopping, Diane von Furstenberg is on top of the fashion world once again.

Born in Belgium, von Furstenberg arrived in New York City in 1972. Her marriage to the glamorous Austro-Italian Prince Egon von Furstenberg and her own charismatic style ensured that her first design—to become the linchpin of her company—was an instant hit. Although the dress was marketed as sexy and feminine, its no-fuss fabric and simple lines made it a natural fit for women desiring clothes to reflect their modern, independent, active lifestyles. By 1976, von Furstenberg landed the covers of Newsweek and the Wall Street Journal, having turned her wrap dress into a successful business featuring her as the face of the product. That same year, she launched her first fragrance, Tatiana, named for her daughter, with a memorable ad campaign featuring the phrase, "For a Woman to Love and a Man to Remember."

During the next few years, von Furstenberg sold five million wrap dresses, until there were too many in the market, forcing her to sell most of her licenses. Although the wrap dress had become such a symbol of its time that one hung in the Smithsonian, von Furstenberg decided to leave the fashion world and go on hiatus. She moved to Paris and founded a French-language publishing house but returned to fashion in 1992 with Silk Assets, a collection sold exclusively on television. Although the line—one of the first for QVC—sold out in two hours and was considered an unqualified success, she was unhappy with the quality and look of the product. Finally, with the help of her daughter-in-law at the time, Alexandra, von Furstenberg relaunched her clothing line in 1997 on her own terms. She founded Diane von Furstenberg Studio to design moderately priced apparel sold at upscale department stores, such as Bloomingdale's and Saks Fifth Avenue. The line has been a hit with consumers and critics, and in June 2005, von Furstenberg was awarded the Lifetime Achievement Award from the Council of Fashion Designers of America for her lifetime of consistent, creative influence over fashion.

Today, Diane von Furstenberg has expanded to a full, comprehensive line of sportswear, dresses, cosmetics, fine jewelry, luggage, swim and beach, a partnership with The Rug Company, and accessories. The collection is sold in retail stores in more than 50 countries, including freestanding shops in New York, Los Angeles, Miami, London, Paris, Hong Kong, Tokyo, and Antwerp. The company headquarters is located in New York City's booming Meatpacking District as is the flagship boutique.

Vital Statistics
Classic Product wrap jersey dress
Established 1972
Founder Diane von Furstenberg

Feel like a
woman,
Wear a dress!
Diane Von Furstenberg

Diaper Genie

Most parents would agree that the Playtex Diaper Genie is one of the best inventions of the twentieth century. Playtex has been making products that improve the lives of families since 1932, although the company is more known for its feminine products than its extensive line of baby products. This may be about to change, thanks to this innovative product: The Diaper Genie is the jewel in the crown of the Playtex baby line, and although it has spawned many imitators, the Diaper Genie reigns supreme.

For three quarters of a century, Playtex has been making spill-proof cups, pacifiers, bottles, and the infamous Diaper Genie for babies all over the world. Founded as the International Latex Corporation, Playtex made its name manufacturing tampons, but has become a major player in the world of infant care. The Diaper Genie System is the top-selling, most recognizable diaper disposal system in the world. It is one of America's favorite baby shower gifts and can be found in nurseries, day care centers, and preschools because of its easy-to-use nature and odor-proof guarantee. Some baby showers build themes around the Diaper Genie, such as making it a table centerpiece and filling it with flowers or turning it into a "wishing well" and filling it with little gifts. In fact, the Diaper Genie has won the American Baby Best of the Year Award seven years running. The Diaper Genie is simple to master. It stands about twenty-one inches tall and is unobtrusive in any room. It requires no batteries or electricity. The diaper gets inserted between the securing clips and then the cap is twisted to push the diaper into the system. The twist cap should be turned several times for maximum efficacy. The system creates a firm barrier between the diapers and the fresh air in the room, allowing no odor to permeate.

One of the many reasons consumers are drawn to the Diaper Genie is its adaptability to the needs of growing babies. In fact, the Diaper Genie System can be used with two different kinds of liners: Stage 1, for babies who are still consuming breast milk and formula, and Stage 2, for older babies and toddlers who have moved on to solid foods. One of the hallmarks of the system is that it can hold up to thirty diapers before needing to be emptied, making it an excellent choice for parents who have better things to do with their time than running back and forth to the garbage can. Each refill lasts about a month, making the system cost-effective as well. The Diaper Genie System is available at large supermarkets, drug stores, baby stores, and discount stores such as Wal-Mart and Target.

Vital Statistics
Parent Company Playtex Products, Inc.
Classic Product Diaper Genie
Inventor John Hall
Employees 1,500
Annual Sales $642.80 million (2005)

Playtex
Diaper
Genie
Easy TWISTAWAY Disposal System
NEW!
Easier in 3 Ways
Easier to Use
Easier to Empty
Easier to Replace Refill
Ultimate Odor Protection
STAGE 1
REFILL INCLUDED
MADE IN U.S.A.

Dixie Cup

Americans who have spent time in a preschool or day care center are familiar with these adorable little paper cups—the first drinking vessels for generations of toddlers everywhere. It is hard to believe that a hundred years ago, no comparable product existed on the market; Dixie Cups, which were developed to improve public hygiene by allowing individuals to avoid sharing cups and glasses, have become an American classic, and for many, an evocative symbol of childhood.

In 1907, a Boston lawyer named Lawrence Luellen became concerned by the spreading of germs involved when people shared cups and dippers at public drinking fountains. At the time, the now ubiquitous "water bubbler" had not been invented, and Luellen rightly believed that thousands, if not millions, were becoming inadvertently sick just by taking a sip of water in certain forums. Luellen developed a new type of drinking fountain that used disposable cups, which he also created, and set out—with the help of another Boston resident, Hugh Moore—to educate the public as to the health concerns of the previous systems. Before long, Luellen's system became standard on trains, and the rest, as they say, is history. Initially, the cups that accompanied the drinking fountains were called "Health Kups," a name destined to turn off—rather than attract—impressionable children. However, in 1919, a line of dolls made by Alfred Schindler's Dixie Doll Company in New York City became suddenly popular. The cup manufacturer decided to ride on the doll company's success and changed its name to the Dixie Cup Corporation, moving company headquarters to a larger facility in Easton, Pennsylvania, at the same time. In 1957, Dixie merged with the American Can Company, which was acquired by the James River Corporation in 1982. In 1997, James River changed its name to Fort James Corporation, before being acquired by Georgia-Pacific in 2000. In 2005, Georgia-Pacific became a subsidiary of Koch Industries, and remains so to this day. Dixie is still owned by Georgia-Pacific, which considers it one of its shining stars.

One of the hallmarks of the Dixie Cup is its eye-catching logo, which was designed by a graphic designer named Saul Bass in 1969. Known for his movie-title sequences, Bass was a coup for Dixie, and the company has retained the image he created for them almost forty years ago. Dixie has expanded greatly and no longer sells just cups. Today, consumers can buy Dixie tabletop products for home and commercial use, including plates, bath cups, hot beverage cups, cutlery, storage containers, bowls, cartons, straws, food wraps, and party supplies. Dixie products come in plain and colored versions, as well as a wide variety of designs suitable for children's parties, holiday celebrations, and everyday meals. Licensing agreements have allowed such beloved characters as Winnie the Pooh, Mickey Mouse, and The Lion King to be featured on Dixie products, bringing a new generation of fans to the Dixie-set table.

Vital Statistics
Parent Company Georgia-Pacific Corporation
Classic Product Dixie cup
Product Launch 1907
Employees 55,000
Annual Sales $19,656 million

A:
CHEETAH.
DIXIE
Q:
SPELL
WITH
THREE
DIXIE
DIXIE

Dole Food Company, Inc.

In 1851, Samuel Northrup Castle and Amos Starr Cooke established a business to sell wholesale goods to missionaries and entered the food business seven years later, investing in Hawaii's sugar industry. In 1894, they incorporated as Castle & Cooke Co., Inc. A few years later, James Drummond Dole, a 21-year-old Harvard graduate, arrived in Hawaii with dreams of making a living off pineapple. His cousin Sanford B. Dole, an influential politician and eventually the governor of Hawaii, encouraged him, and by 1901, James had 60 acres of land and had formed the Hawaiian Pineapple Company.

Dole decided to market his pineapple in cans and set up a cannery near the pineapple groves, enabling him to can the fruit at its peak. Within two years, he was able to ship 1,893 cases of canned pineapple; by 1905 that number increased to 25,000. At that time, few Americans had ever seen, let alone tasted, a pineapple. In 1911, Henry Ginaca, an engineer who worked for the Hawaiian Pineapple Company, invented a machine capable of processing 100 pineapple cylinders a minute, expanding the company's reach nationwide. Toward the end of World War I, Dole's Hawaiian Pineapple Company was producing one million cases annually and was the world's largest processor of pineapples. In 1922, Dole purchased the entire island of Lanai for a pineapple plantation.

In 1961, three years after the death of James Dole, Castle & Cooke purchased the remainder of Hawaiian Pineapple, keeping the Dole name because of its strong brand image. Castle & Cooke introduced new pineapple products, including both fresh and canned pineapple in chunks, slices, or crushed, and began selling citrus fruits, macadamia nuts, vegetables, tuna, and—most successfully—bananas. In 1986, Dole's logo was redesigned, resulting in the yellow sunburst logo known and loved today. Dole Fresh Fruit operations extended its line to grapes, strawberries, nuts, raisins, cherries, and strawberries. In 1988, Dole introduced a new line of dried fruits and nuts, By the 1990s, with busy consumers focused on convenience, Dole's new line of packaged fresh vegetable products became the fastest-growing division in grocery stores. In 1991, Castle & Cooke's stockholders voted to use the Dole name to represent all the company's fruit and vegetable operations, reorganizing under the name Dole Food Company, Inc. Dole began expanding into international markets in the 1990s, including Eastern Europe, South Korea, and the Middle East. By the end of 1995, the company was serving more than 90 countries with a line of more than 170 food products. CEO David Murdock and his management partners took the company private in 2003 and opened the Dole Nutrition Institute, dedicated to educating the public about the health benefits of fruits and vegetables.

Today, Dole is not only the world's leading pineapple seller but one of Hawaii's leading tourist attractions in the form of Dole Plantation, which welcomes more than one million visitors a year and features garden tours, a train through the plantations, and the world's largest maze. With its fully integrated operations of sourcing, growing, processing, distributing, and marketing, it is the world's largest producer and distributor of fresh fruits and vegetables.

Vital Statistics
Established 1851
Founder James Drummond Dole
Annual Sales $5,870 million (2005)
Employees 45,000

ALL NATURAL
Dole
MANDARIN
ORANGES
IN LIGHT SYRUP

Domino's Pizza Inc.

If you want it fast, you've got to get Domino's. Domino's made its reputation on its promise to give customers their pizza for free if it did not arrive within thirty minutes, the promised delivery window. However, Domino's has lasted because of the widespread popularity of its signature offering.

Today, Domino's has more than 8,000 stores in more than fifty countries all over the world. It would be hard to find an individual who has not sampled a slice. Domino's was founded in 1960 by a man named Tom Monaghan and his brother James. The brothers purchased a local pizzeria in Ypsilanti, Michigan, which was—at the time—named Dominick's. James quit after just eight months, trading his half of the business to Tom for a used VW bug. Tom changed the restaurant's name to Domino's, with dreams of expansion. Each pizza box has three dots on it to this day because of Tom's original plan to add a new dot for each new restaurant, though as he expanded he realized this would be impractical.

During the 1960s, Domino's suffered a massive fire that burned down company headquarters and a trademark-infringement lawsuit by Amstar, the maker of Domino sugar. However, under Tom's leadership, Domino's continued to grow, and by 1978, there were 200 Domino's franchises all over the country. In the 1980s, Domino's went international, opening an outlet in Winnipeg, Canada. This was also the decade that Domino's gained widespread attention for its eye-catching advertising campaigns. One popular ad from this time featured "The Noid." Pizza fans were told to "Avoid the Noid" by ordering their pizza exclusively from Domino's. In one of the most bizarre developments in advertising history, a man named Kenneth Lamar Noid held two Domino's employees hostage in an Atlanta pizza parlor for more than five hours, accusing the company of making grand scale personal attacks on him. Before surrendering to the police, Noid forced his two hostages to make him a pizza.

It was not until 1989 that Domino's introduced its first new product: pan pizzas. Four years later, the company discontinued its "30-minute guarantee," offering instead a refund for all dissatisfied customers. In 1998, Tom Monaghan retired with a 7 percent noncontrolling stake in Domino's. He sold the remaining 7 percent when the company went public in 2004. Although Domino's initially sold very basic items built on cheese pizza with a traditional, hand-tossed crust, customer demand and competition has led to countless variations, including the thin and deep-dish crusts, bread sticks, and innovative savory toppings. Domino's has very few outposts offering seating; they are almost all delivery locations.

Other good ideas helped to build the brand. The company was the first to use corrugated cardboard delivery boxes and invented modern belt-driven pizza ovens and the patented "Heat Wave," which used magnetic induction technology to keep pizzas hot during delivery. In 2006, Domino's became the first pizza chain ever to sell a dessert item not made with pizza dough: Brownie Squares. The squares were marketed with the help of mascot Fudgems, a brownie character with arms and legs. Today, company headquarters are in Ann Arbor, Michigan. Global sales exceeded $5 billion in 2006.

Vital Statistics
Inventors Thomas and James Monaghan
Classic Product pizza
Product Launch 1960
Employees 13,500
Annual Sales $5 billion (2006)

Dove

If you have ever seen someone with exceptionally beautiful skin, there is a good chance she is on a first-name basis with Dove. Dove is one of the world's best known moisturizing bars, lauded by dermatologists for its efficacy, gentle nature, and unsurpassed ability to moisturize skin compared to soap.

Owned by Unilever, Dove is one of the most respected, recognizable brands in bathrooms and powder rooms everywhere. The classic, mild Dove formula was developed in the 1940s during World War II to help gently clean the skin of soldiers suffering from burns and wounds. Over the next decade, the original Dove formula was fine-tuned by experts into the Dove Beauty Bar, which so many Americans have come to know and love. Although the Dove Beauty Bar was not available nationwide until the 1950s, the reputation of Dove continued to grow during subsequent years as independent clinical dermatological studies showed that the Dove Beauty Bar was the mildest of the 17 best-selling national bar soaps. Soon, Dove successfully became the number one bar to be recommended by physicians.

In the 1990s, Dove branched out from the bar, creating the Dove Beauty Body Wash, which became a near instant hit with all of those who had come to depend on the quality of Dove, as well as the legions of new fans attracted to the liquid solution. During this decade, Dove introduced a whole new host of products to the marketplace, including the Dove Sensitive Skin Beauty Bar, and Dove Foaming Facial Cleanser. In the new millennium, with its commitment to mild ingredients and customer satisfaction intact, Dove continues to expand its line of offerings with Dove Anti-Perspirant/Deodorants, Dove Hair Care, the Dove Cool Moisture line, Dove Beauty Body Lotions and Creams and Dove pro•age.

In 2004, the brand made a serious commitment to encourage societal change by launching the Dove Campaign for Real Beauty, a global effort to widen the definition and discussion of beauty. The unprecedented campaign supported the Dove mission to make women feel more beautiful every day by widening stereotypical views of beauty. Using real women, not professional models, of various ages, shapes, and sizes; Dove was able to provoke discussion and debate about today's typecast beauty images. In collaboration with the Campaign for Real Beauty, Dove launched the Dove Self-Esteem Fund as an agent of change to support specific charitable organizations that help foster self-esteem in girls. In the United States, the Dove Self-Esteem Fund supports *uniquely ME!*, a Girl Scouts of the USA program that helps build self-confidence in girls ages 8–17 with educational resources and hands-on activities.

Today, Dove continues to inspire real women to be beautiful every day. Dove is sold in more than 80 countries all over the world and sells more beauty bars each year than all other brands combined. More than one billion showers are taken with Dove products each year. That, alone, is a number that speaks for itself.

Vital Statistics
Parent Company Unilever U.S.
Product Launch 1940s

Dove
ULTIMATE CLEAR
cool essentials
Dove
Cool Moisture
CONDITIONER
cucumber & green tea scent
Dove
Cool Moisture
SHAMPOO
cucumber & green tea scent
Dove
Cool Moisture
foaming facial cleanser
moisturizing cream
for normal to combination skin
Dove
Beauty Body Lotion
Cool Moisture
nourishing moisture
normal skin
Dove
Beauty Body Wash
Cool Moisture
hydrating lotion
cucumber & green tea scent
Dove
Dove
cool moisture
beauty bar
hydrating lotion
cucumber and green tea scent
Dove
Nourishing Hand Wash
Cool Moisture
moisturizing cream

Dr. Bronner's Magic Soaps

Dr. Bronner's Magic Soaps are among the quirkiest—and most delightful—products around, with a fascinating history and unique slogans such as "Absolute cleanliness is Godliness!" and "Don't Drink Soap!" Sold primarily at natural foods retailers, Dr. Bronner's liquid and bar soaps are barely advertised, relying instead on word of mouth for sales. Devoted customers claim the soaps can be used for pet shampoos, insect repellant, and more. Founded by master soap maker, world peace visionary, and true eccentric Dr. Emanuel Bronner, the company is still run, lovingly, by his descendants.

Born in 1908 in Heilbronn, Germany, Emanuel Heilbronner emigrated to the United States in 1929, dropping the "Heil" from his name to protest the rise of Hitler. Bronner's parents—soap makers—refused to leave with him and were killed in the Holocaust; his last contact with them was a postcard saying, "You were right.—Your loving father." Bronner decided to start his own soap-making business in his home, carrying on the family tradition. His first product was Dr. Bronner's castile soap, a concentrated liquid that produced an unprecedented amount of lather and provided a vast amount of minuscule text on its packaging. In fact, Bronner's packaging was from the outset a distinctive characteristic. Product labels were crowded with statements of Bronner's personal philosophy, which he called "All-One-God-Faith" and the "Moral ABCs." Many of his references came from Jewish and Christian sources, others from poets such as Rudyard Kipling. Sometimes they contained unusual advice—for example, suggesting a contraceptive use for the soap. When his soap proved popular, Bronner opened a small factory in Escondido, California. His ecological castile soaps and message of peace resonated powerfully with the counterculture of the 1960s and 1970s, and he became an icon of the time. Bronner died in 1997. His factory was by then producing more than a million bottles of soap and other products each year but was still not mechanized. Today, Bronner's family runs the business he began in honor of his parents, supporting charities, and maintaining his inimitable product labels and singular way of doing business.

Dr. Bronner was opposed to the complicated synthetic surfactant formulations that make up most modern body care products, and the products that bear his name are simple, natural, and 100 percent environmentally friendly. All soaps are made with certified organic olive, hemp, and palm oils instead of tallow, and contain three times more organic coconut oil than commercial soaps. Unlike most commercial soap makers who distill the glycerin out of their soaps to sell separately, Dr. Bronner's retains it for its superb moisturizing qualities.

Dr. Bronner would be proud that today, the company's new plastic cylinder bottles are made from 100 percent post-consumer recycled plastic. He might be surprised that Dr. Bronner's sells more than three million hand-poured bottles and bars of soap each year, bringing in more than $9 million in revenue. There are 15 employees, who are paid fairly, made participants in a profit-sharing plan, and given full family health benefits and generous bonuses. One lingering question fans may have: Was Dr. Bronner actually a doctor? The answer is that he earned the title after years of soap making in Germany, and it served as the German equivalent of a doctorate in chemistry. Bronner, however, liked to say, "Ph.D. stands for pile it higher and deeper."

Vital Statistics

Company Name	Dr. Bronner's Magic Soaps
Classic Product	castile soap
Established	1949
Founder	Emanuel H. Bronner

Drāno

For as long as there has been indoor plumbing, there have been clogged drains. And shortly after indoor plumbing became common Drāno came along. Drāno, and several other household cleaning products, became the by-product of a man and his hobby, and has kept American households clean and clog-free ever since.

Born to a Cleveland family in 1854, Philip W. Drackett decided at a young age not to pursue a career in the family shipbuilding business. His intense hobby was experimenting with chemicals, and while he was in high school, he worked in a drugstore, advancing to an apprentice pharmacist upon graduation. Drackett married and opened his own drugstore near Cleveland, but continued his hobby of experimenting with new chemical compounds. He continued with that even after he sold the drugstore and became a sales representative for drug supply houses.

It wasn't until Drackett was well into his fifties with two grown sons that he decided to turn his hobby into a career. In 1910, Drackett and his wife, Sallie, started a brokerage firm that sold bulk chemicals such as soda ash and chlorinated lime to janitor supply companies, laundry companies, and other industrial users throughout the Midwest, South, and West. Drackett's sons joined the family business, and by then the company was packaging the chemicals it sold. In the decade after World War I, P.W. Drackett & Sons was the nation's largest manufacturer of medicinal-quality Epsom salts. At this point, Philip Drackett was already looking to the consumer market and recognized another need that could potentially increase business.

By the early 1920s, indoor plumbing was the standard in America, and with that came the clogged drains. Drackett's experimenting led him to a mixture of caustic soda and aluminum granules that create a chemical reaction that generates heat and a churning action that can clear out drain clogs. With a new product in hand and equipped with glass demonstration pipes, approximately 50 salesmen spread out across the Midwest to demonstrate Drāno's power in department stores and at home shows. Ads were also placed in *Good Housekeeping* and other women's magazines, and within seven years, Drāno went from being unknown to a national best seller.

P. W. Drackett & Sons eventually expanded to include more than 100 household cleaning products, and Drāno would be one of its top sellers. P. W. Drackett & Sons became a subsidiary of Bristol-Myers in 1965. Bristol-Myers sold Drackett to S. C. Johnson & Sons in 1992. Today, S. C. Johnson & Son is one of the world's largest makers of consumer chemical products.

Vital Statistics

Company Name S. C. Johnson & Sons

Classic Product Drāno

Established 1920

Founder Philip W. Drackett

Sales $6.5 billion (2005)

Electronic Arts Inc.

Electronic Arts (EA) is the world's leading independent developer and publisher of interactive entertainment software for advanced entertainment systems such as the PlayStation 3, PlayStation 2 computer entertainment system, the PSP (PlayStation Portable) system, Xbox 360, Xbox video game system from Microsoft, Nintendo Wii, Nintendo GameCube, Game Boy Advance, and the Nintendo DS as well as PC and games for mobile phone devices.

EA has been a leader in its field since the company was founded in 1982. Since then, EA has been a creative leader, and today, the company continues to innovate and improve interactive gaming. By combining diverse media such as computer animation, video, photographic images, motion capture, 3D face and body rendering technologies, computer graphics, and stereo sound with contributions from storywriters, film directors and musicians, EA uses technology and creativity to develop mainstream entertainment through an interactive medium.

EA's broad portfolio of franchises includes global sports blockbusters from its EA SPORTS brand including Madden NFL, FIFA Soccer, and NBA Live. The diverse offering from its EA brand features wholly-owned intellectual properties such as Need For Speed, The Sims, and Burnout franchises, as well as key Hollywood licenses for games based on The Lord of The Rings, Harry Potter, and The Godfather properties. EA SPORTS BIG franchises include: NFL STREET, NBA STREET and FIFA STREET.

EA's five hub studios are in Redwood Shores (US), Los Angeles (US), Orlando (US), Vancouver (Canada) and Warrington (UK), along with development studios in Chicago (US), Montreal (Canada), Stockholm (Sweden) and Tokyo (Japan) and boasts a development team that is more than 5,200 people strong. The company's European corporate headquarters are located in Geneva, Switzerland. With an eye on the global marketplace, EA continues to expand its international presence, most recently having opened offices in Hong Kong, Singapore and Seoul. EA is focused on continuing to grow its business presence in Asia Pacific and Japan.

Additional growth drivers for EA are in online gaming and the mobile cell phone markets. EA supports both the PlayStation 2 online offering from Sony and Microsoft's Xbox Live capabilities and continues to build out its PC online functions including EA Downloader. EA's Pogo.com casual gaming site offers web-based games including a Club Pogo subscription service which has more than 1.26 million active and playing players. EA launched a mobile games initiative in 2004 and in 2006 acquired JAMDAT, making EA Mobile the world's leading game developer and publisher for mobile phones.

EA markets its titles under five brands globally: EA SPORTS, EA SPORTS BIG, EA, EA MOBILE, and POGO. In FY 2006 EA had 27 titles that sold over 1 million units, including games from the Need for Speed, Madden NFL Football, The Sims, FIFA Soccer, NBA LIVE, EA SPORTS Fight Night, Burnout, Tiger Woods PGA TOUR, The Lord of the Rings, and NCAA Football.

Vital Statistics
Established 1982
Major Franchises The Sims, Need for Speed, Madden NFL Football, FIFA Soccer
Annual Sales $3 billion (2006)

Energizer

In 1989, the Energizer Bunny hit the television airwaves with a bang and has kept "going and going" ever since. What started as a parody of a commercial for a rival brand has become one of the most popular and successful ad campaigns of all time.

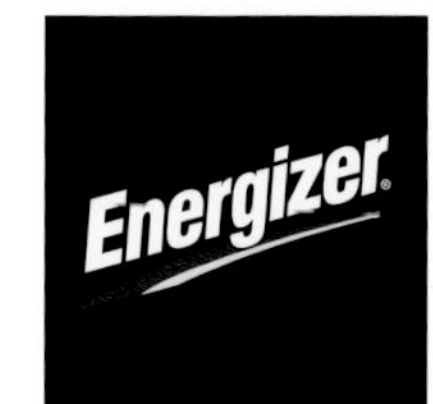

The pink plush bunny, outfitted in shades and banging a marching drum, quickly became Energizer's symbol of long-lasting battery power. The popular ad campaign was one of the most innovative and memorable in advertising history, with the Energizer bunny performing stunts such as barging in on fake TV commercials for breath freshener and beer. He even made appearances on hit TV shows such as *The Simpsons, Cheers,* and *David Letterman*. The Energizer bunny was credited with significantly increasing revenues in the 1990s.

Energizer had come a long way from its 19th-century origins as Columbia dry cell batteries manufactured by the National Carbon Company, a unit of the company later known as Union Carbide. In 1913, National Carbon bought a small company called the American Electrical Novelty and Manufacturing Company, maker of the best-selling Ever Ready flashlight. After the acquisition, Union Carbide dropped Columbia as the brand name of its carbon zinc batteries and renamed them Eveready.

By 1980, as more gadgets such as portable music players were sold and demand for batteries grew, Union Carbide launched a longer-lasting alkaline battery, which they named the Energizer. The Energizer, the first alkaline battery, was invented by Union Carbide employee Lewis Urry and sold alongside the popular carbon zinc Eveready line. The company hired the Olympic gymnast Mary Lou Retton as the spokeswoman for the new Energizer battery, and sales soared. In 1986, the Ralston Purina Company bought Union Carbide's battery division and the Eveready Battery Company became a wholly owned subsidiary of the pet food giant.

Throughout the 1990s, bolstered by the Energizer bunny ads as well as a proliferation of new portable electronic gadgets, the Eveready Battery Company grew at an annual rate of approximately 6 percent. In 2000, Ralston Purina spun off its battery subsidiary as an independent publicly held company and renamed it Energizer Holdings, Inc., which is traded on the New York Stock Exchange.

With markets in more than 165 countries, Energizer Holdings remains one of the world's largest manufacturers of batteries and flashlights. Although its rival Duracell is the market leader in the alkaline battery category, Energizer has expanded its line to include a wide offering of battery technologies from alkaline to lithium to titanium. Meanwhile, the Energizer bunny has still not stopped; it continues to make appearances in commercials for new products such as e2 Titanium Technology batteries. The hip rabbit has become an American icon, the ultimate symbol of perseverance and longevity.

Vital Statistics
Classic Product batteries
Established 1886
Employees 14,800
Headquarters St. Louis, Missouri
Annual Sales $3.1 billion (2006)

AA8
Energizer®
MAX®
+|AA
+|AA
+|AA
+|AA
Energizer®
Energizer®
Energizer®
Energizer®
MEILLEUR AVANT
USAR ANTES DE
USE BY 2012
ALKALINE BATTERIES
PILES ALCALINES
PILAS ALCALINAS
KEEP GOING™ KEEP GOING™ KEEP GOING™

E.P.T.

Johnson & Johnson is one of the world's leading companies, providing over-the-counter drugs; skin, hair, baby, oral, and first aid products; and women's health care products such as the one that revolutionized the way Americans make families: E.P.T.

One of the earliest written records of a urine-based pregnancy test can be found in an ancient Egyptian document dating from 1350 BCE. The test apparently determined pregnancy by having a woman urinate on wheat and barley seeds over the course of several days. If the wheat grew, it meant the woman would have a female child; if the barley grew, a male. If neither grew, the woman was not pregnant. When this ancient method was tested in 1963, testers found that 70 percent of the time, the urine of pregnant women did indeed promote growth in wheat and barley seeds, whereas the urine of nonpregnant women did not. Scientists speculated that the presence of elevated estrogen levels determined the difference. Building on this theory, in 1976 the Warner-Chilcott company sought approval from the Food and Drug Administration for E.P.T., the "Early Pregnancy Test" later known as the Error Proof Test. By the end of 1977, E.P.T. was ready for the American market.

Advertising the revolutionary product was a delicate matter because of the social mores of the time. In 1978, E.P.T. was advertised in major women's magazines, including *Mademoiselle, McCall's, Redbook, Family Circle, Ladies' Home Journal, Good Housekeeping,* and *Vogue*. The original test took two hours, and was more accurate for positive results (97 percent) than for negative (80 percent). Women were finally able to determine pregnancy in the privacy of their own homes, earlier than it took to get into a doctor's office, and with more time to make choices. It also gave women a new opportunity to play an active role in their own health care. Throughout the 1980s and 1990s, technological advances increased the efficacy and popularity of E.P.T. In 2003, the FDA approved the next generation of home pregnancy tests—in place of the classic thin blue line, the test screen could say "pregnant" or "not pregnant."

Today, E.P.T. is more than 99 percent accurate and remains the standard-bearer for women everywhere. It can be used as early as four days before an expected period, and results are available in two minutes. The new E.P.T. Certainty Digital Home Pregnancy Test was an immediate success; it works by detecting levels of hCG, human Chorionic Gonadotropin, a hormone produced by pregnant women. E.P.T. is the market leader in the home pregnancy test category. E.P.T. and E.P.T. Certainty are available through most drug and pharmacy retailers, mass merchandisers, and grocery stores and come in single or double packages.

Vital Statistics
Parent Company Johnson & Johnson
Classic Product home pregnancy test
Product Launch 1977

RESULTS 5 DAYS BEFORE MISSED PERIOD*
*See side panel for accuracy information
e·p·t®
PREGNANCY TEST

e·p·t
OVER 99% ACCURATE**
from the day of your expected period
**Over 99% accurate at detecting typical pregnancy hormone levels. Note that hormone levels vary. See leaflet.
Instructions inside.
Las instrucciones en español adentro.
1 TEST

Ethan Allen Interiors, Inc.

The world-renowned furniture manufacturer and retailer Ethan Allen got its start as a housewares business called Baumritter & Co., formed in the midst of the Great Depression in 1932. Brothers-in-law Theodore Baumritter, a housewares vendor, and Nathan Ancell, a lawyer, committed themselves to making furniture in 1936, when the company purchased its first plant—a 150,000-square-foot factory in Beecher Falls, Vermont. It was here that the company crafted the first colonial-style Ethan Allen brand furniture and the company was able to lay the foundation for what became a vast network of manufacturing and distribution facilities.

At the annual Housewares Show in Chicago in January 1939, the young company introduced its 28-piece collection to buyers. With distribution limited to select dealers, the company shrewdly laid the groundwork for the exclusive dealership network that would set Ethan Allen and its exceptional furniture apart. By 1943, the company's holdings had expanded to 11 plants, and assets were approximately $10 million. In 1954, the company gave its one-millionth piece, a maple chest, to President Dwight D. Eisenhower, and shortly thereafter, the company positioned itself as "one complete source for all your furniture needs in modern or traditional styling."

The company was constantly strategizing to best position its product line of colonial and contemporary furniture, and in 1962, Ethan Allen pioneered the concept of gallery stores by creating freestanding or department store shops to showcase the furniture. Ethan Allen also displayed furniture in complete room settings, enabling the consumers to visualize the possibilities of how their homes could look. In 1964, the instantly recognizable colonial storefront design was drawn for new dealers, quickly becoming Ethan Allen's signature look, and by 1968, 100 galleries were opened across the country. In 1969, the company became Ethan Allen Inc.

Over the years, the company has expanded and diversified its product line from its original early-American heritage to a more contemporary mix to reflect its commitment to style and to attract a wider consumer base. With a consistent emphasis on quality, style, value, and service, Ethan Allen has achieved almost 100 percent brand recognition.

Today, Ethan Allen offers a full range of furniture and accessories through a network of more than 300 interior design centers in the United States and abroad. It has 11 manufacturing facilities throughout the United States.

Vital Statistics
Established 1932
Founders Theodore Baumritter and Nathan Ancell
Headquarters Danbury, CT
Sales $1.1 billion (2006)

ETHAN ALLEN
ETHAN ALLEN

Evercare

So many millions of Americans now own cats and dogs that it is a rare household in which a lint roller is not a necessity, let alone a convenience. But these clever tools have not been around forever—born on the magical eve of a school dance by a quick-thinking parent, the Lint Pic-Up Roller has become an American household staple.

One night in 1955, Nicholas McKay and his wife were preparing to chaperone a local high school dance when McKay noticed his black suit was covered with lint. He looked around, grabbed a roll of masking tape, wrapped it sticky side out around a cardboard toilet paper roll, and affixed it to an unwound wire coat hanger; the rest, as they say, is history. The inventive engineer had fashioned the world's first lint roller. McKay patented his invention as the Lint Pic-Up and launched Helmac Products Corporation—named for his wife, Helen—to manufacture and market it. It was a fitting name, as Helen McKay helped guide the company to steady growth until her death 28 years later. For most of that time, Helmac sold only this one product, until Nicholas McKay Jr. graduated from Harvard Business School and decided to join the family team.

In 1993, McKay Jr. had big dreams for Georgia-based Helmac. In his first few years, he introduced 50 new products to the line, including cedar clothing balls, stain remover, and potpourri. Most caught on with Helmac's retail friends, Kmart and Wal-Mart. McKay Jr. quintupled sales in a matter of years with his innovation and carefully managed expansion. In 1988, however, trouble ensued when 3M began selling a lint roller that was in direct competition with Helmac's, which was selling at the time for $3.50. The McKays turned to Landor Associates, the San Francisco–based brand consultant, to get ideas about how to further diversify Helmac's product mix to stay afloat and get on the right track for the future. Landor disliked Helmac's name, to begin with, and sent out a survey in which consumers were asked what "Helmac" meant to them. A total of 11 percent associated it with mayonnaise, 12 percent said helmets and, worst of all for the conservative McKay family, 9 percent went with actual hell. The name Evercare was suggested—consumers associated this word with hygiene and cleanliness—and both McKays eventually accepted it in 2003, although McKay Sr. was a reluctant convert. McKay Jr. became chief executive in 1997.

Today, Evercare is not only the name to know when it comes to picking up pet hair and lint, but also for laundry, air and pet care. Products include the Bounce Lint & Freshness Roller, Tide Laundry Accessories, and Clorox cleaning accessories, and—of course—the original Lint Pic-Up Roller, which saved McKay Sr. from embarrassment at the dance. Evercare's extensive line has earned legions of fans for its fair pricing, quality, and—most important—effectiveness.

Vital Statistics
Founder Nicholas McKay
Date of Founding 1956
Employees 310
Annual Sales $220 million (2007)

evercare
evercare
AMERICA'S #1
SELLING LINT ROLLER
Lint
Roller
Adhesive Roller
Easy Sheet
Removal!
60
SHEETS

Exxon Mobil Corporation

While many motorists have been to an Exxon or Mobil gas station, some may not know that ExxonMobil is much more than a gasoline supplier and retailer. As the world's largest integrated oil company, ExxonMobil not only provides fuel for our automobiles, but also produces, supplies, and transports fuels to every continent across the globe.

Through its Fuels Marketing company, Exxon Mobil Corporation sells high-quality products to millions of customers around the world. The retail business operates in nearly 100 countries and includes more than 35,000 service stations. In addition to the retail business, ExxonMobil Fuels Marketing also has three business-to-business segments–Industrial and Wholesale, Aviation, and Marine. These segments sell ExxonMobil fuels to more than 1 million customers around the world, including nearly 700 airports and more than 200 marine ports.

In addition to providing fuel for customers, ExxonMobil continues to enhance the strength of its three brands, Exxon, Mobil, and Esso. The company utilizes a targeted capital management strategy focused on selective investments to optimize its retail chain. The company prioritizes focus market investments using sophisticated global tools and models that incorporate factors such as customer demographics and preferences.

Customer preference is a huge priority for ExxonMobil. This is prevalent in the innovative retail products and formats developed to meet drivers' diverse lifestyle needs. Delivering convenience, value, and quality, these tailored programs reflect extensive market research and leading-edge technology, and are designed to optimize site profitability by increasing nonfuels sales and income.

In 2006, ExxonMobil continued the global expansion of the popular, award-winning On the Run convenience store format. The company added more than 250 new On the Run stores, bringing the total to more than 1,500 locations in more than 45 countries.

Vital Statistics
Classic Product gasoline
Established 1882
Employees 83,700
Annual Sales $370,680 million (2005)

EXXON
On the Run
Fast. Fresh. Friendly
Wash at Run
2$1.09
SPORT BOTTLE
DEER PARK

Febreze

If you appreciate a home that smells as fresh as a clear spring morning, you are probably familiar with Febreze–the number one name in household freshness. Produced by Procter & Gamble, Febreze is sold all over North America and Europe and has been freshening rooms and laundry since 1998. Because of its growing popularity and the power of its parent, Febreze seems poised for an even fresher future.

Febreze Fabric Refresher spray was sold in Test Markets in 1996, but took two years to reach store shelves across North America, where it made an immediate impact on the lives of consumers. Initially, Febreze was available only as a Fabric Refresher, although the company soon introduced the Air Effects line of air refresher sprays and small-unit, powered scent diffusers as well. Febreze is safe to use in homes with cats and dogs, which is helpful considering pet odors are a problem for many consumers. One of the newest and most popular products in the lineup is Febreze NOTICEables, an alternating scent oil warmer. This product includes two complementary scents that alternate automatically throughout the day for surprising, long-lasting freshness, and is currently offered in eight different scent combinations and varieties.

Febreze Fabric Refresher spray has been another successful offering from the company. It eliminates odors from fabrics, including clothing, upholstered home furnishings, window treatments, and more. Varieties include Febreze Antimicrobial; Febreze Allergen Reducer, which reduces up to 75% of allergens from cats, dogs, dust mites, and pollen* that may become airborne from fabrics; and Febreze Auto, which helps keep the interior of your car stay as fresh-smelling as your home. The Fabric Refresher is sprayed onto the fabric in question until it becomes damp, and is then allowed to dry. The molecules of the product will be absorbed into the fabric and eliminate any odors. As the product dries, odors will dissipate, leaving only a fresh scent behind. All Febreze products come in a wide range of scents to satisfy many different tastes and preferences. Febreze Original is still the top-selling scent, but newer versions including Febreze Mint & Refresh, Linen & Sky, Spring & Renewal, and Citrus & Light all have their strong consumer support.

The Procter & Gamble Company, which manufactures and distributes Febreze products, is today the world's number one maker of household products, and Febreze is one of the jewels in the company's crown.

Vital Statistics

Parent Company The Procter & Gamble Company

Product Launch 1998

Fidelity Investments

In 2005, Fidelity Investments aired a commercial chronicling musician Paul McCartney's achievements, from Beatlehood to fatherhood to knighthood. To the tune of "Band on the Run," the rock 'n' roll icon's life flashes by, reminding people to invest their money for a secure future for themselves and their children. "I'm really pleased to be working with Fidelity Investments," McCartney said in a statement released with the ad campaign. "We have a lot in common—a commitment to helping people...and a belief that you should never stop doing what you love doing."

"Never stop doing what you love" is Fidelity's advice to clients, and it aims to help them by offering an array of retirement planning, estate planning, mutual funds, wealth management, brokerage, securities execution and clearance, human resources and benefits outsourcing, life insurance, annuities, money management tools, and more. Fidelity emphasizes long-term commitment to its clients, many of whom may, over decades, invest money for homes, college tuition, and retirement.

Fidelity was originally best known as a mutual fund company. Edward Crosby Johnson 2d, a legendary stock-picker, founded Fidelity in 1946 and built the company on an investment philosophy that embraces changing market and economic conditions. In 1947, Fidelity launched the first mutual fund to invest in a portfolio based primarily on common stocks. Johnson's son Edward "Ned" Johnson 3d, who became chairman and CEO in 1977, built on his father's foundation to make Fidelity America's number-one mutual fund company.

The Fidelity brand has been associated with superior customer service made possible by technological innovation. In the 1970s and early 1980s, Fidelity was the first company to offer clients around-the-clock quotes, access to their mutual fund information via a voice-activated system, and tools for clients to initiate their own trades via personal computers. Unlike other mutual fund companies before the 1990s, Fidelity's customer service operators were equipped with mainframe computers that allowed them to easily handle client requests for services and information. In the 1990s, Fidelity became the first mutual fund company to launch an Internet Web site.

Throughout much of the 1980s, until the market crash of 1987, Fidelity's Magellan fund under the management of Peter Lynch was the best-performing mutual fund in the country. Recovering from the crash, Fidelity expanded beyond mutual funds to also offer low-cost personal financial adviser services, including retirement planning.

Vital Statistics
Classic Product Mutual Funds
Established 1946
Founder Edward Crosby Johnson 2d
Headquarters Boston, Massachusetts
Employees 42,000

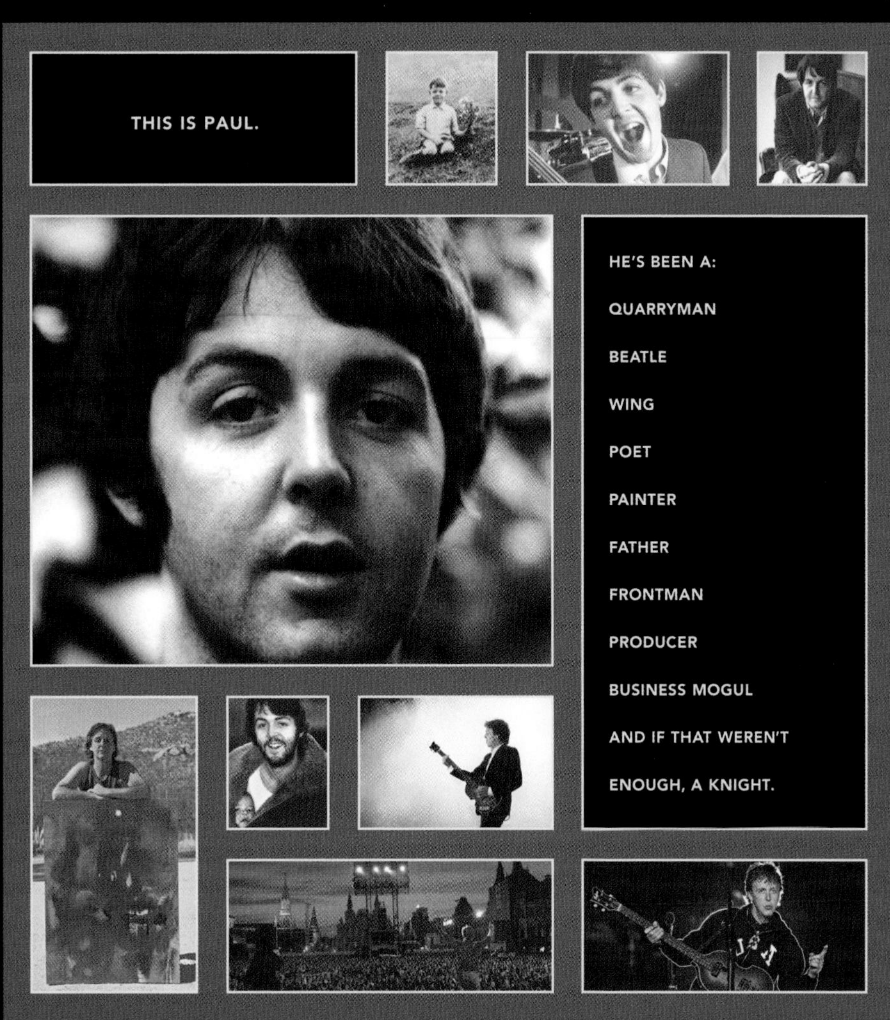

THIS IS PAUL.
HE'S BEEN A:
QUARRYMAN
BEATLE
WING
POET
PAINTER
FATHER
FRONTMAN
PRODUCER
BUSINESS MOGUL
AND IF THAT WEREN'T
ENOUGH, A KNIGHT.

THE KEY IS, NEVER STOP DOING WHAT YOU LOVE.

Whether you're selling out concerts or you're finally going back to music school, we can help you plan for the next part of your life. We have the experience to help you make the most of it. So see if you're on track. **Call 1.800.FIDELITY** and we'll review your plan today.

Smart move.

Fidelity Brokerage Services, Member NYSE, SIPC

424345

Fiesta Dinnerware

Collectors all over the world celebrate this classic dinnerware maker for its simply designed, brightly colored plates and bowls that look stunning in any setting and never go out of style. In fact, Fiesta is now the most collected china product worldwide.

In 1936, English potter Frederick Hurton Rhead introduced a new line of dinnerware, Fiesta, produced by the Homer Laughlin China Company in West Virginia. The original line featured the now-trademark bright, clean colors and eye-catching art deco styling. The plates were designed for maximum plating surface and had six concentric rings built into the design, making it look as though it had been thrown on a wheel and fired in a kiln. Rhead envisioned his line as an alternative to expensive, fussy fine china—everyday dishes that could serve families and dinner parties alike.

Fiesta was discontinued in 1973 and soon gained fame in antique shops and at flea markets from coast to coast. In particular demand—and of greatest value—were the items that had been produced in limited quantities, including vases, nesting bowls, carafes, and compotes. Certain colors were also more desirable, especially gray, rose, and chartreuse. The most popular color for collectors, however, was and continues to be fire red, which was one of the initial offerings and was out of production between 1943 and 1959 for a highly dramatic reason. The government had asked the company to stop using the country's supply of uranium oxide, which the government needed for its work developing the nuclear bomb. The ingredient was also key as a coloring agent in red Fiesta. Until 1972, Fiesta changed its color lineup only five times; however, since the 1980s, seven colors have been retired to make way for eighteen new ones, chosen to meet fashion trends and the desires of consumers. In 1986, to consumer delight, Fiesta was reissued with new, modern colors in celebration of the company's fiftieth anniversary. Today, the line is produced in fifteen colors that can be combined for effect if so desired. There are more than fifty items being manufactured, from plates and bowls to platters and pitchers. A compound called alpha alumina is added to the china to make the items less breakable and allow them to hold heat more efficiently. In 2002, Fiesta discontinued its yellow dinnerware, as it had apricot and lilac in recent years, because of the company policy of introducing new colors, allowing consumers to purchase them, and then replacing them with new, more timely variations. This policy allows Fiesta to remain highly collectible, and the dishes have become one of eBay's more popular items, as collectors strive to buy up the last items of a soon-to-be-discontinued color in anticipation of the newcomer.

Today, Fiesta is the top selection of brides in America for casual dinnerware and remains the country's most collected brand of china. The company is only becoming more popular with modern couples, who want utilitarian but still festive dinnerware they can put in the dishwasher—with a tradition of excellence and innovation besides. Each year at the annual Fiesta convention, a question-and-answer session is held with a hundred fans of the dinnerware in order to give them an opportunity to influence upcoming color selections. Recently, a turquoise onion-soup bowl, of a type that hadn't been made in more than fifty years, sold for a jaw-dropping $8,800 on eBay, but that is hardly the most awesome Fiesta sale: An antiques dealer sold two mixing bowls to a Fiesta fan for $35,000. Fiesta fans, in fact, are the force behind the company, joining Web sites, lobbying company executives, and creating more demand than the company can meet.

Vital Statistics

Parent Company	The Homer Laughlin China Company
Classic Product	Fiesta Dinnerware
Designer	Frederick Hurton Rhead
Product Launch	1936
Headquarters	Newell, West Virginia

Folgers

Each day Americans drink more than 85 million cups of Folgers, the nation's most popular coffee. The brand's tagline, "The best part of wakin' up is Folgers in your cup," is famous in advertising history, and its ad campaigns are among the most memorable. In one, the coffee at a fancy restaurant is replaced with Folgers and snobbish diners can't tell the difference. In another, a well-meaning woman tells her neighbors that a cup of mountain-grown Folgers is the remedy for all of life's little problems. More recently, a popular "viral" Internet ad for the coffee label features yellow-clad dancers singing "Happy Morning" and waking up grumpy sleepers. A Folgers drinker eventually joins in the chorus and welcomes the new day.

The Folgers story begins in 1850 at Pioneer Steam Coffee and Spice Mills in San Francisco, California. In addition to selling roasted whole beans, Pioneer sold ground coffee, which was a novelty at the time. James A. Folger, a hardworking carpenter and handyman at Pioneer, eventually rose in the ranks to become a partial owner of the business. In 1872, he bought out his partners and renamed the business J. A. Folger & Co. When he died in 1889, his son James Folger II inherited the business and ventured into new territories such as Texas and Missouri. In 1963, Procter & Gamble bought J. A. Folger & Co., distributing Folgers around the world and making it America's number-one brand of coffee.

In the 1980s, Folgers expanded its product line to include decaffeinated coffee, a new favorite among coffee drinkers who like flavor without the caffeine. The 21st century ushered in new Folgers varieties, including chocolate silk, cinnamon swirl, French vanilla, and hazelnut. Creamy cappuccino and lattes were also introduced in flavors such as mocha, toffee, and caramel. Recently, in 2006, the "Simply Smooth" line of stomach-friendly coffees was launched for consumers who experience stomach discomfort after drinking coffee. That same year, Folgers also launched a line of gourmet blends for discriminating drinkers in flavors such as vanilla biscotti, hazelnut crème, and chocolate truffle.

One of Procter & Gamble's "billion-dollar brands," Folgers continues to grow and change with the times. In 2005, the company made the switch from its 150-year-old trademark red metal can to the "AromaSeal" canister, a foil-lined package that keeps ground coffee fresh and is easy to hold and to open. The makeover boosted sales of some Folgers lines up to 30 percent and won Folgers several awards, including one from the Arthritis Foundation. Judging from Folgers sales, millions of Americans seem to enjoy the new varieties and the new containers, which make the "best part of wakin' up" even better.

Vital Statistics
Parent Company The Procter & Gamble Company
Product Launch 1972

AromaSeal™
fresh
TASTE
MOUNTAIN GROWN®
Folgers
CLASSIC ROAST
MAKES UP TO
270
MILD
MEDIUM
MED-DARK
DARK

Folgers
GOURMET
SELECTIONS
GROUND COFFEE
Morning Café
LIGHT ROAST
NET WT 11 OZ (311.9g) • COFFEE

Ford Mustang

The Ford Mustang burst onto the scene in 1964, symbolizing American youth and vitality. The first Mustang was a white convertible with a red interior and the most successful product launch in automotive history. It is no exaggeration to say that the Mustang spawned the entire "pony car" genre—sporty, powerful, affordable coupes that provided an exciting alternative to the land yachts that had previously ruled the roads.

From its beginning in 1903, the Ford Motor Company aimed to manufacture cars that most Americans could afford. In the 1960s, Ford's then-general manager, Lee Iacocca, extended this idea to the sports car. His primary goal was to create a product that could compete with GM's sporty Monza. Product manager Donald N. Frey designed a prototype for a two-seat, mid-engine roadster, later remodeled as a four-seat car by David Ash and Joseph Oros in Ford's Lincoln-Mercury Division design studios. The initial Mustang hardtop with an inline six-cylinder engine and three-speed manual transmission sold for $2,368, although it looked much more expensive because of its "long hood/short deck" styling. More than 100,000 Mustangs were sold within the first 100 days of the car's availability, and the Mustang earned many prestigious auto industry awards in its very first year, including Motor Trend Car of the Year, pace car duties for the 1964 Indianapolis 500, and the Tiffany Design Award for "excellence in design."

The Mustang was based on familiar, simple components. Mustang buyers could customize their cars, resulting in higher prices and ensuring profitability for both dealer and manufacturer. In its first two years of production, three Ford Motor Company plants produced nearly 1.5 million Mustangs, a record that has never been topped. The 1968 Mustang fastback became an instant pop culture icon when the ultimately cool Steve McQueen drove it to great effect—racing a Dodge Charger through the streets of San Francisco—in the crime thriller *Bullitt*. In the late 1980s, sales slumped, and Ford announced that the Mustang would be discontinued and replaced by the Probe. Mustang fans wrote hundreds of thousands of angry letters in a combined attempt to save the Mustang. Ford, won over by the pleas, redesigned the Mustang and salvaged the nameplate, and the car is still being produced. In fact, it was named *Motor Trend* magazine's car of the year for the third time in 1994. At the 2004 North American International Auto Show, Ford introduced a completely redesigned Mustang, inspired by the 1960s originals and an aesthetic that J Mays, senior vice president of design, referred to as "retro-futurism." The new Mustang was an immediate success, and half of all "sports" cars sold in the United States are now Mustangs.

Ford continues to sell about 150,000 Mustangs each year. Today, restoring vintage Mustangs is a popular hobby, and parts are easy to find for those inclined. Even the very first production Mustang is still around and on display at the Henry Ford Museum in Dearborn, Michigan.

Vital Statistics
Manufacturer Ford Motor Company
Headquarters Dearborn, Michigan
Established 1903

1964

Ford F-150 Truck

Americans love pickup trucks, a sentiment probably born of our national appreciation of hard work and utility. Almost as soon as Henry Ford was making cars, Henry Ford's customers were tinkering with them, using Model Cs as delivery cars and turning Model Ts into open-air ambulances, fire trucks, taxis, and hearses. Taking a cue from customers, the Ford Motor Company introduced its first factory-produced pickup truck in 1925. It came in one color, black, and was called the Ford Model T Runabout with Pickup Body. It cost $281. Customers could buy the pickup box separately and bolt it onto the chassis of their regular Model T car. Proof of the instant appeal of the truck, Ford produced and sold twice as many pickup boxes as pickup trucks—people couldn't wait to convert their cars.

Ford continued to produce trucks for the next two decades, but it was the F-Series of trucks that really captured America's heart. First introduced in 1948, the F-Series trucks have been the best-selling vehicles in the world for 23 years and the best-selling trucks in America for more than 28 years. There were three trucks in the original F-Series, ranging from the F1 (a half-ton truck) to the F3 (heavy duty). The Coca-Cola Company in Atlanta used Ford trucks to deliver their product—the trucks had custom-built transport boxes with side panels that rolled up. The F-Series quickly became the truck of choice for farmers as well as tradespeople.

The F-Series debuted with the marketing slogan "Ford Bonus Built—Trucks Built Stronger to Last Longer." Then-company President Henry Ford II, like his father, wanted his company's vehicles to project an image of high quality and reliability at an affordable cost. At the same time, with World War II and its sacrifices behind them, Americans were ready for creature comforts. With its bigger cab (marketed as being like a living room), updated styling, and a choice of engines, the F-Series early on had an appeal that extended beyond traditional truck customers. The F-1 Series of trucks were much more comfortable and stylish than anything built in the past.

In 1953, the F-Series was redesigned and renamed the F-100, F-250, and F-350. With their one-piece windshields, integrated headlights, and perks such as armrests and sun visors, these second-generation trucks are today's coveted antiques. Snub nosed and often painted red, antique Ford pickups are often seen proudly rolling down the road in Fourth of July parades, and Ralph Lauren uses them in advertisements displaying the pleasures of country life in fine clothing.

The F-150 made its debut in 1975 and is still the company's best seller. Today's F-150 truck customer is just as likely to live in suburban Atlanta as to own a horse farm in Kentucky, so options include five different trims, three different cab configurations, and several cargo-box lengths, as well as heated leather seats and automatic climate controls.

Vital Statistics
Manufacturer Ford Motor Company
Headquarters Dearborn, Michigan
Established 1903

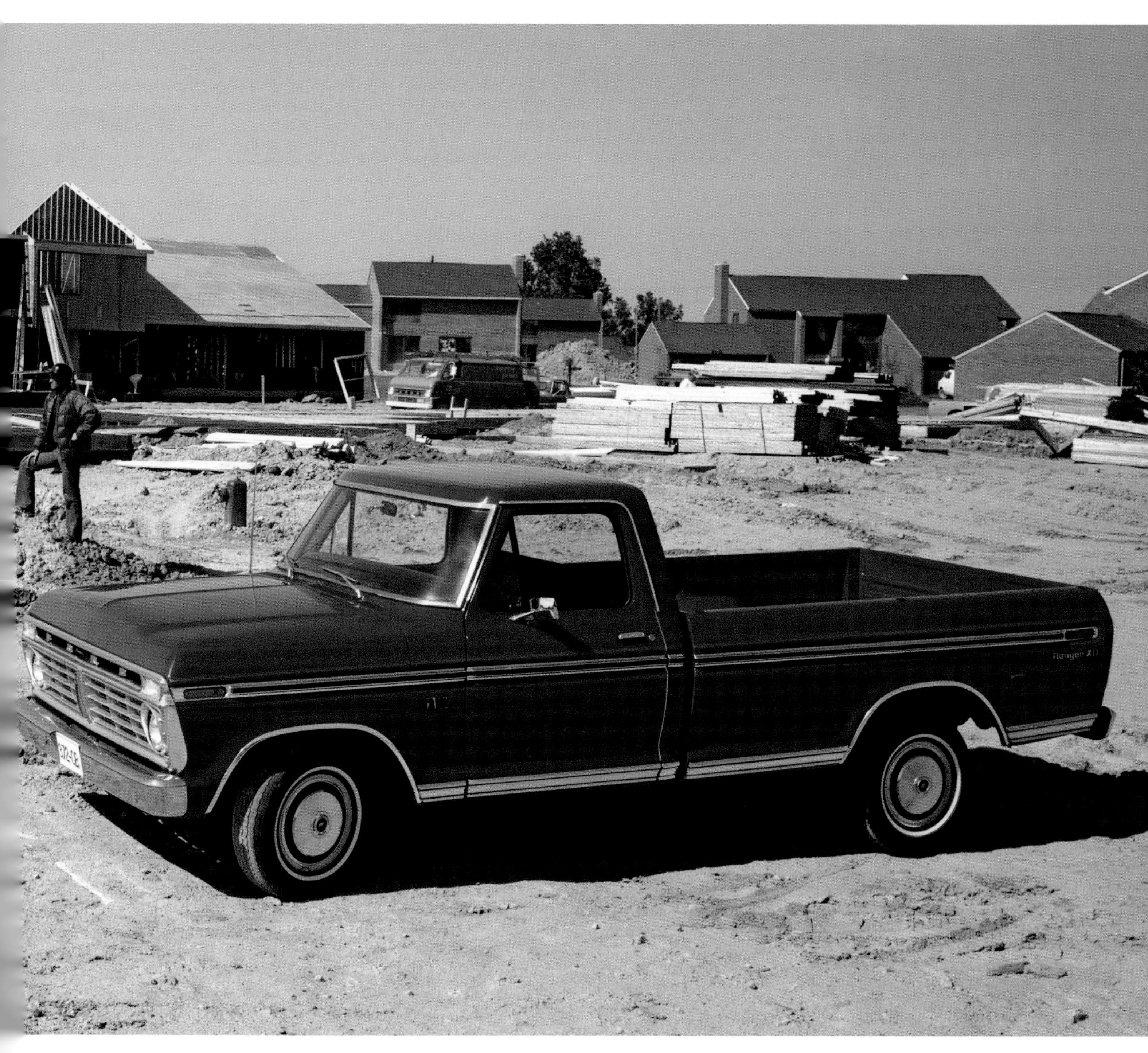

French's Mustard

Two all-American foods were popularized at the 1904 St. Louis World's Fair: the frankfurter (or hot dog, as it would later be called) and its perfect condiment, yellow mustard. The mustard was a vision of the French brothers, Francis and George, who concocted the recipe for a light and creamy spread with a turmeric and mustard seed base. It was an instant success—the new mustard was mild yet flavorful and unlike the hot and spicy varieties that were common at the time.

In 1912, the French brothers expanded their existing business by establishing a new mustard-making facility in Rochester, New York. Although the R. T. French Company existed as a purveyor of spices long before the brothers inherited the business from their father, the popular mustard recipe helped the company grow and thrive even through the Great Depression.

The R. T. French Company not only created cream-style mustard, a new variety of mustard better suited to American tastes, but also led category innovations in new packaging, preparation, and advertising. French's mustard was ready to eat, unlike its dry-powder predecessors that had to be mixed with vinegar and water. The packaging was also novel: by 1915, French's mustard came in clear jars with a trademark pennant logo on the glass bottle and a new government seal indicating that the product fulfilled high standards of quality and hygiene. In 1926, the J&J Colman Company, later to become Reckitt & Colman Ltd., bought the French's brand. By 1980, 100 years after the French Company was first established, French's mustard was selling at a rate of 500,000 bottles a day.

French's became the most popular mustard in the country. As consumer interest in specialty flavors grew, new varieties were introduced in the last decades of the 20th century including Sweet Onion, Horseradish, Bold 'n Spicy, Dijon, Creamy Spread, Sweet 'n Zesty, and Honey Dijon. Most recently, the company innovated with a new squeeze bottle and the first stay clean cap in the mustard category. French's Classic Yellow, however, remains the brand's top flavor. With a 59 percent share of the yellow segment, French's is the overall best-selling mustard in America. Enjoying strong health credentials, the main ingredients of vinegar, turmeric, garlic powder, and mustard seeds haven't changed in the century since the French brothers created the recipe.

Today, French's mustard is more than just yellow mustard, the company markets four leading varieties including Honey, Horseradish, Honey Dijon, and Spicy Brown. French's is the largest brand in the food division of its British parent company Reckitt Benckiser, which has expanded the French's brand to include other products such as Worcestershire sauce, mayonnaise, fried onions, and potato sticks. The company continues to emphasize French's image as "America's favorite mustard" and its mainstream appeal as a healthy, everyday condiment that can liven up ordinary foods such as hamburgers, hot dogs, and sandwiches. French's has recently been introduced into the global market and is quickly becoming a pantry staple in the United Kingdom, Japan, Greece, Mexico, and other countries where American-style sandwiches and hot dogs are gaining in popularity.

Vital Statistics

Company Name	Reckitt Benckiser Inc.
Classic Product	French's Classic Yellow Mustard
Established	1880 (as the R. T. French Company)
Inventors	Francis and George French
Distribution	125 million units/year (est.)
Main Production Site	Springfield, Missouri

Frigidaire

Frigidaire got its start shortly after the first electric refrigerator was produced and sold in 1913. Alfred Mellowes, working in a backyard washhouse in Fort Wayne, Indiana, engineered and created a newer version of the electric refrigerator in 1915. It differed from the original because it was self-contained with a compressor at the bottom of the cabinet. In 1916, the Guardian Refrigerator Company began operations in Detroit to manufacture Mellowes's refrigerator. The company turned out its first "Guardian" through slow and laborious hand operations. Though the quality was exceptional, the company's financial situation soon became dire because of slow production—fewer than 40 refrigerators were produced in two years.

Frigidaire

W. C. Durant, then president of General Motors, purchased the company in 1918 and gave it the name *Frigidaire*. The first Frigidaire refrigerator was built that year in Detroit. Durant applied the mass production techniques of the automobile industry to the building of refrigerators. Production facilities improved and additional sales offices were opened, and Frigidaire was on its way. With an emphasis on developing markets overseas, there was an expansion of manufacturing facilities to accommodate increased sales. Products evolved and prices decreased, and Frigidaire expanded by broadening its production to apply to other uses of refrigeration. Ice cream cabinets and soda fountain equipment were manufactured in 1924, milk coolers and water coolers in 1927, and the first chest-type freezer for the home in 1929.

Despite the hardship of the Depression, Frigidaire production and sales increased. During this time, Frigidaire entered the area of railroad air-conditioning, and in 1937, the company introduced a line of electric ranges. Another achievement at the time was the development and use of freon as a refrigerant. During World War II, all civilian production ceased as the company manufactured .50 caliber Browning machine guns, aircraft propellers and parts, hydraulic controls for airplanes, and other military items. The prosperity of the 1950s boosted consumerism and the desire for the latest in product innovation and design. Frigidaire employed Robert Loewy, one of the best-known industrial designers of the 20th century, to give the kitchens of the 1950s a whole new look. The "Sheer Look" offered contemporary squared corners and bold colors—the first major appliance redesign in years.

Environmentally sound products became a priority in the 1970s and 1980s, which led to the manufacturing of more energy-efficient refrigerators and the elimination of chlorofluorocarbons in refrigeration sealed systems. Consumer needs and concerns were further reflected in products such as the Gallery Tumble Action washer, which operates more quietly and saves energy and water, and the PureSource Ice & Water Filtration System, introduced in side-by-side refrigerators in 1998.

Frigidaire has pioneered many products and design developments in the refrigeration and home appliance industry. With the ability to manufacture and deliver products of high quality and innovative design to a global marketplace, Frigidaire continues to dominate the industry and maintains itself as one of the most recognizable brands worldwide.

Vital Statistics

Parent Company	Electrolux Home Products North America
Established	1918
Founder	W. C. Durant
Annual Sales	$1.6 billion

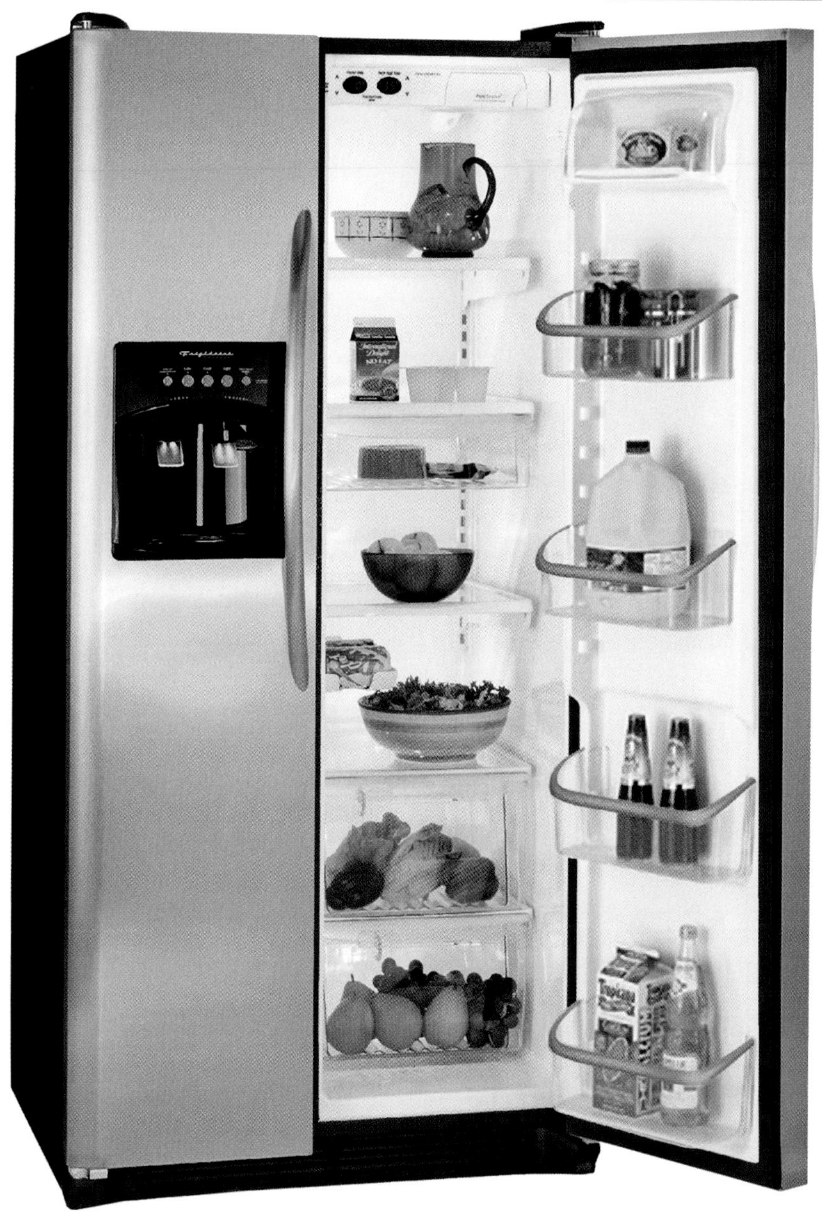

E. & J. Gallo Winery

If you have ever had a glass of wine, it is likely that you have tasted a Gallo wine. For generations, the E. & J. Gallo Winery has been the world's most popular winery and an international authority on winegrape growing, wine making, wine distribution and wine marketing. Today, Gallo has six wineries throughout California accessing grapes from the state's leading grape growing regions. And, perhaps most impressive of all, the E. & J. Gallo Winery is still a family-owned company, as it has been from the start–selling wine in more than 90 countries around the world, making it the largest exporter of California wine.

Co-founders Ernest and Julio Gallo, helped build the American wine industry and, in turn, achieved one of the greatest American business successes of the twentieth century. Ernest and Julio were instrumental in introducing U.S. consumers to wine and creating the modern American wine market. Ernest was among the pioneers of wine advertising on television and he launched many memorable wine advertising campaigns. Working closely together, Ernest and Julio were first in the U.S. wine industry to establish their own national sales force; first to introduce brand management and modern merchandising to the wine industry; first in breakthrough quality initiatives such as long-term grower contracts for varietal grapes and major grape research programs; first to establish a truly significant foreign sales and marketing force to export California wines overseas; and pioneers in bringing new products to store shelves.

Today, the third generation of the Gallo family is working for the winery and standing behind the Gallo brand. Their mission is to develop a diverse portfolio of premium and popular wine brands intended to introduce more people to wine as well as meet the evolving needs of an ever-growing base of wine consumers.

Vital Statistics
Established 1933
Founder Ernest and Julio Gallo
Headquarters Modesto, California
Employees 4,600

1999
RESERVE
Gallo Family's
GALLO of SONOMA
CABERNET SAUVIGNON
SONOMA COUNTY
BARREL AGED

The Gap Inc.

It is ironic that the company that universalized casual dress for all ages was named—at the height of the counterculture movement in 1969—for the notorious "generation gap." When Donald and Doris Fisher opened their first store in San Francisco, they had in mind a place where teenagers could buy their Levi's. Little did they know how ubiquitous their khakis and T-shirts were to become.

When the Fishers' first Gap store took off, they opened a second, in San Jose, eight months later. By the end of 1970 there were six Gaps, and six years later the company went public. The rest is history: today, a Gap store is within driving distance of most homes in America. By the early 1980s, the Gap had 500 stores and was one of the most recognized brand names in the country. Although Levi's still represented about a third of sales, the Fishers had bigger dreams, and in 1983, the company brought in Mickey Drexler, a former president of Ann Taylor, as President and COO of the Gap division. It was Drexler who arrived at today's time-tested formula of durable, brightly colored cotton staples and consolidated the private labels into the brand we now know as the Gap. Drexler also introduced the clean white shelving system to display neatly stacked clothes that was satirized so cleverly by Adam Sandler, David Spade, and others. on *Saturday Night Live*.

In 1983, the Gap bought Banana Republic, a chain of safari-themed clothing stores that has long outlived its theme, and rebuilt it by 1990 into a profitable, more upscale store targeted to young, urban professionals. The first Gap Kids opened in 1986 when Drexler grew frustrated by the clothing options available to his son, and by 1990 BabyGap had been installed in 25 Gap Kids stores. In 1991, the Gap stopped selling Levi's altogether in favor of the increasingly popular private-label items, and in 1994, Old Navy Clothing Co. was launched, bringing the Gap's signature staples to an even wider audience at lower prices. Robert Fisher (the founders' son) became the new president of the Gap division (including BabyGap and Gap Kids) in 1997 and refocused the Gap on basics, with the help of a high-profile advertising campaign. Later in 1997, the Gap opened an online Gap store.

In 1998, the Gap launched what was to become its most famous ad campaign: a trio of unforgettable commercials titled "Khakis Rock," "Khakis Groove," and "Khakis Swing." The ads were designed to appeal to young people turned off by their jeans-wearing, baby boomer parents and aired during hot television shows such as *Ally McBeal* and *E.R.* Amazingly, the Gap succeeded at casting a tired, preppy staple in a new, exciting light. In late 1999, however, Robert Fisher resigned and CEO Drexler took over the helm again, until his retirement in September 2002. Drexler was replaced by Paul Pressler, a veteran of the Walt Disney Company, in 2005; he has since left the company.

Today, Gap Inc. is one of the world's largest specialty retailers, with more than 3,000 stores and fiscal 2005 revenues of $16 billion. It operates the most recognized clothing brands in the world—Gap, Banana Republic, and Old Navy—and has become synonymous with classic, affordable American style.

Vital Statistics
Classic Product jeans and casual wear
Established 1969
Founders Doris and Don Fisher
Employees 153,000 (2006)
Annual Sales $15,943 million (2007)

GAP

The Gatorade Company

It is hard to imagine an athlete these days—amateur or professional—who doesn't have a bottle of Gatorade on hand. But until 1965, many athletes suffered from heat and heat-related conditions. It was in the summer of that year that an assistant football coach at the University of Florida sat down with a team of university doctors and asked them to determine why so many players were adversely affected by heat. Thus Gatorade was born.

Physicians Robert Cade, Dana Shires, H. James Free, and Alejandro de Quesada determined that two major factors were affecting the players. For one, they were losing fluids and electrolytes in sweat that were not being replaced by the body. And, large amounts of carbohydrates their bodies used for energy were not being replenished. The doctors devised a carbohydrate-electrolyte beverage, scientifically formulated to replace all the key elements athletes were losing when exercising in the heat. Because they were the team doctors for the Florida Gators, they called their invention Gatorade. Once the drink was introduced to the football team the following year, the Gators began winning, specifically because of their newfound staying power in the sweltering heat and humidity At 7-4, it was the Gators' first winning season in more than a decade. The Gators kept winning, and in 1967 they went 9-2 and won the Orange Bowl for the first time ever in the history of the school. The scoop on Gatorade began to spread outside Florida, and soon both the University of Richmond and Miami University in Ohio were requesting Gatorade for their athletes. Other teams followed suit, ordering batches for their own football teams all over the country. Gatorade became the official sports drink of more than 70 Division I schools.

In the summer of 1969, the Gators coaches suggested to the Kansas City Chiefs that Gatorade could help them during training camp. The Gatorade was such a hit that the team kept it on the sidelines all season, and the Chiefs won that year, in Super Bowl IV. Gatorade was then made the official sports drink of the NFL, which it remains today. In 1985, the Gatorade Sports Science Institute was founded in Barrington, Illinois, to conduct scientific research in the areas of exercise science, hydration, and sports nutrition. Three years later, the lab was expanded to test new Gatorade products and flavors and develop education materials. Gatorade is now also the official sports drink of the National Basketball Association, the Association of Volleyball Professionals, the Professional Golfers Association, Major League Baseball, Major League Soccer, and many other professional organizations and teams. In 2001, Gatorade and GSSI helped auto racing organizations develop a hydration tool that could withstand 130-degree temperatures: GIDS, the Gatorade In-Car Drinking System, is now considered an essential piece of racing equipment. Also that year, the company introduced Gatorade Performance Series sports nutrition products, including the Gatorade Energy Drink, the Gatorade Energy Bar, and the Gatorade Nutrition Shake.

The Gatorade Company was acquired by the Quaker Oats Company in 1993 and is now owned by PepsiCo, which merged with Quaker in 2001. Gatorade was the world's first isotonic sports drink offering fluid, electrolytes and 6 %–8% carbohydrates. It remains the number-one sports drink with athletes everywhere, thanks to an assistant football coach who was tired of seeing his players suffer in the Florida heat.

Vital Statistics

Parent Company	Pepsi Co
Established	1965
Founder/Inventor	Robert Cade, Dana Shires, H. James Free, and Alejandro de Quesada
Employees	1,210 (2005)
Annual Sales	$183.4 million (2005)

GE

Most of us know that it is GE—General Electric—that brings "good things to life." And many would agree that the lightbulb, symbol itself of inspiration, has truly transformed how people live. Born in the brain of one of the world's great inventors, the lightbulb is a compact marvel of innovation and technology, and the story of how it came to be is an American original.

In 1876, Thomas Alva Edison opened a laboratory in Menlo Park, New Jersey, out of which was to emerge, three years later, one of the most famous inventions of all time: the incandescent electric lamp. The first application of electric lighting was on a steamship called *Columbia* in 1880, and the first full-scale public application was in London, at the Holborn Viaduct. Two years later, the first system in the United States was implemented at New York City's Pearl Street Station, the nation's first central power station. By 1890, Edison had also invented the direct-current generator and combined his various interests into Edison General Electric Company. A competing company caused patent problems, and in 1892, the two merged to form General Electric, headquartered in Schenectady, New York, the only remaining of the original 12 Dow Jones Industrial Average companies. In 1900, General Electric Research Laboratory, the nation's first research lab independent of a university, was founded, and the GE trademark monogram was registered. In 1906, the tantalum filament lamp was introduced. Two years later, a process was discovered to render the durable metal used in metalized carbon filament more pliable, leading to the use of a tungsten filament, and lightbulbs that could be used in cars and trains. In 1935, the first night major-league baseball game was played under GE lights in Cincinnati, and the San Francisco–Oakland Bay Bridge, the world's longest, opened with lighting from 1,000 GE sodium luminaries in 1936.

Of all the lightbulbs GE has created since its inception, none has come close to the debut, in 2001, of the Reveal bulb—the most successful launch in the lighting business' 120-year history. In the first year and a half, more than 100 million Reveal bulbs were sold. GE Reveal bulbs make colors "pop" in a way they don't with standard incandescent bulbs because the rare element neodymium is present in the glass. When Reveal bulbs, bluish in color when not lit, are turned on, the neodymium filters out the yellowish cast of ordinary lightbulbs, creating a clean, pure light. It is likely Thomas Edison would be amazed by these incandescent lights that last 750–1000 hours and are capable of eliminating harsh colors of the spectrum. Today, GE offers 67 GE Edison lighting products, including general purpose, track, and recessed lightbulbs in single and multipacks, table and ceiling-fixture lights, and indoor track and recessed floodlights. Compared to standard reflector lamps, the company's silver coated reflector lamps produce energy savings, a longer life, or both.

General Electric, the parent of the Reveal and other GE lighting products, provides solutions for commercial, industrial, and residential use in more than 100 countries. GE has evolved from Thomas Edison's home laboratory into one of the largest companies in the world. Its recent tax returns have been the largest filed in the United States, spanning approximately 24,000 pages when printed out. Over its century-plus of innovation, General Electric has amassed more than 67,500 patents, and the firm's scientists have been awarded two Nobel Prizes and numerous other honors.

Vital Statistics	
Classic Product	Reveal lightbulb
Established	1892
Founder/Inventor	Thomas Alva Edison
Employees	316,000

GEICO

GEICO, the Government Employees Insurance Company, was founded by Leo and Lillian Goodwin. The Goodwins wanted to provide automobile insurance at reduced rates by selecting prime customer groups and marketing directly to them. Their company was able to drive down operating costs and pass on the savings to policyholders in the form of reduced rates. In doing so, they created what has become one of the best-known car insurers in the United States.

Leo Goodwin was 50 when, in 1936 he and his wife, Lillian, moved their fledgling company's headquarters from Ft. Worth, Texas, to Washington, D.C. Lillian, a bookkeeper, was the accountant, set rates, wrote and issued policies, and marketed auto insurance to GEICO's target customers. From the very beginning, GEICO sought out federal employees and military officers in the greater D.C. area, a strategy that became a company hallmark. By the following year, there were 3,700 GEICO policies, and the Goodwins had a staff of 12. In 1948, Lorimer Davidson, an investment banker and friend of the Goodwins, joined the company and helped the couple find new investors, including Benjamin Graham, a Columbia University business professor who became one of Warren Buffett's teachers. In 1951, Buffett took a train to Washington to learn more about GEICO and had a memorable conversation with Davidson that was to change the future of the company. On the basis of that unplanned meeting, Buffett made his first purchase of GEICO stock. When Leo Goodwin retired in 1958, Davidson took over the helm in time for GEICO's new headquarters to open in Maryland after more than 20 years of success.

The 1960s saw GEICO pass the 1 million policyholder mark, insurance premiums reach $150 million, and net earnings double to $13 million. GEICO opened sales and service offices for walk-in customers and drive-in claims offices that decade as well. Leo and Lillian Goodwin died in 1970 and 1971 respectively, and the company's fortunes temporarily turned sour. However, GEICO took the opportunity to make its underwriting and loss reserving activities stronger, and in 1976, Buffett purchased a reported 1 million shares of company stock. In 1981, GEICO introduced 24-hour, 365-day telephone service for claims, sales, and service. The customer base expanded during the '80s thanks to a new four-company strategy, an increased advertising budget, and greater national visibility. In 1995, Buffett's Berkshire Hathaway investment firm offered to buy the remaining shares of GEICO's stock, and GEICO became a Berkshire Hathaway subsidiary early in 1996.

The GEICO Gecko made GEICO a household name after its initial appearance in 1999. The idea for the gecko grew from a creative session at GEICO's ad agency. Because *GEICO* was so often mispronounced, it became *gecko,* and a quick doodle of a gecko was an instant hit at the agency, which decided to give the gecko a British accent that Americans loved. In 2001, Leo Goodwin was named to the International Insurance Society Hall of Fame, and two years later, GEICO passed the 5 million policyholder mark.

Today GEICO has over 20,000 associates in 12 major locations around the country and maintains a focus on the Goodwins' core values of excellent coverage, low prices, and outstanding customer service. In addition to auto insurance, GEICO offers insurance for motorcycles, ATVs, and RVs, as well as personal umbrella protection. GEICO insures more than 11 million vehicles and is the fourth-largest private-passenger auto insurer in the United States.

Vital Statistics

Parent Company Berkshire Hathaway

Established 1936

Founders Leo and Lillian Goodwin

Employees 20,417 (2005)

Annual Sales $10,101 million (2005)

George Foreman Lean Mean Grilling Machine

George Foreman proves the old adage that brains are better than brawn, at least when it comes to making money. The former two-time world boxing champion has earned more on his George Forman Lean Mean Fat-Reducing Grilling Machine than he has in the ring, despite the fact that he's widely considered to be one of the greatest heavyweights of all time.

The grill was introduced in 1995, during an era when weight-conscious Americans were convinced that reducing fat was the key to staying slim. The machine's slogan, "knock out the fat," alluded to boxing, but the product's real punch for consumers was the promise of patented grooves that carry grease away from food and onto a separate tray. Since then, says grill manufacturer Salton Inc., more than 55 million Foreman grills have been sold. The latest incarnation, the "Next Grilleration," rolled out in 2004, and George Foreman products currently account for about 30 percent of Salton sales.

Foreman became a legend in 1973 when he gained his first world heavyweight title by knocking out then-champion Joe Frazier in only two rounds. But he didn't show his natural bent for salesmanship until his comeback bid for a second world boxing title, which he won in 1994 at age 45 from Michael Moore. On his way up, but still relegated to small fights in the boondocks, he was asked to make a ten-second commercial for a small Florida TV station to promote a fight in 1989. Speaking into a microphone, the strapping, 6-foot-4 Foreman proudly asserted that he wasn't over the hill yet and promised to win. He was so persuasive that the fight immediately sold out. The station asked him to make another commercial the next day.

He rapidly built a career promoting everything from hamburgers to mufflers, fitting it all in between training and fights. Marketing experts attribute his success in sales not to his strength and athleticism, but to his persona as an ordained minister and father of ten children. The angry young man who lost to Muhammad Ali in 1974 in the famous "Rumble in the Jungle" in Congo had evolved into an avuncular, smiling man who was easy to trust.

Recognizing a good thing, Salton Inc., maker of small appliances and housewares, began licensing the George Foreman name in 1995 when it launched the Lean Mean Fat-Reducing Grilling Machine. Under the terms of that early agreement, Foreman received about 60 percent of the profits from every grill sold. In 1999, however, Salton bought the Foreman trademark for $127.5 million in cash and $10 million in stock—at the time an unheard of contract for an athlete. Foreman hasn't argued with published estimates of lifetime earnings of $240 million, about three times the prize money he earned as a boxer.

Vital Statistics
Parent Company Salton Inc.
Product Launch 1995
Headquarters Lake Forest, Illinois

Gerber Products Company

The plump-cheeked image of the Gerber baby has, for generations of Americans, symbolized all that is healthy and pure. Today, more than 200 products in 80 countries bear the Gerber name, including baby cereal, juices, toddler food, bath and skin care products, bottles, teethers, breast-feeding accessories, spill-proof cups, and infant toys and clothing.

A mother's ingenuity is at the heart of the Gerber story. In 1927, Dorothy Gerber started making her own baby food for her seven-month-old daughter, Sally, by hand-straining various solid foods. It occurred to her that this could be done on a much larger scale at the Fremont Canning Company, where her husband and his father produced a line of canned fruits and vegetables. Daniel Gerber did extensive research and testing, and by 1928, peas, prunes, carrots, spinach, and vegetable soup were ready for consumers—and their babies—nationwide. Gerber's brilliant marketing plan, including an advertisement placed in *Good Housekeeping* featuring a novel coupon redemption program and highlighting the nutritional and time-saving value of Gerber's prepared foods, brought it quick success. First-year sales reached 590,000 cans, with gross revenues of $345,000. The Gerber family had revolutionized the way Americans fed their infants at 15 cents a can, affordable for all but the poorest of households. The ad also introduced the now world-famous "Gerber Baby," Ann Turner Cook, who sat for children's portraitist Dorothy Hope Smith and later became a mystery novelist and English teacher. Gerber adopted Cook's image as its official trademark in 1931, and it has appeared on all Gerber packaging and advertisements since.

By 1935, Gerber had competition from more than 60 other manufacturers, but Fremont Canning held its lead, thanks partly to model spokeswoman Dorothy Gerber, whose newspaper column "Bringing up Baby" was wildly popular with mothers from coast to coast. Gerber continued to introduce new innovations, including, in 1959, "quick-twist" jar caps and "shop-easy" labels, with the product's variety name on top of the jar. When Daniel Gerber died in 1974, the company was the world's largest baby-food manufacturer, with sales of $278 million and a domestic market share of almost 70 percent. In 1977, Gerber initiated the "use-by" dating system on its baby-food jars, ensuring freshness, and a decade later it established a consumer help line to answer questions about infant care and nutrition. In the late 1990s, Gerber introduced its first organic products with the Tender Harvest line. The Gerber Organic product line, featuring infant cereal, juice, single-variety 2nd Foods and toddler snacks, came out in 2006. In 1994, Gerber merged with Sandoz Ltd., and today it is part of the Novartis Group of companies.

Gerber offers reassurance to new parents all over the world on many levels, from its Life Insurance Company to the old standbys of pureed carrots and peas. It is the largest supplier of baby products in the world and has dominated the baby-product market since its introduction nearly 90 years ago. Recently, according to a worldwide study commissioned by WPP Group, Gerber beat Nike as the brand with the strongest consumer loyalty among Americans.

Vital Statistics
Classic Product baby food
Established 1928
Founders Dorothy and Daniel Gerber

OPEN
Gerber
Carrots
1ST FOODS
Gerber
nature lock

Gibson Guitars

Orville Gibson was a shoe clerk, but his passion was making mandolins and guitars of his own design. In 1894, when demand for his guitars grew, he quit his job and opened the Gibson Mandolin-Guitar Co., Ltd. in Kalamazoo, Michigan. Gibson, regarded as an eccentric figure, had no interest in running the business end of the company and was listed as a consultant on the official paperwork when the company incorporated in 1902. Before his death in 1918, Orville Gibson was paid $500 a year for his name and many of the most innovative guitar design ideas of all time.

In the following decades, the Gibson Mandolin-Guitar Company established itself as a leading maker of high-precision instruments created for musicians by musicians. In the 1950s, Les Paul, a popular guitar player in America, consulted with Gibson on the design of an electric guitar. For years, the musician had been trying to persuade the guitar manufacturer to consider a new solid body design, but they weren't interested. As Paul became more popular, Gibson began to listen. "Brazil," Paul's 1948 hit, was a demanding piece that featured six guitar parts. Three years later, he sold 2 million records of "Mockin' Bird Hill" and "How High the Moon."

The Les Paul guitar debuted in 1952 as the first guitar that looked like a piece of art. The front of the instrument was made of maple, which gave it a bright sound balanced by the warmth and richness of mahogany in the back. The result was unprecedented sustain and tone. In 1954, Gibson launched two additional versions of the Les Paul: the Les Paul Custom (with more expensive hardware) and the Les Paul Junior. In 1958, the classic gold-top finish was replaced with a cherry-red sunburst, which boosted the popularity of the Les Paul brand even more.

The Les Paul was adopted by America's most famous musicians. Many bands' greatest hits were introduced to the world on a Les Paul, including Led Zeppelin's "Whole Lotta Love," the Allman Brothers' "Ramblin' Man," the Eagles' "Life in the Fast Lane," and "Mama, I'm Coming Home" by Ozzy Osbourne. The Les Paul was also a favorite of Keith Richards, Pete Townshend, Frank Zappa, George Harrison, and Joey Santiago.

Today, the Gibson Guitar Corp., now headquartered in Nashville, Tennessee, is one of the world's top manufacturers of electric and acoustic guitars. In the mid-1990s, Gibson acquired several smaller companies, including those that make resonator guitars, drums, and acoustic pianos, and has plans to expand and explore new digital music technologies. The Les Paul guitar, meanwhile, remains one the best-selling guitars in America and is still made in the United States. Although the mechanics of its design have been relatively untouched since the 1950s, the guitar is available in 13 models, including the Les Paul Standard, the Les Paul Goddess, and the Les Paul Special New Century.

Vital Statistics

Classic Product	Les Paul guitar
Established	1902
Founder	Orville Gibson
Headquarters	Nashville, Tennessee

Gillette

The search for a smoother shave will likely never end, but in the meantime, men are grabbing up Gillette's new Fusion razor as fast as they can. Launched in 2006, Fusion reached a 55 percent market share in razors within months, a remarkable feat for a new product. What's making so many men plunk down the extra money for a new razor and blades? Fusion features what Gillette calls a "shaving surface" created by placing five blades very close together. Ads say the planed surface distributes pressure more evenly than razors with fewer blades and reduces irritation on the skin, making for a more comfortable shave.

It had been seven years since Gillette introduced its last new razor system—in 1998, the Mach3. The Mach3 was the first time a triple-bladed razor had been marketed. Gillette also invented the twin-bladed TracII razor in 1971. But a company spokeswoman says Gillette's breakthrough with Fusion isn't just about the number of blades. It's also about how closely they are spaced (about 30 percent closer than the blades on the Mach3), the coating, and the angle.

The razor also features a single blade on the reverse side that is designed for trimming hair in tricky places including sideburns and moustaches. There's a battery-operated version of Fusion, called Fusion Power, containing a patented microchip that emits electropulses.

Gillette's product launch was meticulously researched, including sales forecasts from three outside vendors. With an 80 percent market share overall in the razor category, some might see that expenditure as overkill. But Gillette wanted to be sure that its large and loyal customer base would be willing to trade up to a more expensive razor and blades. Marketers shrouded the Fusion introduction in secrecy by not giving out customary free product samples. Instead, they invited reporters to a hotel suite where they could see for themselves whether shaving with the Fusion offered advantages over competitors. Reporters were not allowed to take any of the razors home.

Advertising was targeted mostly at traditional media, including commercials on the Super Bowl and the NCAA basketball tournament. Countering observations that unlike many Super Bowl ads, the Fusion spots were not humorous, a company spokesman noted that Gillette's razor ads were not created specifically for the Super Bowl.

Global Gillette is the world's number one manufacturer of shaving products. It was acquired in 2005 by The Proctor & Gamble Company and together the two companies boast 17 brands which are each worth over $1 billion in annual sales.

Vital Statistics
Parent Company Global Gillette
Product Launch 2006
Headquarters Boston, Massachusetts
Employees 28,700
Annual Sales $10,477 million (2004)

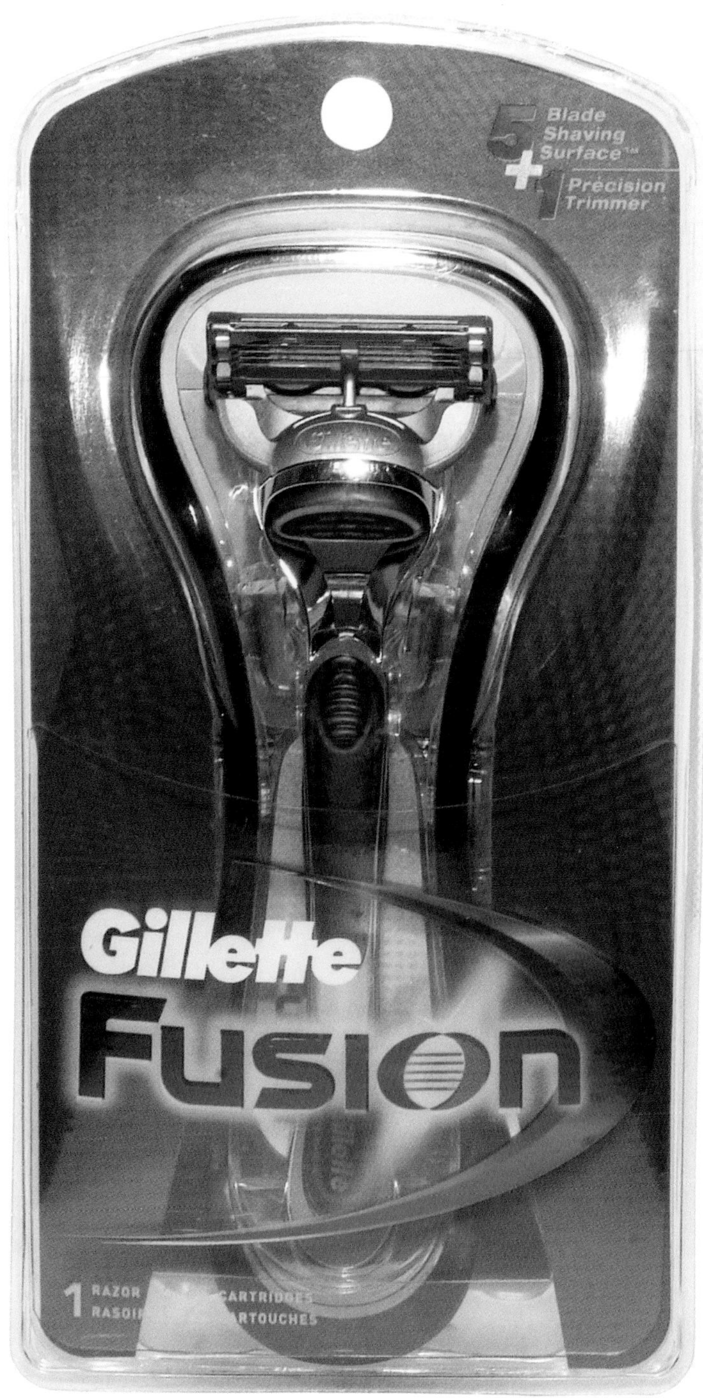
5 Blade Shaving Surface™
+1 Precision Trimmer
Gillette
Fusion
1 RAZOR
RASOIR

Glacéau

In the early 1990s, New York City suffered from a water-contamination scare. As a result, the water in J. Darius Bikoff's Upper East Side building was shut off, an inconvenience that prompted the thirtysomething metals supplier to buy bottled water for the first time. He quickly noticed that all of the bottled waters available seemed to make the same vague promises of mountains and streams. After that, Bikoff began to research water and eventually concluded that the type of water he wanted to be drinking—pure, fresh water developed in nature (before it picked up contaminants from the sky or ground)—didn't exist, so he decided to make it himself. In 1996, Bikoff launched his own beverage start-up, Glacéau, which represents "a fresh new approach to water."

Every day, more and more Americans are waking up to the importance of good health and wellness. They are seeking out things that make them feel better—physically, mentally, and emotionally. They're exercising more and adopting additional healthy practices, including seeking out fresher, healthier, and more nutritious foods and drinks. With Vitaminwater, Smartwater, and Fruitwater, Glacéau is helping people feel and function better through better hydration.

Smartwater, introduced in 1998, is vapor-distilled (a simulation of the hydrologic cycle found in nature) for purity you can taste, and electrolyte-enhanced for hydration you can feel. In 1999, Bikoff introduced Fruitwater, a low-calorie, flavor-enhanced water.

Glacéau's third product line, vitaminwater, enhanced water that is all-natural, low calorie, and packed with nutrients, quickly became a hit when it debuted in 2000, and today is the leader of the enhanced water category. It has since become an iconic brand, recognized by *Advertising Age* in 2006 as one of "10 Brands that Have Rocked the World."

In 2005, a 30% stake of Glacéau was acquired by the Tata group, India's most respected business conglomerate. This transaction valuates Glacéau at $2.2 billion, and ensures that Glacéau continues to meet the explosive demand for its Vitaminwater brand fueled by America's health and wellness revolution.

Glacéau is the pioneer and leader of the enhanced water category and its brands represent 84% growth of the segment. Vitaminwater is leading the enhanced water category, and is trumping competitive brands.

As of 2006, more than 5 million bottles of Glacéau water were being sold daily across the United States in grocery stores, gyms, yoga studios, drugstores, and beyond.

Vitaminwater is the first of its kind, and its potential is endless.

Vital Statistics

Parent Company	Energy Brands, Inc.
Established	1996
Founder	J. Darius Bikoff
Distribution	more than 5 million bottles every day nationwide
Headquarters	Queens, New York

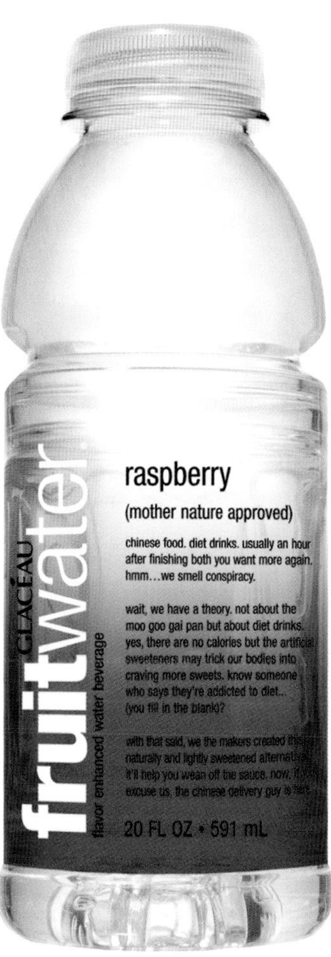

GLACÉAU
fruitwater
flavor enhanced water beverage
raspberry
(mother nature approved)
chinese food. diet drinks. usually an hour after finishing both you want more again. hmm...we smell conspiracy.
20 FL OZ • 591 mL

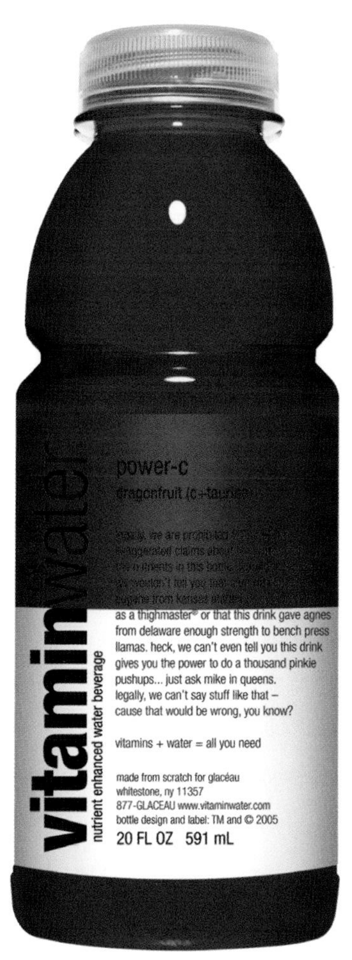

vitaminwater
nutrient enhanced water beverage
power-c
as a thighmaster® or that this drink gave agnes from delaware enough strength to bench press llamas. heck, we can't even tell you this drink gives you the power to do a thousand pinkie pushups... just ask mike in queens. legally, we can't say stuff like that – cause that would be wrong, you know?
vitamins + water = all you need
made from scratch for glacéau
whitestone, ny 11357
877-GLACEAU www.vitaminwater.com
bottle design and label: TM and © 2005
20 FL OZ 591 mL

Gold's Gym

What do Muhammad Ali, Nicolas Cage, Anna Kournikova, Dr. Phil, and Barbara Mandrell have in common? Along with millions of others, they've all worked out at Gold's Gym! Gold's Gym International, Inc. is one of the largest fitness club chains in the world and operates primarily through franchising. Its first establishment became the center of the sport of bodybuilding in the United States, and although for years Gold's was known as a no-frills gym for serious weight lifters, today it appeals to a much broader group of exercisers with classes such as yoga, Pilates, and Spinning, as well as personal training and pure weight lifting.

GOLD'S GYM

Joe Gold was born near the famed Muscle Beach in Los Angeles in 1922, and built his first gym at his parents' house as a teenager, using junked car parts for weights. Gold joined the navy during World War II and served in the Korean War as well, bringing his homemade weights with him whenever he shipped out. Gold opened his first gym—Ajax Gym—in New Orleans in 1951 but soon abandoned the venture. By 1954, he was back in Los Angeles, where he landed work performing as an extra with Mae West. In 1963, Gold contracted with the Muscle Beach Weightlifting Club in Santa Monica to build an indoor facility, but when the relationship went sour, he left and opened Gold's Gym, in Venice, California, in 1965. Gold designed and built all the equipment himself, and the club attracted serious bodybuilders from California and all over the world. In 1970, Gold grew tired of running the gym and sold it to Bud Danitz and Dave Sachs for $50,000. Gold went back to being a merchant marine until 1977, when he opened another facility called World Gym. Although Joe Gold had owned Gold's Gym for only five years, he gave the chain its image and its intrinsic tie to the sport of bodybuilding.

In 1977, thanks to the movie *Pumping Iron* and its star, Arnold Schwarzenegger (who'd been training at Gold's Gym since 1968), bodybuilding skyrocketed in popularity. That same year, Gold's Gym was bought by bodybuilder Ken Sprague and was host of the Mr. America contest. In 1979, another group of investors bought Gold's and began franchising the Gold's name. By 1988, there were 220 Gold's Gyms in the United States and another 50 in foreign countries. Gold's began selling clothing in 1980, and then added a line of nutritional supplements sold exclusively through the gyms until 1988. By that year, 80 percent of the company's revenue was from clothing sales. By 1993, the chain had about 400 gyms worldwide, all franchises, except the original Venice, California, location. In 1999, Kirk and John Galiani, who owned eight Gold's franchises in the Washington, D.C., area, bought the parent company and made significant changes, adding 100 franchises in two years. Yet the Galiani brothers stepped down from leadership of Gold's in 2001, wanting to return to operating individual gyms. In 2004, Gold's Gym was acquired by the Texas-based investment group TRT Holdings.

Gold's Gym has been the authority on fitness for more than 40 years. Today, it is the largest coed gym chain in the world, with more than 600 facilities in 43 states and 25 countries. Gold's Gym members climb 1,700,000 flights of stairs a day, the equivalent of 11,000 Empire State Buildings, run 556,800 miles a day, 23 times around the Earth, bike 236,670 miles a day, 750 times across the United States, lift 3.6 billion pounds a day, more than all the gold bars in Fort Knox, and—most impressively—lose 43,835 pounds of body fat a day, enough to make a difference in the health of the world.

Vital Statistics

Classic Product gym franchises

Established 1965

Founder Joe Gold

Annual Sales $48.6 million (2005)

Goodyear

Frank Seiberling, the founder of the Goodyear Tire & Rubber Company, could clearly see the future. In 1898, with the bicycle craze booming and horseless carriages beginning to turn heads, Seiberling had the foresight to found a business that made bicycle and carriage tires, horseshoe pads, and poker chips—the latter perhaps to symbolize the gamble he was taking. Seiberling had borrowed $3,500 from his brother-in-law to buy an old factory in Akron, Ohio, despite the fact that it was thousands of miles away from the rubber and cotton that had to be imported to make the company's products. In 1899, the visionary Seiberling added automobile tires to the product line. By the time Henry Ford's assembly line was producing affordable cars for the mass market a decade later, Goodyear was well positioned to become the country's leading tire manufacturer.

In the meantime, Seiberling's employees were busy making innovations in the still-fledgling tire manufacturing business. They developed the first straight-side tire in 1901, the universal rim in 1904, and the first quick, detachable tire in 1906. Then they came up with the all-weather, diamond-studded tread pattern (which remained in use for 40 years) and a pneumatic rubber airplane tire (which replaced the sled runners and bicycle tires currently being used).

All of this was being advertised using the by-then-familiar Goodyear logo, with the winged Mercury foot separating the first and second syllables of the Goodyear name. The logo was first used in 1901 and was the brainchild of Seiberling, who had a winged statue of the Roman god Mercury on a newel post in the stairway of his Akron home. Mercury was the god of trade and commerce, but he was especially known for being the swift messenger bearing good news.

Perhaps even better known than the Goodyear logo are Goodyear blimps. The first was built in 1925. Filled with helium and painted on the side with the Goodyear name, it crisscrossed the country. During World War II, blimps were used by the navy for aerial surveillance. Floating high above navy convoys, blimps could spot enemy subs and radio their position to troops, providing early warning. Over the decades, Goodyear built more than 80 blimps, which served primarily as floating billboards. Today, the company operates three ships based out of Akron, California, and Florida and three ships based in Europe.

After World War II, Goodyear was an innovative leader in polyester tire cord and the bias-belted tire. But in 1977, Goodyear hit it big when it introduced the Tiempo, a tire for year-round use in all climates. The tire was immediately successful, and in 1978 the company topped $8 billion in sales, led by the Tiempo, which sold 3.5 million units.

In 1991, Goodyear began selling tires through Kmart, Wal-Mart, and Sears in addition to selling them through their dealerships. Today, with more than 100 plants in 29 countries, Goodyear is one of the world's leading tire companies and is the market leader in North America and Latin America.

Vital Statistics
Established 1898
Founder Frank Sieberling
Headquarters Akron, Ohio
Employees 80,000 (2005)
Sales $20,258 million (2006)

Google

The Internet search site Google is named after the word *googol,* a term invented to represent the humungous sum of 1 followed by 100 zeros. But it was no fewer than "googol" sites on the World Wide Web that Stanford students Larry Page and Sergey Brin sought to categorize and make searchable. The two friends, both PhD candidates in computer science, built their first search engine in Page's dorm room in the mid-1990s and maxed out their credit cards in the process. In 1998, finally secured by starter capital, they dropped out of school and founded Google, Inc.

From the start, Google was different from other Internet search engines. Whereas others were slow, Google could search millions of sites on the Web in less than a second by harnessing the power of networked PCs. Whereas other search engines were often inaccurate, Google seemed intuitive, calling up results that matched the user's needs. Whereas others based their search results on the number of times a key word is used on a site, Google uses "Page Rank" technology created by Brin and Page to sort sites according to how often they're referred to, or "linked to," by other sites. Not merely counting links, Google assigns each link a value that is determined by the referring page's importance, or the number of Web sites that in turn link to it. Each Web site is further scanned in full for relevancy to the user's key words, factoring in fonts and other textual clues.

Google quickly became regarded as the world's best search engine. In 2004, amidst much publicity and fanfare, Google went public. On opening day its stock rose to $100 a share with more than 22 million shares traded. Brin and Page became billionaires.

Brin and Page's motto is "don't be evil," and by that they mean that Google should aim to improve, not exploit, the world. Google searches and other tools are free of charge. Google's Web site is clean, without offensive blinking ads and pop-ups. Although Google depends on advertisers for income, ads on Google are placed discreetly in the margins and are relevant to the user's key word search. The company has also established a foundation and grant program to address issues such as human rights and the environment.

Each day, Google performs more than 200 million searches in more than 35 languages of 3 billion searchable Web sites. Its users total nearly 400 million people worldwide. While its core search engine business thrives, Google has ventured into dozens of new areas, buying and/or developing technologies, including Blogger for personal online journals, YouTube for video sharing, Picasa for image editing, Gmail for e-mail, and Google Earth for viewing satellite images of the earth and navigation. Other tools under development include those for scanning books, news reporting, instant messaging, word processing, Web site creation, and telephony. The future for Google seems to be infinitely large, or, in other words, a googol.

Vital Statistics
Established 1998
Founders Sergey Brin and Larry Page
Employees 5,680 (2005)
Headquarters Mountain View, California
Annual Sales $10,604 million (2006)

Google™

Goya Foods

If you've prepared Latin American cuisine in your home lately, chances are that you've used Goya products. Maybe it was a classic like Rice and Beans, or maybe it was something more intriguing like Ecuadorian Shrimp Ceviche. The company distributes over 1,500 Latin American foods and ingredients, making it the largest Hispanic-owned food company in the United States. Goya's Latin specialties include a variety of canned and dry-packaged beans, rice, and rice mixes, nectars, seasonings, and frozen entrees. If you're cooking a dish from Spain, Mexico, the Caribbean, or Central or South America, you'll most likely be reaching for something with a Goya Foods label.

There's no doubt Goya is well-positioned as the Latino population in the U.S. continues to rise and interest in Latin American cuisine among non-Latinos grows. Goya comes to the table prepared to meet the needs of the highly diverse Latino community, as the company is owned and operated by Hispanics with unprecedented expertise in Latin American food products, preparation, and usage.

The company was founded by Prudencio Unanue and his wife Carolina in 1936. He had been working as an agent for food companies from Spain. When the Spanish Civil War erupted, he could no longer bring in products from his native homeland. "Don Prudencio," as he is affectionately known, bought the name Goya from a Moroccan Sardine company for $1.00 and began importing a handful of products. Within 30 years, Goya went from a small storefront in lower Manhattan to a company providing its own food processing, canning, and packaging.

Goya's consumer base grew exponentially as the numbers of immigrants from the Caribbean and other parts of Latin America increased throughout the 1940s, 50s, and 60s. Goya advertised in Spanish-language media and participated in Latino community events. Goya established a significant presence in Latino communities and has become a staple of kitchen shelves in the U.S. In 1974, the company moved to its current headquarters in Secaucus, New Jersey. Today, with an offering of over 1,500 products, Goya is known as the largest Hispanic-owned food company in the United States. Goya has 15 facilities and distribution centers throughout the United States, Spain, and the Caribbean.

Goya's Web site is complete with product information, recipes, and the Goya eStore, making Goya products available online. The company is still owned and operated by the Unanue family and is expanding its distribution to Europe and Latin America.

Vital Statistics

Classic Product Latin American Food Products

Product Launch 1936

Headquarters Secaucus, New Jersey

Employees 3,000

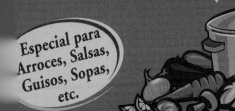

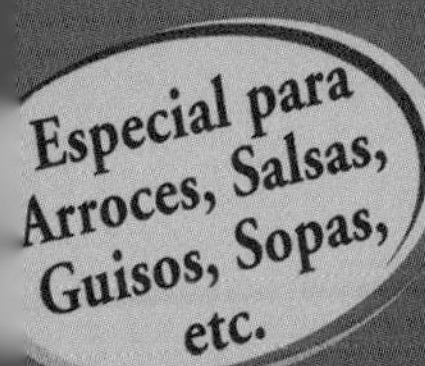

Greyhound Lines

Greyhound's beginnings go back to 1914, when Carl Wickman, a Swedish immigrant living in Minnesota, wanted to be a car salesman. When he couldn't sell a single Hupmobile, the durable, mid-range touring car of the time, he started the first U.S. bus transportation company. Wickman began transporting miners from his hometown of Hibbing to Alice along the Mesaba Iron Range. He would load 18 miners into a seven-seater Hupmobile for 25 cents round-trip. Wickman took on partners to help purchase larger vehicles, and in 1916, Hibbing Transportation began to run Studebakers and Packards that were sawed in half and elongated.

Hibbing Transportation wasn't the only motorcoach business in town, and when a competitor, run by a motorcycle racer named Ralph Bogan, offered a round-trip fare of 50 cents from Hibbing to Alice, Wickman responded by offering the same trip for 40 cents, beginning the first-known fare war of the industry. Wickman eventually offered Bogan a share in Hibbing Transport, establishing a longtime tradition of merging with competitors that eventually resulted in the formation of the largest bus company in the world.

Post–World War I was a prosperous time for small, independent bus lines, and the company, now named Greyhound, competed for passengers with other bus lines such as Golden Eagle, Jack Rabbit, and White Swan. The stock market crash of 1929 nearly bankrupted the company, but Greyhound saw a boost in sales with the 1933 World's Fair in Chicago, and in 1934, the Clark Gable and Claudette Colbert movie *It Happened One Night* featured a cross-country bus trip on a Greyhound bus.

During World War II, Greyhound mainly transported workers to munitions plants and shipyards and also carried military personnel to their bases. Wartime responsibilities and gas shortages made it difficult for Greyhound to serve all its civilian customers, so the company used advertisements to discourage ridership. It also began training women to drive buses, because more than 40 percent of its staff was called into military service.

Over the years, Greyhound continued to expand and add state-of-the-art equipment to accommodate a country that was taking to the roads. With strategic mergers and partnerships, such as the one with Amtrak to provide destinations that are not served by passenger trains, Greyhound is able to compete with airlines on price and serve more destinations.

Greyhound is the only nationwide intercity bus company. Carrying more than 20 million passengers annually to more than 1,700 destinations in the United States, Greyhound has a fleet of 1,200 buses. In addition to its regularly scheduled trips, Greyhound offers charter bus services and express package delivery. Greyhound is an innovative leader in bus transportation, having provided safe, comfortable, and affordable travel for more than 90 years.

Vital Statistics
Established 1914
Founder Carl Wickman
Employees 8,400
Annual Sales $1.24 billion for Greyhound Lines, Inc. and Greyhound Canada Transportation Company

308
SEATING CAP. 47

H&R Block, Inc.

The idea for the world's largest tax services company, having served more than 20 million people in the United States and several other countries, was sparked when co-founder Henry Bloch read a pamphlet in the Harvard library.

Henry was a junior in college when Pearl Harbor was bombed. He enlisted in the Army Air Corps and was eventually sent to Harvard Business School to pursue a military career. While in the library one day, he read a pamphlet of a speech that a professor had delivered to a group of insurance men. It said that there were three kinds of business: big business, small business, and labor. And whereas big business and labor were powerful, small business had no one to turn to. The future, the professor claimed, would be in helping small businesses. Henry wrote to his brothers Leon and Richard about his idea of providing a wide range of services to small businesses. His complete list consisted of more than 100 services, including tax preparation.

Henry returned to Kansas City after the Air Force, and after a brief stint as a stockbroker, he rented a storeroom office for $50 a month and opened the United Business Co. in 1946. With the help of his older brother Leon, Henry landed a bookkeeping account for a hamburger stand a few blocks away. More accounts followed, and when Leon returned to law school, Richard became Henry's business partner.

The business continued to grow, and by 1954, United Business Company had 12 employees keeping books for several clients, with Henry and Richard working around the clock. They had been doing taxes for one of their clients, John White, who worked in display advertising at the *Kansas City Star.* They told him they couldn't continue doing his taxes because they were too busy with other work. White suggested they try making a business out of taxes before abandoning it altogether.

White made up a small ad that showed a man behind an eight ball with the headline "Taxes, $5." He persuaded Henry and Richard to run the ad twice, and on the day the first ad ran, the office was overrun with customers. It seemed timing could not have been better. Until the mid-1950s, the IRS filled out tax returns at no charge for anyone who went to the local IRS office. Errors were common, and when people complained, the service was eliminated. The first ad appeared at the same time the people of Kansas City discovered the IRS would no longer provide that service.

In January 1955, United Business Company became H&R Block Inc., specializing in tax return preparation. The first tax season was a huge success, and when the IRS was about to stop filling out tax returns in New York also, H&R Block opened seven offices there the following year. That was the beginning of a nationwide chain.

Known as the leader in tax preparation, H&R Block, through its electronic filing service called Rapid Refund, files almost half the total number of returns filed electronically with the IRS. The company has grown to accommodate the financial needs of its clients by offering comprehensive financial, mortgage, and business products and services.

Vital Statistics

Classic Product Tax Preparation

Established 1946

Founders Henry and Richard Bloch

Annual Sales $4,872 million (2006)

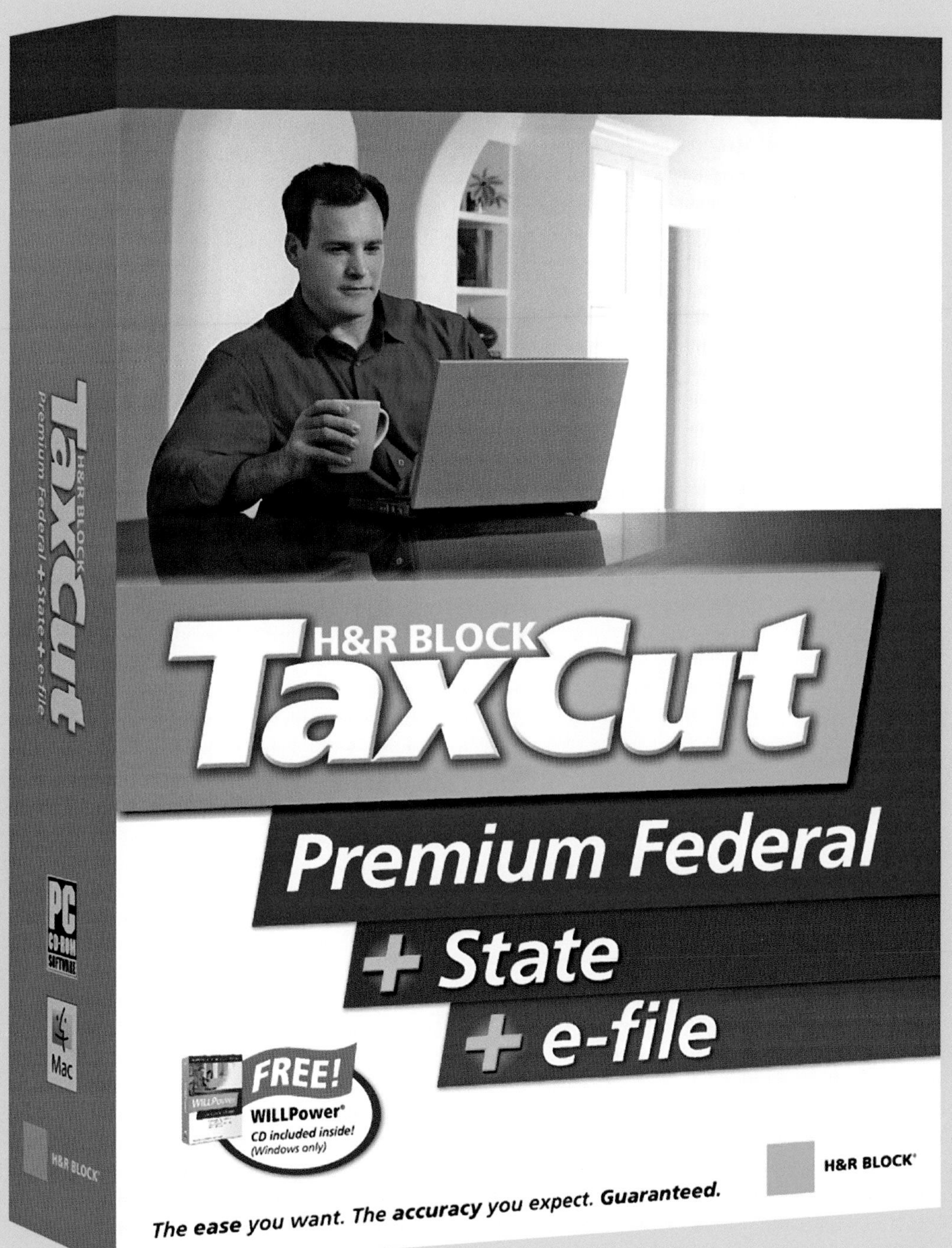
H&R BLOCK
TaxCut
Premium Federal
+ State
+ e-file
FREE!
WILLPower®
CD included inside!
(Windows only)
H&R BLOCK®
The ease you want. The accuracy you expect. Guaranteed.
PC
CD-ROM
SOFTWARE
Mac

Hallmark

As the world's number-one producer of greeting cards, Hallmark encompasses every emotion and situation imaginable. Hallmark cards are sold under brand names such as Hallmark, Shoebox, and Ambassador and are found in more than 42,000 retail stores. Hallmark also owns Crayola, maker of crayons and creative art supplies, offers electronic greeting cards and flowers through its Web site, and produces movies.

Even as a teenager, founder Joyce C. Hall knew the power of a card. He began selling picture postcards out of shoe boxes in his room at the YMCA in 1910 in Kansas City, Missouri. The following year, he was joined by his brother Rollie, and the pair added greeting cards to the line in 1912. The young company, called Hall Brothers, sold cards and stationery, but the office and all the inventory were destroyed in a 1915 fire. Undeterred, the Halls applied for a loan, bought an engraving company, and produced their first original cards in time for Christmas that year. In 1921, a third brother, William, joined the firm, and by the next year, Hall Brothers had salespeople doing business in all 48 states. By 1928 the back of each card read "A Hallmark Card," and the company's first ad appeared in *Ladies Home Journal.* In 1931, the company entered its first international venture, five years before patenting the now-ubiquitous "Eye-Vision" display cases for greeting cards. In 1939, Hall Brothers introduced a "friendship card" featuring an image of purple pansies that became the company's best seller and virtually created a new market for cards.

During World War II, when so many other companies suffered, Joyce Hall persuaded the government to let Hall Brothers keep making cards, claiming they were essential for national morale. The first production of Hallmark Hall of Fame, winner of more Emmy awards than any other program, aired in 1951. In 1954, Hall Brothers changed its name to Hallmark Cards, and introduced the Ambassador line for mass channel stores in 1959. Joyce Hall's son Donald was made company CEO in 1966. Hallmark then opened Crown Center, a retail complex that surrounds company headquarters in Kansas City. When Joyce Hall died in 1982, Donald Hall became both chairman and CEO. Under his leadership, Hallmark acquired Binney & Smith (now called Crayola) in 1984 and introduced Shoebox Greetings, a line of nontraditional cards, in 1986. Irvine Hockaday replaced Donald Hall as CEO the same year, although Hall continues as chairman today. Hallmark introduced its Web site in 1996 and took its cards online—making it easier than ever to send a Hallmark. Hockaday retired as president and CEO at the end of 2001, and Donald Hall Jr., grandson of the founder, became CEO.

Some literary types may be unaware that in 2002 Hallmark developed a line of cards and products with Maya Angelou, Pulitzer Prize nominee and poet. In 2006, the company launched a women's lifestyle magazine called *Hallmark Magazine.* "When You Care Enough to Send the Very Best" is not just Hallmark's trademark slogan, featured regularly in Hallmark print and broadcast advertising, and as part of Hallmark Hall of Fame productions—it was the idea behind Joyce Hall's boyhood dream come true. Today, Hallmark Cards, Inc. creates 48,000 different products each year in more than 30 languages, and distributes them in more than 100 countries.

Vital Statistics

Classic Product	greeting cards
Established	1910
Founder	Joyce C. Hall
Employees	16,000 (full-time)
Annual Sales	$4,200 million (2006)

Harley-Davidson

In 1903, William Harley and Arthur Davidson of Milwaukee began selling the first Harley-Davidson motorcycles—bikes with motors that needed to be pedaled uphill—based on a blueprint drawing of Harley's. The bikes sold well, leading to continually improved products. In 1909, the trademark Harley-Davidson two-cylinder, V-twin engine hit the market, and America's highways have not been the same since.

By 1913, more than 100 companies were competing with Harley-Davidson, but none managed to capture the American imagination like Harley-Davidson. During World War I, the demand for American motorcycles grew overseas, and by the 1920s, the company was a world leader in innovative engineering. The company's bikes first became known as "hogs"—a nickname that stuck—when a racing team's mascot of a pig was carried on victory laps in 1920. Harley front wheel brakes and "teardrop" gas tanks became part of the company's signature innovation and style. During the Great Depression, however, the market for motorcycles dropped. Harley-Davidson was one of two companies to survive, largely by exporting bikes to Europe and selling them to police and military personnel. During these lean years, the company began using art deco decals and two-tone paint in its design schemes. The 1936 EL model, with its "knucklehead" engine (named for the shape of its rocker boxes), was a preview of modern bikes. The tide turned during World War II, when military orders reached an all-time high. In 1947, Harley-Davidson began selling a black leather motorcycle jacket that still epitomizes style in American pop culture, thanks to Elvis, James Dean, the Fonz, and countless others. New bike models were introduced after the war to appeal to the leisure class then growing in America: the K-model in 1952, the Sportster "superbike" in 1957, and the Duo-Glide in 1958. Harley-Davidson became America's most significant motorcycle manufacturer, with little competition.

Harley-Davidson merged with American Machine and Foundry (AMF) in 1969. But by the late 1970s, sales and quality were slipping. AMF put the company on the market, but it was eventually purchased in 1981, by a group of 13 Harley-Davidson executives led by Vaughn Beals. The Harley Owners Group (H.O.G.) was founded in 1983 and immediately became the largest factory-sponsored motorcycle club in the world, numbering more than one million members by 2006. Harley-Davidson's comeback, helped by updated manufacturing methods, improved quality, expanded product lines, financial restructuring and tariff relief on Japanese imports, was one of the greatest in American business history. The company went public in 1986 with its listing on the American Stock Exchange, followed by a New York Stock Exchange listing in 1987. In the early 1990s, the company introduced the popular FLSFT Fat Boy, Dyna line, and FLHR Road King, and acquired a 49 percent share of Wisconsin-based Buell Motorcycle, a performance-motorcycle company. Toward the end of the century, Harley-Davidson expanded several facilities and built new ones to increase production and development. In 2001, Harley introduced the V-Rod, inspired by Harley's legendary drag racing heritage.

Harley-Davidson celebrated 100 years in business in 2003 with parties around the world and celebrations in Milwaukee attended by more than a quarter of a million Harley lovers. In 2004, Harley-Davidson's production increased by nine percent over 2003, reaching more than 300,000 bikes. The company recently unveiled plans for a Harley-Davidson Museum in Milwaukee, to open in 2008, and appointed Beijing Feng Huo Lun (FHL) as the first authorized Harley-Davidson dealer on mainland China, as another important step toward bringing the Harley-Davidson passion, adventure, and lifestyle to the motorcycle world.

Vital Statistics

Established 1903

Employees 9,700 (2005)

Annual Sales $6,185.6 million (2006)

Harrah's Entertainment Corp.

In 1930, William Fisk Harrah, the son of a lawyer and real estate operator in Venice, California, was caught cheating on his college chemistry exam. Humiliated, he dropped out of school to run his father's semi-illegal gambling parlor in Venice Beach. By 1937, he had moved to Reno, Nevada, where gambling had been legalized. Two years later, he opened his first profitable casino complete with blackjack, craps, and slot machines. Harrah distinguished Harrah's Club by making it classier and sleeker than other casinos. Unlike the dubious betting parlors that surrounded it, Harrah's Club was clean and carpeted, with spotless glass fixtures.

By the 1950s, Harrah had made enough profits to open a new casino in Lake Tahoe, California. Harrah's Tahoe offered much more to the casino experience than gambling. The casino included an 850-seat dinner theater that featured gourmet food and all-star entertainment, luxurious hotel rooms, and child care facilities. Harrah set up an extensive bus network to transport thousands of customers to the casino from surrounding cities. Suddenly, the casino had become a vacation destination for thousands of middle-class families. Harrah's casinos and hotels made tremendous profits, with nearly full occupancy. By the time William Harrah died in 1978, he had become the world's biggest gambling operator.

In 1980, Holiday Inn acquired Harrah's, and the Harrah's brand became a wholly owned subsidiary of the hotel chain. Holiday Inn opened a Harrah's casino, now called Harrah's Atlantic City, which includes not only theaters and restaurants, but also conference rooms and entertainment for teens. In 1989, Holiday Inn became Promus Cos., Inc., with Harrah's as the conglomerate's casino-entertainment division, later named Harrah's Entertainment Corp. Harrah's then aggressively expanded its brand to include dozens of dockside and riverboat casinos and casinos on American Indian–owned land. In 2004, Harrah's bought rival Caesars Entertainment for $9.4 billion and became the world's largest gaming company.

In the 1990s, Harrah's introduced a loyalty card, the Harrah's Gold Card, which bolstered the brand and gave the company valuable insight into the gambling and purchasing habits of more than 3 million customers. The cardholder program became even more successful with the introduction of a Total Gold Card, which offered larger rewards to its best customers and incentives to visit Harrah's casinos across the country.

Today, there are nearly 40 million individuals that carry a Total Rewards card, and 80% of Harrah's gaming revenue is tracked to a Total Rewards member. This has enabled Harrah's to implement a sophisticated relationship management approach that has dramatically increased customer loyalty and the company's profitability. With nearly 40 casinos in the United States with such well-known brands as Caesars, Horseshoe, and Paris, among others, customers have a plethora of choices. In addition, Harrah's plans to expand internationally in the United Kingdom, Spain, and Slovenia.

Vital Statistics
Classic Product casinos
Established 1939
Founder William Fisk Harrah
Annual Sales $9,673 million (2006)
Employees 85,000 (2005)

TOTAL
REWARDS®

Harvard University

Harvard University is the oldest institution of higher learning in the United States and considered among the best. Founded in 1636, merely 16 years after the pilgrims arrived at Plymouth, it was established by vote of the Great and General Court of the Massachusetts Bay Colonies. Its name comes from the university's first benefactor, John Harvard of Charlestown, a young minister who left his library and half his estate to the new institution in 1638.

Harvard's first scholarship fund was created with a gift from Ann Radcliffe, Lady Mowlson in 1643. In 1650, the Great and General Court approved the charter of incorporation establishing the President and Fellows of Harvard College (Harvard Corporation), which was made up of a seven-member board. Harvard is the oldest corporation in the Western Hemisphere.

Harvard took a turn toward intellectual independence with the election, in 1708, of John Leverett, the first president of Harvard who was not a clergyman. During the 18th and 19th centuries, the college grew and the curriculum broadened, thereby attracting many respected scholars to Harvard. But it was Charles W. Eliot, president from 1869 to 1906, who turned the small-town college into a modern university.

It was during Eliot's tenure that the schools of business, dental medicine, and arts and sciences were established and the schools of law and medicine were revitalized. Under Eliot, enrollment tripled from 1,000 to 3,000 students, and the faculty expanded from 49 to 278. Harvard's endowment, the largest of any university in the country with $2.6 billion today, increased from $2.3 million to $22.5 million.

Among the many notable achievements of Eliot's time as president, perhaps most effecting was the establishment of Radcliffe College. Spearheaded by a group of women with ties to the Harvard faculty, the women, among them Alice Mary Longfellow, daughter of the famous poet, were looking to make higher education more accessible to women. The result was a women's college where Harvard courses were taught by Harvard faculty, and Radcliffe degrees approved by the president and fellows of Harvard were conferred. Other women's colleges existed, but such close affiliation with a men's college was unprecedented at the time, and it enabled women to receive a comparable education.

Harvard boasts many famous alumni, including seven U.S. presidents and many renowned scholars such as the elder Oliver Wendell Holmes, William James, and Gertrude Stein. The student body represents men and women from a wide range of ethnic, religious, and political groups coming from every region of the United States and more than 100 other countries. Harvard's effect on the local economy is just as impressive as the education it offers. With an annual budget of $2.4 billion, Harvard is one of the largest employers in Massachusetts, with more than 15,000 employees, including more than 2,000 faculty members.

Opposite: Photo by Justin Lacey

Vital Statistics
Established 1636
Founder Great and General Court of the Massachusetts Bay Colonies
Endowment $25,900 million (2005)

HBO

As a subsidiary of Time Warner, HBO programming includes original series, original movies from HBO Films, concerts, stand-up comedy, documentaries, and sports, and is available in more than 50 countries around the world.

It began in 1972, when Time Inc. launched Home Box Office on a single cable system in Pennsylvania as an incentive for people to subscribe to cable. Distributed by local cable operators in a small section of the northeast, the service typically cost subscribers $3.50 per month on top of their cable subscription to get HBO's selection of recent films and sporting events telecast for just a few hours a day. HBO grew slowly, encumbered by poor infrastructure, uneven film distribution policies, and stringent federal regulations—some of which were sponsored by TV broadcasters who were fearful of cable eating into their revenue and audience.

In 1975, HBO made a commitment to full-time satellite carriage—making it the first TV programmer to do so—which gave the service a national presence overnight. With court victories removing many regulations and studios easing their policies on releasing films to pay-TV, subscribership boomed, from less than 300,000 at the end of 1975 to 10,000,000 by the end of 1982. The explosive growth of HBO drove the national expansion of cable, and the two were so closely associated that for decades subscribers often took their cable company and HBO to be one and the same, and even assumed competing pay-TV services to be a part of HBO.

Original programming had always been a part of the HBO programming mix, but often in a supporting role behind movie offerings. However, in the 1980s, HBO became more aggressive in its original programming strategy, attracting top talent with the offer of unprecedented creative freedom and none of the content restrictions which marked broadcast TV. Critics and audiences alike were impressed with the growing quality of what HBO had to offer with original movies like *And the Band Played On* and *If These Walls Could Talk*, and series such as *The Larry Sanders Show* and *Oz*, its first hour-long drama series. HBO's original programming hit its stride in the late 1990s with the appearance of series like *The Sopranos* and *Sex and the City*, and in 1997 the company received 90 Emmy nominations, the first time a cable network received more nominations than any broadcast network.

Subscribers to the commercial-free service, which now offers over a half-dozen channels of programming, typically pay $12-15 each month to see original series like *Big Love, Entourage, Curb Your Enthusiasm, Real Time with Bill Maher, The Wire,* mini-series like *Rome,* documentaries like *Baghdad ER* and Spike Lee's *When the Levees Broke: A Requiem in Four Acts*, and original movies like *Elizabeth I* and *Empire Falls*, as well as theatrical movies, some of which have been produced by the company such as *American Splendor* and *Real Women Have Curves.*

HBO's identification as a quality programmer not only keeps the service at the forefront of the industry domestically, but has propelled the brand on an international expansion dating back to 1991. Today, with $3 billion in annual sales, HBO is the world's largest premium television company, and offers multiple networks to almost 50 million subscribers around the world, from the U.S. to Europe, Latin America, and the Pacific Rim.

Vital Statistics

Classic Product	Original Programming
Established	1972
Parent Company	Time Warner Inc.
Annual Sales	$3 billion

Heinz Ketchup

In 1869, approximately 200 years after English sailors in southeast Asia discovered a briny sauce known as *ketsiap*, 25-year-old Henry J. Heinz opened his first business. Although Heinz would become best known for tomato ketchup, his first product was his mother's grated horseradish, grown in the family garden in Sharpsburg, Pennsylvania.

In 1876, ketchup was added to the company's condiment line. Unlike other ketchup varieties at the time, Heinz's was made with savory, ripe tomatoes and vinegar, and had a sweeter overall taste.

Henry was dedicated to producing only the best. "Quality is to a product what character is to a man," he said. His ketchup, pickles, jams, jellies, and condiments were made of the finest ingredients (never adulterated with preservatives), picked when fresh, monitored by quality standards, and packed in clean factories.

By 1896, the H. J. Heinz Company was selling more than 60 food products when Henry noticed a shoe store sign that advertised "21 Varieties" of footwear. He liked the ring of the slogan and came up with his own version: "57 Varieties" of Heinz foods. Legend has it that he liked the number 57 much more than 60 or 61, so "57 Varieties" it was, and to this day the number is still featured on the labels of all Heinz-branded products.

Henry also conceived one of the most popular promotional ideas in American history: the Heinz Pickle Pin, which he introduced at the World's Fair in Chicago in 1893. With a knack for attracting attention, he plastered the Heinz name on billboards, magazines, newspapers, and even on hillsides. In 1899, he built the Heinz Ocean Pier at Atlantic City, which was later destroyed by a hurricane. Heinz is also credited with erecting the first large electric promotional sign in New York City.

The H. J. Heinz Company prides itself on offering "Good Food Every Day" and has become one of the world's leading marketers and producers of nutritious foods. Heinz currently has 150 number-one and number-two brands on five continents, showcased by Heinz ketchup, The World's Favorite Ketchup. The company is the most international of all U.S.-based food companies and reports $8.91 billion in global sales. Heinz is a global family of leading brands, including Heinz ketchup, sauces, soups, beans, pasta and infant foods (representing nearly one-third of total sales or close to $3 billion), Ore-Ida potato products, Weight Watchers Smart Ones entrees, Boston Market meals, T.G.I. Friday's snacks, and Plasmon infant nutrition.

The H. J. Heinz Company continues to expand its presence in global markets, which now make up approximately 40 percent of the company's sales. Key markets to Heinz's expansion plans are China, Indonesia, and Singapore—the same countries that first introduced ketsiap to the world.

Vital Statistics
Founder Henry J. Heinz
Distribution worldwide
Headquarters Pittsburgh, Pennsylvania

HEINZ
57
VARIETIES
HEINZ
EST'D 1869 EST'D
TOMATO
KETCHUP
HEINZ
America's Favorite Ketchup™
NET WT 14 OZ-397 GRAMS

HEINZ
57
VARIETIES
HEINZ
EST'D 1869 EST'D
TOMATO
KETCHUP
HEINZ
America's Favorite Ketchup™
NET WT 14 OZ-397 GRAMS

HEINZ
57
VARIETIES
HEINZ
EST'D 1869 EST'D
TOMATO
KETCHUP
HEINZ
America's Favorite Ketchup™
NET WT 14 OZ-397 GRAMS

HEINZ
57
VARIETIES
HEINZ
EST'D 1869 EST'D
TOMATO
KETCHUP
HEINZ
America's Favorite Ketchup™
NET WT 14 OZ-397 GRAMS

Hellmann's Mayonnaise

Although mayonnaise—an emulsion of egg yolk, vinegar, oil, and salt—had been popular in Europe since the 18th century, it took nearly another 200 years for it to be readily available in the United States. In 1903, Richard Hellmann, a German immigrant, opened a delicatessen in New York City where his wife prepared several varieties of homemade mayonnaise.

The dressing they sold from a jar with a blue ribbon was such a hit that Hellmann realized he could make it a side business. In 1912, the Hellmanns began to sell the mayo in jars that featured a blue bow on a label that read, "Richard Hellmann's Blue Ribbon Mayonnaise." By 1915, demand for the mayonnaise was so great that Hellmann incorporated the business and opened a manufacturing facility. In 1927, Hellmann's merged with the Postum Company, and the mayonnaise benefited from increased distribution throughout the East Coast.

In 1932, Best Foods, Hellmann's biggest competitor, bought the Hellmann's brand. Although the Best Foods mayonnaise recipe was revised to be similar to Hellmann's, to this day the company labels mayonnaise sold west of the Rockies under the Best Foods brand, and the Hellmann's brand is sold east of the Rockies and throughout the world. Hellmann's became Best Foods' best-selling product, and over the years the company expanded the market to other countries, including Central and South America and Asia. Mayonnaise became integrated into recipes around the world, including chocolate mayonnaise cake in the United States, a vinegary dip for fish-and-chips in the United Kingdom, and tacos poblanos in the Spanish-speaking market.

In the 1980s, as Americans became more diet conscious, mayonnaise was considered by some to be unhealthful because of its high oil and egg content. In response, Best Foods, then a division of CPC International, introduced a light mayonnaise in 1987, and a few years later, a cholesterol-free version. Another new product, Canola Mayonnaise, is made with real canola oil and is low in saturated fat. To boost sales, the company launched an advertising campaign with the tagline, "Bring out the best."

Today, Hellmann's is the best-selling mayonnaise in the world. In 2000, CPC International became a division of the Dutch-Anglo conglomerate Unilever. The company has expanded the brand's presence by introducing new flavors in new markets, including Hellmann's Dijonnaise made with Dijon mustard, and Honey Mustard. Recognizing that new markets have different tastes, Best Foods has also launched a lime-juice-infused mayonnaise to the Hispanic market and a hot red-pepper variety in Brazil. The Hellmann's brand continues to offer new condiments sold alongside mayonnaise, such as tartar sauce and deli mustard.

Vital Statistics

Parent Company Unilever U.S.

Founder Richard Hellmann

EAT SMART
'BRING OUT THE BEST'®
HELLMANN'S
PARVE
REAL
MAYONNAISE
30 FL OZ
(887mL)
NATURALLY RICH IN
OMEGA 3
ALA

Hershey's

There is truth in advertising, at least if you use Hershey's milk chocolate bar as your example. Called "the great American chocolate bar" in its advertising campaigns, Hershey's classic chocolate bar has ranked among the 20 most popular American candies every year since its national launch in 1905. And the story of its creator, Milton Hershey, is a classic tale of a poor young man who persevered, succeeded in his dream of making chocolate delicious, affordable, and available, and used the fruits of his success to improve the lives of others.

Milton Hershey, a Mennonite from Derry Church, Pennsylvania, was running a small caramel business in nearby Lancaster when he chanced upon the recently invented machinery to produce milk chocolate. Chocolate had been invented about 50 years earlier, but it was still expensive and usually sold in large blocks. Intrigued, he sold his caramel business in 1900 and plowed the profits into making chocolate.

His goal was to produce a "wrapped, milk chocolate bar which would be purchased with the nickel in a man's pocket." His pioneering idea of making a high-quality, single-serving milk chocolate bar struck a chord with the public, and the bars sold as fast as they came off the production line. The product was so immediately successful that in 1906, just a year after the bar was introduced, the town fathers of Derry Church decided to rechristen their town Hershey, Pennsylvania.

Hershey's Kisses chocolates were born in 1907, and in the next decades Hershey's Syrup and the Mr. Goodbar and Krackel bars were introduced. A massive sales force fanned out, charged with the task to "put Hershey's milk chocolate bars on every counter, shelf, stand, and rack in every retail establishment in the United States—food store, restaurant, drug store, ice cream parlor, and soda fountain." This distribution strategy, combined with the consistency and quality of the product, was so successful that the Hershey Chocolate Corporation dominated the industry and did not advertise at all for its first 68 years.

In the meantime, Milton Hershey was pioneering more than chocolate. Feeling strongly that workers who were treated fairly and lived well would be more productive, Hershey developed a model community for his employees that included housing, schools, churches, parks, and even a department store and an amusement park. He also ran a school for orphans, now named the Milton Hershey School, which he later endowed with the majority of his personal wealth.

In the 1960s, realizing the value of their brand, company executives opened the factory for public tours and installed streetlights shaped like giant Hershey's Kisses along town streets. Hershey also purchased the H.B. Reese Candy Company in the 1960s.

The company, renamed the Hershey Foods Corporation in 1968, and renamed The Hershey Company in 2005, diversified in the 1970s into pasta products and also purchased other confectionary makers, including Y & S Candies (the makers of Twizzlers) and Peter Paul/Cadbury. With a presence in Canada, Germany, and the Far East, Hershey is the largest North American manufacturer of chocolate candy. The factory in Hershey is the biggest chocolate factory in the world, and the air on East Chocolate Avenue just might be the sweetest-smelling air anywhere.

Vital Statistics

Founder Milton Hershey

Established 1894

Employees 13,750 (2005)

Annual Sales $4,994.2 million (2006)

Hertz Rent-A-Car

The yellow-and-black Hertz sign is one of the most recognizable global logos, welcoming travelers at airports and in neighborhoods the world over. Hertz is the world's leading car rental company, operating approximately 7,600 rental locations in 145 countries. Hertz's Worldwide Reservations Center handles 40 million calls and 30 million reservations annually.

The Hertz story begins with Walter L. Jacob, who in 1918 opened a Chicago car rental business with 12 Model T Fords that he had repaired and painted himself. Within five years, Jacob's business had expanded to the point of generating $1 million annually, and in 1923, John Hertz, president of both Yellow Cab and Yellow Truck and Coach Manufacturing, bought the company. Jacob stayed on as an executive of the company that was renamed Hertz Drive-Ur-Self System. Within two years, it was a coast-to-coast operation. In 1926, General Motors Corporation acquired Hertz when it bought Yellow Truck from John Hertz. At the first national convention of the American Drivurself Association that same year, Hertz introduced the first car rental charge card, called the National Credential card. Hertz opened the first rent-a-car facility at Chicago's Midway Airport in 1932 and also initiated the first rent-it-here/leave-it-there program, thereby helping customers adjust to travel by air.

In 1970, Hertz established its Worldwide Reservations Center in Oklahoma City, and a year later, opened Hertz Data Center. Hertz opened its phone lines, 24 hours a day, 365 days a year, all over the world. Among other firsts in the industry, Hertz, in 1984, developed and introduced Computerized Driving Directions (CDD), and was the first car rental company to offer this feature. CDD was made available at more than 100 airport and downtown locations throughout the United States and Canada. Available at customer rental locations with easy-to-use, self-service, touch-screen terminals, Hertz offered directions in six different languages.

Always looking to improve and streamline business, Hertz Instant Return was introduced in 1987, expediting the return process by having a Hertz agent meet the returning customer with a Hertz Return handheld computer, enabling customers to quickly execute the return transaction. Furthering its focus on customer service, Hertz introduced the #1 Club Gold Service in 1989, quickly becoming the symbol for fast service. This premium rental service, available at 1,000 locations, is the ultimate in speed and high-quality service, eliminating paperwork and long lines.

Hertz continued to grow and dominate the car rental business with international expansion in Russia and all Eastern European countries as well as Africa, Asia, the Middle East, and Latin America. Other businesses in the Hertz portfolio include construction and industrial equipment rental and third party liability claims administration to corporations. Through more than 80 years of growth and change, the oldest company in the car rental business is also the largest general use car company in the world.

Vital Statistics
Parent Company Hertz Holdings
Established 1923
Founder John Hertz
Employees 32,200 (2005)
Annual Sales $8,058.4 million (2006)

Hertz #1 Club Gold
Hertz #1 Club Gold
130 131

Hewlett-Packard Company

Hewlett-Packard came to be in a small garage behind a rented house in Palo Alto, California, thanks to a good idea and about $500. After their graduation from Stanford University's engineering school in 1934, Bill Hewlett and Dave Packard went on a camping trip together during which they cemented what was to become a lifelong friendship. Although Bill was off to graduate school at MIT and Dave had a job lined up at General Electric, the pair—encouraged by Stanford professor Fred Terman—decided just a few years out of school to go into business together.

Hewlett-Packard Company (the order of the names was decided with a coin toss) was founded on New Year's Day 1939. Once ensconced in their cozy garage, Bill and Dave began work on their first project: a resistance-capacity audio oscillator (HP 200B), a machine used for testing sound equipment. When Walt Disney ordered eight for the production of ***Fantasia,*** they were up and running. Shortly after their first year in business, Bill and Dave agreed that all employees should share directly in the company's future success, instituting what was to become the trademark companywide profit-sharing plan in 1962. Hewlett-Packard Co. (HP) was incorporated in 1947, and in 1951, the HP 524A, a high-speed frequency counter used by radio stations to maintain accurate broadcast frequencies, was released. Net revenue soon reached $5.5 million. Six years later, Hewlett-Packard stock was offered for public trading for the first time. In 1964, Dave Packard was elected chairman of the board, and Bill Hewlett company president. The company developed a cesium beam standard instrument accurate to one-millionth of a second, which became famous as the "flying clock."

The 1960s saw Hewlett-Packard's transformation from manufacturer of instruments for analysis and measurement to electronic research, with the advent of its first computer, the HP 2116A. Soon, almost in spite of itself, Hewlett-Packard was one of the world's leading electronics research centers. In 1972, Hewlett-Packard introduced the first handheld scientific calculator, the HP-35, allowing the company to enter the business computer market, dominated by IBM and Digital Equipment Corp., with the HP 3000 minicomputer. Concerned by rapid growth, Bill and Dave decided to refocus on product leadership in the mid-1970s, establishing a new, highly decentralized structure. By 1978, John Young had replaced the original founders as president and CEO, although Bill and Dave remained on the board for much of their lives. In 1980, Hewlett-Packard produced its first personal computer, the HP-85, and saw subsequent net revenues of $3 billion while establishing itself as a major computer vendor. In 1985, the company's most successful product of all time was introduced: the HP LaserJet computer printer. Two years later, the original garage in Palo Alto became a California state landmark. By 1988, Hewlett-Packard was 49th among Fortune 500 companies with orders of more than $10 billion. The year 1995 saw the introduction of the CopyJet color copier and printer, at one-tenth the price of standard color copiers, and the first desktop scanner to operate from a network. In 2001, Hewlett-Packard merged with Compaq Computer Corp., and by 2004, profits had reached $3.5 billion, with overall sales near the $80 billion mark. In 2005, the company acquired online photo service Snapfish.

Hewlett-Packard remains on the cutting edge of technology, providing consumers with high-quality products and employees with outstanding benefits. Bill and Dave—who designed their first real offices so they could be transformed into a grocery store if the company failed—would surely be amazed by the continued growth and productivity of their $500 dream.

Vital Statistics
Established 1937
Founders Bill Hewlett and Dave Packard
Employees 156,000
Annual Sales $91,658 million (2006)

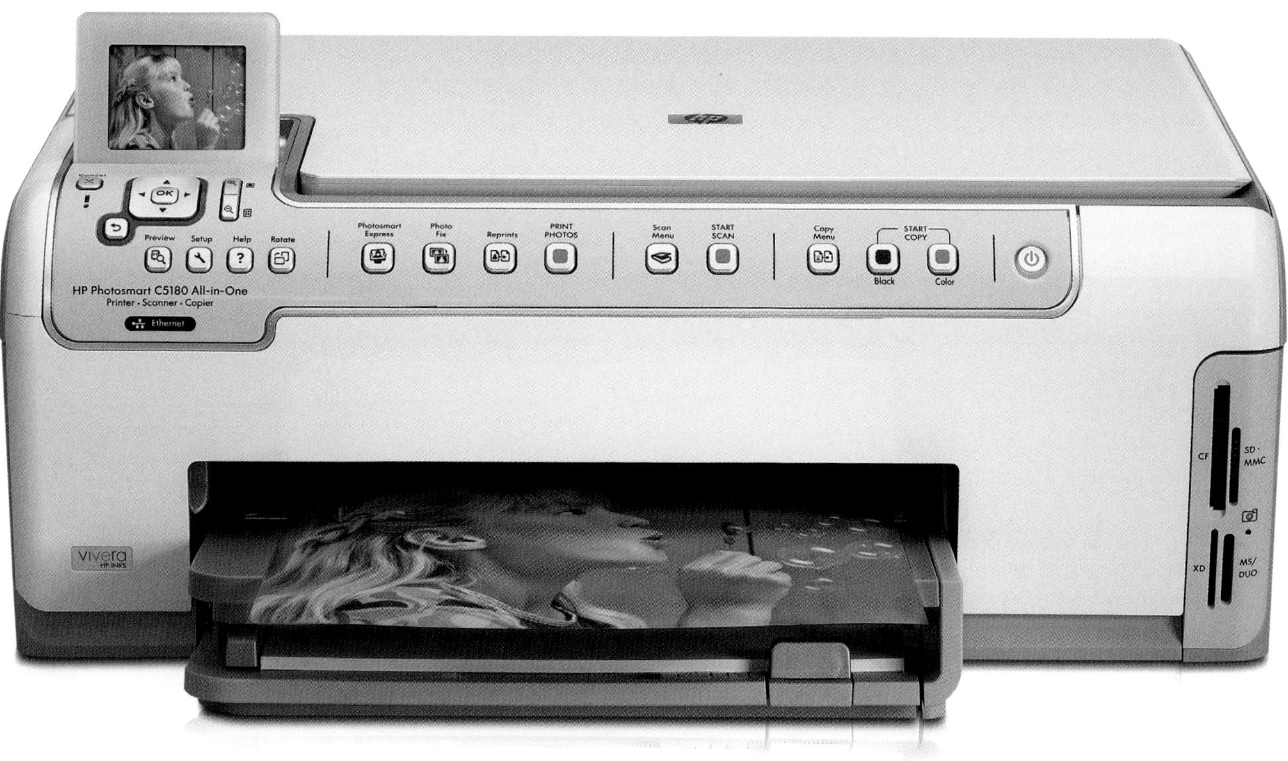

The Home Depot

How many companies can claim to have changed the habitats and daily activities of millions of people? The Home Depot—the world's largest home improvement chain and second-largest retailer in the United States—sure can.

The Home Depot was founded in 1978 by Bernie Marcus and Arthur Blank, two home center executives who had been fired from their jobs at Handy Dan. Along with investment banker Ken Langone and merchandising guru Pat Farrah, the founders' vision of one-stop shopping for the do-it-yourselfer came to fruition when they opened the first two Home Depot stores on June 22, 1979, in Atlanta, Georgia. The first stores, at around 60,000 square feet each, were cavernous warehouses that dwarfed the competition.

The story of The Home Depot is one of growth, as the company is the fastest growing retailer in U.S. history. In 1981, the company went public on NASDAQ and moved to the New York Stock Exchange in 1984. The 1980s and 1990s spawned tremendous growth for the company, with 1989 marking the celebration of its 100th store opening. The company arrived in Canada with the acquisition of Aikenhead's home improvement centers in 1994, began flying its flag proudly in Mexico in 2001 through the acquisition of Total HOME, and in 2006, acquired Home Mart's 12 stores in China.

In 2000, Bob Nardelli joined the company, becoming president and CEO. For the next six years, The Home Depot continued its leadership in serving DIY customers, while aggressively widening its span of interest to builders, contractors, municipalities, industrial customers and maintenance professionals with its HD Supply business. In addition, the company successfully pursued other profitable areas, such as home services and the direct-to-customer business, while celebrating its 2,000th store opening, 50th store in Mexico and 10-year anniversary in Canada. As a result, over the six-year period, annual sales doubled to more than $90 billion, encompassing retail and wholesale.

In January 2007, Frank Blake was named chairman and CEO. His goal is unmistakable: to instill the "sense of entrepreneurship, excitement and competitive fun that built the company from the ground up," a blueprint for the next chapter of The Home Depot story of growth and innovation.

Twenty-two million people visit a Home Depot each week, and although The Home Depot is the youngest retailer in the Fortune 50, it is safe to say it is a child prodigy—virtually assured of a bright tomorrow.

Vital Statistics
Classic Product Home Improvement
Year Founded 1978
Employees 364,000
Annual Sales $90,800 million (2006)

Hoover

In 1907, Murray Spangler, an inventor who worked nights as a janitor at a Canton, Ohio, department store, found a way to keep the dust from his broom from aggravating his asthma. With a tin soapbox, a fan, a sateen pillowcase, and a broom handle, Spangler created a contraption that managed to pull dust away from the air he breathed. He quickly realized that his "suction sweeper" had great sales potential and began seeking financial backing for his invention.

He turned to Susan Hoover, a family friend, who agreed to test the machine in her home. Before long she was singing its praises to her husband, W. H. "Boss" Hoover. Hoover, owner of a leather goods manufacturing shop, bought the patent from Spangler in 1908, retained Spangler as partner, and soon had six employees assembling six units a day in a corner of his leather shop.

To educate the public about the product, Hoover took out an ad in the *Saturday Evening Post* offering the machine for 10 days of free use to anyone who wrote and asked for it. Instead of sending a machine to the potential customer, he chose a reputable merchant in each city to take requests and deliver the machine. If the request resulted in a sale after the trial period, the merchant received a commission, thereby making the merchant a dealer. This forethought laid the groundwork for a national network of dealers that continues to be the main channel of distribution of Hoover products today.

"Boss" Hoover looked for new markets in which to sell his electric suction sweeper from the very beginning. The first Hoover plant opened in Canada in 1911, and in 1919, a manufacturing facility was established in England. By 1921, Hoover was selling products all over the world. Hoover is the number-one–selling vacuum cleaner in America and the leading manufacturer of floor care appliances.

From its very first product, innovation has been a mainstay at Hoover. Engineers continuously find improved methods of carpet cleaning, starting at the beginning design stage through production. As a result, the Hoover Company boasts many "firsts" aside from producing the first portable electric upright vacuum cleaner. Hoover produced the first vacuum cleaner headlight, the first disposable paper bag, the first side-mounted attached hose feature, and the first dual tanks for wet and dry pickup on wet/dry utility vacs, just to name a few. Hoover's "Intelligent Innovation" is a consumer-driven process in which traditional consumer research is supplemented by actual in-home observations of people as they clean. Trained observers look for behaviors that people do to make up for the shortcomings of the products they use. Engineering and manufacturing work closely with product development, enabling them to identify and resolve concerns before getting to the production stage. Such synergy ensures product excellence and customer loyalty that keeps Hoover at the front of the pack.

Vital Statistics
Parent Company Whirlpool
Product Launch 1908
Founders Murray Spangler and W. H. Hoover
Classic Product Hoover Upright Vacuum Cleaner

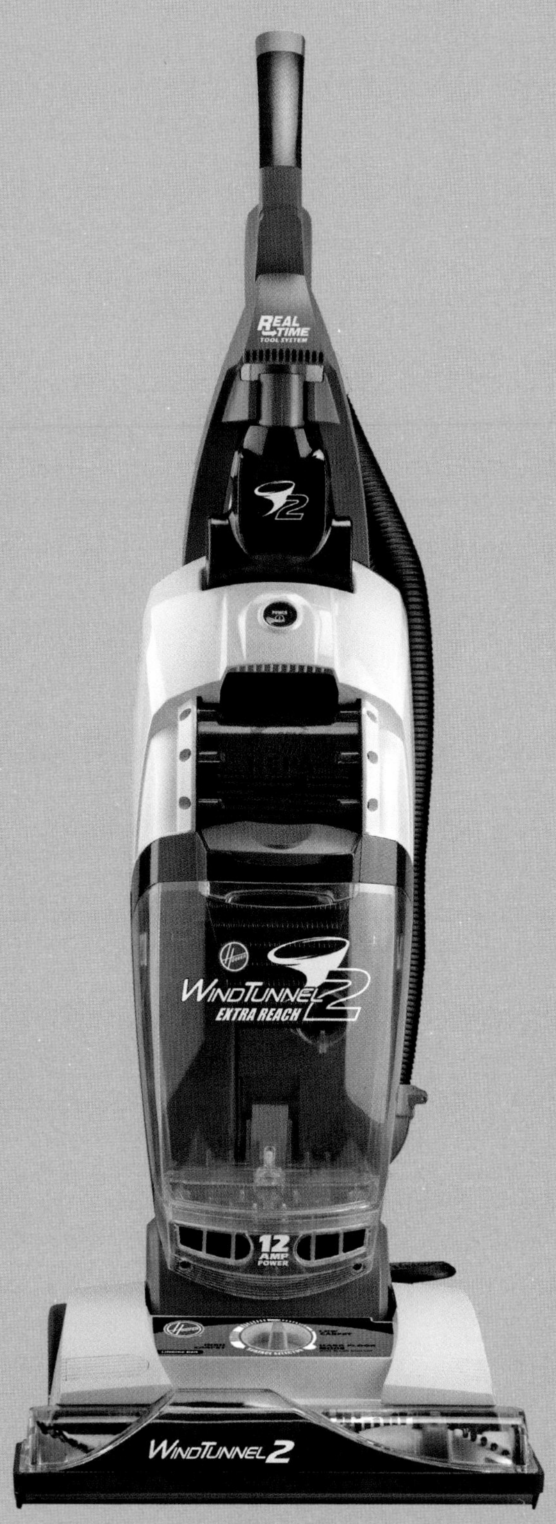
REAL TIME
TOOL SYSTEM
WINDTUNNEL 2
EXTRA REACH
12 AMP POWER
WINDTUNNEL 2

Igloo

Igloo is the number-one manufacturer of ice chests worldwide, and an estimated three out of four households own an Igloo cooler. It all started in 1947, when a group of Houston investors saw a market that had great potential. At that time, drinking water for oil riggers and construction workers was brought into the hot, humid oil fields in the area surrounding Houston in wooden buckets.

The small metal workshop where the company began developed an insulated metal container to replace the wooden buckets, and after a series of joint ventures and mergers and acquisitions, the Igloo Manufacturing Company was producing and distributing three brands of metal water coolers: Horton's, Polar King, and Igloo. The company's first ice chest, a 22-quart metal unit with a plastic liner, was introduced in 1960.

In 1962, when the company was known as Texas Tennessee Industries (TTI), the first all-plastic ice chest was produced. Offered as an alternative to metal coolers, the plastic cooler was initially sold to beer manufacturers. In 1963, Oshman's Sporting Goods in Houston became the first retailer to buy the plastic cooler and offer it to consumers. The Giant Sea Chest, introduced in 1967, was a 155-quart ice chest that was a huge success with Gulf Coast fishermen. It was the second all-plastic ice chest that Igloo produced, and it was stain and odor-resistant on the inside with a rust-proof exterior. After the Giant Sea Chest came the 25-quart model.

In 1971, TTI changed its name to Igloo Corporation to acknowledge its success with the brand. That same year, Igloo patented and introduced one of its most innovative and successful products: the Playmate ice chest. The new product featured a "tent-top" design and could be carried with one hand. This personal-size ice chest was a favorite with consumers, and the unique push-button lock and release was added in 1972. Because of the overwhelming response to the Playmate, Igloo introduced the Little Playmate in 1977 and the Lunchmate in 1978. Other products that were introduced included Sturdy Jug utility containers, Jerry Jug containers for gasoline and other flammable liquids, and the Kool line of specially designed containers for cars and trucks.

Igloo has always been committed to customer service. It is known for its ready supply of replacement parts and for offering a three-year warranty, for many years the only company in the cooler business to do so. Many consumers didn't need a warranty—they experienced Igloo's quality and durability firsthand. According to the company, Igloo coolers have survived maulings by wild animals and remained intact in burning buildings. Playmate coolers have even been used to transport human organs for transplant operations.

Igloo is a worldwide leader known for its quality, durability, and commitment to improving its existing line of products while developing new products to meet consumer needs. With more than 500 products sold throughout the United States and around the world, Igloo continues to be the market share leader in the industry it created.

Vital Statistics
Established 1947
Headquarters Katy, Texas

IGLOO
playmate

iPod

If the first computer you ever owned was an Apple, you are far from alone. Apple Computer, Inc.'s user-friendly personal computers are among the world's favorite products. Today, Apple's extensive product line includes Macintosh desktop and notebook computers, iPod digital music players, the Mac OS X operating system, the iTunes Music Store, the Xserve G5 server, and Xserve RAID storage products. Apple products are sold online, through third-party wholesalers, and at its own chain of stores, which attract crowds 24 hours a day in major urban centers around the world. Apple owns approximately 125 retail stores in the United States, as well as stores in Canada, Japan, and the United Kingdom.

Apple was founded in April 1976 by Steve Wozniak, then 26, and Steve Jobs, 21, who had both dropped out of school. The men had known each other for a few years, since Wozniak, a self-taught electronics expert, had designed a box that enabled him to make free long-distance phone calls. Jobs was intrigued when he learned Wozniak was working on another box for a computer club, a box that was to become the Apple I computer and change the world. The pair sold a van and two calculators for the total grand sum of $1,300 and launched the Apple Computer Co. to manufacture the boxes. The name was inspired by an orchard Jobs had worked at in Oregon. An area store ordered 50, and the men built them in Jobs's garage. The computers, with no monitors or keyboards, retailed for $666 each. A year later, the computers had user-friendly color monitors, keyboards, and device slots, rendering them more versatile than others on the market. In 1980, Apple went public, and sales were more than $100 million. Wozniak left Apple in 1983, and the Macintosh made its first appearance a year later. Jobs left, too, in 1985, and founded NeXT Software, leaving the company in the hands of then-president John Sculley. Competition from Microsoft proved challenging in subsequent years. The handheld device called the Newton, introduced in 1993, was a failure, and in 1997, Jobs agreed to come back in an attempt to save the company. The adorable, colorful iMacs made their debut in 1998, and Apple was again on an upward path. The portable ibook followed, then CD and DVD burners, and a super-thin Powerbook. The most significant new product, however, was the iPod, in 2001.

Apple greeted the new millennium with unprecedented success, largely because of its line of portable digital music players: iPods. The original iPods featured five gigabytes of storage, allowing customers to record 1,000 songs on a device the size of the palm of a hand. The first iPods sold for $399, making them affordable for a range of music and gadget lovers, and the iPods became one of the most successful new products of all time.

A 10-gigabyte iPod was introduced in 2002, then the iPod Mini, iPod Shuffle, and iPod Nano—each launch seemingly more popular than the previous one. In 2005, Apple brought out 30- and 60-gigabyte versions that could store and play video files, and iTunes began selling episodes of popular programs to be watched at the viewer's convenience. By this point, iPods represented 35 percent of Apple's sales, which had tripled in the years since 2001. In 2006, Jobs, still at Apple's helm, announced that iTunes had sold its billionth song—Coldplay's "Speed of Sound."

Vital Statistics

Company Name	Apple Computer
Established	1976
Founders	Steve Wozniak and Steve Jobs

Iron Horse Ranch and Vineyards

Most American sparkling wines have had a hard time living up to their French cousin, champagne. But not Iron Horse Sparkling Wines, which have been praised by a range of people, from experts such as Robert Parker to famous connoisseurs such as William Paley. Iron Horse Sparkling Wines have been served by four consecutive presidential administrations, starting with the Reagan-Gorbachev summit meeting in Geneva in 1985, which resulted in the end of the Cold War.

Founders Audrey and Barry Sterling had lived in California, London, and Paris during Barry's career as a lawyer, spending considerable time touring vineyards as well as entertaining for both business and pleasure. In the late 1960s, they decided to find "a place we could call our own forever where we could have the satisfaction of seeing the full circle—of making something and enjoying it—like a vineyard."

They searched in vain in Europe. It wasn't until they came back to California that they found what they were looking for in Iron Horse. The Sterlings fell in love with the 300-acre property at first sight in 1976, but they knew they were taking a gamble in buying it. Situated just 13 miles from the Pacific Ocean, the land was prone to late frosts, which could jeopardize crops. The cold, foggy climate was perfect for growing chardonnay and pinot noir grapes, though, so the Sterlings bought the property and hired veteran grape grower Forest Tancer to manage it. They set about restoring the existing grapevines, building the winery, and fixing up the dilapidated but lovely 1876 redwood Victorian house. Most important, they installed an elaborate frost-protection system.

The estate was named Iron Horse after a train that stopped at the nearby Ross station at the turn of the 20th century. The distinctive Iron Horse logo, featuring a rampant horse on a weather vane, was developed after a similar weather vane was unearthed during the restoration process.

The Sterling family uses the precision-farming method for growing their grapes. Precision farming uses the latest technology, including GPS mapping and CAD computer models, to focus on small, tightly delineated blocks of land, which are marked by soil type, orientation to the sun, and elevation. Vine-pruning, canopy-trimming, irrigation, and harvesting decisions are all determined on a block-by-block (and sometimes even vine-by-vine) basis. The data is so specific that, for one block, growers changed the direction in which the rows of vines were planted.

Today, there are 170 acres of chardonnay and pinot noir grapes planted on the property, and the Sterlings' children are partners in the winery. Joy Sterling oversees marketing and public relations and lives on the estate, and brother Lawrence, director of operations, also lives on the property with his wife and children.

Vital Statistics
Established 1969
Main Production Site Sebastopol, California
Employees 33
Annual Sales $11.2 million (2003)

ESTATE BOTTLED
SPARKLING WINE
IRON HORSE
SONOMA COUNTY • GREEN VALLEY
Classic Vintage Brut
2000
ALC 13% BY VOL

J.Crew

The J.Crew catalogue, featuring beautiful twentysomething models who appear to be at a permanent house party, sets the standard for young, affluent Americans looking for style as well as comfort in their clothing. The line features updated favorites, including madras shorts, chinos, and cashmere sweaters, for a look that's casual and collegial. There are small animal embroideries and plenty of bright colors, but an overall air of sophistication distinguishes J.Crew from its competitors.

J.CREW

The company was founded in 1947 by Mitchell Cinader and Saul Charles and originally sold a low-priced line of women's clothes to customers in their homes. In 1983, company head Arthur Cinader (Mitchell's son) decided that catalogue sales were the way to go. Cinader's daughter, Emily Cinader (later Woods), who had recently graduated from college, was instrumental in creating the look and feel of the clothing and catalogue.

Quality was the company watchword, for both its clothing and its catalogue. A design staff not only designed clothing but also carefully monitored garment production to be sure it met company specifications. For the catalogue, 8,000 rolls of film were shot every year, and in-house copywriters penned every word. The result, a glossy catalogue with up to 100 pages at certain times of year, was mailed to customers 14 times a year.

The catalogue often featured an item of clothing more than once and on different models. Customers were able to see how a piece fit and draped, and how to pair it with other items. The company targeted educated customers with a median age of 32 and average household income above $62,000. Sales grew 25 to 30 percent a year through the mid-1980s, according to Emily Cinedar, who in 1986 was promoted to president. But by the end of the decade, with growth slowing, J.Crew management realized that a new strategy was necessary. Hoping to capitalize on its strong brand identity, J.Crew decided to expand into retail. Management initially slated only 22 stores for development because they worried that the stores might cannibalize catalogue sales. They also decided to make most of the clothing offered in their stores unavailable in the catalogue.

Growth strategies in the early 1990s included a push to increase sales from existing buyers and movement into international markets. A catalogue mailing in Canada was extremely successful, and in 1993, J.Crew reached an agreement with the Japanese retailers ITOCHU and Renown, Inc., to open 46 stores in Japan. By this time, the company had learned that opening stores didn't harm catalogue sales and in some markets, such as New York City, actually improved them.

In 1994, when both postal and paper rates sharply increased, the company committed to opening more retail stores. In 1997, with 47 stores operating, Texas Pacific bought J.Crew in a leveraged buyout. In 1999, J.Crew began doing business over the Internet, and by 2004, it had 167 stores and 48 factory outlets. The company filed documents in June 2006 with the Securities and Exchange Commission to go public.

Vital Statistics
Catalogue launch 1983
Employees 6,800 (2006)
Annual Sales $1,152 million (2007)

J.CREW

Jack Daniel's

In the late 1850s, seven-year-old Jasper Newton "Jack" Daniel, one of 13 children born to a poor family, was sent to work for a minister and whiskey maker in Lynchburg, Tennessee. The minister taught Daniel everything he knew about whiskey, including the tricky, time-consuming, and costly process of mellowing the alcohol with hard maple charcoal. Years later, when he decided to devote himself full time to the ministry, he sold the whiskey still to his teenage apprentice. Only five foot two, Jack Daniel became a larger-than-life promoter of his whiskey as he walked around in his trademark formal black frock coat and wide-brimmed hat.

Jack Daniel's whiskey was originally sold in stenciled earthenware jugs. When glass bottles became the rage in the late 1870s, Daniel switched over, but he wasn't satisfied with a generic round shape for his distinctive whiskey. In 1895, Daniel found something more appropriate for his whiskey—a square-shaped bottle with fluted neck. The unique square bottle remains one of the key identifiers of the Jack Daniel's brand.

In the years to follow, Daniel perfected the charcoal mellowing process, making a whiskey that was outstandingly smooth and mellow. Charred white oak barrels imparted a soft brown color and unique flavor to the drink. Daniel entered his Old No. 7 Tennessee at the 1904 World's Fair in St. Louis, Missouri, and the international judges awarded it the gold medal. Until Jack Daniel died in 1911 from gangrene (that set in after he broke his toe kicking his safe) his motto was, "Each day we make it, we will make it the best we can."

Jack Daniel's nephew Lem Motlow took over the thriving business and soon introduced Black Label whiskey, a special aged variety that became a trademark of the brand. In 1956, the Jack Daniel's Distillery was sold to Brown-Forman Beverage Worldwide, Inc., which also owns spirits such as Southern Comfort and Finlandia, and wines such as Fetzer and Bolla. Brown-Forman created a marketing campaign for Jack Daniel's Tennessee whiskey that highlights homespun images of Lynchburg. The advertising emphasizes how Jack Daniel's transcends socioeconomic class, with slogans such as "Served in Fine Establishments and Questionable Joints Everywhere." Fans of Jack Daniel's have included Frank Sinatra, Keith Richards, President Theodore Roosevelt, and Slash.

Today, with sales of just under nine million cases a year, Jack Daniel's is the top-selling whiskey brand in the world and the fourth-largest selling premium spirit in the United States. Brown-Forman expanded the Jack Daniel's brand of Old No. 7 Black Label and Green Label whiskeys to include new super premium varieties called Single Barrel and Gentleman Jack. They have also introduced Jack Daniel's Country Cocktails. Today, nearly half of Jack Daniel's sales are international, especially in the United Kingdom, Eastern Europe, China, and Japan. The Jack Daniel's brand is the driving force behind Brown-Forman's recent double-digit growth in gross profits, even as sales of other whiskey brands have remained flat. Brown-Forman intends to continue to expand into new global markets and further increase its market share abroad and at home.

Vital Statistics

Parent Company Brown-Forman Company

Founder Jasper Newton "Jack" Daniel

Established 1866

Headquarters Louisville, Kentucky

Jell-O

Jell-O has long been a popular food, as much for the fun of watching it wiggle on a spoon as for its taste. Whether chock full of mini-marshmallows and canned peaches, molded in the shape of a mermaid as a centerpiece, or infused with vodka in the form of Jell-O shots, the product has earned its claim of being "America's Most Famous Dessert."

Patented in 1845, the confection didn't gain notice until 1897 when a carpenter named Pearle Wait added fruit flavoring. The first flavors were strawberry, raspberry, orange, and lemon. His wife, May, named it Jell-O. Without experience in manufacturing or marketing, Wait decided to sell his fledgling business to the Genesee Pure Food Company in LeRoy, New York, in 1899. He received $450.

The first ad for Jell-O appeared in *Ladies' Home Journal* in 1902. But Genesee hit pay dirt in 1904 with another *Ladies' Home Journal* ad, which this time included recipes. Recipe booklets proved a big hit with consumers, with stars such as Ethel Barrymore including their favorite concoctions, and in later years as many as 15 million Jell-O recipe booklets were distributed annually. Over time, experienced Jell-O cooks learned that fresh fruits such as apples, bananas, orange sections, and sliced peaches float, while sinkers include seedless grapes and fruits packed in heavy syrup.

Cherry and chocolate flavors were added to the product line in 1904, and peach was added in 1907. Chocolate was discontinued in 1927. The cola flavor had an even shorter life span, introduced in 1942 and removed a year later.

Lime was launched in 1930 and was immediately popular. The new lime flavor lent itself well to gelled salads, which were en vogue. Capitalizing on the green color, company executives sponsored a *Wizard of Oz* radio show and a series of children's books by Frank L. Baum that included recipes in the back pages. Today, residents of Salt Lake City, Utah, consume the most per-capita lime-flavored gelatin. It was declared the "Official State Snack" of Utah by the state senate in 2001.

Other marketing successes included Jell-O's sponsorship of the Jack Benny radio show between 1934 and 1944 and the use of famous artists, including Maxfield Parrish and Norman Rockwell, to illustrate the ease of making family desserts with Jell-O. Bill Cosby was named the Jell-O spokesman in 1988. Cosby officiated at the inaugural opening of the Jell-O Museum in LeRoy, New York, in 1997, when the brand turned one hundred years old.

Purchased in 1925 by what came to be known as General Foods, today Jell-O is manufactured by Kraft Foods Inc. and includes more than 158 products ranging from gelatin and puddings to ready-to-eat snacks and desserts. Products including Gelatin Pops, Jigglers, and recipes for playful edibles such as Dirt Cups and Aquarium Cups have helped Jell-O secure a place on the shelves of 68 percent of American kitchens.

Vital Statistics

Parent Company Kraft Foods Inc.

Founder Pearle Wait

Product Launch 1897

Jelly Belly Candy Co.

In 1869, Gustav Goelitz, a 24-year-old German immigrant, bought a candy store in Belleville, Illinois. The business prospered until it went bankrupt in the Great Panic of 1893. Gustav's sons, Adolph and Gus, Jr., had learned the candy trade working in their father's business, and promptly launched their own candy company, which became Goelitz Confectionary Company of Cincinnati, specializing in buttercreams and candy corn. Herman, a third brother, came to work in the family business and then opened the Herman Goelitz Candy Company in Oregon in 1918. The two Goelitz candy companies experienced the same ups and downs over the decades: a deep dip during the Great Depression, a spike in sales during World War II, and a plummet in the 1960s when the price of sugar surged.

Everything changed in 1975 when Herman Rowland, the grandson of Herman Goelitz, met David Klein, a driver for a candy distributor. Klein introduced the concept of a gourmet jelly bean. Rowland developed the recipe and the Herman Goelitz Candy Company soon came out with the first eight flavors of jelly beans: Very Cherry, Lemon, Cream Soda, Tangerine, Green Apple, Root Beer, Grape, and Licorice. The new candy was called Jelly Belly, inspired by a rhyme with Leadbelly, the 1920s blues singer. Jelly Belly candies not only had a unique and vivid taste, but also came in bags of individual flavors rather than a mix, and at a much higher price point. By 1977, the jelly beans were selling so well that Rowland asked his cousin at the Goelitz Confectionary Company in the Midwest to help produce the candies.

The craze for Jelly Belly jelly beans intensified in 1981 when Ronald Reagan, whose favorite flavor was licorice, ordered 7,000 pounds of Jelly Belly jelly beans for his inauguration. Reagan was Jelly Belly's biggest fan and greatest publicist—he was often photographed with the candies and credited them for helping him quit smoking. The president sent Jelly Belly jelly beans to the *Challenger* astronauts and offered them to visiting dignitaries. He told Rowland that he couldn't start a meeting at the White House or make a decision without passing around a jar of jelly beans. Rowland could not keep up with demand, and retailers were put on two-year waiting lists. The Herman Goelitz Candy Company and the Goelitz Confectionary Company merged into a single corporation in 1978, and renamed it the Jelly Belly Candy Company in 2001.

Today, the Jelly Belly Candy Company has plants in Fairfield, California, and Chicago that produce jelly beans, candy corn, and 150 other gourmet confections including candy covered treats, licorice, chocolate covered nuts and candies, jells, gummies, and seasonal sweets. The company has also expanded to include new jelly-bean lines, such as Sport Beans jelly beans. In early 2006, Rowland began to build the company's first overseas plant in Thailand. Despite stiff competition from larger companies, Rowland has declined several appetizing offers for Jelly Belly. He says he wants to keep it for his children—the fifth generation of candy sellers.

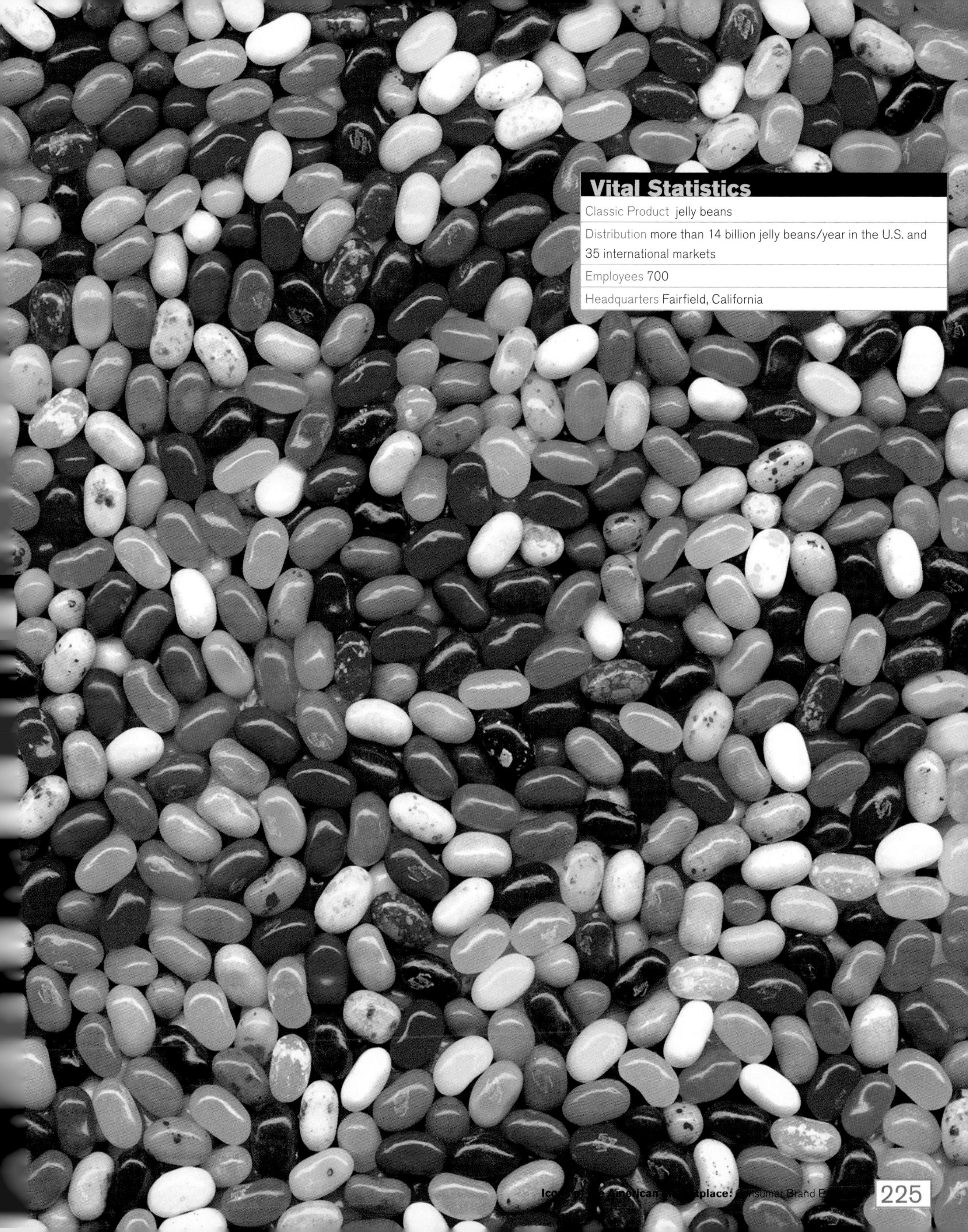

Vital Statistics

Classic Product	jelly beans
Distribution	more than 14 billion jelly beans/year in the U.S. and 35 international markets
Employees	700
Headquarters	Fairfield, California

JetBlue

JetBlue's innovative ticketing, seating, and in-flight entertainment system combined with low-cost fares have revolutionized airline travel. The airline has been chosen by J.D. Power and Associates, the Federal Aviation Administration, *Travel + Leisure,* and *The Wall Street Journal,* among many others, for awards ranging from best value to highest customer satisfaction. Founder and Chief Executive Officer David Neeleman says the secret is in keeping costs low while maintaining a high level of service. That philosophy has put newcomer JetBlue, which began flying in 2000, in the ranks of the top ten U.S. carriers based on passenger revenue miles. And with JetBlue constantly adding new destinations (sixteen new routes were added in 2006), that ranking is likely to rise.

Why do so many people like JetBlue so much? To start, their fleet of Airbus A320s boast wider seats and aisles and greater legroom than any other planes in the same class. The carrier offers only one class of service, with comfortable leather seats, each with its own TV screen with 36 channels of free DIRECTV and more than 100 channels of XM satellite radio. There are free snacks, including blue potato chips and gourmet biscotti. All ticketing is electronic, all fares are one way, and an overnight stay is never required. That level playing field, where every customer is created equal and the rules never vary, improves the experience for travelers weary of the vagaries of other big airlines.

Keeping fares low while still offering luxuries such as individual TVs also accounts for JetBlue's popularity. Costs are kept in check because the airline is not unionized and customer support is handled by employees working from their homes in Salt Lake City, Utah. Also, 80 percent of tickets are sold online. As for the TVs, JetBlue was among the first customers for the prototype in-flight entertainment system, so it paid for the equipment but installation was free.

JetBlue developed a strong brand identity by using every contact with a customer as an opportunity to establish a company personality. The original on-hold message used when people called the toll-free number was, "We know you hate being on hold, but we forgot to tell you that you look great today." The language used at the electronic check-in kiosks is friendly to the point of being folksy. And nearly every airplane in the fleet has a name incorporating the word blue, such as "Absolute Blue," "Rhapsody in Blue," and "Blue Suede Shoes."

JetBlue also places heavy emphasis on friendly and efficient customer service. From the start, applicants were hired more for attitude than experience. There are exceptions: Candidates for technical jobs such as pilots and mechanics are evaluated based on their specific skills and experience. But the primary qualification for most service personnel is a positive attitude.

Based in New York's John F. Kennedy International Airport, JetBlue has grown to become the airport's largest airline. The carrier originally flew to less-crowded airports outside of larger cities, but has recently expended to larger airports like San Francisco and Chicago's O'Hare. The airline serves more than fifty destinations and takes delivery of a new A320 or Embraer 190 every few weeks to meet its growing need for passenger capacity.

Vital Statistics

Product Launch	1998
Headquarters	Forest Hills, New York
Employees	12,000
Annual Sales	$2,363 million (2006)

Johnson's Baby Shampoo

It would be difficult to find a baby whose first shampoos were not administered with a product that has been cherished by generations of parents: Johnson's Baby Shampoo. Of course, Johnson's entire line of baby products can be found in nurseries everywhere, from lotions to swabs and everything in between—not to mention hundreds of other products that proudly bear the J&J name. In fact, Johnson & Johnson (J&J) is one of the largest, most diversified health care firms in the world.

Johnson's®

J&J began in the late 1800s, when Joseph Lister discovered that airborne germs were causing infections in operating rooms, and a man named Robert Wood Johnson, a New England druggist, decided to take action. In 1886, Johnson joined forces with his brothers, James Wood and Edward Mead, producing dressings to keep wounds clean. J&J was incorporated in 1887 and found a ready market for its product, introducing Johnson's Baby Powder in 1893 in response to a doctor's complaints of patient skin irritation caused by the company's plasters. This led to the introduction of a number of other baby products, including shampoo, and the memorable tagline, "Best for your baby, best for you." R.W. Johnson died in 1910 and was succeeded as chairman by his brother James, as the company continued to grow. In 1921, Band-Aid brand adhesive bandages and Johnson's Baby Cream made their first appearances, and Modess sanitary napkins were made available in 1927. The younger Robert Johnson, who came to be known as "the General," was elected president in 1932, and in 1944, the company was listed on the New York Stock Exchange. The General was the driving force behind J&J's unique organizational structure, in which divisions and affiliates are given autonomy to direct their own operations; he was also a champion of social issues. Under his leadership, J&J moved into pharmaceuticals, hygiene products, and textiles and annual sales grew from $11 million to $700 million at the time of his death in 1968. In the 1990s, J&J pioneered several progressive programs including child care, family leave, and "corporate wellness," which were beginning to be recognized as health care cost reducers and productivity enhancers. In 2000, William C. Weldon became the sixth chairman in the history of J&J.

J&J Baby Shampoo, with its reassuring "No More Tears" formula, is perhaps the best-loved, most well-known J&J product of all. The shampoo is clinically proven to be as gentle and mild as water on a baby's skin and will not irritate the eyes. It is soap-free, alcohol-free, hypoallergenic, and allergy- and dermatologist-tested. J&J's acquisition of BabyCenter LLC, the leading online pregnancy and parenting resource, shows its continued commitment to parents and infants, providing customizable information and resources. Recently, the company has introduced botanical versions of classic products, including Bedtime Baby Bath, with lavender and chamomile.

J&J is organized into three business segments: pharmaceutical, medical devices and diagnostics, and consumer. The consumer products include the Neutrogena skin and hair care line, o.b. and Stayfree feminine hygiene products, the Reach oral care line, Band-Aid brand adhesive bandages, Imodium A-D diarrhea treatment, Mylanta gastrointestinal products, Pepcid AC acid controller, Tylenol, Motrin, and St. Joseph pain relievers, Benecol and Splenda sweeteners, and, of course, the J&J baby care line. J&J generates about 40 percent of its revenues outside of the United States, through its network of 200 operating companies in fifty-seven countries, and has been named one of the best employers for Hispanic women, working women, people with disabilities, and biopharmaceutical employees.

Vital Statistics

Parent Company	Johnson & Johnson
Classic Product	Baby shampoo
Date of Founding	1886

K2

K2 skis, like the many mountain peaks and alpine summits where they've been used, are widely considered to be top of the line. K2 founder Bill Kirschner is credited for pioneering fiberglass ski technology, which made skis significantly lighter and livelier than their wood and metal counterparts.

Kirschner's first experiment in making skis in the early 1960s was the perfect way to combine his love of the outdoors with his stake in the family business founded by his father near Seattle, Washington. Kirschner Manufacturing used early fiberglass technology to make splints for fractured bones, plastic skeletons for teachers, and other products. Always in search of new ideas, Kirschner came up with the concept of fiberglass skis while he was on the slopes at Sun Valley in 1960 using a pair of then-popular metal skis. By the following winter, in time for his vacation again at Sun Valley, Kirschner had produced a pair of fiberglass skis. Pleased with their performance, he decided to try to manufacture them. He refined his product during the week at the manufacturing facility and tested it on weekends when he took his family skiing at nearby Crystal Mountain. The first iterations weren't always successful because the many fiberglass layers tended to peel apart in the cold. But he solved the problem by winding fiberglass fabric around a lightweight core of spruce and then heating the ski to stabilize the shape. In 1964, Kirschner brought 250 pairs of skis to market, and in 1965, he manufactured 1,600 pairs. Kirschner spun the ski business off from Kirschner Manufacturing in 1967 and named it K2 for the world's second-highest mountain and for the two Kirschner brothers, Bill and Don. Just a year later, K2 had boosted sales to 21,000 pairs of skis.

Kirschner decided that in addition to producing an intermediate ski, he wanted to develop a world-class racing ski. Company engineers developed two prototypes, and in 1969, Marilyn Cochran skied her way to a gold medal in the World Cup Giant Slalom on a pair of K2s. It was the first time a World Cup had ever been won on American-made skis, and the publicity pushed K2 into the limelight. People loved the signature K2 design of red, white, and blue stripes, which was in stark contrast to the all-black Head metal ski. K2 sales skyrocketed, spurred on by world champion skiers and Olympic medalists, including Spider Savich, Jean Claude Killy, and Phil and Steve Mahre, who all raced and won gold on K2s. The company doubled its shipment every year between 1966 and 1970.

Today K2 Sports is a part of a multinational manufacturer of sporting goods called K2 Inc., located in Carlsbad, California. In addition to being the number-one maker of skis in the United States with its K2 and Völkl brands, the company has a diversified product line, including competition snowboards, in-line skates, and fishing gear. Recent K2 ski models still feature triaxial-braided glass wrapped around wood, but design changes include deep sidecuts, short length, fat width, twin tips, and ultraviolet ink graphics. Bill Kirschner was inducted into the U.S. National Ski Hall of Fame in 2001, cited as being one of the country's great ski entrepreneurs.

Opposite: Skier: Shane Szocs. Photo by Alex O'Brien.

Vital Statistics
Company Founding 1967
Headquarters Carlsbad, California
Employees 4,700 (2005)
Annual Sales $1,394 million (2006)

Kellogg Company

The world's leading producer of cereal got its start back in 1894, when Will Keith (W. K.) Kellogg was working with his brother, Dr. John Kellogg, at the famous homeopathic sanitarium in Battle Creek, Michigan. The two men were experimenting with grains for patients' meals, but set their dough aside when they were interrupted. When they returned, they found that the dough had absorbed a great deal of water. They decided to roll the dough anyway and baked it, and the result was the first flaked cereal. John Kellogg sold the flakes through a mail order business that W. K. managed, and in 1906, W. K. started his own company to produce cornflakes.

At that time, America was moving away from heavy, high-fat breakfast fare in favor of a lighter grain-based breakfast. With a strong interest in health and nutrition, William Kellogg discovered how to make a better cornflake by using the corn grit, or heart of the corn. In an effort to enable customers to distinguish his cornflakes from the other 42 cereal makers in Battle Creek at the time, Kellogg put his signature on every box, noting that Kellogg Corn Flakes were "The Original."

The cereal business really took off with the introduction of milk pasteurization in 1910, and Kellogg kept pace with innovative marketing and packaging. Kellogg was an excellent marketer of the product he cared so deeply about, distributing free samples of his cornflakes and advertising in magazines and on billboards to maximize brand awareness and keep the consumers coming back for more. Kellogg even held a children's art contest, with the best entries being used for Kellogg advertisements.

Kellogg has continuously worked at accommodating ever-changing consumer needs, introducing new products and marketing them in new and interesting ways. Kellogg expanded into new markets when the country sank into the Depression, and responded by investing in the country and its people. He doubled his advertising, which increased sales, and reduced the number of hours in shifts to create more jobs for those in need. Additionally, he employed a number of people to develop a 10-acre park on the grounds of the Battle Creek plant. In 1930, he created the W. K. Kellogg Foundation.

Kellogg kept investing in his company, creating new products and forging partnerships to enhance business. During World War II, Kellogg provided packaged K-rations for U.S. armed forces, and engineering personnel used the Kellogg machine shop to manufacture parts for the Manhattan Project, which aimed to develop an atomic bomb, in 1945. Kellogg's Rice Krispies Marshmallow Treats recipe appeared in 1940 and became a favorite food for mailing to service members abroad.

W. K. Kellogg died in 1951 at the age of 91, but the company continued to maintain the tradition of its founder by constantly striving to provide the best products in the most effective ways. After Kellogg's death, some of Kellogg's best-loved cereals were introduced, such as Kellogg's Special K, Kellogg's Corn Pops, Kellogg's Cocoa Krispies, and Kellogg's Frosted Flakes. Tony the Tiger, the famous spokescharacter for Frosted Flakes since 1952, was an immediate success and is one of the most recognized characters in advertising.

Today Kellogg manufactures in 17 countries and sells its products in more than 180 countries around the world.

Vital Statistics

Classic Product Frosted Flakes

Established 1906

Founder W. K. Kellogg

Kenneth Cole

Kenneth Cole has a motto: "To be aware is more important than what you wear." Coming from the owner of a $500 million shoe and clothing corporation, those are bold words. But Kenneth Cole has made a name for himself as much for his socially conscious marketing campaigns as for being a fashion magnate. His unexpected taglines often tie together his products with a message. "Today is not a dress rehearsal." says a recent one. Another of his lines reads, "It's okay to be clothes minded."

KENNETH COLE
new york

Cole, the son of a Brooklyn-based shoe manufacturer, grew up cutting patterns and gluing soles for his dad. Fresh out of Emory University, he agreed to help out his family's company El Grecko Leather Products, while contemplating law school. After a brief stint studying shoe design in Europe and making contacts with factories there, he returned home intent on opening his own shop. In 1982 he wanted to debut his shoes at the prestigious New York Shoe Show, held every year at the Hilton Hotel. But with very little money, Cole couldn't afford to rent space at the show.

Instead, he called a friend in the trucking business and asked to use his truck. Then he called Mayor Ed Koch's office and asked how to get a permit to park in Midtown, across from the Hilton. The mayor's office said it was impossible—the only permits issued for parking there were for utility trucks or to movie production crews. Cole changed his company letterhead from Kenneth Cole, Inc., to Kenneth Cole Productions, Inc., and applied the next day to shoot a movie called *The Birth of a Shoe Company.* The day of the shoe show, the Kenneth Cole Productions truck parked on Sixth Avenue across from the Hilton, fully furnished with a director, several models serving as actresses, and samples of Cole's shoes. They sold the entire production of forty thousand pairs of shoes in two days, and the company was launched.

After establishing the company in 1982 as a women's shoe designer, Cole added accessories and men's and women's apparel. But despite his company's success, he hasn't shied away from notable controversies in his marketing campaigns, including reproductive rights, gun control, and nuclear power. In 2005, Cole worked with Viacom and the Kaiser Family Foundation to create the "We all have AIDS" public service campaign to help erase the stigma associated with having AIDS. The campaign tagline "We All Have AIDS...If One of Us Does" is written across a photograph that includes Nelson Mandela, Desmond Tutu, Elton John, Alicia Keys, and Sharon Stone stepping into wet concrete to demonstrate their commitment to fighting AIDS.

Married to ex–New York governor Mario Cuomo's daughter, it's unlikely Cole will give up his sometimes controversial marketing tactics anytime soon. In fact, he feels so strongly about the importance of taking a stand that he's willing to risk fallout from customers who may disagree. "I can come to terms with that," he says.

Vital Statistics
Company Name Kenneth Cole Productions Inc.
Classic Product shoes
Established 1982
Annual Sales $536.5 million (2006)
Employees 1,900

Kiehl's Since 1851

The cognoscenti have long known about the little shop in Manhattan's East Village with the luxurious skin and hair care products in simple, elegant packaging. Today, however, Kiehl's has gone international and can be found in some of the world's most exclusive department stores as well as freestanding boutiques in more than 40 cities and communities. Many consumers are probably unaware that Kiehl's has been around for more than 155 years.

Indeed, Kiehl's was established in 1851. From its earliest years, a Mr. John Kiehl served patrons of his humble apothecary virility creams, baldness cures, and a formula called Money Drawing Oil, likely believed effective at the time. In 1921, Mr. Irving Morse—who had worked as an apprentice at Kiehl's and earned his pharmacology degree—bought the company from the retiring John Kiehl, transforming it into a full-scale pharmacy and adding homeopathic cures and herbal remedies. Irving's son, Aaron, himself a scientist, started his own business, Morse Laboratories, and would produce a fluoride therapy still in use today. During the 1950s, he began assisting his father at Kiehl's and by 1961 had taken the helm of the family business. It was Aaron Morse who transformed Kiehl's into the store we know today. He phased out the pharmacy and homeopathic products, developing the natural skin and hair formulas that have become Kiehl's staples. Kiehl's introduced its classic Original Musk Oil in 1963 and its iconic Blue Astringent—purported to have been a favorite formula of Andy Warhol—in 1964. Morse preferred generic containers with simple handwritten labels and straightforward product names like Creme de Corps and Lip Balm #1. He also established Kiehl's longstanding policy of distributing complimentary samples, largely due to his gregarious nature and confidence in his formulas.

Over 35 years ago, Morse wrote "The Mission of Kiehl," expressing noble beliefs and setting the course for his company. He wrote: "A worthwhile firm must have a purpose for its existence. Not only the everyday work-a-day purpose to earn a just profit, but beyond that, to improve in some way the quality of the community to which it is committed." Morse created a small, in-store library of scholarly tomes such as Gray's Anatomy, and introduced a real human skeleton to assist the pharmacists in explaining to patrons what was ailing them and why. He added a makeshift museum displaying several vintage motorcycles, a Lamborghini, and two "Kiehl Squadron" stunt planes, which he piloted himself. There was a xylophone and timpani on hand in case he—or a customer—was inspired to pick up the energy in the store environment, something it rarely lacked. In 2000, French cosmetics giant L'Oréal bought Kiehl's and has adhered to the business formulas which made Kiehl's products so popular.

Kiehl's still uses the finest natural ingredients available, refuses to test products on animals, and tests all formulas thoroughly in laboratory environments to assure safety, quality, and efficacy for its customers. Nearly thirty years ago, Kiehl's was recognized by the Smithsonian National Museum for its contributions to American history—incorporating 103 relics and products into the permanent pharmacological collection. In 2003, the museum welcomed three new formulas, Kiehl's Abyssine Cream, Cryste Marine Cream, and Original Musk Eau de Toilette—firmly establishing the company as an American institution.

Vital Statistics
Parent Company L'Oréal
Classic Product Blue Astringent Herbal Lotion
Established 1851
Founder John Kiehl

Kleenex

Kleenex, one of the world's most famous and useful paper products, was introduced in 1924 as a replacement for the cloths that were being used at the time to remove cold cream from the face. Promoted by movie stars such as Helen Hayes and Jean Harlow, Kleenex became popular quickly and has never released its hold on American consumers.

Kimberly, Clark & Company—which built Wisconsin's first paper mill—was founded in 1872 by four men: John A. Kimberly, Charles B. Clark, Frank C. Shattuck, and Kimberly's cousin Havilah Babcock. Its initial product was newsprint made from linen and cotton rags, which sold well enough that after six years the company was able to acquire a majority interest in the nearby Atlas paper mill, which converted ground pulpwood into manila wrapping paper. In 1889, the company constructed a large pulp- and paper-making complex on the Fox River, and in 1914, company researchers working with bagasse, a pulp by-product of processed sugarcane, came up with what was to become the base of Kleenex: creped cellulose wadding, or tissue. During World War I, this product, called cellucotton, was used to treat wounds and as a disposable feminine napkin. Realizing the potential of cellucotton just in time, the company introduced the Kotex feminine napkin in 1920 and, four years later, a disposable tissue they called Kleenex. Two years after that, Kleenex facial tissues were introduced in Canada and marketed as a disposable substitute to the handkerchief.

In 1928, the now-staple pop-up cartons with perforated openings hit the market, and a year later brought the first colored Kleenex tissues, which could be matched to bathroom décor. Nationwide advertisements promoting Kleenex for its current use began in 1930, and sales doubled within a year. Kimberly & Clark created a separate sales company, International Cellucotton Products, which it contracted to manufacture Kotex and Kleenex. Throughout the decade, consumers kept contacting the company, advocating the use of Kleenex tissues for colds. The company responded with its new slogan: "the handkerchiefs you can throw away." Further developments followed, keeping up with consumer demand—the Pocket Pack in 1932, Mansize tissues in 1941, the Kleenex Chubby in 1943, and Eyeglass tissues in 1949. Advertising campaigns became an essential component of company strategy, from the True Confessions campaign in 1941, to Little Lulu's endorsement in 1944, to the now-famous Tissue Quadrant Design at the Museum of Modern Art in 1949. During the 1960s, Kleenex switched its television advertising from evening to daytime, anticipating the wild popularity of daytime soap operas—which often featured tear-jerking, Kleenex-needing moments. Additional products appeared: Space-Saver packs, Juniors, Purse Packs. Subsequent innovations—from holiday-themed tissues to designer graphics—carried the company solidly through the 1980s and 1990s.

By the time the new millennium arrived, Kleenex was one of America's most reliable, recognizable brands. Manufactured by the world's leading tissue company, Kimberly-Clark Corporation, Kleenex Brand is available in more than 150 countries. To meet consumer demands, varieties such as Kleenex with lotion, Anti-Viral—one of the first tissues available to consumers that kills 99.9 percent of cold and flu viruses in the tissue—and Moist Cloths have been developed, and it is certain that Kleenex will continue offering the tissues their customers desire.

Vital Statistics

Company Name Kimberly-Clark, Corporation

Classic Product tissues

Founders John A. Kimberly, Charles B. Clark, Frank C. Shattuck, Havilah Babcock

Established 1872

Kodak

With the slogan "you press the button, we do the rest," George Eastman gave the world its first simple camera in 1888. Since that time, Kodak has changed the way we record images used in leisure, medical, business, entertainment, and scientific applications, as well as, increasingly, the way we combine images and information. In short, it is a brand justifiably recognized in virtually every country around the world.

Kodak

George Eastman, Kodak's founder, was a high-school dropout who began his business career as a 14-year-old office boy. At 24, he made plans for a vacation to Santo Domingo, purchasing a photographic outfit to record his trip. The "outfit" included a camera the size of an oven, a tripod, a tent so that he could spread photographic emulsion on glass plates before exposing them, chemicals, glass tanks, a heavy plate holder, and a jug of water. Although Eastman never made it to Santo Domingo, he did make a fateful decision: to simplify the way people took pictures. He began making gelatin emulsions in his mother's kitchen at night and, after three years, had a formula that worked. In 1880, he began the commercial manufacture of dry plates, impressing businessman Henry A. Strong. On January 1, 1881, Eastman and Strong formed a partnership called the Eastman Dry Plate Company. Late that year, Eastman resigned from his position at the Rochester Savings Bank, inspired to, in his words, "make the camera as convenient as the pencil."

In 1883, Eastman began selling film in rolls and, in 1888, came out with the $25 Kodak camera, preloaded with enough film for 100 exposures. The word "Kodak" was first registered as a trademark in 1888 and was invented by Eastman, who had always liked the letter "K." In 1896, the 100,000th Kodak camera was manufactured, and film and photographic paper were being made at the rate of about 400 miles a month. In 1900, the first in a long line of popular Brownie cameras was introduced to the masses. Eastman's basic business principles, which have become the Kodak standard, included research to foster growth, respect for employees, reinvestment of profits, and mass production at low cost. In 1919, Eastman gave one-third of his own holdings of company stock, $10 million worth, to his employees. He died in 1932 at the age of 77. The impact of Eastman's dream, however, has outlived him. It enabled Thomas Edison to develop the first motion picture camera in 1891. All Oscar-winning "Best Pictures" have been shot on Kodak film. In 1896, Kodak introduced a photographic paper designed specifically for X-ray image capture. Kodak technologies touch about 40 percent of the world's commercially printed pages. And Kodak technology also went along on Apollo 11, with the first astronauts to walk on the moon. Photos of the lunar soil taken by Neil Armstrong enabled scientists to see soil particles smaller than two one-thousandths of an inch. It was in 1963 that Kodak's most successful camera, the Instamatic, was introduced. Kodak engineers invented the world's first consumer digital camera in 1975. By 2000, Kodak was the number one brand in the United States.

Kodak is the world's leading imaging innovator; the name has become synonymous with photography, and the company provides its innovative products to the photographic, graphic communications, and health care markets. Consumers use Kodak's systems for digital and traditional picture-taking in daily life, while businesses use Kodak to communicate with customers worldwide with prepress, conventional, and digital printing and document imaging. Creative professionals rely on Kodak technology for moving and still images alike, and health care organizations use Kodak's innovative products to help improve patient care. Kodak's reach is wide indeed.

Vital Statistics

Classic Product camera/film

Established 1881

Founder/Inventor George Eastman

Annual Sales $13, 274 million (2006)

Kohler Co.

An innovator in bathrooms around the world, creating products of exceptional quality and design, Kohler Co. got its auspicious start producing cast iron and steel implements for farmers, castings for furniture factories, and ornamental iron pieces, including cemetery crosses and urns. The company was founded in 1873, when Austrian immigrant John Michael Kohler purchased Sheboygan Union Iron and Steel Foundry in Sheboygan, Wisconsin. J. M. Kohler, an excellent craftsman, was able to find immigrants like himself, with a tradition of European craftsmanship and eager to find success in their new homeland.

In 1883, in an effort to improve the quality of life of his customers, Kohler applied baked enamel coating to a Kohler horse trough, thereby creating the first Kohler bathtub and kicking off a strong growth period for the company. Kohler's plumbing business was born. When J. M. Kohler died in 1900, the company had more than 250 employees, and almost all the company's revenues came from the sale of enameled products such as sinks and tubs.

Kohler's three sons inherited the business, and the subsequent deaths of two of them left the entire business in the hands of Walter Kohler by 1905. Known for his strong sense of corporate responsibility, Walter took steps to help the early employees by creating the American Club, a boarding hotel for new immigrants. He also established a benefit organization for employees, offered lessons to enable employees to pass citizenship exams, and commissioned architects and city planners to establish a community to be built around the company. The village of Kohler, Wisconsin, had 40 houses and a population of 254 when it incorporated in 1911.

By 1923, Kohler was the third-largest plumbing products company in the United States, with new products such as the vitreous china toilets and washbasins, brass faucets, and others propelling sales. Although quality and craftsmanship were founding principles of the company, Kohler is equally known for its artful design and functionality. In 1929, Kohler products were selected to be part of a Museum of Modern Art exhibition showcasing artistry in the bathroom. Always a pioneer, Kohler took a bold step by introducing vibrant colors and shapes, changing the look of the American bathroom forever.

Known for its superior quality and craftsmanship, Kohler incorporates high-quality materials with cutting-edge design and technology to create function and beauty in everyday life. Kohler constantly invests in its company, which includes 11 manufacturing facilities in North America as well as businesses in China and Australia. The largest is still in Kohler, Wisconsin, where the company operates a vitreous china pottery, a cast iron foundry and enamel shop, a faucet manufacturing operation, and a 200-acre plumbing distribution center.

The dedication of Kohler and his employees helped create one of the oldest and largest private companies in the United States. It supplies bathrooms around the world with its bathroom products, cabinetry, and tile.

Vital Statistics
Established 1873
Founder John Michael Kohler
Employees 31,000 (2005)
Annual Sales $3,000 million (2005)

Kool-Aid

If you were young during the 1970s, you will recall the image of the cheerful Kool-Aid Man bursting through a wall to quench the thirst of waiting children. In fact, the very mention of this advertising icon may conjure up the sweet-tart taste of a glass of America's classic kids' drink.

Kool-Aid Man appeared on the scene in 1975, to be exact, with his trademark, "Oh yeah!" but the beverage itself has been on the market for almost 80 years. Entrepreneur Edwin Perkins, the son of a Nebraska grocer, was a lifelong admirer of Jell-O, impressed since childhood by its six flavors and commercial success. He dreamed of inventing a similarly innovative product, and in 1914 was on his way when he established a small mail-order business called Perkins Products Company, which sold small bottles of perfume and calling cards through magazine advertisements. Eventually, his company included more than 125 products; the most popular item was a concentrated soft drink syrup called Fruit Smack that came in six flavors: strawberry, cherry, lemon-lime, grape, orange, and raspberry, just like Jell-O. Door-to-door sales agents sold the product in four-ounce glass bottles. However, the glass packaging meant significant breakage and high shipping costs. Perkins decided to transform the Fruit Smack syrup into a concentrated powder and package it in envelopes. He changed the product's name to Kool-Ade, which soon became Kool-Aid, and sold it in one-ounce envelopes. All that was required of consumers was to add water and voila: a new, refreshing, fruit-flavored beverage.

Perkins soon discontinued all other products to focus exclusively on Kool-Aid. In 1931, the company relocated its headquarters and production facilities to Chicago, bringing it closer to suppliers and improving national distribution. Packaging improvements allowed for a price reduction from a dime to a nickel per package in 1933, and that price stood for more than 30 years, thanks to continuous enhancements. After the war, Perkins expanded the Kool-Aid factory further, and by 1950, 300 production workers produced nearly a million packets of Kool-Aid each day.

In 1953, the Perkins Products Company was acquired by General Foods Corporation, one of Kraft Foods' predecessor companies, and Perkins retired, his dream fulfilled. General Foods, however, had even bigger dreams for Kool-Aid and brought it to Canada, then Latin America. Within a year, General Foods introduced a new advertising campaign for Kool-Aid, featuring the Smiling Face Pitcher that remains Kool-Aid's trademark today. Root beer and lemonade flavors were added to the original six flavors in 1955, and presweetened Kool-Aid was developed in 1964 and redeveloped in 1970. General Foods, which merged with Kraft in 1989, continued to target the 6- to 12-year-old market. In the 1990s, hip flavors such as Surfin' Berry Punch and Rock-a-dile Red were introduced, as the Kool-Aid Man took up skateboarding and other modern pastimes.

Today, Kool-Aid comes in dozens of flavors and varieties and in many sizes, to continue to meet the changing needs of consumers. The Kool-Aid Man has become one of the country's most beloved mascots, featured in dozens of commercials and on millions of Kool-Aid packets. He even has been honored with a footprint ceremony at Mann's Chinese Theatre in Hollywood, and Kool-Aid was named the official soft drink of the state of Nebraska. Thanks to its low cost per serving, appealing advertising campaigns, and ease of purchase and preparation, Kool-Aid is the number-one-selling powdered drink mix on the market.

Vital Statistics
Parent Company Kraft Foods
Established 1927
Founder/Inventor Edwin Perkins

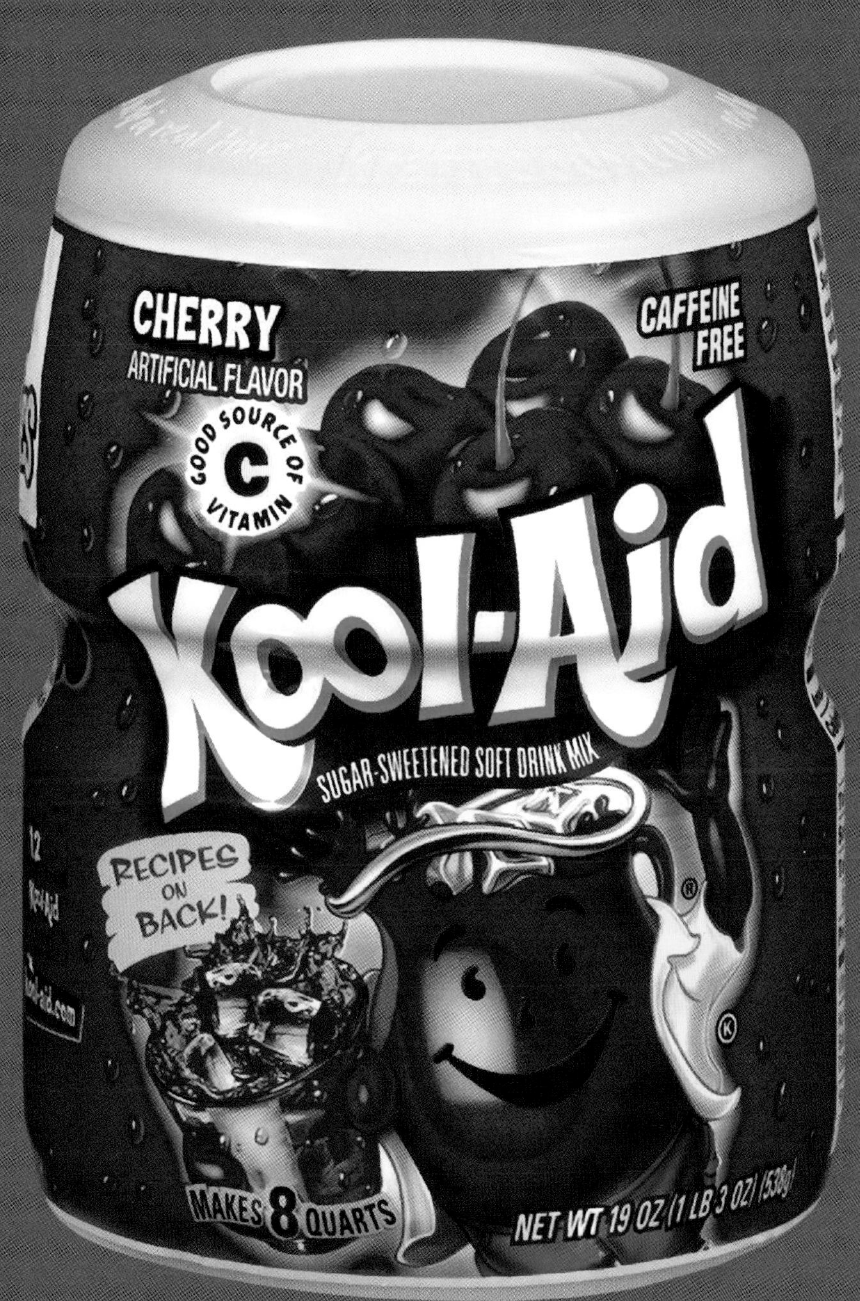
CHERRY
ARTIFICIAL FLAVOR
CAFFEINE FREE
GOOD SOURCE OF C VITAMIN
Kool-Aid
SUGAR-SWEETENED SOFT DRINK MIX
RECIPES ON BACK!
MAKES 8 QUARTS
NET WT 19 OZ (1 LB 3 OZ) (538g)

Krazy Glue

Krazy Glue is a substance called cyanoacrylate that was discovered by Dr. Harry Coover while working for Kodak Research Laboratories to develop an optically clear plastic for gunsights in 1942. Coover rejected cyanoacrylate because it was too sticky and stuck to all apparatus used to handle it. In 1951, cyanoacrylate was rediscovered by Coover and Dr. Fred Joyner, who were researching a heat-resistant acrylate polymer for jet canopies when Joyner spread a film of ethyl cyanoacrylate between refractometer prisms and discovered that the prisms were glued together. Coover finally realized that cyanoacrylate was a useful product and in 1958 the Eastman compound #910 was marketed to consumers as a product named Eastman 910. Cyanoacrylates are now a family of adhesives based on similar chemistry.

The company Jadow & Sons were the first to market and distribute Krazy Glue in the U.S. and entered the market with this brand in 1970. Elmer's became the marketer and distributor of the Instant Krazy Glue brand of cyanoacrylate in 1990.

Consumers quickly found many uses for Krazy Glue. A wife Krazy-Glued herself to her foreign-born husband to prevent him from being deported. Veterinarians have used it to piece together the cracked shells of accident-prone tortoises, reattach fins to fish, and mend split hooves on horses. Physicians have used it as a substitute for sutures. A woman who won the "How Krazy Glue Saved the Day Contest" used the powerful adhesive when she woke up from taking a nap in her rowboat and found herself knee-deep in water that had been pouring in from a leak in the bottom. Unable to swim, the boat owner Krazy-Glued a piece of leather over the hole, which stopped the leak and saved her life.

Elmer's Products, Inc., marketer of the popular water-soluble white Elmer's Glue-All, markets and distributes Krazy Glue, which has become America's best-selling instant adhesive. In recent years Elmer's, now owned by the investment management company Berwind Group, has expanded the brand and introduced new varieties of Krazy Glue. In 1995, in response to the number of emergency calls from people who inadvertently glued their fingers together, Elmer's introduced a skin-guard formula that will bond practically anything except skin. In 2005, the company introduced a Color Change formula that goes on purple and dries clear, which makes it easy to see where the glue has been applied. They have also recently developed an advanced formula as well as single-use tubes of Krazy Glue. The company maintains its lead as the number-one superglue, with plans to continue developing new formulas and applicator technologies that will permanently fix the brand in its enviable position.

Vital Statistics

Parent Company Elmer's Products, Inc.

Established 1956 (cyanoacrylate patented)

Inventor Harry Coover

Headquarters Columbus, Ohio

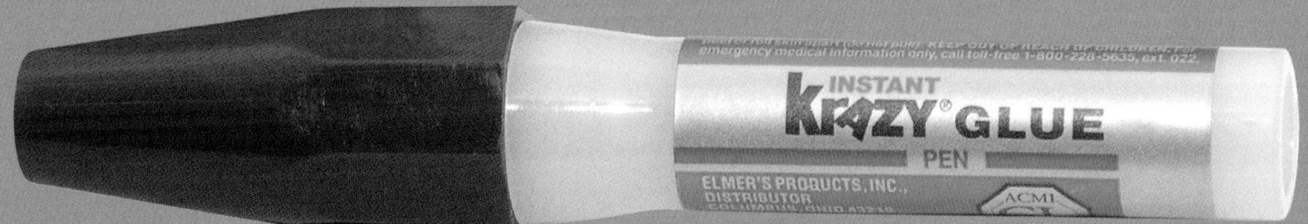

Lawn-Boy

For almost three-quarters of a century, Lawn-Boy has helped homeowners maintain their lawns to green perfection. The Lawn-Boy walk power mower has surprisingly romantic origins: a Wisconsin man named Ole Evinrude conceived of its motor one hot summer in 1906 in hopes of more quickly reaching an ice cream shop across a lake that was favored by his future wife. His invention led to the birth of Evinrude Motors, then to Outboard Marine Corporation, and ultimately to the Toro Company, the walk-behind lawn mower company homeowners have come to trust and love.

The original Lawn-Boy was manufactured by the Evinrude Company and became the first one-handed reel power mower the American public had ever seen. Evinrude's design consisted of a horizontal cylinder, a vertical crankshaft, and a driveshaft with direction-changing gears housed in a submerged lower unit. In 1956, the company's corporate name was changed to Outboard Marine Corporation. Two years later, Lawn-Boy introduced the QUIETFLITE mower, which featured sealed and insulated engines that reduced sound. OMC focused on research and development throughout the 1960s, and expansion continued in the Unites States and abroad. Lawn-Boy snow throwers, rototillers, and ride-on products were developed. During that decade, the Lawn-Boy headquarters and manufacturing facilities were moved from Missouri to Illinois, and by 1970, Lawn-Boy lawn mowers were considered the standard-bearer because of a new two-cycle engine that produced 20 to 30 percent more power with less weight, fewer parts, and easier servicing. The company was also developing the world's first cordless mower, key electric starting systems, and CD ignition systems that would change the lawn-mower landscape forever.

Groundbreaking production of Consumer Product Safety Commission (CPSC) compliant lawn mowers, featuring three blade-stopping systems, began in 1983. The blade-stopping systems included zone, electric start, and blade brake clutch systems. Two new manufacturing plants were established in Mississippi and Tennessee, and the company's sales/marketing and engineering divisions relocated to Memphis, Tennessee. In the late 1980s, seeking expansion opportunities, Lawn-Boy bought Gilson Brothers, a manufacturer of garden tractors, single- and two-stage snow throwers, rototillers, and space heaters, and moved headquarters again, this time to Wisconsin. Lawn-Boy's destiny changed when, in 1989, Outboard Marine Corporation was purchased by its greatest competitor, the Toro Company. The Toro Company expanded Lawn-Boy distribution to the mass retail market, most markedly Sears and Montgomery Ward. Distribution channels soon encompassed home centers, hardware co-ops, and other select mass retailers.

In the late 1990s, Toro aligned its business units around a centralized operations group and a strategic business units group. Lawn-Boy secured the lead in the market for walk power mower repurchase rates in 1996, by which point 58 percent of Lawn-Boy users were previous Lawn-Boy owners. In 2005, Lawn-Boy launched a new line of walk-behind mowers and introduced an unprecedented line called Zero Radius Turning Mowers, which are specially engineered to best meet each user's individual needs, and in 2006, golf legend Jack Niklaus signed a multiyear contract to appear in ads promoting Lawn-Boy mowers. Today, Lawn-Boy mowers are sold all over the world.

Vital Statistics

Company Name	TORO Company
Founder/Inventor	Ole Evinrude
Founded	1914
Employees	5,185 (2005)
Annual Sales	$1,836 million (2006)

Lay's Potato Chips

There is almost nothing more addictive than a potato chip, and Lay's Potato Chips have been capitalizing on this for more than sixty years. The H.W. Lay & Company Inc. was founded by entrepreneur Herman W. Lay, a North Carolina native whose business career launched at the age of 10 with his first ice cream stand. In 1932, he took a job as a route salesman at the Barrett Food Products Company, an Atlanta-based potato chip manufacturer. Later that year, Lay borrowed $100 to take over Barrett's small warehouse in Nashville on a distributorship basis, and the rest is snacking history.

Lay began selling Barrett's Gardner brand products from his 1928 Model A Ford. In 1933, he hired a salesman and, three years later, employed a staff of 25. In 1938, however, as a result of some financial problems suffered by the Barrett company, Lay borrowed money from friends to buy Barrett and all of its plants, changing the company's name to H.W. Lay & Company Inc. and moving its headquarters to Atlanta. Lay began expanding, building manufacturing plants throughout the southeast. Most notably, he opened a plant in Atlanta with one of the world's first continuous potato chip production lines, making large-scale production possible and, in 1944, began marketing potato chips under the Lay's name. He began advertising on television that year, with an ad campaign featuring Oscar, the Happy Potato. Lay also hired Bert Lahr—the lovable Cowardly Lion from *The Wizard of Oz*—as the company's first celebrity spokesperson. Lahr's signature line, "so crisp you can hear the freshness," became the chips' first slogan.

In 1949, Lay founded a research laboratory to develop new products and subsequently expanded its product line to include barbecued potato chips, corn cheese snacks, fried pork skins, and a variety of nuts. The company also expanded to the rest of the country. In 1956, Lay went public with more than a thousand employees, manufacturing facilities in eight cities, and branches or warehouses in thirteen cities. By the late 1950s, Lay's was the largest maker of potato chips and snack foods in the United States. The change that rocked the snack world came in 1961, when Lay's merged with the Frito Company, which had been founded the same year Lay had founded his company, to form Frito-Lay Inc., the world's largest and most successful snack food company. Lay's then introduced its best-known slogan: "Betcha can't eat just one." New versions of the Lay's chip continued to appear, including barbecue, sour cream & onion, salt & vinegar, wavy, baked, fat-free, kettle cooked, stackable, and countless other flavor varieties in other countries, ranging from Poutine (a regional concoction of French fries with gravy and melted cheese) in Canada to Magic Masala in India and Prawn Cocktail in the United Kingdom.

Today, Frito-Lay, which is owned by PepsiCo. Inc., controls more than half of the United States' salty snack foods market, selling Lay's along with Fritos, Doritos, Ruffles, Cheetos, and Rold Gold pretzels. The basic, original potato chip is still the top choice of 81 percent of consumers.

Vital Statistics
Parent Company Frito-Lay Inc.
Established 1932
Founder/Inventor Herman W. Lay
Employees 40,000 (2005)
Annual Sales $10,322 million (2005)

0 grams
Trans Fat
Lay's
BRAND
Classic
POTATO CHIPS
2005
BEST
TASTE
AWARD

La-Z-Boy Incorporated

In 1925, Edward Knabusch quit his job as a carpenter to create his own business. He set out to develop a new band-saw guide and hired his cousin Edwin Shoemaker, who was also a carpenter, to help him. They established Kna-Shoe Manufacturing Co. in 1927 to sell novelty and custom furniture, which they built in Knabusch's garage at home in Monroe, Michigan. The partners borrowed money and built a factory to accommodate the rapid growth, and in 1928, developed a folding porch recliner made of wood slats. The new product was the first of its kind and was an instant attraction. At the suggestion of a customer, they made an upholstered version of the porch recliner for indoor use that could be marketed year-round. The chair was a big hit—but it needed a name. To generate even more attention, the partners held a contest. Some of the suggestions they received were the Sit-N-Snooze, Slack-Back, and Comfort Carrier, but it was La-Z-Boy that won the contest.

LA-Z-BOY®

Business started to really take off with the stock market crash of 1929. With a hit product and a reputation as honest men and excellent woodworkers, Knabusch and Shoemaker's business thrived during the volatile period after the crash. Money was tight for everyone, and payment for furniture often came in the form of wheat, coal, and even cows.

Upon realizing that their retailers were making twice the profit they were, Edward and Edwin converted the company into a retail store. After joining the Michigan Chair Company, Floral City Furniture—as it was then called—tripled in size and had to expand production space. A circus tent was pitched in front of the building to display furniture, and people came from miles around to their "furniture shows." While other companies were focused on the hard sell, Floral City focused on entertaining the fearful public during the Depression. Manufacturers across the country tried to copy the popular La-Z-Boy, and ultimately they complained that Floral City was both a manufacturer and a retailer, thereby creating unfair competition. So in 1941, Edward and Edwin decided to separate the La-Z-Boy reclining chair factory from Floral City Furniture, and La-Z-Boy Chair Company was on its way and in a building of its own. But World War II began soon afterward, and the new building didn't produce a single recliner from 1941 to 1946. Instead, La-Z-Boy rented out garages to make tank seats and crash pads for the war.

The wooden outdoor recliner was just the beginning for the company that is now a leading U.S. furniture company and the leading global producer of reclining chairs. Through the years, La-Z-Boy has maintained its commitment to quality and innovation while expanding its product line, which now includes a complete line of upholstered furniture, wood furniture for bedrooms, dining rooms, rugs, and accessories—all in styles that range from traditional to contemporary. La-Z-Boy's success is a testament to its dedication to quality, style, and value and has, for almost 80 years, evolved with the consumer into a brand that is favored across every demographic.

Vital Statistics
Established 1925
Founders Edward Knabusch and Edwin Shoemaker
Employees 13,404 (2006)
Annual Sales $1,916.8 million (2006)

Levi Strauss & Co.

For more than 100 years, the name *Levi's* has been synonymous with "jeans." Even in today's overcrowded world of designer denims, Levi's stand out for their timeless quality, affordability, durability, and classic style.

The story behind the company is also classically American: Levi Strauss was a German immigrant who arrived in New York with his mother and sisters in 1847 to join his two older half-brothers in the dry goods business. His American dream changed the way people dress.

In 1853, during the California gold rush, Levi Strauss headed for San Francisco and established his own successful dry goods business. In 1872, a tailor in Nevada named Jacob Davis, who had bought fabric from Strauss, wrote him a letter describing his recent invention: a new way to rivet pocket corners onto men's pants. Davis suggested that the two men patent the process and go into business together. Strauss agreed, and with the help of Davis, who soon joined him in San Francisco, began manufacturing copper-riveted jeans—then called waist overalls—with denim from a mill in New Hampshire. When Strauss died at the age of 73, his nephews took over the business, with expansion in mind, and by the 1920s, Levi's waist overalls were the best-selling clothing product in the western states.

In 1928, the company registered the name *Levi's* as a trademark. With the success of western movies and the popularity of the iconic cowboy, sales of western clothing skyrocketed in the 1930s, and denim reached mainstream consumers for the first time. During World War II, American soldiers took their denim pants overseas, introducing the wardrobe staples to an expanding international audience. When the war was over, Levi's became associated worldwide with the leisure activities of a suddenly prosperous America. In the 1950s, Levi's went national. The pants gained notoriety as a symbol of youth, captured in enduring images of Marlon Brando and James Dean. The portrayal of young denim-clad "juvenile delinquents" in movies and on television led many principals to ban denim in schools, fearing mass rebellion against authority, but they were up against too big a force. One 1958 newspaper article reported, "About 90% of American youths wear jeans everywhere except 'in bed and in church.'" It was around this time that the word *overalls* was replaced by the word *jeans* in advertising and on labels because teenagers had cemented the change in their everyday vernacular.

Levi Strauss's original model of charitable giving, fair labor practices, and consistent quality carried the company through booming expansion and public ownership in subsequent decades, and when members of the Haas family, descendents of Levi Strauss, staged a leveraged buyout in 1985, Levi Strauss & Co. was the largest manufacturer of pants in the world. Today, the company is privately held by descendants of the family of Levi Strauss, one of the few companies of its kind to retain family ownership. In 2003, Levi Strauss & Co. celebrated the 150th anniversary of its founding and the 130th anniversary of the invention of blue jeans. Today, it is one of the world's largest brand-name clothing manufacturers, with sales in more than 110 countries around the globe.

Opposite: the oldest 501 jeans, dating to circa 1879. "XX" was the original name for the 501 jeans. Levi's® is a registered trademark of Levi Strauss & Co.

Vital Statistics
Classic Product Denim blue jeans
Established 1853
Founders Levi Strauss and Jacob Davis
Employees 9,635 (2005)
Annual Sales $4,125.2 million (2005)

Life Savers

With only ten calories each, Life Savers pack a satisfying sweetness into a neat little round package. Invented in 1912 by Clarence Crane, father of famous poet Hart Crane, Life Savers are distinctive because of their shape as well as their flavor. Cleveland-based Crane invented the ring-shaped hard candy because his main business, chocolate-making, suffered during the warm summer months. He came up with a round peppermint-flavored disc that wouldn't wilt in the heat, but he didn't have the proper machinery to manufacture it. He asked a pill-maker to press the candy into the proper shape. The pill-maker obliged, but found that his equipment worked more efficiently if the candies had a hole in the middle.

Crane decided to call the little white rings "Crane's Peppermint Life Savers" because of their resemblance to life preservers. The sinking of the Titanic that year had made life preservers foremost in peoples' minds. Popular myth has it that Life Savers were so named because Crane's daughter died by choking on a hard candy and the hole was included to prevent further instances of choking, but there is no evidence supporting that story.

Edward Noble bought the candy formula from Crane in 1913 for $2,900, renaming the business Mint Products Company and moving it to New York City. Noble also renamed the candy, calling it "Pep-O-Mint Life Savers," packaged it into rolls covered in tin foil, and sold each roll for five cents. To boost sales, he got shopkeepers in saloons, drug stores, barber shops, and restaurants to put the candy right next to the cash register. In 1924, Noble invented the first fruit-flavored Life Savers, lemon, lime, and orange, but he could manufacture them only as solid discs. By 1929, however, he was making them with holes in the middle.

The classic "Five Flavor" rolls made their debut in 1935. In addition to the original fruit flavors of lemon, lime, and orange, Noble added cherry and pineapple. This combination remained intact until 2003, when consumers were asked to vote on a new assortment of flavors. More than two million voters weighed in, ultimately keeping only cherry and pineapple from the original group, and adding raspberry, watermelon, and blackberry. Blackberry disappeared quickly, however, when consumers begged to have orange returned to the mix.

More than fifty flavors of Life Savers have been produced over the years. Butter Rum, Spear-O-Mint, and Wint-O-Green are among the more popular. When eaten in a dark room, Wint-O-Green Life Savers produce visible sparks caused by grinding wintergreen and sugar together. Discontinued flavors include Cola, Anise, Vi-O-Let, and Cl-O-Ve.

Life Savers was acquired by Wrigley's in 2004, and production is in Canada.

Vital Statistics
Parent Company Wm. Wrigley Jr. Company
Product Launch 1912
Headquarters Chicago, Illinois

ROLL CANDY
LIFESAVERS
PEPOMINT
14 CANDIES

ROLL CANDY
LIFESAVERS
BUTTER RUM
ARTIFICIAL FLAVOR

NEW FLAVORS!
ROLL CANDY
LIFESAVERS
5 FLAVOR
14 CANDIES

Lillian Vernon Corporation

Lillian Vernon is not your fusty great-aunt—in fact, much about this company, founded in 1951 by entrepreneur Lillian Vernon, is cutting edge. Today, Lillian Vernon is one of the country's most well-known mail and online catalogue, offering more than 6,000 gift, household, gardening, children's, and holiday items to gratified customers. Lillian Vernon sends out more than 80 million copies of its two mail-order catalogue titles, Lillian Vernon and Lilly's Kids, each year. In 2006, Lillian Vernon was acquired by Sun Capital Partners, and Lillian Vernon herself became a nonexecutive chairperson to maintain her strong ties to the company she created.

Lillian Vernon®

In 1937, Lillian Vernon and her family left Amsterdam to escape the Nazis, settling in New York City. In 1951, four months before the birth of her first child, Lillian decided to start a business out of her home. She set up shop at her kitchen table and, with $2,000 in wedding gift money, designed a belt and a purse. She placed a single advertisement in *Seventeen* magazine, offering her products with what was at the time an unusual twist: free monogramming. This ad provided $32,000 in sales, and her business was off and running. In 1954, the company was named formally—after Lillian herself and the town she lived in: Mount Vernon, New York. Lillian rented a warehouse, a building for the now extremely popular monogramming services, and another building to serve as a shipping department. Because of the reputation it garnered in a short time, Lillian Vernon soon began manufacturing and wholesaling stock for other, more well-established companies such as Revlon, Avon, and Elizabeth Arden.

The major shift in the company's fortunes came in 1956 when Lillian published her first catalogue. It was 16 pages long and sent out to 125,000 customers. The product line was simultaneously expanded to include personalized cufflinks, combs, buttons, and collar pins. By 1970, Lillian Vernon reported its first million dollars in sales. Before too long, the Mount Vernon operations could no longer house the business, and in 1988, a national distribution center was constructed in Virginia Beach, Virginia. The following year, a computer center was opened there, as well as the first Lillian Vernon outlet store where customers could buy heavily discounted overstock and discontinued items. The company went online in 1995, and expanded its distribution center one year later, bringing the total square footage to 821,000. That same year, HarperCollins published Lillian's autobiography, called *An Eye for Winners.* By the turn of the century, Lillian was named one of the 50 top female entrepreneurs in the world by the National Foundation for Women Business Owners.

In 2001, Lillian Vernon celebrated its 50th anniversary and launched its new Web site, a venture that was giving the print catalogue a run for its money. The company was named "One of the 100 Best Corporate Citizens" by *Business Ethics Magazine,* and the catalogue was named one of America's ten most popular. By 2002, the Web site was hailed by *Internet Retailer* as one of the top 25 retail Web sites. Lillian Vernon continues to offer free personalization and boasts one of the largest personalization departments in America. In 2006, more than 3.5 million products were customized using any one of 14 different types of personalization. Since its founding, the company has offered its 100% Customer Satisfaction Guarantee. If not fully satisfied, customers may request a replacement or refund, no questions asked, even if the product is personalized. When in 2006 Lillian Vernon was acquired by Sun Capital, it was firmly established as one of America's retail success stories, thanks to a soon-to-be mother who wanted a way to keep busy and earn some extra money for her growing family.

Vital Statistics
Parent Company Sun Capital Partners
Classic Product mail-order catalogue
Product Launch 1951
Annual Sales $175 million (2006)

Lipitor

Lipitor—the top cholesterol-lowering drug on the market—has saved countless lives since its inception and will save millions more in years to come. Manufactured by pharmaceutical giant Pfizer, Lipitor is fighting one of America's great health problems: high cholesterol. One in five American adults suffers from cholesterol that is dangerously high, and some people with high cholesterol have inherited the tendency and cannot control their cholesterol levels by exercise and diet alone. In fact, for up to two-thirds of high cholesterol sufferers, this is the case, which is why Lipitor has become such a lifesaver.

Lipitor is a drug called a statin, and the history of statins began in Japan in 1971. A doctor working for a drug company in Tokyo decided he wanted to create a drug that would lower cholesterol, which is made by the body in the liver with the assistance of an enzyme called HMG-CoA. Until Dr. Endo began his undertaking, no researchers had been able to find a compound that would keep the enzyme from being vigorously produced. After years of work, Endo and his team discovered mevastatin, the first compound found to fight cholesterol. The chief scientist at Merck, P. Roy Vagelos, was intrigued by Endo's findings and duplicated his experiments in the United States. His team also discovered another cholesterol-fighting compound: lovastatin. Merck had the difficult job of convincing Americans that high cholesterol was a deadly problem once it put lovastatin on the market. People began to use terms such as HDL (high-density lipoprotein) and LDL (low-density lipoprotein), and other drug companies began exploring the possibilities of statins.

In 1982, a man named Bruce Roth, a post-doctoral fellow in chemistry at the University of Rochester, synthesized a statin that was very similar to Endo. Warner-Lambert, the company known for Visine, Listerine, and Schick, invited him to join the pharmaceutical branch of the company. By 1984, Roth was the head of an eighteen-person team of scientists devoted to researching statins. In 1985, Roth synthesized Lipitor, forever changing the health of millions of people all over the world. After some skepticism from company executives, tests proved conclusively that even the lowest effective dose for humans, 10 milligrams, reduced bad cholesterol by 38 percent. Knowing it needed a big gun in pharmaceuticals to help it market Lipitor, Warner-Lambert joined forces with Pfizer to market Lipitor as a team. Lipitor was significantly more effective than its rapidly encroaching competition, making it very appealing to medical professionals. It was also priced lower, making it more affordable for a greater number of people. Lipitor was first available to consumers in early 1997. Between mid-1997 and mid-1998, the stocks of Warner-Lambert and Pfizer rose 83 percent and 102 percent respectively, causing Wall Street to nickname Lipitor the "Turbostatin." In 1999, Pfizer acquired Warner-Lambert in the biggest drug company takeover of all time.

The future looks bright for Lipitor—and the millions of people whose cholesterol is kept in check with it. Today, Pfizer focuses on physicians and patient education about the benefits of Lipitor in reducing the risk of heart attacks and strokes by lowering bad cholesterol in your blood. Lipitor's sales grow every year, and Roth remains at Pfizer, responsible for a large part of the company's $7.6 billion research and development budget. The product he gave to the world, however, is likely to be his greatest accomplishment in terms of the number of gratified customers.

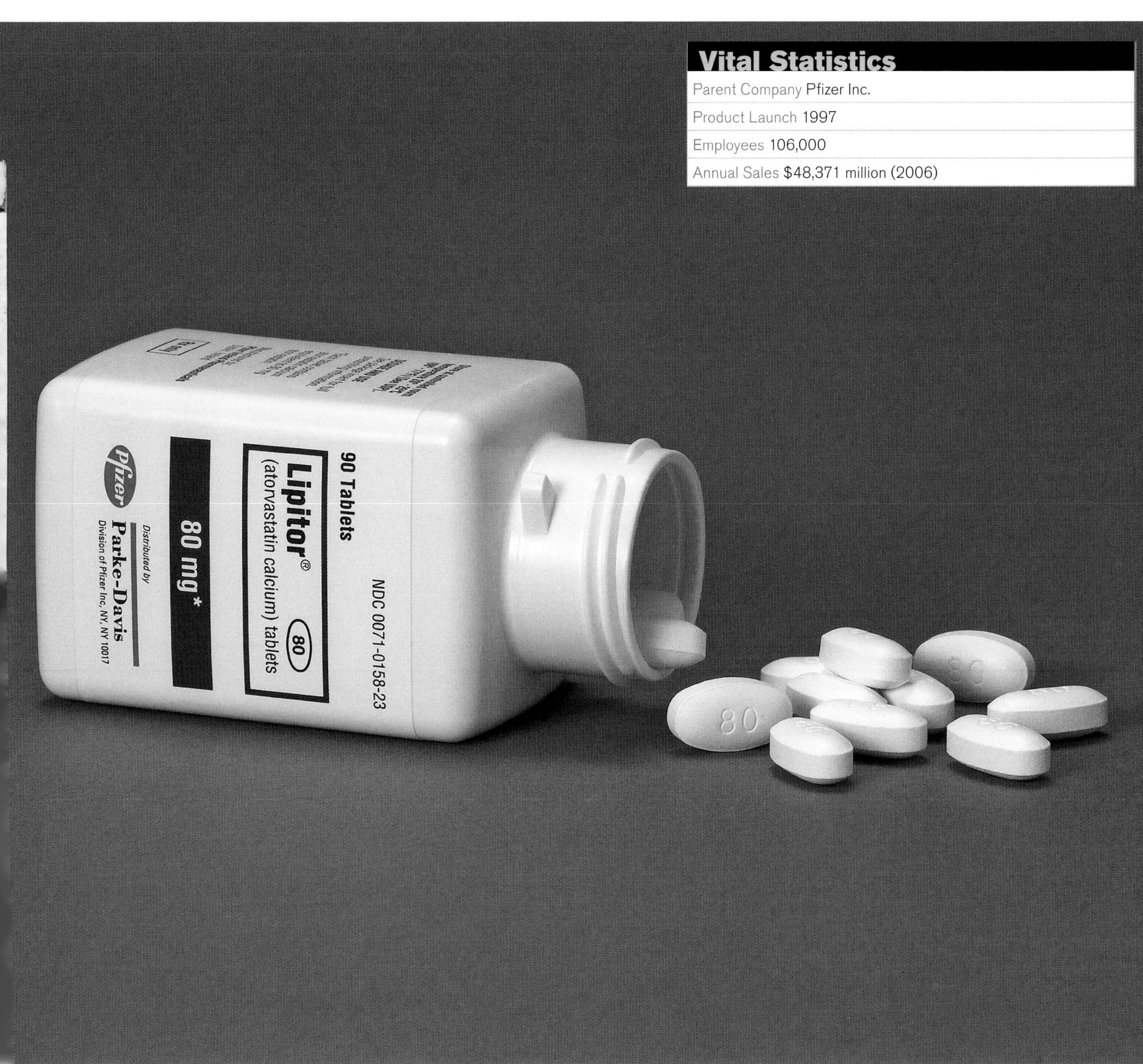

Vital Statistics

Parent Company Pfizer Inc.

Product Launch 1997

Employees 106,000

Annual Sales $48,371 million (2006)

Lipton

Lipton is virtually synonymous with tea. In fact, it is the standard-bearer, the first tea many people ever try, and a staple in kitchen cabinets all over the world. Owned by British and Dutch company Unilever, Lipton is one of the world's most recognizable brands, from classic tea bags to more current offerings, such as canned and bottled iced teas, leaf teas, and infusions. Lipton is the global leader in tea.

The Lipton tea company was started by a British man named Sir Thomas Lipton. It grew quickly into the largest producer of tea in the world, and the company owns tea plantations in India, Tanzania, and Kenya. Lipton also buys tea on the world's tea markets. The best-selling variety of Lipton tea is Lipton Yellow Label, which is sold with a band reading "Quality Number 1." Today, Unilever sells about 20 percent of the world's tea, with brands such as Beseda and PG Tips, although Lipton represents half of that amount—a full 10 percent of the world's market. Lipton teas are available in 110 countries in North America, Europe, the Middle East, Africa, and Asia. The company's Pure Leaf Iced Tea is sold through Lipton's partnership with Pepsi. In the past, Lipton has sold other products with the Lipton name, including soups and pastas. However, because of the company's desire to focus on tea, Unilever has switched these products to other brand names, such as Knorr.

In recent years, Lipton has made a real commitment to environmental issues. In growing their tea, and in deciding who to buy it from, Lipton is a firm believer in sustainable farming practices. Lipton has instituted a number of special programs worldwide to support these causes. One program is called the Trees 2000 program, which entails Lipton planting 40,000 indigenous trees each year in Kenya as a way to help combat deforestation caused by modern society. Lipton is also enjoying increasing success because of recent studies touting tea's health benefits. One independent panel of nutrition experts determined that unsweetened leaf tea is a smart beverage choice to help consumers limit their calorie intake from beverages. Tea has also been found to contain flavonoid antioxidants, which can help the body protect itself against free radicals. Lipton's current slogan, "Drink Better, Live Better," reflects this information and the company's desire to spread it. Lipton is also making a strong stand in the ready-to-drink category. Its classic Lipton Iced Tea has much less sugar than carbonated beverages, and consumer demand has led Lipton to lower it even further, by 10 percent. The Lipton Brisk and Lipton Fusion lines are growing in popularity; other options can be served either hot or cold, and still others are available in exotic fruit flavors, as well as green tea. Old-fashioned leaf tea is making a comeback too. New Lipton Pyramid tea bags with long leaf tea and real fruit pieces deliver a better tea infusion and the invention of Cold Brew bags allows users to brew iced tea in minutes without boiling any water.

Besides being the world's second-favorite beverage after water, tea is healthful, affordable, simple to prepare, and delicious. Unsweetened tea naturally has zero calories, and studies show that drinking tea may well, over time, be good for the heart. A cup of tea has less than half the caffeine of a cup of coffee, and as for Lipton's role in spreading the word, the numbers speak for themselves: 1,649 cups of Lipton tea are drunk every second of the day.

Vital Statistics

Parent Company Unilever U.S.

Founder Thomas Lipton

Lipton
100% Natural Tea
NEW LOOK
Same Great Taste
150mg PROTECTIVE ANTIOXIDANTS
NATURALLY PER SERVING
SEE BACK FOR DETAILS
AOX
Lipton
100% Natural Tea
FINEST QUALITY TEA
SINCE 1879
100 TEA BAGS NET WT 8 OZ (226g)
Serve HOT or ICED

Listerine

Necessity is the mother of invention, they say, and Listerine—like so many great inventions—was discovered almost by accident. The year was 1879, and two men, Dr. Joseph Lawrence and Jordan Wheat Lambert, concocted an amber-colored liquid to be used as a disinfectant in surgical procedures. They named their product Listerine, after English physician Sir Joseph Lister, who performed the first-ever antiseptic surgery in 1865. At the time, Listerine filled an important niche, and in 1884, Lambert formed the Lambert Company to produce Listerine for the medical community.

Listerine's destiny was changed, however, when hospital workers discovered how effectively it killed germs in the mouth. In 1895, the Lambert Company began marketing Listerine to dentists as a powerful oral antiseptic. Designed to kill the germs that cause plaque, gingivitis, and bad breath, Listerine is a blend of four oils: thymol, menthol, eucalyptol, and methyl salicylate. By 1914, Listerine was one of the first prescription products available over the counter and had effectively created the new world of mouthwash. Soon, competitors appeared. Lambert's son Gerard, who had taken over leadership of the company, launched an advertising campaign to tout Listerine's superiority. He introduced Americans to the concept of (and the word itself) halitosis—and began a nearly century-long promotion of Listerine as bad breath's most powerful foe. In the 1930s Listerine created such famous slogans as "Always a bridesmaid, never a bride," and in the 1970s "The taste you hate twice a day." It was not until 1983 that Listerine felt the need to add new claims to distinguish it from the competition; "Listerine fights plaque" then became the siren song to consumers. In 1987, Listerine was the first nonprescription mouthwash to earn the American Dental Association's Seal of Acceptance for fighting plaque and gingivitis. In 1992, Listerine reached out to a younger audience with its wildly popular Cool Mint flavor. When Cool Mint was launched, television commercials featured a bottle swinging through the trees like Tarzan. These commercials won both the youth market and Effie Awards for advertising effectiveness. Another successful ad campaign was created by Australian J. Walter Thompson. The first commercial showed Listerine exploding inside a man's mouth along with the slogan "It's dynamite against germs." These commercials have been largely responsible for generating consumer acceptance of mouthwash as an important part of everyday hygiene and have made Listerine the world's most popular mouthwash. In the mid-1990s, when Scope listed Rosie O'Donnell as America's least-kissable celebrity, she teamed up with Listerine to give money to charity every time she kissed someone on her talk show. This provided positive publicity for Listerine and harsh publicity for Scope, which O'Donnell disparaged on her show. In 2000, Pfizer acquired Warner-Lambert, the company formed in 1955 when Lambert joined forces with William Warner to form the Warner-Lambert Pharmaceutical Company.

Today, Listerine has a wide range of products in many sizes to meet every mouthwash need, from Cool Mint to Antiseptic, FreshBurst to Whitening, and more. In 2006, Johnson & Johnson bought Pfizer's consumer health care unit, including one of its most famous offerings: Listerine. More than one billion people have tried Listerine.

Vital Statistics

Parent Company Johnson & Johnson

Inventors Dr. Joseph Lawrence and Jordan Wheat Lambert

Established 1879

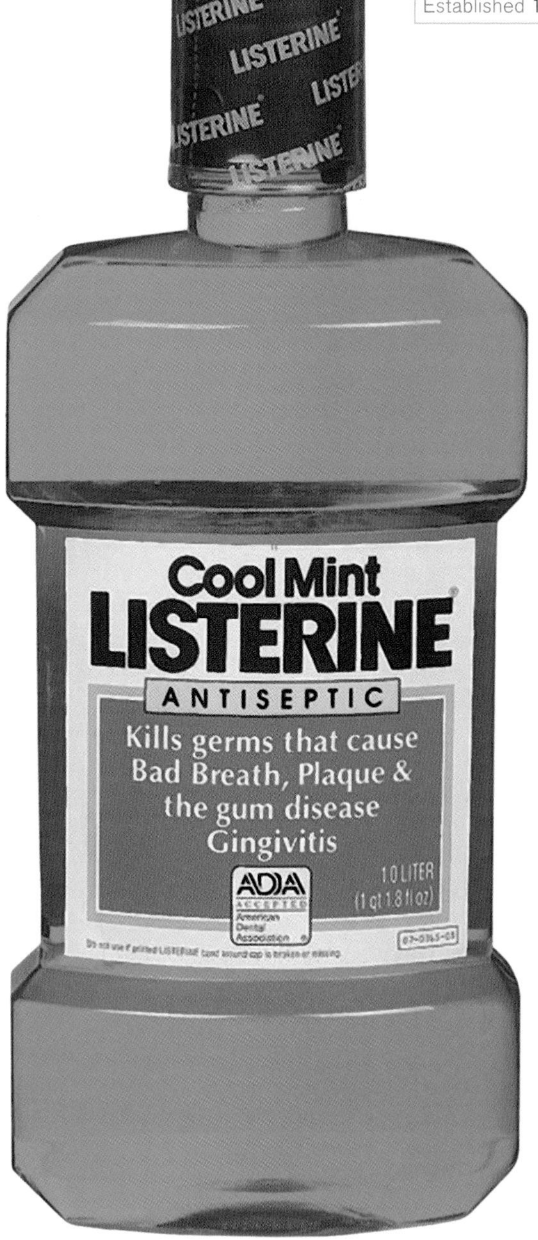

L.L. BEAN

Nothing evokes the rugged outdoor life like L.L. Bean. For decades, L.L. Bean has provided the wardrobe and gear to comfortably tackle the great outdoors. It all started back in 1911, when Leon Leonwood (L.L.) Bean, an avid outdoorsman, returned from a hunting trip with cold, damp feet. He decided to create a comfortable, durable boot for exploring the woods of Maine. He got a local cobbler to stitch leather uppers to workmen's rubber boots, and the Maine Hunting Shoe was born. This innovative boot changed outdoor footwear forever and was the start of one of the most successful family-run businesses in the country.

L.L.Bean

L.L. began his business in the basement of his brother's apparel shop in Freeport, Maine. In 1912, he obtained a mailing list of nonresidents of Maine with a Maine hunting license and prepared a three-page flier that proclaimed, "You cannot expect success hunting deer or moose if your feet are not properly dressed." He went on to extol the virtues of his new Maine Hunting Shoe, which was created by a hunter with satisfaction guaranteed. The public liked this approach, and he received 100 orders for the boot. Unfortunately there was a problem. The rubber bottoms separated from the leather uppers, and 90 of the 100 pairs were returned. L.L. kept his word and refunded the full price of the boot, and went back to the drawing board. He borrowed money, fixed the problem, and sent out more brochures. Though this episode nearly put him out of business, he learned the importance of personally testing the product, honesty in advertising, and that the customer must always be satisfied, no matter what. The customer-based service, created back in 1912, set L.L. Bean apart and is still a fundamental part of the company nearly 100 years later.

The company grew and quickly became the place for high-quality outdoor equipment and expert advice. The product line expanded to include nonshoe apparel, sporting gear, and fishing and camping equipment. Its focus was simple: provide high-quality products backed by excellent customer service. By 1934, the company had increased its factory size to 13,000 square feet and their flier had evolved into a 52-page catalogue. Although most of the sales came from the catalogue, the company generated more than 70 percent of the volume of the Freeport Post Office, hunters and visitors regularly stopped by, and a night bell allowed for late-night visitors to call on a watchman or L.L. himself. In 1951, L.L. opened the store 365 days a year, 24 hours a day, a schedule the flagship store in Freeport, Maine, continues to keep.

In 1967, L.L.'s grandson, Leon Gorman, took the beloved Maine company and grew it into a multi-channel outdoor retailing giant with sales surpassing one billion dollars per year. In 1992, the company opened its first store in Japan and in 1995, it entered the electronic commerce market by launching llbean.com. In 2000, L.L.Bean expanded its retail presence beyond its famous flagship store for the first time. With retail stores in Virginia, Maryland, and New Jersey, L.L. Bean continues to be a world leader in the mail order and retail industries. L.L.Bean's commitment to customer service and quality, firmly established by its founder, L.L., has made it the premier place to shop for outdoor apparel and sporting goods equipment for nearly a century.

Vital Statistics

Established	1912
Founder	Leon Leonwood Bean
Employees	3,900 (2005)
Annual Sales	$1,440 million (2005)

M&M'S

M&M'S Plain Chocolate Candies—yes, the ones that "melt in your mouth"—have rather romantic origins. Legend has it they were conceived of by Forrest E. Mars, Sr. during the Spanish Civil War when he encountered soldiers eating pellets of chocolate encased in a hard sugary coating that kept the chocolate from melting. Mr. Mars returned to his kitchen in the United States and invented what the whole world now knows as M&M'S.

The small chocolate candies were first manufactured in 1940, when Forrest E. Mars Sr. formed the company in Newark, New Jersey, after a falling-out with his father Frank Mars, who owned the Mars company. Mars took the initials of his and his colleague Bruce Murrie's last names to form the company name and what were to become the defining letters on the namesake candy. The candies were originally made in six colors: red, orange, yellow, green, brown, and violet. In 1949, violet was replaced by tan. M&M'S were first sold in cardboard tubes in 1941 and as Mars had foreseen, became a favorite of the American soldiers serving in World War II. By the end of the decade, M&M'S were widely available to the public, and in 1948, they were first sold in the characteristic brown pouch that has barely changed since. Television helped the candy's popularity skyrocket.

In 1954, the country met the M&M'S characters for the first time on television—giant M&M'S with arms, legs, voices, and personalities—and heard the catchy slogan "The milk chocolate melts in your mouth—not in your hand." This year also saw the debut of the wildly popular Peanut M&M'S. Many Americans will recall the controversy of 1976, when the red-dye scares caused red M&M'S, which did not actually use the dangerous coloring, to be removed from the traditional color mix because of consumer fears. Even more will be aware of the racy reputation of green M&M'S, although there are no known facts to back up claims that the candy has aphrodisiac qualities. In 1981, M&M'S were included in the food supply of the first space shuttle astronauts by their unanimous choice—the candies are now on permanent display at the space food exhibit of the National Air & Space Museum in Washington, D.C. The early 1980s saw the launch of the first holiday lines: red and green for Christmas, and pastel colors for Easter. Also in the 1980s, M&M'S went international, targeting Europe and competing with tubes of similarly designed Smarties. In 1987, red was returned to the mix because of the overwhelming number of customer requests, and in the 1990s, Peanut Butter and Almond M&M'S made their debuts. In 1995, the company launched an unprecedented project, asking consumers to help select a new color of M&M'S. Blue won by a landslide, with 54 percent of the more than ten million votes cast. Also in 1995, M&M'S Chocolate Mini Baking Bits and Minis, which are sold in reclosable plastic tubes, were introduced. Recent developments have included COLORWORKS, displays in specialty stores allowing buyers to select up to 20 colors of M&M'S to tie into any occasion; Crispy M&M'S; and a partnership with the Susan G. Komen Breast Cancer Foundation involving the creation of a temporary pink and white color blend to raise awareness of the cause.

In 1964, Forrest merged M&M'S with his father's business. Today Mars is an $18 billion business and M&M'S one of its the flagship brands. The company operates in more than 65 countries and—amazingly for a company of this size—is still privately owned by descendants of the original Mars father and son. It is one of the largest "small family businesses" in the world.

Vital Statistics

Classic Product	Chocolate Candies
Inventor	Forrest E. Mars, Sr.
Employees	39,000
Annual Sales	$18 billion
Year Founded	1925

Macy's

Macy's is the classic American department store. It would be difficult to find an American who has not set foot in a Macy's branch, and each year millions of people from all over the world visit the flagship New York Macy's, one of the largest department stores anywhere. There are more than 400 Macy's in thirty-three states, and Macy's, under the auspices of parent company Federated Department Stores, also owns Rich's/Lazarus/Goldsmith's, Bloomingdale's, Burdines, The Bon Marché, and Stern's. The recent addition of Macy's.com and Macy's by Mail have allowed to company to reach even more consumers worldwide.

In 1858, an entrepreneur named Rowland Hussey Macy opened a dry goods store on the corner of 14th Street and 6th Avenue in New York City. It was called R.H. Macy & Co., and was to become one of the most significant department stores in the world. Macy had been a sailor and chose a red star to symbolize his company and its success. On the first day the store was open, Macy took in a mere $11.06 in sales, but had grossed almost a hundred thousand dollars by the end of the first year of operations. By 1887, Macy's was one of the city's leading department stores. By 1902, Macy's had grown so substantially that it needed new space. The company relocated to its present location at Herald Square. In 1922, Macy's went public and began its march toward expansion, opening its first regional stores and acquiring other, smaller stores under the Macy's umbrella such as Toledo-based LaSalle & Kock and Atlanta-based Davison-Paxton. By this point, the company was selling more than $36 million in merchandise annually. By 1924, Macy's was billing itself as "The World's Largest Store," with more than a million square feet of retail space. That same year, the company held its first Christmas Parade, which later became the famous Thanksgiving Parade, featuring floats, zoo animals, and more than 10,000 fans, lining the streets in support of the store. In 1946, Macy's introduced another event in California that was to become a world-famous trademark: the annual flower show, which hit New York for the first time in 1950. In 1970, the Macy's in New York City's Union Square became the first to organize its lower level into "The Cellar." The flagship store followed five years later, and other Macy's outposts have adopted the format since. Macy's was acquired by Federated Department Stores in 1994, allowing the company to exceed founder R.H.'s wildest dreams, with Macy's stores all over the country. In the following years, A & S Department Stores, I. Magnin stores, Jordan Marsh stores, Sterns stores, and others, all were converted into Macy's.

Today, Macy's is a household name, but it has never strolled far from the dreams and beliefs of its founder, even in its widespread expansion. Macy's was the first retailer to make a woman a top executive, pioneered the one-price system, promoting fairness and equality yet again, and has been at the forefront of retail innovations such as the tea bag and colored bath towels. Macy's also was the first retailer to hold a New York City liquor license. Macy's future looks as bright as the lights of New York City, where it began so many decades ago.

Vital Statistics
Parent Company Federated Department Stores
Product Launch 1858
Employees 232,000
Annual Sales $ 22,390 million (2006)

MACY'S

Maidenform

The story of Maidenform is far more than a history of a dynamic company. It is the story of a company founded on innovative products, consumer-driven marketing, inventive advertising, and an emotional connection with women. It began in 1922 with Ida Rosenthal and Enid Bissett, partners in Enid Frocks, a custom dress business in New York. The country was just coming out of the flapper era, and the flat-chested look was popular. But Bissett believed that a dress fit better over a natural bust line. She restructured the boyish form bandeau to have two cups separated by a center piece of elastic. Ida's husband, William Rosenthal, further refined the style, filing the patent for the first uplift brassiere in 1926.

MAIDENFORM®

The "Maiden Form Brassiere" was born, and was then built into each dress. Clients started requesting separate brassieres, prompting Enid Frocks to offer a bonus undergarment with every dress sold. To create a demand for their products, the Rosenthals placed ads in newspapers, national magazines, and other media, making Maidenform the first intimate apparel company to advertise. The company continued to innovate and develop new and better brassieres. In 1942, William Rosenthal filed the patent for the adjustable strap fastener, a design that is still used today. Then, in 1949, Maidenform launched the ground-breaking "I Dreamed" advertising campaign. These ads, which ran for 20 years, revolutionized intimate apparel advertising by featuring women in their bras acting out fantasies of independence in public places. In the late 1970s, Maidenform introduced a new campaign geared toward the new attitudes of women entering the workforce. The ads pictured women wearing Maidenform products in unexpected settings and carried the tagline, "The Maidenform Woman. You Never Know Where She'll Turn Up." In the 1990s, Maidenform made a strategic move in the marketplace by purchasing Flexees and Lilyette, enabling the company to expand its product line with other, non-conflicting brands. Flexees is still the number one brand in shapewear, while Lilyette, designed for the full-figured woman, has become the company's fastest growing brand. As Maidenform entered the 21st century, it continued its quest to reinvent and challenge itself by once again re-inventing the bra. The company's One Fabulous Fit line, combining the latest innovations in comfort and support with technologically advanced fabrics, quickly became the number one selling bra in department stores nationwide. Maidenform also introduced an updated "Dream" advertising campaign that recalled the heritage of the original "I Dreamed" campaign and reinforced Maidenform's emotional bond with many different types of women.

Today Maidenform sells some of the most recognized brands in the intimate apparel industry: Maidenform, Flexees, Lilyette, Sweet Nothings, Self Expressions, Bodymates, Rendezvous, and Subtract. Maidenform has had a long and rich history. And, as Maidenform's unrelenting commitment to innovation and understanding what women want makes clear, its future promises to further build upon its successful products and brands.

Vital Statistics
Sstablished 1922
Founders Enid Bissett and Ida Rosenthal
Annual Sales $382 million
Headquarters Bayonne, New Jersey

Manischewitz

Manischewitz has been providing premium kosher foods for more than a hundred years and can be found in virtually every kosher kitchen worldwide. In fact, Manischewitz is the world's top producer of matzo and sells many other types of kosher food as well. If you shop and cook kosher, you know this company's quality, variety, and overall excellence. Its reputation speaks for itself.

In 1888, a Cincinnati rabbi named Dov Behr opened a bakery to make and sell matzo. He had been making it at home for friends and family for years, and the positive response inspired him to go into business to make his beloved matzo available to a wider audience. Behr was observant, and his desire to provide matzo for Passover was motivated by his religious beliefs. As his business, somewhat unexpectedly, took off, he pledged to maintain his commitment to the devout Jews who had been his earliest customers. By the turn of the century, Behr's matzo had become so popular that the company began producing it in gas-fired ovens instead of coal stoves. The gas-fired ovens allowed for much greater temperature control, ensuring a consistently satisfying product. Behr also introduced portable traveling-tunnel ovens and began packaging his matzo so that it could be shipped outside of the vicinity of the bakery's neighborhood. As a result of international demand, Behr began shipping his matzo overseas to countries such as England, France, Hungary, Egypt, New Zealand, and even Japan.

In 1932, a second factory was built in Jersey City, New Jersey, to meet the growing demand. The Jersey City location introduced Behr's product to large Jewish communities throughout the northeast. Before long, Manischewitz foods were being sold in ethnic grocery stores and delis in all of the large cities along the East Coast. Soon, the Cincinnati factory closed, and all operations were shifted to the new location. In 1940, Manischewitz introduced its first non-matzo product: the Tam Tam cracker. That year, the company also made a licensing agreement allowing it to sell Manischewitz wine. In 1954, the company acquired a large processing plant in Vineland, New Jersey, which allowed it to begin manufacturing a wide variety of new products, from canned chicken soup to jarred gefilte fish and borscht. Today, workers at the Vineland facility pack about 2 million pounds of fish and 1 million pounds of beets each year. Manischewitz continued to grow, adding products to its line of kosher foods and creating generations of loyal, grateful customers who wanted to prepare and serve the foods of their childhood and heritage but didn't necessarily have the skill or the time to do so in their busy, modern lives. In 1998, the Manischewitz Company was acquired by R.A.B. Holdings, a private company. R.A.B. owns and oversees Manischewitz. In 2004, the company changed its name from The B. Manischewitz Company LLC to RAB Food Group LLC.

Manischewitz is poised for a bright future as the leader in the kosher food market worldwide and is making steps to bring its products to a non-kosher audience as well. Manischewitz makes high quality kosher foods, from the original matzo to pasta, cookies, preserves, and soup, some of which are sold in the general sections of grocery stores. Manischewitz wine has become a staple at celebrations. The company shares its profits with Jewish organizations everywhere and prides itself on its good works in the Jewish community and beyond.

Vital Statistics
Parent Company R.A.B. Holdings Inc.
Classic Product matzo
Product Launch 1888
Employees 1810
Annual Sales $508.5 million (2005)

MANISCHEWITZ
MANISCHEWITZ
יין מבושל
AMERICAN
CONCORD
GRAPE
SPECIALLY SWEETENED, CONTAINING
NOT LESS THAN 51% CONCORD
כשר לפסח
KOSHER
FOR PASSOVER
UNDER STRICT SUPERVISION BY THE UNION OF
ORTHODOX JEWISH CONGREGATIONS OF AMERICA
ALC. 11% BY VOL • 750ML

Master Lock

At the beginning of the 20th century, most padlocks were flimsy pieces of metal, hollow and easily broken. Harry Soref, a military consultant in World War I, thought a tough padlock made of the same layered laminated steel as a battleship would revolutionize the household lock. In 1921, he opened his company, Master Lock, and he patented the world's first laminated padlock in 1924. His tiny Wisconsin headquarters housed a drill press, a punch press, and a grinder. Each Master Lock padlock was imprinted with the company's logo—a lion's head with bared teeth.

Demand for heavy-duty locks skyrocketed in the Prohibition years that followed. Federal authorities across the country ordered hundreds of thousands of Master Lock padlocks to lock down bars and clubs that served alcohol. Business was so good that Soref moved his company from a one-room shop to the Pabst Brewery, which had been shut down during Prohibition. In 1931, Harry Soref received the gold medal from the American Association of Master Locksmiths for making the greatest contribution to the development of locks in more than 50 years.

The toughness of Master Lock padlocks intrigued escape artist Harry Houdini. Legend has it that Houdini consulted with Soref on how to escape from a set of handcuffs. (Soref advised him to put the key under his tongue and between his fingers.) Until his death in 1957, Soref continued to consult on padlock construction, develop stronger and tougher padlock designs, and expand his product offerings to include specialty locks for use in schools, hospitals, and offices, and on vending machines. By that time, Master Lock had become the biggest manufacturer of locks in the country.

In 1970, Master Lock was purchased by American Brands (renamed Fortune Brands in 1997), which perpetuated Master Lock's reputation for toughness and durability. Super Bowl commercials in the decades to follow featured the Master Lock padlock being blasted by a high-power rifle, abused by hammers and crowbars, and crunched by a huge truck. Nothing succeeded in defeating the Master Lock, reinforcing the iconic "Tough Under Fire" brand positioning.

Today, Master Lock is the world's largest padlock manufacturer, with approximately 65 million locks sold each year. The company, challenged by inexpensive overseas competitors, seeks to compete through innovation rather than mere cost cutting. In recent years the company has introduced rust-proof locks, Titanium padlocks, and light-up dial combination locks, and has extended the brand into adjacent security categories including automotive, storage security, TSA-accepted luggage locks, and bicycle and power sports locking products. The Master Lock brand is guaranteed by a limited lifetime warranty. The company plans to grow and strengthen its brand by focusing on automotive and sporting-goods products.

Vital Statistics
Classic Product padlocks
Established 1921
Founder Harry Soref
Headquarters Oak Creek, Wisconsin
Annual Sales $300 million

Match.com

Match.com is the world's number one dating and relationship site. Launched on the web in April 1995, Match.com is at the forefront of a cultural shift that has fundamentally changed the way that people connect, communicate, and find love. On Match.com, single adults post profiles with photos and information about themselves, as well as their preferences regarding a potential date. At the click of a mouse, they can see and read about their most likely matches, often numbering in the hundreds, and paid subscribers can elect to contact the members they find most appealing.

match.com®

Contact between members on the site is done using an anonymous username and a Match.com email address. Every profile and photo is screened for appropriateness before it is posted to the site. Match.com is a fun, efficient, and effective way for eligible single people to meet and get to know each other. The company boasts more than 15 million members in 240 countries and has local country sites in 18 different languages. More than 60,000 new people regiser on Match.com every day, and each month, on average, March.com receives news of more than 400 marriages or engagements from members or former members.

Match.com was one of the first online dating sites, pioneered by Gary Kremen in San Francisco, with help from Peng Ong and Simon Glinsky in 1995. In 1998, Match.com was purchased by IAC/InterActiveCorp, giving it even greater resources. Match.com is now known to be the world's leading online relationship site, according to industry-leading independent measurement firm comScore Media Metrix and Guinness World Records.

In 2006, Match.com launched its partnership with Dr. Phil McGraw. Created specifically for Match.com, *MindFindBind* with Dr. Phil is a Web-based program designed to educate singles about the ins and outs of dating and relationships. Dr. Phil's signature insight is delivered via video modules, podcasts, audio tips and techniques, workbooks, and more.

Additionally, the company offers Match.com Mobile, a wireless dating service, available through Cingular/AT&T Wireless, Nextel, and Sprint. People can search, flirt, and connect with other eligible singles—all through their mobile phones. Match.com powers online dating for MSN across the U.S., Europe, Asia, and Latin America, and is the premier personals provider for Love@AOL, offering the Match.com service on both AOL and Netscape.

The company, led by CEO Jim Safka, based in Dallas, with offices all over the world, continues to grow and innovate. March.com reported revenue of $311.2 million in 2006, and nearly 1.3 million paying subscribers in 2006.

MindFindBind™ is a trademark of Match.com, L.P.

Vital Statistics

Parent Company	IAC, InterActiveCorp.
Classic Product	dating service
Established	1995
Founder	Gary Kremen
Employees	250
Annual Sales	$311.2 million (2006)

Maytag Dairy Farms

Maytag Dairy Farms started producing its world-famous blue cheese in Iowa in 1941 with milk from a prizewinning herd of Holstein cattle. The herd of show cattle was established in 1919 by E. H. Maytag, son of the founder of the Maytag appliance company. The Maytag Holsteins gained famed from competition across North America in the 1930s.

Fred Maytag II, who succeeded his father in 1940, had heard about a new process for making blue cheese. Developed by Iowa State University, the process is still used by Maytag today. Using fresh, sweet milk from Iowa dairy farms, it is a slow process that entails making cheese by hand in small batches. The mold that colors and flavors the distinctive veins in the cheese, *penicillum roqueforti,* is added to the milk and then sprinkled on the curds as the cheese solidifies. Then the cheesemaker pierces each wheel with needles to give the mold air channels to bloom in. Each batch of cheese, in the form of 4-pound wheels encased in wax, is meticulously monitored during the long months of aging until the optimal flavor is reached and it is ready for market. Its uses are myriad. Professional and home cooks from coast to coast delight in the creamy texture and tangy taste of this classic American food. It is featured in the classic blue cheese salad dressing, in blue cheese stuffed olives for Martinis, blue cheese and watercress soup, dipping sauce for Buffalo chicken wings, and even blue cheese quesadillas.

Considered by cheese experts and food editors to be the finest American blue cheese and ranked among the best cheeses in the world, the famed Maytag blue cheese is still made by hand, aging in caves twice as long as most other blue cheeses. In fact the some of the cows that produce the milk to make the cheese, though no longer raised by the farm, are direct descendants of the original herd.

Maytag cheese is still made in the tradition that it was when the farm started making it back in 1941. The Maytag family still owns and operates the farm, where they make and age blue cheese. Maytag Dairy Farms also produces Swiss cheese, Edam, and Natural White Cheddar, at other locations.

Vital Statistics
Classic Product Maytag Blue Cheese
Established 1941
Founder E. H. Maytag

CAVE RIPENED
Maytag
BLUE CHEESE
INGREDIENTS:
MILK, CHEESE CULTURE, SALT,
ENZYMES, PENICILLIUM
ROQUEFORTI
NEWTON, IOWA 50208

McCulloch

McCulloch is one of the world's top producers of garden tools that operate with two-stroke gas engines, and many yards look beautiful thanks to the company's trimmers, brush cutters, chainsaws, and hedge trimmers. Owned by AB Electrolux, the company responsible for some of the most well-known household appliances, including Eureka and Frigidaire, McCulloch is a force to be reckoned with in its own right. Electrolux products can be found in ninety countries worldwide and counting, and McCulloch aspires to reach such impressive numbers in years to come.

The year was 1946, the product: power tools. Robert Paxton McCulloch launched his company with a line of small, two-stroke gasoline engines, producing its first chainsaws in 1948. The chainsaws took off, and McCulloch decided to focus on other household power tools, filling a niche in the market at the same time. McCulloch then developed a centrifugal supercharger for use in automobiles. In 1956, the division producing these was renamed and then eventually sold, but they helped McCulloch's reputation grow. In the 1970s, McCulloch began making hedge and string trimmers and leaf blowers, expanding the line while maintaining the focus on yard and garden equipment. A difficult year for McCulloch was 1998, as the company had to declare bankruptcy. However, a miraculous recovery was not long in coming.

In 1999, McCulloch was acquired by a Taiwanese company called Jenn Feng Industrial Co. Ltd. Under the auspices of Jenn Feng, McCulloch began manufacturing new electric power tools with a wider focus, including drills and sanders. The company then introduced a greatly expanded line, featuring upgraded, modern, electric lawn and garden tools, power tools, and lighting products. Today, only two employees remain from the 2,000 who had been employed prior to the company's Chapter 11 days. Because of customer-friendly steps such as all-encompassing warranty-reimbursement and the honoring of all dealers' claims, as well as the solid grounding of McCulloch's new parent company, the McCulloch name has maintained its integrity. In fact, the rebounding has been so thorough and impressive that even industry experts have been taken by surprise. It seems clear that a firm commitment to exceptional customer service, quality parts, and relationships with dealers built on a foundation of mutual trust are factors that consumers don't take lightly. The McCulloch Dealer Hotline, staffed by technical experts and customer service professionals, is still another indication of McCulloch's desire to remain a force to be reckoned with.

For more than sixty years and counting, McCulloch has been ensuring Americans that they are capable of maintaining homes and yards on their own, with reliable power equipment and a company's commitment on their side.

Vital Statistics

Parent Company	Jenn Feng Industrial Co. Ltd.
Classic Product	chainsaw
Product Launch	1946
Employees	57,000
Annual Sales	$100,000 million (2005)

McDonald's

Every day, more than 52 million people around the world eat at McDonald's, the world's leading fast food retailer. "Billions and billions served" is its slogan—and, from the looks of it, McDonald's will serve billions more in years to come. With more than 31,000 restaurants in more than 100 countries and ambitious plans in China and India, McDonald's is just about everywhere.

In 1948, the McDonald brothers opened their first restaurant in San Bernardino, California, and sold burgers, fries, milk shakes, soft drinks, and apple pie. Richard and Maurice (Dick and Mac) McDonald, had engineered a kitchen assembly routine so fast and efficient that they were able to reduce the price of their food, which in turn attracted more diners. In 1954, a visiting Multimixer salesman named Ray Kroc admired the operation and advised the brothers to replicate it in franchises. When they declined, Kroc said he would do it himself. In 1955, he opened his first McDonald's restaurant in Des Plaines, Illinois, and incorporated McDonald's Corp. By the time Kroc passed away in 1984, McDonald's had expanded to more than 8,000 locations across the United States and in 35 countries.

McDonald's introduced fast, affordable food to America at the same time as Americans began to buy automobiles and move to the suburbs. Nearly everything about the McDonald's franchise was standardized for consistency—the food, kitchen, cooking technique, and even the restaurant's exterior and interior design. In 1961, McDonald's launched the "Look for the Golden Arches" campaign, and in 1963, the kid-loving clown Ronald McDonald. The Big Mac debuted in 1969 and the children's Happy Meal in 1979.

French fries are one of McDonald's most profitable menu items. Every day in the U.S., more than five million pounds of Russet Burbank potatoes are peeled, sliced, cooked, and frozen in the processing plants of the company's suppliers. McDonald's fries—golden brown, slightly crispy, and lightly salted—repeatedly win taste tests. Even celebrity chefs James Beard and Julia Child praised them. Ray Kroc had admired the McDonald brothers' shoestring fries and experimented with various drying, blanching, and frying methods. McDonald's fries were originally fried in beef tallow but, in 1990, the chain switched over to vegetable oil. Since 2002, McDonald's has experimented with heart-healthy oil blends that contain fewer trans-fatty acids and, after extensive testing, the company has found the right oil—that delivers the same great taste—and is preparing to roll it out.

McDonald's continues to evolve its menu to include more choice and variety. In recent years, the chain introduced salads, grilled chicken sandwiches, and apple dippers to its menu. McDonald's is a global brand that operates as a local company and adapts to local cultural norms: in Israel there's kosher, in Arab countries there's Halal, in India lamb is substituted for beef, and in Japan Fish McDippers are on the menu. As people around the world ask for Big Macs, fries, Egg McMuffins, Happy Meals, Chicken McNuggets, and drive-thrus, McDonald's creates something like a common tongue.

Vital Statistics
Classic Product French Fries
Established 1955
Founder Ray Kroc
Employees 1.6 million
Annual Sales $21.6 billion (2006)

McDonald's®
DRIVE-THRU

Mead

Every fall, tens of millions of children head back to school with brand new notebooks in their backpacks. Chances are that most of them have been made by MeadWestvaco. Originally founded as The Mead Corporation in 1846 by Colonel Daniel E. Mead and partners Ellis, Chafflin & Company, the company began as a paper mill in Dayton, Ohio, that produced book and other printing papers. Mead shared in the ownership and operation of the company until 1881, when he became sole owner and changed the name to The Mead Paper Company. The company acquired The Chillicothe Pulp and Paper mill of Ingham Mills & Company, thereby creating a second division at Mead, which kicked off several decades dedicated to growing its paper and paperboard manufacturing capabilities.

A period of rapid expansion started in 1955, when Mead began a series of steps that enabled it to become a diversified, billion-dollar corporation in less than 20 years. Mead acquired the controlling interest in Jackson Box Company of Cincinnati, a manufacturer of corrugated shipping containers. Mead acquired the company the next year, and the company became the nucleus of Mead's Containers division. In 1957, the Atlanta Paper Company became part of the corporation, adding a new market to the growing corporation.

That same year, Mead's acquisition of Hurlbut Paper Company moved Mead into the technical and specialty papers area. The company's Specialty Papers division manufactures a variety of papers used for furniture and countertops and other industrial applications. A few years later, Mead acquired Gilbert Paper Company, a leader in the manufacture of cotton fiber, letterhead and stationery papers, cover and text papers for business, and security papers for stock certificates and legal documents—adding to its already extensive paper empire. Further expansion proved to create one of the most popular brands in school supplies. In 1966, Mead acquired Westlab, now part of the company's Consumer & Office Products division, which is the largest manufacturer and distributor of school supplies in the country. This division also manufactures and distributes home and office supplies.

Mead's Five Star line of school supplies provides everything a student could possibly need, including notebooks, student planners, binders, pencil cases, and more. Mead continued to broaden its scope by moving into the industrial and high-technology markets. Mead Technology Laboratories developed technology that led to new businesses in electronic information storage and retrieval. Using this technology, Mead Data Central was formed in 1973 and developed Lexis, the world's leading computer-assisted legal research service, and Nexis, a leading full-text search and retrieval service of news and business information. Mead merged with packaging company Westvaco Corporation in 2002 to form MeadWestvaco Corp., and over the last several years, the company has streamlined its businesses by focusing on its packaging division. In 2005, MeadWestvaco divested its Coated Papers division, allowing the company to focus more intently on building its packaging division, its largest and most profitable segment, while maintaining industry leadership with its widely celebrated school supplies and office products brands.

Vital Statistics

Parent Company	MeadWestvaco Corporation
Classic Product	school supplies
Established	1846
Founder	Colonel Daniel Mead
Annual Sales	$6 billion

Meow Mix

Many Americans—and their cats—grew up on the famous ad campaign in which a cat asked for its food by name. In fact, it is likely most cat owners can easily sing along in tune to, "Meow, meow, meow, meow." Meow Mix has long been America's most popular cat food and now, thanks to its 2006 acquisition by the Del Monte Foods Company, it's poised to satisfy even more cats and owners. Del Monte acquired Meow Mix from the New York-based private equity firm Cypress Group, which had acquired the business in 2003 for $425 million from J.W. Childs Associates.

The original Meow Mix spot was created in the early 1970s by New York's Della Femina, Travisano & Partners agency and firmly established Meow Mix as the country's top choice. According to Jerry Della Femina, the shot of the cat "singing" was unintentional—the cat was actually choking on cat food when it was recorded, and executives later decided to set the scene to music. Meow Mix has become known for clever, sometimes truly offbeat advertising campaigns, such as 2004's search for America's Top Cat Lover at the Meow Mix Gold Level Games. This was an eight-city tour on which cat lovers competed in events such as "Hairball Toss" and "Litter Box Cleanup." Kerri Strug, Olympic gold medal gymnast, was the master of ceremonies at the New York games. Meow Mix donated one pound of cat food to local shelters for each person who participated. Another unusual project was Meow Mix's launching on the Oxygen network of Meow TV, stemming from research that showed that one-third of all cats enjoy watching television. The show was hosted by Annabelle Gurwitch and her cat Stinky and featured segments such as The Squirrel Alert and The Cat Critics. In 2004, Meow Mix also opened the temporary Meow Mix Café in midtown Manhattan

Del Monte, which also owns 9 Lives, Snausages, and Kibbles 'n Bits, has big plans for Meow Mix, which has come on strong post-millennium. Its competitors include Nestle, which makes Purina pet food, and Mars, which makes Whiskas. One change Del Monte instituted was the introduction of wet food to the Meow Mix line, which previously featured only dry food. One fifteen-second commercial touting the wet offerings showed an orange tabby wearing a yellow rain slicker and hat and singing the good old "Meow-meow-meow-meow" jingle. Another showed a cat wearing goggles and water wings while singing the Meow Mix tune with a voiceover claiming, "Now, cats can't wait to get wet. Introducing new Meow Mix wet pouches in seven deliciously fresh flavors." Both commercials share the vintage Meow Mix tagline, "Tastes so good, cats ask for it by name." Meow Mix Wet Pouches are available in flavors such as Fillet Meow (beef); Hook, Line and Sinker (fish); and Upstream Dream (salmon). Other Meow Mix offerings include Meow Mix Original, Seafood Middles, Hairball Control Formula, Indoor Formula, and Kitten Formula.

Thanks to its dancing, singing cats—and the excellent quality of its products—Meow Mix is a leading player in the world of cat food, as well as the only major pet food company devoted solely to cat food. The Meow Mix jingle is now part of American popular culture.

Vital Statistics

Parent Company Del Monte Foods

Main Production Site Decatur, Alabama

TASTES SO GOOD CATS ASK FOR IT BY NAME!®
Meow
MIX
brand
CAT
FOOD
High Quality
Ingredients for 100%
Complete Nutrition
Original
Choice
Fresh
Irresistible
Taste!
CHICKEN, TURKEY,
SALMON & OCEAN FISH
FLAVORS
NET WT
3.5 LB (1.59 kg)

Milk-Bone

Milk-Bone is synonymous with dog biscuits. Although plenty of other companies make and sell dog treats today, for more than a hundred years, Milk-Bone has been the standard benchmark. Today, Milk-Bone dog biscuits are made by Del Monte Foods and its Del Monte Pet Products division, which bought the brand from Kraft Foods, Inc. in 2006. Regardless of ownership Milk-Bone continues to be a staple in the homes of millions of dog owners nationwide.

In 1908, commercial dog biscuits were virtually unheard of when the F.H. Bennett Biscuit Company opened a bakery to make and sell them on Manhattan's Lower East Side. The biscuits were shaped like bones and made from meat, minerals, and milk, ingredients that were known to be healthy for dogs. At first called Maltoids, between 1915 and 1926 the name was changed to Milk-Bone, because of the large amount of milk used in the recipe. In 1931, food giant National Biscuit Company, which was to become Nabisco, purchased the F.H. Bennett Biscuit Company, although the only product they continued manufacturing after the acquisition was the Milk-Bone dog biscuit. Nabisco was later purchased by Kraft Foods, which continued to produce Milk-Bone alongside other famous brands like Oreos and Chips Ahoy.

Over time Milk-Bone gained a national presence. Different flavors of biscuits were introduced to appeal to the palates of different dogs and the bones were marketed as healthy treats that freshen breath and were beneficial for their teeth. Until this marketing strategy took off, dog biscuits were seen as food supplements or rewards, not as healthy shacks.

Milk-Bone is constantly redefining the category and raising the bar for its competition. Now available in many different shapes, sizes, and flavors, Milk-Bone maintains the essence and brand identity that helped to make it the success it is today.

Generations of Americans have fed millions of dogs these classic, nourishing snacks. Developed by experts with the input of veterinarians and nutritionists and tested on dogs, Milk-Bone dog biscuits are healthy, satisfying, affordable treats that has been pleasing dogs—and their owners—for the last century.

Vital Statistics
parent company Del Monte Foods
classic product Milk-Bone dog biscuits
product launch 1908

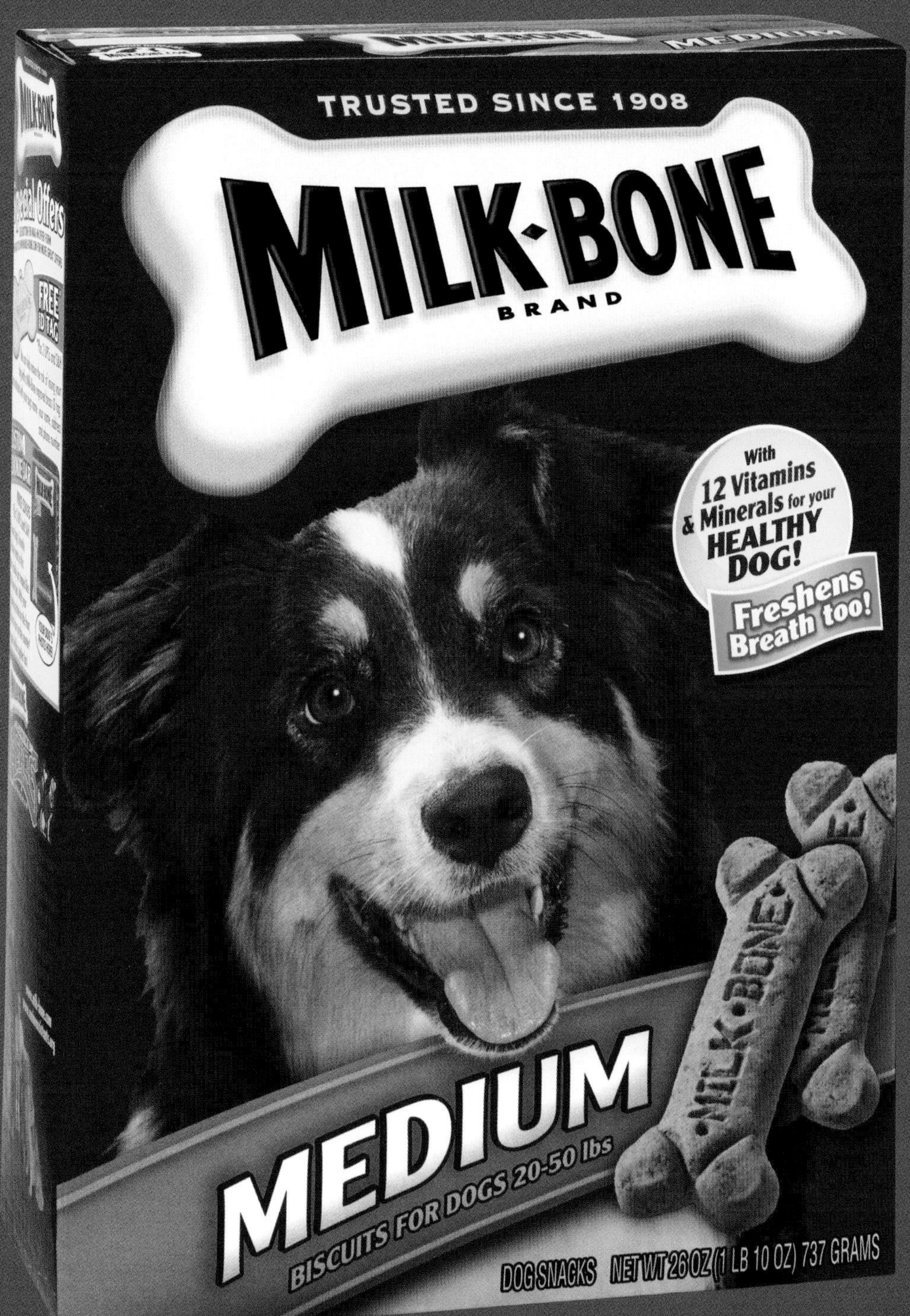
TRUSTED SINCE 1908
MILK-BONE
BRAND
With
12 Vitamins
& Minerals for your
HEALTHY
DOG!
Freshens
Breath too!
MEDIUM
BISCUITS FOR DOGS 20-50 lbs
DOG SNACKS NET WT 26 OZ (1 LB 10 OZ) 737 GRAMS

Monopoly

It's hard to imagine life without Monopoly, the best-selling board game in the world with more than 200 million sets sold in 27 languages. The popular game, created during the depths of the Depression in 1934, was initially rejected by Parker Brothers because of "52 design errors." The creator of Monopoly, an unemployed man named Charles B. Darrow from Germantown, Pennsylvania, wasn't deterred. Driven by the promise of fame and prosperity that his new game offered, he decided to make it himself. With the help of a friend who was a printer, Darrow created the game and sold five thousand handmade sets to a department store in Philadelphia.

Monopoly was a huge success. But the ongoing demand for the game became too much for Darrow to handle on his own, so he went back to talk to the executives at Parker Brothers again. Thus began the phenomenon of Monopoly. In its first year, 1935, Monopoly was the best-selling game in America.

Evidence of the game's popularity has been illustrated in the vast ways in which it has been used, or banished. During World War II, Monopoly game boards, inserted with escape maps, files, and compasses, were smuggled into POW camps in Germany and real money for escapees was slipped into packs of Monopoly money. When Fidel Castro came to power in Cuba, he had all known sets of the popular board game destroyed.

The total amount of money in a standard Monopoly game is $15,140, and since Parker Brothers introduced the game in 1935, 20 tokens have been cast such as the dog, the lantern, the purse, and the elephant. The tokens, made of metal since 1937, were made out of wood from 1943 to 1947 because of the World War II metal shortage. The race car was voted the Favorite Classic Token in 1998.

Over the years, America's best-loved board game has been honored in many ways. In 1978, Neiman Marcus offered a chocolate version of the game in their famous Christmas catalogue. The price...$600. Not to be outdone, Alfred Dunhill created a set that included gold and silver houses and hotels that sold for $25,000.

Monopoly is published in 27 languages and licensed in more than 81 countries around the world. Among them is a Braille edition for the visually impaired that was introduced in the 1970s. An estimated 500 million people have played Monopoly since 1935.

Monopoly is manufactured by Hasbro, the No. 2 toymaker in the United States.

Vital Statistics
Company Name Hasbro
Classic Product Monopoly
Established 1934
Creator Charles B. Darrow
Annual Sales $3.1 billion (2005 sales for Hasbro)

Property Trading Game from Parker Brothers®
MONOPOLY®
The World's Most
Popular Board Game
Plan a Family Game Night
COLLECT $200.00 SALARY AS YOU PASS
GO
PARKER BROTHERS
BOARDWALK
PRICE $400
TAX
PAY $75.00
PARK PLACE
PRICE $350
PENNSYLVANIA AVENUE
PRICE $200
COMMUNITY CHEST
AGES 8 to Adult

Monster.com

Looked for a job lately? You probably came in some contact with Monster Worldwide Inc. The company oversees Monster.com, the leading global online careers property, that has changed the way people look for jobs; the way employers look for people; and the way companies connect with their target audience. The company continues to define and expand an industry that did not exist a mere 10 years ago. Monster works for everyone by connecting quality job seekers at all levels with employers and providing the best career advice available online.

Over 75 million visitors have established personalized accounts that take advantage of Monster's wide breadth of services, including its global resume database or proprietary job search agent technology, that enable them to better manage their careers. Monster Worldwide is consistently ranked among the top 20 most visited sites on the Internet.

In 1967, former CEO Andrew McKelvey founded TMP, Telephone Marketing Program, a specialist in placing advertisements in Yellow Pages telephone books, and began acquiring additional Yellow Pages ad agencies. By the end of the 1980s, TMP was running smoothly, and the company began to investigate other related areas of business.

In the 1990s, TMP entered the recruitment classified advertising market by purchasing Bentley, Barnes & Lynn. Over the next five years, TMP bought more than 40 recruitment ad shops. In 1993, TMP hit the Internet with its Online Career Center Web site, which listed 150,000 jobs from a variety of companies. Two years later, TMP bought Boston-based ad agency Adion—and its Monster Board online job posting site—for $3 million. TMP went public in 1996 and soon became a darling of investors. In 1998, TMP combined its Online Career Center and Monster Board sites to form Monster.com—the site Americans rely on today for the most comprehensive database of job listings in existence.

Monster.com rose to the top relatively quickly. By late 1998, Monster Board was listing 50,000 job postings and receiving more than two million visitors a month, making it the Internet's top job-search site. In 1999, the company bought LAI Worldwide, one of the top American job recruitment companies, and TASA Worldwide. Monster.com also solidified its position as one of the most innovative advertisers around with its first-ever Super Bowl ad, "When I Grow Up," which asked job seekers: "What did you want to be?" This was the only commercial named to Time magazine's list of the "Best Television of 1999." Monster.com has since run clever ads during every Super Bowl. In 2000, TMP bought two British executive recruiting firms; Florida-based information technology recruiter System One Services; and online relocation service VirtualRelocation.com. Later that year, Monstermoving.com and ChiefMonster.com were launched. In 2003, TMP spun off its eResourcing and Executive Search business units and changed its name to Monster Worldwide. The company came full circle in 2005 when it sold its Yellow Pages division for $80 million to the Audax Group, deciding to focus exclusively on Monster.com.

Today, with approximately 5,000 employees and operations in 38 countries, Monster Worldwide has an unparalleled international reach. The company has aggressively expanded its global footprint, becoming the only pan-European recruitment website in 2004, entering developing markets such as India and China in 2005, and most recently launching Monster Mexico and Monster Gulf, spanning eight countries throughout the Middle East region.

Vital Statistics

Classic Product	job search board
Established	1998
CEO	Sal Iannuzi
Employees	4,800
Annual Sales	$986.9 million

Employers Click Here
First time here?
Post jobs
Search resumes

My Monster | Find Jobs | Post Resume | Money | Education | Career Advice

Double your chances of getting a job

It's a fact. When you post your resume, you double your chances of getting the interview and the job.* It's fast, easy and free.

Post Now!

My Monster

Job seekers access your account.

Log In

Sign up for a free monster account today or learn more.

Sign up today

Find the right job

Keywords: (e.g., sales, Java, nurse, marketing)

Select Job Category | Select Job Location | Search

Advanced Search | Company Search | Diversity Search

Earn Your Degree... and Earn MORE!

Subject: Select Your Degree

Zip Code: Search Degrees

monster learning

Featured Employers

SHELL
Discover a world of opportunities with a global company.
Learn more >

Be The Boss
Search exciting franchise opportunities and be your own boss!
Learn more >

Monster Features

Get Your Resume Out There
Executive Agent is a premier resume distribution service provided by Kennedy Information, a leading recruiter resource.
Learn more

Get Hired with Monster's Resume Writing Service
Your resume is the most important part of your job search. Let our experts create a job-winning resume for you in three days or less.
Learn more >

Ready to Grow Up and Lead?
You've made it to management, but that doesn't mean all the fun's behind you. Learn how to take charge while still enjoying yourself.

Monster Poll

If your CEO had an approval rating, what would it be?
- 0% to 25%
- 25% to 50%
- 50% to 75%
- More than 75%

Results

Share Your Comments

Questions?

Need help with anything on this site? I can answer questions or direct you to solutions.
Click Here >

Morton Salt

Morton Salt has been around for more than a century and a half and has added that little something extra to countless dishes in homes throughout the United States. Morton is the best-selling salt in the U.S. and sells table salt, canning salt, and salt for controlling ice on roads, water conditioning, and the food and chemical industries. Along with its Canadian sister company, Windsor Salt, Morton became part of chemical giant Rohm and Haas with acquisition of Morton International in 1999, but the Morton Salt brand—symbolized by the little girl with a yellow umbrella—has retained its homespun appeal.

In 1848, Morton Salt was founded in Chicago as a small, Midwestern sales agency. It grew into North America's leading producer and marketer of salt for home, water conditioning, industrial, agricultural, and highway use and was incorporated as the Morton Salt Company in 1910. By that point, it had become a manufacturer and seller of salt. As a result of consumer demand, Morton developed a salt that would not clump in damp conditions and introduced it to the public in 1914 with a national consumer advertising campaign featuring a little girl with an umbrella and the now-famous slogan, "When It Rains It Pours." Two prominent features of the package have remained the same through the decades, the pouring spout and the dark blue label. Although the Morton Salt girl has changed her appearance to fit the times, being updated in 1921, 1933, 1941, 1956, and 1968, she has remained largely intact and is one of the nation's most recognizable company symbols.

A Morton hallmark has been regular innovation to meet market demand. From basic salt blocks for industrial agricultural use (first marketed in 1918), came blocks with special additives, such as calcium, sulfur, phosphorus, and trace minerals such as iron, cobalt, copper, iodine, zinc, and manganese to promote faster growth and healthier animals. Later, feed-mixing salt products, including various combinations of minerals and vitamins and several medicaments, were developed. In 1924, Morton became the first company to produce iodized salt for the table to help prevent goiters, a widespread health problem at the time. In the 1950s, the boom in building superhighways and increase in traffic brought about an increased demand for rock salt for ice control and also during that decade, Morton developed the world's then-deepest salt mine. In 1951, Morton Pellets were introduced for the recharging of home water softeners, and in 1958, a separate water conditioning product group was established, for water softener dealers and homeowners alike. Morton Salt Substitute, appearing in the 1970s, was indicative of health trends at the time, and subsequent concoctions—Morton Seasoned Salt Substitute and Morton Nature's Seasons Seasoning Blend, a balanced blend of popular seasonings—met the needs of experimenting home cooks. In the 1980s, Morton Seasoned Salt and Morton Garlic Salt were added to the specialty line. Over the next few decades, Morton became increasingly involved in various phases of the chemical processing industry as a major supplier of basic inorganic chemicals derived from salt. This led to the formation of a separate chemical division that now produces organic chemicals, polymers, and chemical formulations used in industry and agriculture.

In 1999, Morton was acquired by Philadelphia-based Rohm and Haas Company Inc. and operates as a division of that company today. Under the impressive auspices of Rohm and Haas, Morton—still symbolized by the little girl with the yellow umbrella—remains a household staple and a significant player in American commerce.

Vital Statistics

Parent Company Rohm and Haas Company

Classic Product salt

Product Launch 1848

Employees 1,500

Annual Sales $268 million

Motorola, Inc.

Most of the people flipping open sleek Motorola cell phones worldwide would be surprised to learn that the company that made their perfectly designed device was launched almost 90 years ago as a storage battery firm. It was 1921 when Paul V. Galvin and his friend Edward Stewart went into business, although it was not until nine years later that Galvin and his brother Joseph really got the company rolling, with the first commercially successful car radio, called Motorola—a combination of *motor* and *victrola.*

Motorola dominated the car-radio business throughout the 1930s, although Paul Galvin added to the company's repertoire with the soon-to-become-ubiquitous "Police Cruiser": an AM auto radio preset to a single frequency to receive police broadcasts. Galvin Manufacturing then formed a police-radio department and added a home-radio division, as more than half of American homes owned a radio by the end of the decade. In 1936, after a tour of Europe, Galvin returned convinced that war was imminent, so he directed the company's research into areas that would be helpful to the military, resulting in the Handie-Talkie two-way radio and its offspring, the Walkie-Talkie. These were to be among the most important pieces of communications equipment used in World War II. The company's focus returned to the car radio after the war, however, and it was the first to feature push-button tuning, a vibrator power supply, fine-tuning, and tone controls. Galvin Manufacturing installed the first complete two-way AM police-radio system and introduced the first commercial line of two-way FM radio communications products—FM because it allowed for greater distances and quieter use. A subsidiary sales corporation to market the new product called Motorola Communications and Electronics, Inc., was created.

One of Motorola's glory moments occurred when Neil Armstrong's 1969 message to the world from the moon was delivered via a transponder designed and manufactured by the company's government electronics division. By 1982, development was completed on the Dyna-TAC cellular system, which was to revolutionize the way the world communicated. Two years later, 200,000 Motorola pagers were in use in Japan, and the first 32-bit MC68020 microprocessor, with 200,000 transistors accessing up to four billion bytes of memory, went on the market. The world's first commercial handheld cellular phone, the Motorola Dyna-TAC, received approval from the U.S. Federal Communications Commission, and the 28-ounce cordless phone was on the market for the first time in 1984. In 1989, Motorola introduced the world's smallest portable telephone, and in 1991, a satellite system called Iridium Inc. was set up to allow mobile telephones to operate worldwide. Motorola-Nortel Communications was formed to market cellular telephone network systems, and Motorola began developing the first pen-based, handheld wireless computers in a joint venture with Samsung. By the millennium, Motorola's $17 billion merger with General Instrument Corp. was complete, forming the core of Motorola Broadband Communications Sector, an end-to-end broadband solutions provider. In 2004 Motorola's RAZR V3 cellular phone was an instant hit with consumers from teens to celebrities and was a Gold Winner in *Business Week* magazine's Industrial Design Excellence Awards.

Today, Motorola, Inc. is ranked among the 25 largest companies in the world and sells almost half of the world's cellular phones and 85 percent of its pagers, with more than 50 percent of sales outside the United States. Motorola has proven itself a global leader in wireless, broadband, and automotive communications technologies and embedded electronic products, and is recognized everywhere for its dedication to ethical business practices and pioneering role in important innovations.

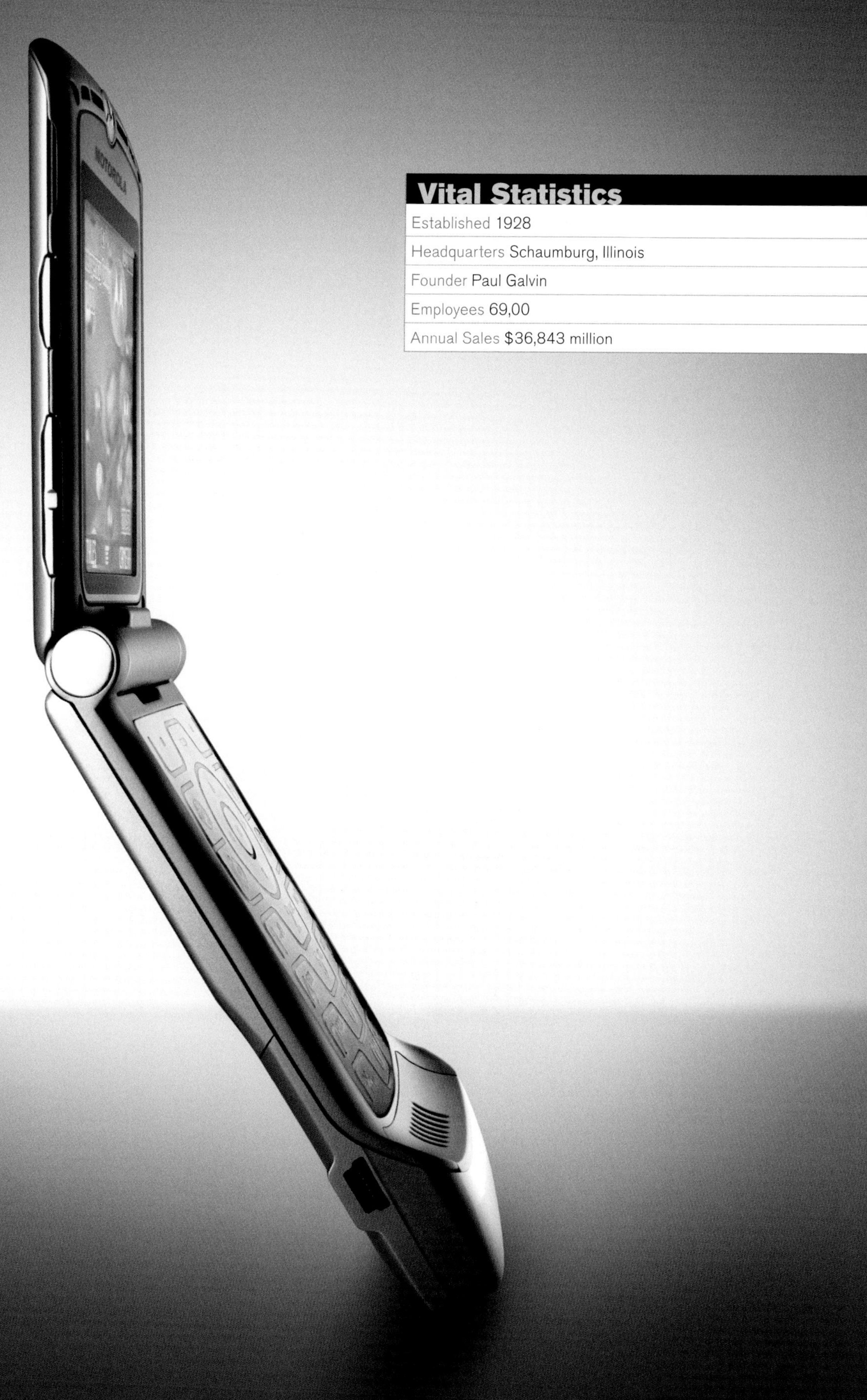

Vital Statistics

Established	1928
Headquarters	Schaumburg, Illinois
Founder	Paul Galvin
Employees	69,00
Annual Sales	$36,843 million

Mr. Clean

"Mr. Clean, Mr. Clean. . . ."Are you humming yet? Can you picture company spokesman Mr. Clean? Mr. Clean household cleaner is one of the most beloved products around, thanks in part to the company's clever advertising campaigns. Today owned by giant Procter & Gamble, the world's top manufacturer of household goods of all kinds, Mr. Clean is in good company with other Procter & Gamble products such as Bounty, Tide, Folgers, Pampers, and Pantene.

In 1958, hearth and home were center stage, and the American housewife was a household goddess—passionate about keeping surfaces sparkling and windows and floors as spic and span as could be. This was the year Mr. Clean was introduced to the market, and although there is no stereotypical household cleaner, Mr. Clean is certainly still helping all those doing the lion's share of the work. Mr. Clean achieved speedy success, partly because of its charismatic mascot: Mr. Clean. Mr. Clean is a bald, muscular man who resembles a genie or a sailor and is an amazing cleaner who shows up just in the nick of time to take care of a household mess. Mr. Clean is known for his kindly nature, although there was a brief period in the 1960's when he was shown frowning on the product packaging; it is not known why. The Mr. Clean jingle was written by Thomas Scott Cadden and has been associated with the product for generations, sometimes with lyrics, sometimes as an instrumental version. The catchy lyrics read, "Mr. Clean gets rid of dirt and grime, and grease in just a minute, Mr. Clean will clean your whole house, And everything that's in it. Mr. Clean, Mr. Clean, Mr. Clean. (ping-ping-ping of xylophone)". In 1998, Mr. Clean was voted by People magazine as one of its "Sexiest Men Alive."

Mr. Clean is also popular because of its versatility in the home. It can be used to clean countertops, walls and floors, appliances, vinyl siding, patio furniture, and sinks and bathtubs. It is known for its clean, fresh scent. In fact, Mr. Clean multipurpose cleaners are available in five popular fragrances, including Spring Garden, Invigorating Breeze, Sparkling Apple, Summer Citrus, and Ultimate Orange. Mr. Clean is also sold in other forms besides the most familiar spray. The Mr. Clean MagicReach includes scrubbing tub/shower pads that are extremely effective on porcelain and tile surfaces. Mopping floor/multipurpose pads can be affixed to the Mr. Clean MagicReach pole and used to clean floors. The company's latest offering has quickly won over legions of fans: the Mr. Clean Magic Eraser. These deceptively simple-looking little white rectangles are capable of cleaning marks and grime off walls. They can wipe scuff marks off tile floors, remove crayon marks from surfaces.

Mr. Clean has fans all over the world, although he goes by different names depending on where the cleaning is taking place. For example, in most of Europe, he is Mr. Proper; in the United Kingdom, he is called Flash; and in Spain, he goes by the romantic-sounding Don Limpio, although *limpiar* means simply "to clean". One thing, however, never changes about Mr. Clean—its ability to meet changing household needs with innovative products, refreshing scents, and reliability that household cleaners have come to depend on.

Vital Statistics

Parent Company The Procter & Gamble Company

Product Launch 1958

Nalgene Outdoor Products

Nalgene Outdoor Products go wherever you go. Nalgene products first experienced the outdoors when scientists would take them from laboratories and into the wilderness. Recognized by explorers and adventurers worldwide, Nalgene bottles and containers come in a variety of shapes and sizes to accommodate everyone—even if your closest encounter with wilderness is on your television screen.

It all started in 1949 in Rochester, New York, when a chemist named Emanuel Goldberg developed the first plastic pipette holder. He and three other colleagues started the Nalge Company. Goldberg and his growing team spent years developing the Nalgene line of state-of-the-art polyethylene labware, including centrifuge bottles, filter units, and storage tanks. Rumor had it that some of the scientists were taking the smaller bottles out of the lab to use on hikes. By the 1970s, word of the bottles' "unofficial" use got back to Nalge president Marsh Hyman.

Marsh had a son who was a Boy Scout, and he and his fellow Scouts used Nalgene lab bottles on the trail as water bottles, for storing pancake mix and snacks, and for carrying shampoo. These containers were lightweight, leak-proof, and highly functional—perfect for camping. When Marsh heard about this new use for his bottles, he had an idea. He moved the product line to the Specialty Products Department. The objective: spread the word about the new line of high-quality camping equipment to hikers and campers far and wide. And Nalgene Outdoor was born.

Since then, Nalgene has become a global brand with presence in North America, Europe, and Asia Pacific. The Nalgene bottle has become a fashion statement on college campuses, with students sporting their own personally decorated bottles everywhere they go. Campus bookstores have provided yet another successful market outlet for the predominantly scientific company. There are even Internet chat rooms where proud owners extol the virtues of their Nalgene bottles. Although the 32-ounce gray wide mouth with blue top is the "classic" edition, sizes and styles range from 16 to 48 ounces and come in a variety of colors, depending on the size. Nalgene has even expanded into hands-free hydration packs, offering two- and three-liter designs. Hailed for its portability and durability—the Nalgene bottle is virtually indestructible—laboratory equipment has never been so cool.

The Nalge Company merged with Nunc in 1995 to create Nalge Nunc International, a worldwide manufacturer of plastic products for use in laboratory, environmental, life science, and outdoor applications. Now part of Thermo Fisher Scientific, Nalgene is part of a global organization poised to help make the world healthier, cleaner and safer.

Vital Statistics
Parent Company Thermo Fisher Scientific
Classic Product Nalgene Outdoor 32-ounce Wide-mouth Bottle
Established 1949 (Nalge Company)
Founder Emanuel Goldberg

nalgene®
MADE IN USA

New York Yankees

Love them or despise them, there isn't a man, woman, or child in the country, probably much of the world, who hasn't heard of the New York Yankees. The winningest team in baseball, the ever-confident Yankees have won a record-breaking twenty-six World Series titles and thirty-nine American League pennants. In fact, the Yankees are the winningest franchise in the history of professional sports. Legends such as Babe Ruth, Mickey Mantle, Joe DiMaggio, and Lou Gehrig have ensured that the Yankees—a.k.a. the Bronx Bombers because of the location of their stadium—will go down in history.

When the American League came to be in 1901, New York was already established as a National League team. The American League was soon faced with a disastrous Baltimore team, and it dealt with the situation by essentially giving a mismatched group of players from a number of teams to Frank Farrell and Bill Devery of New York to see what they could come up with. Farrell and Devery moved their new crew into a stadium that had been quickly assembled in the Bronx at 168th Street. The baseball park was at the top of a hill, so it became known as Hilltop Park, and the team itself became the Highlanders. The Highlanders ended their first season with a winning 72-62 record to the shock of league executives. The next year, the team went 92-59, and the Yankee magic—although still not by that name—had begun. That second season, the Highlanders came within spitting distance of overtaking the Boston Red Sox, launching a rivalry in professional sports that exists to this day and has few real peers.

The team's fortunes took a turn for the worse in subsequent seasons. Up until 1919, the Highlanders rarely could claim a winning record and had two atrocious 100-loss seasons. In 1912, however, the team started wearing its now-trademark striped uniforms and in 1913 changed their name to the Yankees, both harbingers of things to come. The Yankees were sold to Jacob Ruppert in 1915. The most significant event in the life of the team came in 1920, right after New Year's, when the Yankees acquired Babe Ruth from the Red Sox, a move that in Red Sox lore has been known ever since as the Curse. During his first year as a Yankee, Babe Ruth hit fifty-four home runs, and the Yankees won ninety-five games. By this point, the team was playing in the Polo Grounds, and more than 1,200,000 fans attended games that year. In 1921, the Yankees won their first American League pennant, and construction began on what was to be the world-famous Yankee Stadium—the House that Ruth Built—which opened for business in 1923. That year, fittingly, the Yankees won their first World Series. From 1936 to 1964, the Yankees dominated baseball, playing in twenty-two World Series and winning sixteen. The years from 1965 to 1993 were less successful. Then now-notorious team owner George Steinbrenner—who came on board in 1973—brought in the big gun: manager Joe Torre. Torre led the Yankees to four World Series titles and counting, including three in a row from 1998 to 2000.

The next move on the horizon for the storied team is a new stadium, something fans have been wanting for decades. The stadium will be built in Macombs Dam Park, next to and close to the existing stadium but with vastly updated facilities and 51,000 seats. The Yankees continue to attract some of the largest crowds in baseball, and if Steinbrenner has anything to say about it, the best is yet to come.

Vital Statistics

Established	1903
Employees	130
Annual Sales	$315 million (2004)

New York City Transit Authority

New York City is known as much for its transportation system as it is for its skyscrapers and inhabitants. New York's famous subway has played a role in pop culture for decades, with notable appearances on the big and small screen alike; on the hit television show ***Seinfeld,*** in the classic chase scene in the movie ***The French Connection,*** and as the inspiration for Billy Strayhorn's "Take the A Train," which later became a signature song for Duke Ellington and his orchestra. It even has its own museum. The New York Transit Museum is the largest museum in the United States devoted to urban public transportation history.

New York City's transportation history goes back to 1827 with a 12-seat stagecoach that ran along Broadway from the Battery to Bleecker Street. In 1870, the city's first regular elevated railway service began along Greenwich Street and Ninth Avenue in Manhattan. By the end of the century, electric trolley cars were developed using overhead lines of power and soon replaced horses. The first subway opened on October 27, 1904, with 28 subway stations in Manhattan. At that time, the transit lines that previously existed were consolidated into two privately owned systems, the Brooklyn Rapid Transit Company (BRT, later BMT) and Interborough Rapid Transit Company (IRT). The number of subway stations quickly reached the current number of 468 stations, with most being built by 1930.

The first line of the city-owned and city-operated Independent Subway System (IND) opened in 1932. This system was meant to compete with the private systems and to allow for some of the elevated railways to be torn down. In 1940, the two private systems were bought by the city, and in 1953, the New York City Transit Authority was created to take over subway, bus, and streetcar operations from the city.

The subway token was also introduced in 1953. Before that, customers bought tickets to pay their fare until 1920. When the fare went up to 10 cents, coin-operated turnstiles were installed to accept first nickels and then dimes. Tokens were introduced when the fare went up to 15 cents, because turnstiles couldn't handle two different coins.

The New York City Transit Authority provides subway and bus transportation 24 hours a day throughout the five boroughs of New York City, carrying more than seven million passengers on an average day. The subway system handles two-thirds of the passenger traffic and consists of more than 25 routes over 660 miles of track, with the largest subway car fleet in the world. The New York City Transit Authority also operates a fleet of about 4,700 buses, more than any other public agency in North America.

Over the years, NYCTA has continued to successfully upgrade its image with safer trains and stations, new MetroCard vending machines, easy-to-read maps, and cleaner trains. Cars are better maintained, and all trains have reliable air-conditioning and heat. The New York Transit Authority is the largest operating unit of New York's government-owned Metropolitan Transit Authority, which also operates the Staten Island Railway (part of New York City Transit Authority), the Long Island Rail Road, MTA Long Island Bus, Metro-North Railroad, MTA bridges and tunnels, and MTA Capital Construction.

Vital Statistics

Classic Product New York City Subway

Established 1953

Employees 47,956

Sales $1,569 million

Newman's Own

Paul Newman always enjoyed cooking and eating but never aspired to professional status. In 1982, he and writer A. E. Hotchner, a close friend, decided almost as a joke to ask their friend Stew Leonard to sell their salad dressing in his eponymous stores. To their shock the product took off, and Newman's Own was born. Today, the company is still best known for its salad dressings, but it also sells popcorn, salsa, pasta sauce, lemonade, and steak sauce—all made with natural ingredients and marketed with Newman's winning image on the labels. Newman's Own foods are sold all over the world, and all after-tax profits are donated to charities.

Picture, if you can, Paul Newman and A. E. Hotchner in Newman's Connecticut basement mixing up batches of salad dressing and decanting them into old wine bottles. Then, picture them showing up on your doorstep Christmas caroling, passing out bottles of the dressing as they move from house to house, probably providing some people with the thrill—and gift—of a lifetime. After some years of this, local gourmet shops began making requests, and "limited editions" of the dressings could be purchased, although it's safe to say neither purveyors nor customers had any idea of what was to come. The two men decided to market the dressing, inspired by its cult popularity, and each contributed $40,000 to the job. They asked their friends to choose their favorites from the available offerings, and Newman's Own Olive Oil & Vinegar Salad Dressing made its debut at Stew Leonard's in 1982. Newman was the president and owner, and Hotchner his partner, vice president, and treasurer. Newman realized that he had a potential opportunity in his fledgling business and pledged to give every penny the business earned to charity—in particular to his Hole in the Wall Gang camps for terminally ill children. Although experts had warned Newman to expect $1 million in losses his first year, the business turned a profit immediately, with almost $500,000 in after-tax profits.

Other dressings followed, including caesar, creamy caesar, balsamic vinaigrette, Italian, ranch, and others. Pasta sauces were introduced in seven varieties, followed by steak sauce, three types of salsa, Old Fashioned lemonade, and popcorn. The company continued to grow, showing increased earnings each year and grossing $36 million in 1988. Products were manufactured at different locations nationwide; the popcorn was packaged in Iowa, for example, and the salad dressing bottled in California. Newman's Own foods were sold largely in supermarkets and chain stores such as Kmart and Wal-Mart, which together were responsible for 90 percent of sales. Industry publication *Grocery Marketing* reported that the company's tremendous success was because of Newman's image on the packaging, the high quality of the products, and an effective public relations campaign. In 1990, the company made an agreement with Burger King to sell its salad dressings with BK salads, a deal that led to a doubling of dressing sales in the first month. Although Newman's Own doesn't advertise, Newman's image serves the same purpose, and the copy on the labels—written by Newman and Hotchner themselves—has created a cult following. The Sockerooni spaghetti sauce touts itself as delivering a "zesty twist that will knock your socks off," and the Virgin lemonade is "made from lemons that have never been squeezed." In 1993, Newman's daughter Nell introduced a new division: Newman's Own Organics.

Although Newman still professes amazement at the success of his company, its future seems limitless, along with its potential to do good. Recent additions to the line include seven-grain pretzels, organic chocolate bars, sandwich cookies, and fat-free Fig Newmans. Paul Newman is still at the helm as company spokesman, approving all new recipes and products himself and opening a restaurant in his hometown of Westport, Connecticut, to showcase his informal, natural approach to food.

Vital Statistics

Creator	Paul Newman and A.E. Hotchner
Classic Product	salad dressing
Product Launch	1982
Headquarters	Westport, Connecticut
Annual Sales	$190 million

Nickelodeon

Launched on April Fools' Day in 1979, Nickelodeon Network was designed to be a home on television that was just for kids. What started as a kids' programming block on the Qube network, available to 600,000 viewers in Columbus, Ohio, has become the most-watched television network by kids in the United States. In 1982, Nickelodeon acquired the popular Canadian kids' television show You Can't Do That on Television, which was a big hit. Even bigger was the green slime that would become a Nickelodeon hallmark.

In 1985, Nickelodeon launched Nick at Nite, providing classic television shows from prime time into the early morning hours for an older audience. Early shows included old favorites such as The Donna Reed Show and My Three Sons and have come to include many popular sitcoms from the last 40 years such as I Love Lucy, The Cosby Show, and Cheers. Nickelodeon has spun off other affiliated networks, including Nick Game and Sports (Nick GAS), Nicktoons Network, Noggin, a commercial-free educational channel for preschoolers, and The N, the nighttime network for teens.

Nickelodeon offers a creative and diverse mix of original programming that includes comedy, variety, adventure, news, and game shows created especially for kids. Its wildly popular Nicktoons, a lineup of creator-driven original animation, was started in 1991 with three cartoons: *Doug, Rugrats,* and *The Ren and Stimpy Show.* The network soon moved toward providing more animation programming, many of which are created at the network's state-of-the-art animation studio in Burbank, California.

Among Nickelodeon's many top-rated animated television series are *Dora the Explorer, The Fairly OddParents,* and the number-one kids' television show, *SpongeBob SquarePants.* Introduced in 1999, SpongeBob SquarePants and pals from Bikini Bottom has been the top rated show for kids on television for five years. With a worldwide appeal to both young and older viewers, *SpongeBob SquarePants* has become a pop culture phenomenon, selling billions of dollars in merchandise. Nickelodeon has also introduced a live-action slate for tweens called TEENick, featuring well known stars such as Emma Roberts (*Unfabulous*), Jamie Lynn Spears (*Zoey 101*), Romeo (*Romeo!*), Devon Werkheiser (*Ned's Declassified School Survival Guide*), Drake Bell and Josh Peck (*Drake & Josh*), and newcomers Nat and Alex Wolff (*The Naked Brothers Band*).

Nickelodeon was founded with the commitment to providing high-quality entertainment for kids. This mission has made Nickelodeon the number-one kids' entertainment brand and the top-rated cable network for twelve consecutive years. In addition to its original television programming for kids, Nickelodeon has expanded to include ventures in feature films, consumer products, music, the Internet, and publishing. Nickelodeon is seen in 92 million households in the United States and 471 million households globally in 161 territories through channels, branded program blocks, and international program sales.

Image courtesy of Nickelodeon

Vital Statistics
Parent Company MTV Networks
Classic Product *SpongeBob SquarePants* and *Dora the Explorer*
Established 1979
Annual Sales $1.7 billion (2005)

NicoDerm CQ

Kicking the smoking habit is one of the hardest things to do. But the recognition that smoking produces addiction to nicotine has enabled new products to be tested and marketed to effectively help people combat the addiction. Smoking is a very fast and effective way of getting nicotine to the brain. Nicotine changes the brain's chemical structure and thereby triggers cravings, which causes the smoker to continue to smoke—to satisfy the need for nicotine. Because smoking is a physical addiction as well as a habit, quitting is difficult without the help of some kind of smoking-cessation program.

NicoDerm CQ, the number-one doctor-recommended nicotine patch, was approved by the Food and Drug Administration in 1991 and is considered the original nicotine transdermal system. At the time, nicotine gum was very popular because it was the only smoking-cessation product being offered to help smokers quit by attacking the nicotine addiction. NicoDerm CQ is a nicotine patch that is a form of nicotine replacement therapy, which provides nicotine to the user's system. NicoDerm CQ contains SmartControl, a patented technology that monitors the controlled release of nicotine for up to 24 hours. A NicoDerm CQ patch each day protects the user from cravings for up to 24 hours and works by reducing nicotine withdrawal symptoms until the body no longer craves the nicotine. NicoDerm CQ helps calm the cravings by gradually weaning the body off the nicotine over a period of time. After following the 8- or 10-week quit-smoking system, determined by the smoker's usage, the user will be free from nicotine and cigarettes.

To support its users, NicoDerm CQ additionally provides the Committed Quitters program. With more than 50,000 participants, Committed Quitters is an individualized plan, created from information provided by the user that is used to create a calendar and diary that helps them move through the program and kick the smoking habit for good.

NicoDerm CQ has become the most popular topical nicotine alternative. NicoDerm CQ is marketed by GlaxoSmithKline, one of the top five pharmaceutical companies in the world.

Vital Statistics
Parent Company GlaxoSmithKline
Manfacturer Alza Corporation
Established 1991
Sales $3.7 billion (2005) (GSK)

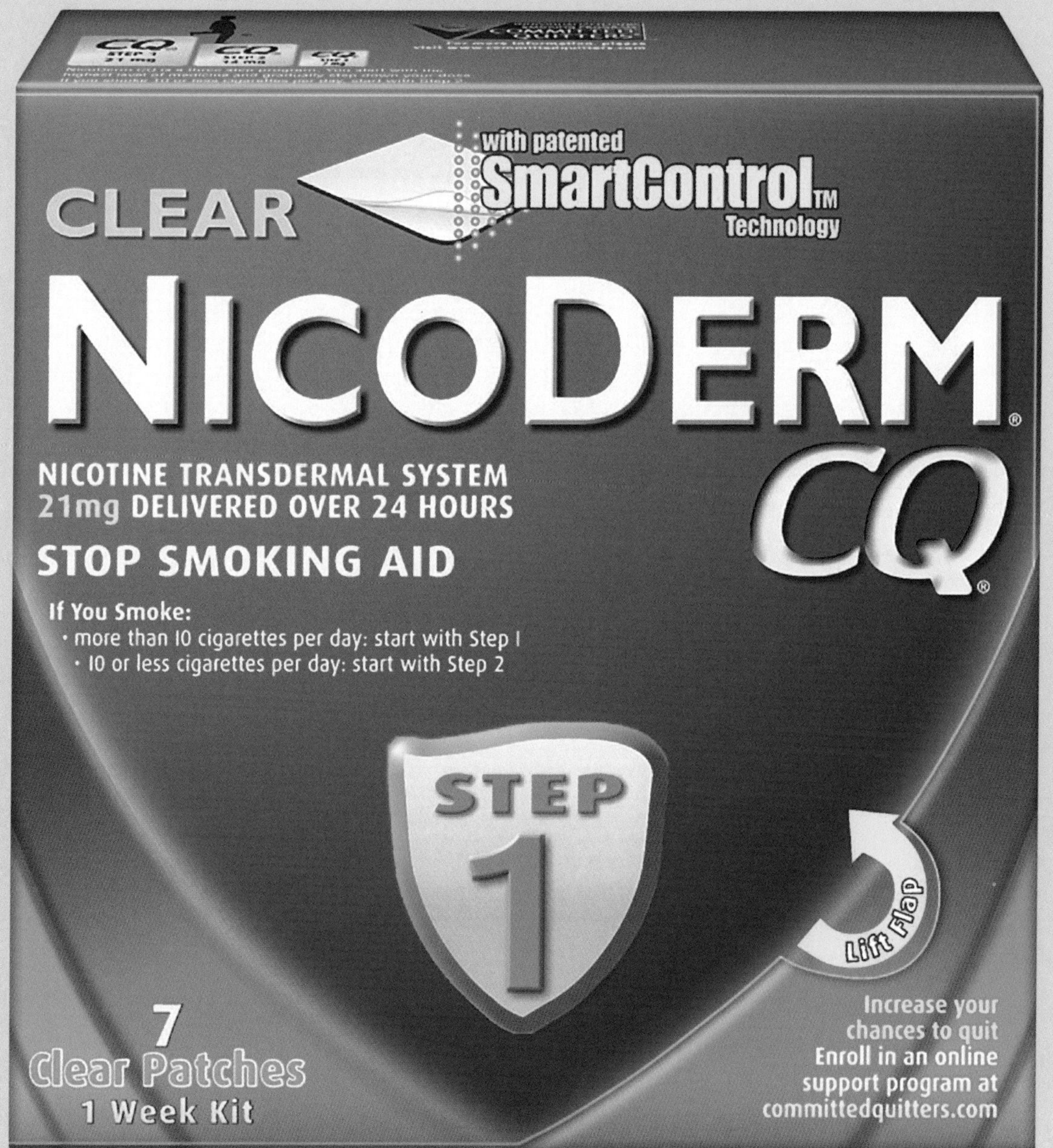
with patented
SmartControl™
Technology
CLEAR
NICODERM®
CQ®
NICOTINE TRANSDERMAL SYSTEM
21mg DELIVERED OVER 24 HOURS
STOP SMOKING AID
If You Smoke:
• more than 10 cigarettes per day: start with Step 1
• 10 or less cigarettes per day: start with Step 2
STEP
1
Lift Flap
7
Clear Patches
1 Week Kit
Increase your
chances to quit
Enroll in an online
support program at
committedquitters.com

The North Face

Since the late 1960s, The North Face has built the most technically advanced apparel, equipment, and footwear that will endure the harshest environs on the planet. The world's most accomplished climbers, mountaineers, snowsports athletes, endurance runners, and explorers turn to The North Face to outfit their outings and expeditions, from the sky-piercing peak of Mount Everest to 135-mile runs across Death Valley.

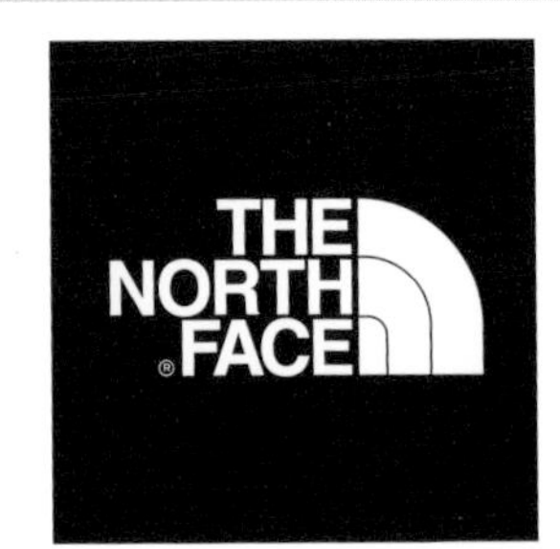

In 1966, two outdoor enthusiasts founded a small mountaineering retail store in the heart of San Francisco's North Beach. Two years later, the company changed hands and moved across the Bay, where it began manufacturing its own products. The North Face, a retailer of high-performance climbing and backpacking equipment, was born. The company name is a reverent nod toward the north-facing slopes of mountains in the Northern Hemisphere, known to be the coldest and most formidable for mountaineering. An instant outerwear classic, The North Face Sierra Parka was designed with such places in mind and began selling in 1969. Subsequent product releases—including the geodesic dome tent in 1975—consistently raised the bar of performance and underscored The North Face commitment to applying the most cutting-edge design principals and materials to better equip explorers. During this time, The North Face inaugurated a proud tradition of expedition and athlete support, sending its products to the most demanding places on the planet. The North Face Half Dome logo, homage to the famed granite Half Dome that stands guard over Yosemite National Park, has appeared on the planet's highest peaks, steepest rock walls, and most historic journeys.

The 1980s saw the further introduction of many successful new products at The North Face, including the first technical ski apparel line, and new, expedition-worthy apparel systems, outerwear, sleeping bags, and tents. At the decade's end, The North Face recognized the growing need to encourage environmental awareness and co-founded the Outdoor Industry Conservation Alliance. The 1990s continued a track record of product innovation—including Tekware, the company's foray into technical sportswear. The North Face also introduced freestanding The North Face stores, and continued opening new ones well into the 21st century. The company tagline, Never Stop Exploring, still encourages everybody to head outdoors and challenge their perceived limits, whether on an 8,000-meter peak or a mountain half marathon. In celebrating its 40th Anniversary in 2008, The North Face emphasized the staying power of high-quality outdoor gear, a rich tradition of exploration, and a brand devoted to the core athlete, while already planning the next wave of innovative products due for release in 2009 and beyond.

Opposite: Photo Courtesy Kristoffer Erickson/The North Face

Vital Statistics

Parent Company VF Corporation

Founded 1968

OfficeMax Incorporated

OfficeMax, the company formerly known as Boise Cascade, is one of the nation's largest office-supply distributors with almost 1,000 superstores, 25,000 products, and a wide range of business services to meet the needs of enterprise-level, small, and midsized businesses, as well as individual customers in the United States, Canada, Mexico, Europe, Australia, and New Zealand.

Boise Cascade was created in 1957 with the merger of two small lumber companies: Boise Payette Lumber Company and Cascade Lumber Company. In 1964, the company moved into the distribution of office products, and shortly thereafter, several acquisitions helped Boise Cascade diversify into several areas, including building materials and paper products.

While keeping a hand in the paper industry, Boise Cascade moved with the flow of business beyond paper to provide small and midsize businesses with office solutions.

A leader in business-to-business and retail office products, OfficeMax distributes office supplies, paper, technology products and services, and office furniture. It also provides print and document services through CopyMax, its store-within-a-store. Customers are served through direct sales, catalogues, the Internet, and its nearly 1,000 OfficeMax superstores. With a strong, customer-driven focus, OfficeMax is known for its excellent service, superior products, and exceptional value—all while saving the customer valuable time.

OfficeMax provides business-to-business solutions through OfficeMax Contract, offering a broad line of office products and services. Selling directly to enterprise-level and midsize businesses, customers are served by salespeople in the field, catalogues, e-commerce, and, in some areas, retail stores. In 2005, OfficeMax caught the eye of the International Academy of Digital Arts & Sciences, and it received a "Webby Worthy" distinction for its e-commerce Web site for contract business customers.

OfficeMax Retail distributes office supplies, paper, technology products, office furniture, and print and document services with retail operations in the United States, Puerto Rico, and the U.S. Virgin Islands as well as a joint venture in Mexico. Products for OfficeMax Contract and Retail are purchased from outside manufacturers or industry wholesalers.

The success of OfficeMax is rooted in its emphasis on unparalleled customer service, with more than 40,000 OfficeMax associates providing the best experience—whether serving customers on the Internet or in a superstore.

Vital Statistics

Established 1957 (as Boise Cascade)

Employees 40,000+

Annual Sales $9.2 billion (2005)

OfficeMax®

Old Town Canoes

Old Town Canoe Company of Old Town, Maine, goes back to 1900, when it formed to create a wood-and-canvas canoe. This was a revolutionary idea evolving from the birch-bark canoes used by the local Penobscot Indians.

The Indian Old Town Canoe Company, as it was then called, had backing from the Gray family, entrepreneurs with ventures in logging, hardware, and Bickmore's Gall Cure, a very successful salve for horses that would exist for more than 100 years. The first canoes were made behind the Gray's hardware store, but production quickly moved to two floors of an industrial building. Several more moves were made to larger facilities to accommodate demand for the product, and the company built 250 canoes in the first year. The company targeted a large market, advertising in recreation publications and producing an annual catalogue. Its large distribution network and easy access to rail service contributed to the company's success. Early models featured sails, and customers had their choice of different designs and three grades of materials and finish. Soon after, the company was offering rowboats of canvas-covered construction as a lightweight alternative to the traditional all-wood models.

Within five years, Old Town was making between 200 and 400 canoes a month, and the product line was expanded to include shorter (15-foot) and longer (34-foot) models. By 1908, the company was also selling motorized models. Old Town was the largest canoe manufacturer, with 50 employees, of more than a dozen in the area, selling crafts to customers as far off as Europe and South America.

As the logging industry was faltering, people were heading into the woods and out onto the water, and the company was prospering. Soon after, World War I saw many men off to war, and the company supplied the military with paddles. Advertising was tailored to the women left at home who went to work and were earning money for the first time. By 1931, despite the Depression, Old Town was producing about 1,600 canoes a month, half the total made in the state of Maine, and its products were available in 50 different designs. In 1940, Old Town introduced its kayak—a more durable version of the sealskin kayak made of wood and canvas.

Although World War II saw a shortage of workers and materials, the postwar years produced many new models to appeal to the newly affluent society. Old Town's all-wood motorboats with an emphasis on speed were the popular items of the 1950s and 1960s. Technological advances saw the production of canoes at Old Town plummet to 200 per year until the company started making fiberglass canoes to compete with the popular aluminum canoes that Grumman was turning out by the thousands.

One of the largest changes to the canoe and kayak industry in the past century has been the move to plastic boats (which make up a very large majority of the boats sold). Old Town was the brand that enabled this, when Lew Gilman borrowed rotomolding technology from the chocolate industry and applied it to the manufacture of canoes and kayaks.

Old Town Canoe Company has continually evolved by creating new designs with new materials while constantly inspired by the classic boatbuilding tradition that helped establish the company. Old Town Canoe is the world's largest supplier of canoes and kayaks and is a key part of Johnson Outdoors Inc.'s Paddlesports division. The canoes are sold at about 900 dealers throughout the world, mainly at specialty stores.

Vital Statistics

Parent Company	Johnson Outdoors Inc.
Headquarters	Old Town, Maine
Established	1900
Founder	George and Herbert Gray
Sales	$380 million

Omaha Steaks

At Omaha Steaks, filet mignon, boneless strips, and other specialties are hand-cut and packaged, and sold to more than 2 million customers worldwide. In addition to its signature beef, Omaha Steaks also offers a complete line of pork, poultry, seafood, side dishes, appetizers, and desserts. The company sells through a variety of marketing channels including direct mail, online, business-to-business, food service, and at nearly 80 Omaha Steaks retail stores. An American classic, Omaha Steaks is still owned and operated by the fourth and fifth generations of the Simon family.

In 1898, J.J. Simon and his son, B.A., left Latvia to escape religious persecution, bound for the United States and its promised opportunities. They settled in the place that most resembled their homeland: Omaha, Nebraska. The men, who had been butchers, started working in the meat business and, in 1917, bought a building in downtown Omaha from the Table Supply Company and founded their own business. B.A. brought in a cooler and a freezer and inserted the word "Meat" between Supply and Company on the sign, creating the Table Supply Meat Company. The Simons focused on selling flavorful, grain-fed Midwestern beef primarily to restaurants and grocers in the surrounding area. B.A.'s son Lester Simon joined the company in 1929, becoming president in 1946 and expanding on the family's original dream. In the 1940s, Lester suggested that he personally hand-pick Table Supply Meat Company's well-aged steaks for the Union Pacific passenger trains that traveled between Omaha, Los Angeles, San Francisco, and Seattle, spreading the company's reputation throughout the West. Customers nationwide started calling to find out how they, too, could purchase the steaks. By 1952, Lester Simon had launched the company's first mail order venture, shipping meat in dry ice-filled, wax-lined cardboard cartons by train.

In the following decades, the direct mail business took off, aided by the introduction of direct shipping, polystyrene coolers, and vacuum packaging. In 1961, Nebraska Governor Frank B. Morrison sent Table Supply Meat Company steaks to President Kennedy and the governors of every state. In 1963, the first catalogs were sent to customers. Three years later, after continued growth, Table Supply Meat Company built a new plant and headquarters in Omaha and changed its name to Omaha Steaks. In 1975, the Simon family launched the company's 800 number for easy ordering and added one of the nation's first toll-free customer service lines. A year later, the first Omaha Steaks retail store opened in Omaha. Expansion in the 1980s and 1990s led to an increase in retail stores and the development of a Web site, www.omahasteaks.com, in 1995.

Today, Omaha Steaks are well-known as a leading personal and corporate/client gift. The product line now includes more than 400 gourmet food items. Thousands of Omaha Steaks employees share in the success, as the company has won public recognition and awards for its benefits package and family-friendly policies. Lester's sons are still involved in operations and two of them currently serve in executive leadership roles. Omaha Steaks epitomizes the American dream fulfilled.

Vital Statistics
Classic Product steaks
Established 1917
Founders J.J. and B. A. Simon
Employees 1,800
Annual Sales $439 million (2006)

Oneida Ltd.

Oneida is the number-one maker of stainless steel and silver-plated flatware in the world. It supplies flatware both to household consumers and the food industry and produces sterling, silver-plated, and stainless flatware, as well as china dinnerware, coffee sets and trays, crystal products, and gift items. The company also licenses its name to makers of linens, cookware, and utensils. Oneida owns Kenwood Silver Company, Inc., which operates more than 60 Oneida Factory Stores nationwide. Oneida is the only flatware that is available for a lifetime; customers are guaranteed that their pattern of choice will never be discontinued.

In 1848, a Christian leader named John Humphrey Noyes founded the Oneida Community in upstate New York. The community espoused shared property and labor, the communal raising of children, and the end of monogamous marriage. To survive, the community produced goods, including high-quality silverware. A split led to the founding in 1880 of the Oneida Community, Ltd., a company operated by former members of the community and focused on making the business a success. In 1916, Oneida opened its international factory, in Niagara Falls, contributing to the boom in upstate New York. By the 1920s, the company was almost exclusively manufacturing silverware and in 1935 changed its name to Oneida. During both World Wars and the Korean War Oneida grew because of its work as a defense contractor, making goods such as surgical instruments, parachute parts, rifle sights, parachute releases, hand grenades, shells, survival guns, bayonets, aircraft fuel tanks, and chemical bombs.

In the 1960s, Oneida became more interested in design, at a time when American homeowners were equally interested in entertaining. By the 1980s, Oneida had produced an astonishing half of the flatware in use in the country. In 1987, when sales lulled, Oneida sold its limousine fleet and corporate jet, cut management by 15 percent, and strove to improve its factories. In 1996, the company decided to expand to tableware in general. In 2000, Oneida began selling its product range on the Internet. Oneida continued expansion, purchasing Sakura, Delco International, and Viners of Sheffield Limited.

Oneida is a household name and standby all over the world. Today, the company imports flatware, dinnerware, and glassware, with its trademark metal products factoring in about 60 percent of sales. The company also sells cookware, china, linens, picture frames, and other home accessories in department stores and other outlets.

Vital Statistics
Employees 1,240
Annual Sales $417.5 million (2005)
Headquarters Oneida, New York

Ore-Ida Tater Tots

It's hard to know whether there's a correlation, but in 1953, just a year after Mr. Potato Head arrived in toy stores, Ore-Ida came out with Tater Tots. The genius of the small deep-fried cylinders of shredded potatoes wasn't just that they tasted good, but that they were made with the slivered remains of the potatoes used to make Ore-Ida's french fries.

Company co-founder F. Nephi Grigg came up with the idea to use the pieces left over from shaving potatoes into french fries, leftovers previously considered so worthless that they sold for next to nothing to be used as livestock feed. Grigg ground the leftovers together, stirred in flour and spices, and then pushed the mix through holes cut in a plywood board. He cooked the little cylinders in hot oil and then froze them. Nephi and his brother and co-founder Golden T. Grigg were so enthusiastic about their product that they traveled to potential customers with briefcases filled with samples of Tater Tots packed in dry ice.

Frozen foods at that time were a new concept, and the brothers had a hard time raising the money to run their business. Ore-Ida Potato Products Inc. had been formed just a year earlier on the border between Oregon and Idaho, which was the basis for its name. Potential lenders balked, fearing the potatoes would turn black during processing, or that people would prefer fresh food. The Griggs secured their loans with raw potatoes and raised the cash to move ahead.

Ore-Ida was distributing its potato products nationally when it went public in 1961, and in 1965, H. J. Heinz Company bought Ore-Ida to diversify into the frozen foods business. In 1978, the signature advertising campaign "When It Says Ore-Ida, It's All Righta" was introduced, and it remained the company slogan for a decade. With the acquisition that same year of Foodways National, Inc., the producers of Weight Watchers frozen entrees, the company was able to double profits over the next decade. By 1991, with a product line that included other favorites such as Golden Fries and Golden Crinkles, Ore-Ida had 50 percent of the market share in frozen potato products.

In 2004, Ore-Ida launched their new Extra Crispy Tater Tots based on consumer research that showed that people wanted the taste of a true fried potato that could be prepared at home in the oven. Today, about 70 million tons of Tater Tots are consumed each year. Parents like them because they're a snap to prepare, kids love the taste, and they've so clearly earned their place in popular culture that they were featured in a scene in the movie *Napoleon Dynamite.*

Vital Statistics
Established 1952
Headquarters Boise, Idaho
Employees 41,375
Annual Sales $8,643.4 million

Ore Ida
NEW! FAMILY SIZE!
Ore-Ida
EXTRA CRISPY
Fast Food Fries™
FRENCH FRIED POTATOES
NET WT 4 LB (1.81 kg)

Oreo

American pie? Many generations of Americans would argue that Oreo cookies are the ultimate American treat. It would be hard to find a person without a personal philosophy on how to eat an Oreo, from those who twist open and eat the filling first to those who need milk for dunking and every other conceivable possibility. After almost a hundred years on the market and in our homes, Oreos have become a classic American treat.

In 1912, Nabisco (now part of Kraft Foods) introduced a new cookie consisting of two chocolate rounds sandwiched together with a crème filling, almost identical to today's Oreo. The first Oreos were sold in bulk in tin cans with glass tops for 30 cents a pound. These tin cans were the first in their day to have glass tops to allow consumers to view the cookies. Oreos became the best-selling cookie on the marketplace during their first year of existence, a position they have never relinquished. Many believe this is because Oreos were one of the earliest interactive foods, affording people choices of consumption style and authorizing—even encouraging—playing with food. The flavor and texture contrasts were also novel for the time. Nobody is sure exactly how Oreos got their name; because "oreo" is the Greek word for mountain, one theory is that because the founder of Nabisco was a classics buff, it was after a hill-shaped test version of the cookie!

The design of the Oreo was inspired by a medieval Italian printer's mark: an oval surmounted by a cross with two horizontal lines instead of the typical one, symbolizing the triumph of good over evil A two-stage process is used to make the cookies. First, the base dough is formed into the familiar round cookies by a rotary mold at the entrance of a 300-foot-long oven. Then, the white, creamy, frosting-like filling is placed between two cookies, creating the "sandwich." Over the years, Oreo has offered variations on its untouchable original. Mini Oreos, for example, appeared in 1991 in response to a growing demand for bite-size, snackable foods. The minis were named one of the best new products of 1991 by *Business Week* magazine. Today, there are many types of Oreo cookies, including Chocolate Creme Oreo, Reduced Fat Oreo, Fudge Covered Oreo, Fudge Mint Covered Oreo, Double Delight Oreo with Peanut Butter 'n Chocolate Creme, Double Delight Oreo with Mint 'n Creme, and Double Delight Oreo Coffee 'n Creme. Seasonal varieties appear throughout the year, including the Candy Cane Creme Oreo, which has become a holiday classic. Oreos are enjoyed in more than a hundred countries around the world.

Surprisingly few changes have been made to the original Oreo cookie, since a grocer named S.C. Thuesen bought the first batches on March 6, 1912. Oreos remain the number one choice of American cookie buyers and the best-selling cookie of the twentieth century. More than 362 billion Oreo cookies have been sold.

Vital Statistics
Parent Company Kraft Foods Inc.
Product Launch 1912

NABISCO
America's Favorite Cookie
OREO
Chocolate Sandwich Cookies
NET WT 1 LB (453g)
SERVING SUGGESTION
3 STAY FRESH PACKS

Oscar Mayer Foods Corp.

Most Americans have not only tasted Oscar Mayer's products, but sung the company's most famous jingles. Oscar Mayer's sliced meats and other offerings are available in almost every supermarket in the country and have been providing lunches for generations. What people may not know is that Oscar Mayer began as a small family business.

In 1873, 14-year-old Oscar F. Mayer came to America from Bavaria and found work as a butcher in Detroit. In 1876, he moved to Chicago and took an apprenticeship in Armour & Company's stockyards. Soon he contacted his brother Gottfried back in Germany, suggesting he learn the art of sausage making, with the idea that they could start a business together in the States. In 1883, Oscar and Gottfried opened their own store. Five years later, the brothers borrowed $10,000 and bought a building with room for a shop and living space. A third brother, Max, soon joined. By 1900, the company had more than 40 employees and was well known throughout Chicago and its suburbs. In 1911, they incorporated as Oscar F. Mayer & Bro. and began the process of expansion.

Oscar Mayer sales reached $11 million by 1918, including significant sales to the government for the military in World War I. A year later, the company changed its name to Oscar Mayer & Co. The following year, Oscar Mayer bought a meatpacking plant in Madison, Wisconsin, and by 1925 they expanded into Milwaukee. In 1936, the company introduced Little Oscar and his Wienermobile, a perennially popular promotion. Oscar Mayer again provided food for the troops, this time during World War II, and—in 1944—introduced the first hot dogs sold in self-explanatory "Kartridg-Paks," the way nearly all hot dogs are sold today. Later that decade, they started selling meats in vacuum-sealed packages, which could be stored longer in the refrigerator. By 1958, the company was selling more than 200 varieties of sausages, lunch meats, and smoked and canned meat products. In the 1960s, Oscar Mayer went international, and in 1963, it released the "Wiener Jingle," with the words familiar to any kid who has ever watched TV: "Oh, I wish I were an Oscar Mayer wiener. That is what I'd truly like to be."

The company's common stock was listed on the New York Stock Exchange for the first time in 1971, the same year it became the first meat processor to put "use-by" dates on its labels. That year, the second of Oscar Mayer's unmistakable jingles was also released, beginning, "My bologna has a first name. It's O-s-c-a-r." In the late 1980s, Oscar Mayer introduced the groundbreaking Lunchables, prepackaged options for school lunches.

Although the health-conscious 1990s and post-millennium years have been challenging for the meat industry, Oscar Mayer has stayed on top thanks to its outstanding reputation for excellence in product, packaging, and marketing. New products, such as low-fat chicken breast strips and other ready-to-cook offerings, will ensure that the little butcher shop Oscar Mayer founded more than a century ago will remain a leader well into the next.

Vital Statistics
Parent Company Kraft Foods, Inc.
Established 1883
Employees 3,000
Headquarters Madison, Wisconsin
Annual Sales $1,300 million (2005)

Oscar Mayer®
BEEF
Franks
Quality Meat,
No Fillers
U.S. INSPECTED AND PASSED BY DEPARTMENT OF AGRICULTURE
KEEP REFRIGERATED
NET WT 16 OZ (1 LB)
BEEF

OshKosh B'Gosh

OshKosh B'Gosh is more than a hundred years old and counting. Many generations of kids have grown up in the famous bib overalls that made this company a household name. Today, OshKosh operates about 170 outlet and specialty stores and an online shopping site, and sells its products through retailers in the United States and abroad. And although children's clothing giant Carter's bought OshKosh in 2005, the company's classic, durable clothing will never change.

Oshkosh, Wisconsin—where Grove Manufacturing was founded in 1895 to produce striped bib overalls for farmers and railroad laborers—could not have foreseen that its name was to become synonymous with classic children's style. In 1896, the business changed its name to Oshkosh Clothing and Manufacturing; it did not add the "B'Gosh" until a company owner heard the phrase in a vaudeville skit on a visit to New York. In 1910, the company first started making child-size overalls. One of the earliest advertising slogans was: "Work Clothes for Dad, Play Clothes for Sonny." Throughout the '20s and '30s, OshKosh promoted its products on radio shows, featuring the OshKosh B'Gosh Radio Boys, and at county fairs. In 1930, OshKosh ran testimonial ads crediting the durability of OshKosh clothing for saving a man's life! OshKosh continued to gain a reputation for quality, presenting bib overalls to such prominent figures as Dwight Eisenhower and John F. Kennedy. However, until the late 1960s, it remained primarily a regional producer of work clothes, in particular the original overalls.

OshKosh's future took a different turn, however, when in 1962 it advertised a pair of children's overalls in a national catalog almost on a whim. Some 15,000 orders poured in immediately, and catalog sales skyrocketed. In 1975, OshKosh began producing the children's overalls in bright colors and stripes. By 1978, children's apparel accounted for 15 percent of OshKosh sales. Three years later, Oshkosh B'Gosh opened its first outlet store in Wisconsin and then began to expand its product line, introducing such items as knit tops and shorts, all with the characteristic clean lines and comfortable yet play-hardy materials. OshKosh went public in 1985, and demand for its clothing became so great that the firm had to contract with private manufacturers. OshKosh opened forty-six stores in 1994, including showcase stores in London and Paris, and was online by late 1999. In 2004, the company moved its design team to New York City, a year before it was acquired by Carter's.

Although the rugged, hickory-striped trademark bib overalls are a perennial best-seller, the entire line is consistently ranked as one of the favorite children's wear brands in research studies. In addition to the OshKosh B'Gosh name brand for boys and girls, the OshKosh B'Gosh family of brands also includes OshKosh Baby and a layette line for newborns. OshKosh B'Gosh products are available in more than fifty countries around the world.

Vital Statistics
Parent Company Carter's
Classic Product bib overalls
Date of Founding 1895
Employees 5,100
Annual Sales $398.7 million

Oster

The John Oster Manufacturing Company was started by John Oster, in his garage in Racine, Wisconsin, in 1924. He saw an opportunity to market a hand-operated hair clipper—a new product designed to cut and style women's hair. Four years later, the John Oster Manufacturing Company introduced a new motor-driven clipper, which quickly became the industry standard for professionals in the grooming industry.

In 1946, John Oster decided to diversify from grooming equipment to small electrical house appliances. He purchased the Stevens Electric Company, the company that had invented the liquefier blender in 1923. Stevens Electric manufactured drink mixers for soda fountains and bars. At the time, Steven Poplawski, owner of Stevens Electric, had already begun experimenting with a mixer to blend and chop food. With this acquisition, John Oster instructed engineers to find ways of improving mixers for other uses. The Oster engineers completed the experiments that Poplawski started, and a new product was introduced. The Osterizer blender has become a classic product and the staple of Oster blenders.

With the success of this one model, Oster Manufacturing Company began building its reputation in the small appliances industry. In 1948, Oster introduced the Osterett mixer, a forerunner of the portable hand mixer. The Osterett was a huge success then and is still produced in some markets today. Oster followed with the Oster Model 202 hair dryer in 1949, a knife sharpener in 1950, and an updated and improved Osterizer blender in 1955. New products were being produced and sales were soaring. And Oster expanded its facilities to accommodate the company's growth.

In 1960, the John Oster Manufacturing Company became a wholly owned subsidiary of Sunbeam. Oster was a natural fit for Sunbeam, and it was business as usual for Oster, with the same officers in charge. Complementing Sunbeam's stable of well-known brands, they continued to make high-quality, high-performance appliances. Over the years, innovative new products were introduced and the small appliance marketplace was teeming with shiny new wares for the home. Among the offerings were humidifiers, can openers, irons, automatic juice extractors, sandwich makers, bread makers, and toaster ovens. Worldwide recognition for its innovation, design, and style enabled the company to reign as the leading manufacturer and designer of small kitchen appliances for nearly 60 years, recognized in kitchens worldwide.

The Oster business was acquired by Jarden Corporation in 2005, complementing Jarden's diverse group of branded consumer goods. They continue to introduce exciting and innovative products into the marketplace.

Vital Statistics
Parent Company Sunbeam Products, Inc.
Headquarters Boca Raton, FL
Established 1924
Founder John Oster
Classic Product Oster Classic Beehive Blender

Osterizer
BLENDER
Classic
OFF

Pampers

The Procter & Gamble Company is the world's number-one maker of household products, with approximately 300 brands available in 180 countries around the world. With more than 20 brands in the billion-dollar sales range, the Procter & Gamble Company was created when candle maker William Procter and soap maker James Gamble merged their businesses in 1837 in Cincinnati, Ohio. By 1859, Procter & Gamble had become one of the city's largest companies.

Pampers disposable diapers were introduced in 1961. Pampers were the invention of Victor Mills, a chemical engineer at Procter & Gamble. He was looking for a better and easier way to diaper his grandson than using cloth diapers. Mills realized that the pulp mill owned by Procter & Gamble might be able to provide a clean, absorbent paper that could be used for a disposable diaper. A group researched the possibility of designing a diaper that was disposable, absorbent, and prevented leaks. Mills used his grandson to test his first disposable diaper. In 1959, the unnamed diaper was tested in Rochester, New York. After several names were discarded, the company settled on Pampers brand. Pampers brand was tested in the Peoria, Illinois, market and though it was unsuccessful, it led to a more improved disposable diaper and a lower cost. Pampers eventually became the preferred way to diaper a baby.

Early disposable diapers were bulky and heavy, but they were a big hit with consumers. This new and innovative product was a success, but there was confusion about where to stock it in grocery and drug stores. Pampers were found everywhere from the food aisle to the drug section. In 1966, Pampers introduced a new design, called the C-fold design, and a third design came along in 1969. With that, Pampers became a national brand in the United States.

New ideas continued to improve and expand the Pampers brand, and in 1971, the diaper pin design was replaced by strips of adhesive tape , which allowed for easier access and made changing a diaper less hazardous. A variety of styles were introduced in the 1970s, including Pampers Toddler Size, Extra Absorbent Daytime, Improved Newborn, and Premature Infant Size. Procter & Gamble continued to improve the brand, changing the diapers to an hourglass design in 1984. Two years later, the first thin diaper with absorbent gelling material, elastic leg gathers, and tabs that could be refastened was introduced, reducing the diaper's weight considerably. Cushion Quilted lining and Value Packs were also introduced in the 1980s. With new technology enabling improved and advanced products, Pampers continued to evolve and expand its product line, introducing new styles such as training pants and larger-sized diapers. New technology led to styles such as Ultra Dry Thins designed to pull moisture away from the baby and stretch panels for a more comfortable fit. Pampers brand created the disposable diaper market and has led the way ever since.

Vital Statistics

Parent Company The Procter & Gamble Company

Product Launch Date 1959

Jumbo
Pampers
Baby Dry
FLEX
3
16-28 lbs
7-13 kg
SESAME STREET
40
DIAPERS
COUCHES
PAÑALES

Parkay

Although Parkay margarine was introduced in 1937, the brand really hit its stride in 1973, when its "Talking Tub" commercial made its first appearance on television. The amusing spot featured a plastic Parkay tub with a talking lid that quickly uttered the word *butter* to convey that the flavor was more like butter than margarine. The advertising campaign was immediately successful in positioning the product as a tasteful and healthful alternative to butter and its saturated fats, the dangers of which newly health-conscious Americans were beginning to be aware. Over the years, celebrities such as the pranksters Laurel and Hardy, football star Deacon Jones, and comedian Al Franken have been featured on the Talking Tub ads.

Margarine has been manufactured in this country since 1873, when Hippolyte Mège-Mouriez , a Frenchman who first developed margarine in Provence, received a patent to make the product in the United States. He first developed the product in 1870 in response to an offer by the Emperor Louis Napoleon III for the production of a satisfactory substitute for butter. But shortly thereafter, the dairy industry successfully lobbied for legislation that for years placed expensive taxes and fees on the product, making prices artificially high. In 1941, the National Nutrition Conference published a study on margarine's health benefits, and consumers began to take notice. The federal government repealed the margarine tax system in 1951, and lower prices caused margarine consumption to double over the next 20 years. Today Americans consume twice as much margarine as butter, and research studies have shown that the shift away from the saturated fats in butter can reduce the risk of heart disease.

The Parkay brand, which was bought by ConAgra Foods in 1978, has continued to innovate and expand. Parkay products include Original spread and stick, Light spread and stick, Parkay Squeeze, and Parkay Fat-Free Spray. The company once even experimented with blue and pink-tinted squeeze margarine aimed at children. The product had accompanying local marketing efforts, including a kids' photo contest.

The marketing strategy has also continued to evolve. In 2002, the company used technology to animate the Talking Tub, making him seem more lifelike. That same year, they placed talking tubs in supermarkets. Shoppers approaching the dairy case, detected by electronic sensors, would hear, "The label says Parkay: the flavor says butter." The in-store promotion targeted 500 million shoppers, making the technology investment in developing a real in-store talking tub a smart buy.

Vital Statistics
Parent Company ConAgra Foods, Inc.
Product Launch 1937
Headquarters Omaha, Nebraska

Patagonia

Patagonia is totally unique in its ability to create clothing and accessories that are aesthetically appealing, suited for the most rugged conditions, and environmentally conscious. Patagonia products are beloved by extreme sports lovers and all of those who love their singular quality and distinctive style. Patagonia sells its lushly colored, technically advanced clothes, gear, accessories, and luggage through specialty retailers, a catalogue, a Web site, and its own stores.

Maine-born Yvon Chouinard was a mountain climber before he ever became a businessman and a lifelong advocate of "clean climbing," scaling rock walls without leaving behind any paraphernalia. He began selling his own design of hard steel pitons in 1957 because there was nothing comparable on the market. By 1966, he had formed Chouinard Equipment and was selling items through the mail and specialty stores in California, where he could surf as well as work. By 1970, Chouinard Equipment had captured 80 percent of the American climbing market. Clothing followed close behind and in 1976, the first clothing bearing the Patagonia logo, named for a rugged area of Argentina, hit the market. The following year saw the introduction of Patagonia's signature offering: the pile jacket, designed to insulate well and repel moisture. Polypropylene long underwear and a children's line followed in the early 80s. In 1985, Chouinard announced that his companies, grouped under the Lost Arrow umbrella, would begin donating 1 percent of sales—more than Patagonia spends on advertising!—to environmental causes. Subsequent rapid growth caused the original equipment company to go Chapter 11 by 1990, and it was eventually sold to employees.

The 1990s saw an even greater focus on environmental issues and employee benefits. The company introduced PCR Synchilla pile, made from post-consumer recycled plastic drink bottles, and has saved almost 90 million soda bottles from the trash heap since then. It launched a global campaign focused on wild salmon as an indicator species of stream and river health worldwide. And in 1996, Patagonia began using only organic cotton to avoid the pesticides used in most cotton fields, avoiding the toxified soil and air and groundwater pollution of traditional methods. By the turn of the century, Patagonia was one of the world's major providers of high quality equipment for outdoor enthusiasts, as well as a recognized leader in environmental causes. In the year 2000, Patagonia ranked eightieth on Fortune magazine's annual listing of the "100 Best Companies to Work For" because of its casual work environment, flexible hours, onsite child care, encouragement of outdoor pursuits, and donations to environmental causes.

Today, Patagonia has initiated a groundbreaking garment recycling program, in conjunction with Japanese fabric maker Teijin, in which customers may return old Capilene base layers, Patagonia fleece, and any manufacturers' Polartec-branded fleece to Patagonia to be broken down and made into new garments using Teijin's EcoCircle fiber-to-fiber recycling system, which breaks down the fiber to its molecular level and creates new raw material for polyester. Patagonia also accepts and recycles Patagonia-branded cotton tees which have reached the end of their lifecycle. Patagonia was the first major retail company to switch all of its cotton clothing over to organic, the first to make fleece from recycled soda-pop bottles, and the first to pledge 1 percent of its annual sales to grassroots environmental organizations. Chouinard has created a multimillion dollar company without going public and has maintained his integrity every step of the way.

Vital Statistics

Classic Product	fleece jacket
Founder	Yvon Chouinard
Employees	1,000
Annual Sales	$2,403 million

Pepperidge Farm Goldfish Crackers

Goldfish crackers have been making new eaters happy for generations. Owned by Campbell Soup Company, Pepperidge Farm is part of the Baking and Snacking division, which brings in 25 percent of Campbell's sales each year. Although Pepperidge Farm breads, cookies, puff pastry, and stuffing account for some of that percentage, it is hard to imagine that any of the other products pack the emotional wallop of those little smiling fish.

The Pepperidge Farm label came about in 1937, when Margaret Rudkin, the mother of a young boy with allergies, couldn't find bread made without preservatives or additives in local Connecticut grocery stores. She decided to take matters into her own hands, the result of which was a delicious loaf of whole wheat bread made entirely of natural ingredients. She launched a small business, with her doctor's encouragement, baking bread in her own home kitchen. In 1947, once the rationing and shortages of World War II had ended, Rudkin opened her first modern bakery, in Norwalk, Connecticut. She added products such as dinner rolls, stuffing, and oatmeal bread. Rudkin went on to produce cookies, including Bordeaux, Brussels, and Milano. Television advertising began in earnest around this time, with Margaret Rudkin serving as the company spokeswoman. Rudkin was later replaced in ads by the grandfatherly horse-and-wagon driving delivery man "Titus Moody," who remained a TV favorite for more than 40 years. Pepperidge Farm was acquired by Campbell's in 1961.

Rudkin discovered Goldfish in Switzerland in the late 1950s and launched them in the U.S. in 1962. Today, Goldfish crackers are found in half of all American households with children under 12 and consumed at a rate of more than 85 billion per year! Parents and kids alike love them for their appealing friendly shape, and the fact that they are made with real cheese and contain no artificial preservatives or trans fats.

Goldfish crackers are sold in 40 countries worldwide. Their popularity transcends the Earth itself, with the crackers having traveled aboard the *Apollo* XII and XIV space missions and on the Space Shuttle *Discovery*.

In 1997, Goldfish became "The Snack That Smiles Back" when smiles were added to some—not all—of the little fish in each back. The latest brand milestone came in 2005 when the Goldfish icon was brought to life as the endearing animated character "Finn" who appears in television ads with his engaging band of fish cracker friends.

Cheddar is by far the most popular Goldfish flavor, but many others have been added through the years. Today's varieties include parmesan, pretzel, and pizza, plus a range of zingy Flavor Blasted favorites like Nothin' But Nacho and Burstin' BBQ Cheddar. Other popular offerings are Baby (mini) Goldfish, Goldfish Colors, Whole Grain Goldfish, and Goldfish 100 Calorie Packs in both savory and sweet flavors. Pepperidge Farm sales curretly exceed $1 billion.

Goldfish® is a registered trademark of Pepperidge Farm, Incorporated.

Vital Statistics
parent company Campbell Soup Company.
product launch 1962
company founder Margaret Rudkin

Poland Spring

Created by a retreating glacier 20,000 years ago, the Poland Spring aquifers are among nature's most effective purification systems. Continuously fed by rainfall and melting snow, the water is filtered through layers of fine sand to produce salt-free spring water with a crisp, invigorating taste. If the words *Poland Spring* conjure up the refreshing image of a clean, clear, bubbling spring, the Ricker family would be very pleased. It was in the late 18th century when the Rickers settled in Maine and opened a small inn near the popular local Poland Spring. When Joseph Ricker was supposedly saved from his deathbed by the spring water (he lived another 52 years!), word of its restorative properties spread far and wide, and the Ricker family's inn was transformed into a major health spa.

In 1845, Hiram Ricker opened the first bottling plant for Poland Spring water. The first shipment was a three-gallon clay jug that sold for 15 cents to local grocers. The water was also sold to travelers and sea captains, enabling word to spread of the water's marvelous healing powers. Throughout the Victorian era, the inn—and the Poland Spring water—grew increasingly popular. In the 1880s, national demand was so high that the company decided to establish a principal sales and distribution depot in New York City. Poland Spring water was featured at the World's Columbian Exposition in 1893 and the 1904 St. Louis World's Fair; in both cases it was awarded honors. In 1907, the first spring and bottling houses, the largest and best-equipped in the United States, were completed, and in 1913, the more formal Riccar (i.e., Ricker) Inn opened with first-rate facilities and national appeal. The Poland Spring resort hosted presidents Cleveland and Taft, business leaders such as Joseph Kennedy, and movie stars such as Mae West, who posed in a provocative ad for the water with a caption reading, "Is that a bottle of Poland Spring in your pocket, or are you just happy to see me?"

Poland Spring water remained a top seller with northeasterners in particular until the company was acquired by the Perrier Group of America in 1980, which committed to ensuring the brand's survival in a new corporate environment and started the Poland Spring route delivery business in 1982. Perrier was acquired by Nestlé Water, North America Inc., which featured Poland Spring water, in a large variety of bottles and packages, as its premier product.

Now headquartered in Greenwich, Connecticut, Poland Spring has been a subsidiary of Nestlé Source International since July 1992. By 2004, Poland Spring annual sales were $628 million and innovative new products, such as the 24-ounce Sport-Pack and 8-ounce half pint, had been introduced. Today, Poland Spring Natural Spring Water is one of the country's leading bottled water brands. Its spring water sources have been chosen for their likeness to the original Poland Spring water in taste and mineral composition. The company's slogan, "Poland Spring—what it means to be from Maine," is now familiar to several generations.

Vital Statistics
Parent Company Nestlé Source International
Classic Product spring water
Established 1845
Founder Hiram Ricker

Thirst Quencher
Poland Spring
BRAND
NATURAL SPRING WATER
FROM MAINE SINCE 1845

Polaris

Folks living in the Snow Belt know that since you can't beat winter, you might as well enjoy it. And riding a snowmobile made by Polaris, the world's number-one manufacturer of snowmobiles, is a surefire way to thumb your nose at the cold. Polaris makes snowmobiles in all shapes and sizes, for enthusiasts who want acceleration and power to race long distances and for those who just need a cruising vehicle to get out to the middle of the lake to do some ice fishing. There are snowmobiles in the Trail Luxury, Mountain, and Crossover categories, and certain models sport the Rider Select Steering system, which allows drivers to adjust the steering post to suit their stature. One particular model, the 900-RMK, is engineered to float on top of the deep snows in the western United States. And the Polaris 750 four-stroke engine already meets the Environmental Protection Agency's proposed standards for model year 2012 and is certified for use in Yellowstone National Park.

The company was started in Minnesota in 1945 by Edgar Hetteen and David Johnson, two friends who were welders and did repair work. Hetteen was a hunter and needed a way to travel the long snow-covered distances out to his winter hunting grounds. He invented a gas-powered sled in the early 1950s that became the envy of his neighbor. The neighbor offered to buy it, and a new industry was born. In the winter of 1954–55, Hetteen and Johnson made five snowmobiles under the Polaris brand name, and by 1957 the duo made upward of 300 of the machines a year. Hetteen's younger brother Allen joined the company.

But people viewed the machines as utility vehicles, good for transporting people and things but nothing more. Knowing that the company needed to expand its market, Edgar Hetteen decided to try to attract the attention of adventurers by leading a 1,000-mile expedition to Alaska in 1960. He received attention from sportsmen, but also the ire of his backers, who complained that the trip cost too much money. Edgar left in 1960 to found a competing company, and his brother Allen assumed the presidency. As snowmobiling grew in popularity Polaris enjoyed strong growth. Executives made frequent product improvements and sponsored snowmobile racing teams.

Now Polaris, which subsequently added all-terrain-vehicles and motorcycles to its product line, is working closely with state snowmobiling associations and clubs to build customer relationships. The volunteers belonging to the associations and clubs maintain the trails necessary for riding. With states such as New York boasting 10,000 miles of designated trails and Minnesota with 20,000 miles, the task of trail maintenance is critical and costly. As a way to support the sport, for each 2006 Polaris snowmobile sold, Polaris contributed money to the association in the state where the transaction occurred. The association can use the money as it sees fit. Additionally, Polaris sent a letter to every new customer with detailed information on how to make a donation or become a member of the state association.

Vital Statistics

Product launch 1954

Headquarters Medina, Minnesota

Employees 3,600

Annual Sales $1869.8 million (2005)

Post-it Notes

Post-it Notes are one of 3M's numerous iconic products. Minnesota Mining and Manufacturing (3M) was started by John Ober and Lucius P. Ordway and three other businessmen back in 1902 to mine and sell corundum to grinding-wheel manufacturers. Mining stopped in 1905 when what they thought was corundum was actually anorthosite. The firm moved from Two Harbors, Minnesota, to Duluth and used the rock they had mined to make sandpaper to accommodate a large and expanding market caused by numerous furniture factories and the fast-growing industrial economy in the Midwest. William L. McKnight and A. G. Bush joined the company in 1907 and worked together for the next 60 years, developing the customer-oriented sales method that has helped create 3M's success.

In the decades that followed, they introduced numerous products, including Scotch Tape. In the 1970s and 1980s, 3M moved into pharmaceuticals, energy control, and office supplies, where it went on to introduce one of the company's most innovative and useful products: Post-it Notes.

Post-it Notes came about in the 1970s when 3M scientist Art Fry felt a need for a new kind of page marker. As a singer in his church choir, he often lost his place when his bookmark fell out of his hymnal. Back in 1968, colleague Spencer Silver had developed an adhesive with a low grade of stickiness but couldn't find a use for it. Recalling this, Art Fry brushed some of the adhesive onto paper to create a marker that would stay in place but wouldn't damage the pages of a book and could easily be repositioned. This led to the creation of a line of products that generates hundreds of millions of dollars each year.

Without actual samples, it was difficult for those involved in early marketing efforts to show consumers just how useful Post-it Notes could be. In 1978, the company launched the "Boise Blitz," a marketing campaign that blanketed the city of Boise, Idaho, with Post-it Notes. When people got to sample the product, 90 percent said they would purchase it themselves, and two years later, Post-it Notes were being sold nationally.

Originally made in canary yellow—the color of American legal notepads—Post-it Notes are available in more than 60 colors and come in eight standard sizes and 25 different shapes. One survey found that the average professional receives 11 messages on Post-it notes every day. The Post-it line has more than 600 products sold in more than 100 countries. The Post-it phenomenon has spawned numerous imitations around the world, and many software companies have electronic versions to grace computer desktops, but the original Post-it product remains the leader in the category.

Vital Statistics
Parent Company 3M
Classic Product Post-it Notes
Introduced 1978-1980
Inventor Art Fry
Headquarters St. Paul, Minnesota

Prozac

In 1987, a green-and-cream-colored pill was launched by Eli Lilly & Co., the global pharmaceutical company. The drug was guaranteed to be safer and more effective than any existing medication of its kind. It seemed to offer the impossible—to alleviate the feelings of despair and anxiety that chronically afflict more than 12 million Americans each year. By 1990, psychiatrists were prescribing the green-and-cream pill more frequently than any other drug. That year, the pill, already an icon, was featured on the front cover of *Newsweek.* The banner headline over it read, "Prozac: A Breakthrough Drug for Depression."

Prozac was a completely new type of drug to counter depression. Since 1970, Eli Lilly & Co. had been on a mission to develop a better, safer medicine than the potentially lethal tricyclic antidepressants on the market. In 1972, the team working on the project—chemists Ray Fuller, Bryan Molloy, and David Wong—synthesized fluoxetine hydrochloride, an off-white crystalline substance. The company named it Prozac based on the positive connotations of the Latin prefix *pro* combined with a succinct and zippy suffix.

Prozac works by increasing levels of serotonin—the brain's "feel good" neurotransmitter that affects sleep, appetite, and aggression. It is the first of a class of drugs known as selective serotonin reuptake inhibitors (SSRIs). By preventing the absorption or "reuptake" of serotonin, the brain's concentration of neurotransmitters changes, which in turn affects a person's mood. Prozac is used to help treat not only depression but also obsessive-compulsive disorder, bulimia, anorexia nervosa, and panic disorder. By 2000, millions of patients in nearly 100 countries were on Prozac.

Unlike any drug before it, Prozac captured the public imagination. In the years after it appeared on the market, psychiatrist Peter Kramer wrote *Listening to Prozac,* a best seller that gushes about how the antidepressant makes timid people confident and have the "social skills of a salesman." Harvard freshman Elizabeth Wurtzel wrote *Prozac Nation,* a best-selling book about teenage depression and drugs that later became a movie starring Christina Ricci. Celebrities spoke publicly about their struggles with depression, and Americans seemed more comfortable in general discussing depression publicly. Prozac gained a reputation as a "celebrity drug"—not only did it seem like a lot of stars were taking it, but it was a celebrity in its own right. It became a household name.

In August 2001, Eli Lilly lost patent protection on Prozac, which allowed other companies to manufacture generic versions of fluoxetine. By that time, the pharmaceutical giant had made $21.1 billion in Prozac sales. More than 54 million people worldwide have been prescribed Prozac, which makes the antidepressant one of the most successful drugs in pharmaceutical history. Eli Lilly is researching newer, safer, more effective forms of SSRIs and other antidepressants that will replace Prozac.

Vital Statistics
Parent Company Eli Lilly
Established 1987
Inventors Ray Fuller, Bryan Molloy, and David Wong
Headquarters Indianapolis, Indiana

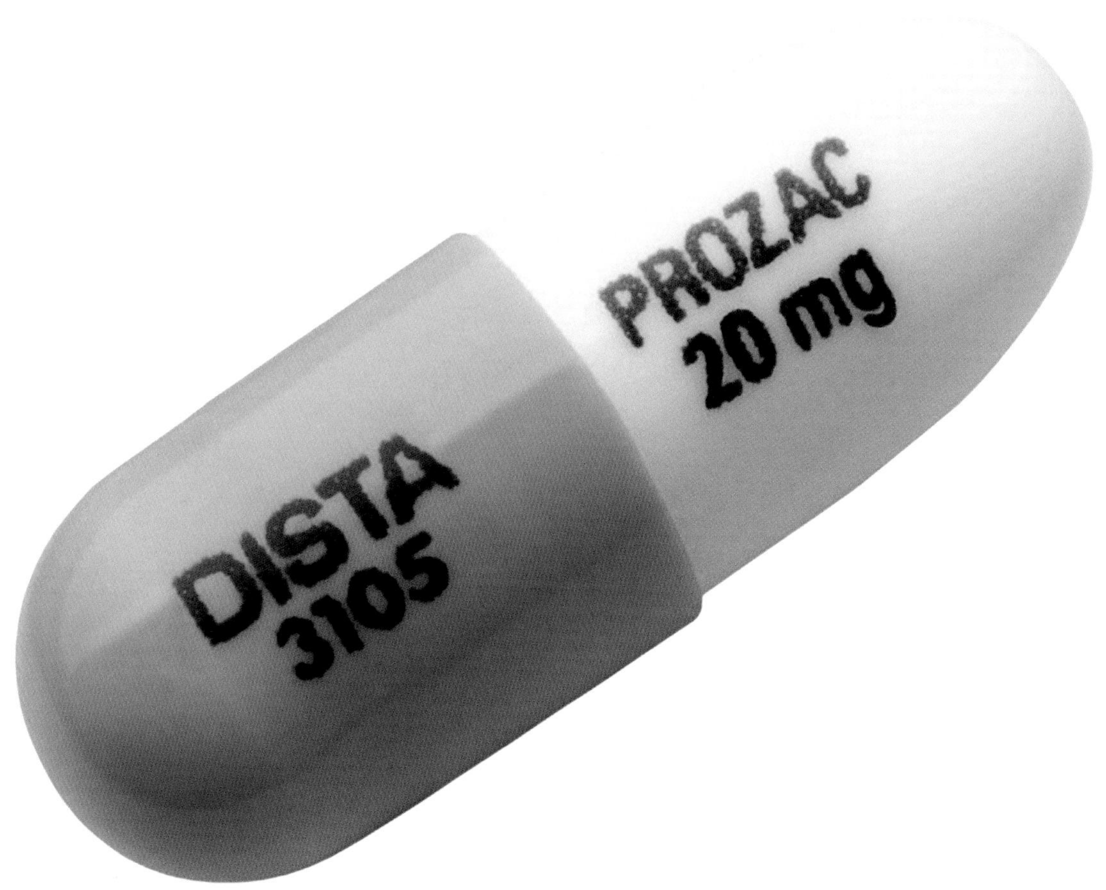
PROZAC
20 mg
DISTA
3105

Purell

Goldie Lippman, a worker at a rubber factory during World War II, had a problem. At the end of the workday her hands were black with tar, graphite, and carbon—substances that wouldn't easily wash off. Her husband, Jerome "Jerry" Lippman, contacted a chemist at Kent State University who created a powerful grease-cutting soap that Goldie and her co-workers loved. In 1948, the Lippmans decided to open an Akron, Ohio–based business selling the soap to factory and automobile workers. They named their company GOJO—a combination of their first names—and sold hand-mixed batches of the product out of the back of Jerry's car. By the 1950s, GOJO had become the leading seller of heavy-duty hand cleaner.

In 1988, GOJO developed Purell—an ethyl alcohol–based hand cleaner that kills 99.99 percent of common germs that may cause illness. The new waterless hand sanitizer was targeted to food and health care workers who regularly wash their hands as part of a hygiene regimen. Health care workers found the hand cleaner particularly useful in emergencies and at times when it was inconvenient to get to a sink—which, when moving quickly from patient to patient, was almost all the time. In 1997, GOJO launched Purell as a consumer product. In 2001, the company launched a two-in-one product with moisturizer containing aloe and vitamin E. Purell became the best-selling hand sanitizer in the United States. It caught the attention of pharmaceutical giant Pfizer, which bought the brand in 2004.

Purell's success paralleled the increasing number of consumer warnings about viruses and bacteria that cling to hands, doorknobs, desks, subway handrails, kitchen sponges, and other surfaces. The case for Purell also comes from no less an authority than the Centers for Disease Control and Prevention, which issued a recommendation that alcohol-based instant hand sanitizers be used when soap and water are unavailable. Scientists shocked the public when they voiced that far fewer germs are found on public toilets than on playground equipment, escalator handrails, picnic tables, and other unexpected places. Studies showed that absenteeism in schools was lowered when teachers made their students use hand sanitizer.

Purell commercials successfully targeted a geared-up germ-phobic public. In one, to the tune of MC Hammer's "U Can't Touch This," a young man violently sneezes all over the handle of a shopping cart. Moments later, a young mother and her child use the same cart. In another ad with the same rap music, a kid with a bad cold wipes his moist hands on a playground ball.

In 2006, Pfizer sold its Home and Healthcare division, which included the Purell brand, to Johnson & Johnson, which made the latter the largest over-the-counter pharmaceutical company in the world. The Purell brand is sold throughout the Americas, Europe, and Asia—and Johnson & Johnson plans to increase its presence wherever germs spread, which is just about everywhere.

Vital Statistics
Parent Company Johnson & Johnson
Established 1948 (GOJO)
Founders Goldie and Jerry Lippman
Headquarters New Brunswick, New Jersey

New Value Size!
Purell
BRAND®
Instant Hand Sanitizer
ALOE
with
VITAMIN E
Great for:
• Refilling smaller bottles
• High traffic areas

Q-tips

The year was 1923. The product was the unfortunately named Baby Gays. Leo Gerstenzang, a Polish-American entrepreneur, invented what the world now knows as Q-tips and founded the Leo Gerstenzang Infant Novelty Company to market his product. In 1926, Baby Gays became Q-Tips Baby Gays, and soon thereafter Baby Gays was dropped from the name altogether. Q-Tips—with the Q for "quality," and *tips* referring to the cotton ends—can now be found in bathroom cabinets all over the world.

Gerstenzang came up with his idea while watching his wife wrap bits of cotton around toothpicks to make a homespun cleaning device. He figured there would likely be a market for a ready-to-use swab and perfected the design we are familiar with today based on his wife's model. Initially, his (also awkwardly named) Leo Gerstenzang Infant Novelty Co. marketed baby care accessories. The Q-tips were what really took off, however, and the company's focus turned to expansion. In 1948, because of increased consumer demand, Q-tips, Inc., moved its manufacturing facility from New York City to a new facility in Long Island City, New York, where greater numbers could be produced. Ten years later, Q-tips purchased Paper Sticks Ltd. of England, a manufacturer of paper sticks for the confectionery trades. Q-tips brought the machinery to the United States and adapted it to manufacture Q-tips' new "Paper Applicator" cotton swabs, making Q-tips available for the first time with both wooden and paper sticks. In 1962, after decades of success, Q-tips, Inc., was acquired by Chesebrough-Pond's, which relocated the production facility to Jefferson City, Missouri. The Missouri plant continued to produce all Q-tips cotton swabs for the domestic market until 1974, when Chesebrough-Pond's moved some production to Puerto Rico.

The 1980s saw an important development as Q-tips began using 100 percent cotton in all their swabs, solidifying the quality consumers have come to expect from the brand. The most significant change in Q-tips' fortune, however, came in 1987, when Unilever—the industry giant founded as Lever Brothers in 1885—acquired Chesebrough-Pond's, including Q-tips cotton swabs. Unilever had big ideas for the brand, introducing the Q-tips Vanity Pack in 1995 and Q-tips Antibacterial cotton swabs in 1998. Today's line offers packaging for a variety of occasions, from the 285-count Vanity pack to the 54-count Travel package, small enough to fit in a travel case, and the 30-count pack, which can be tucked into a pocket or purse.

Q-tips cotton swabs are perfect for cleaning the outside parts of ears, applying, blending, or removing makeup, helping families care for babies, and cleaning hard-to-reach places around the house. Q-tips are the number-one cotton swab on the market and have more cotton on the tip than any other cotton swab, from the end of the stick to the top of the swab. In fact, the word *Q-tip* has become synonymous with cotton swabs throughout North America, where people use it to refer to any and all brands.

Vital Statistics
Parent Company Unilever U.S.
Year Introduced 1923
Founder Leo Gerstenzang

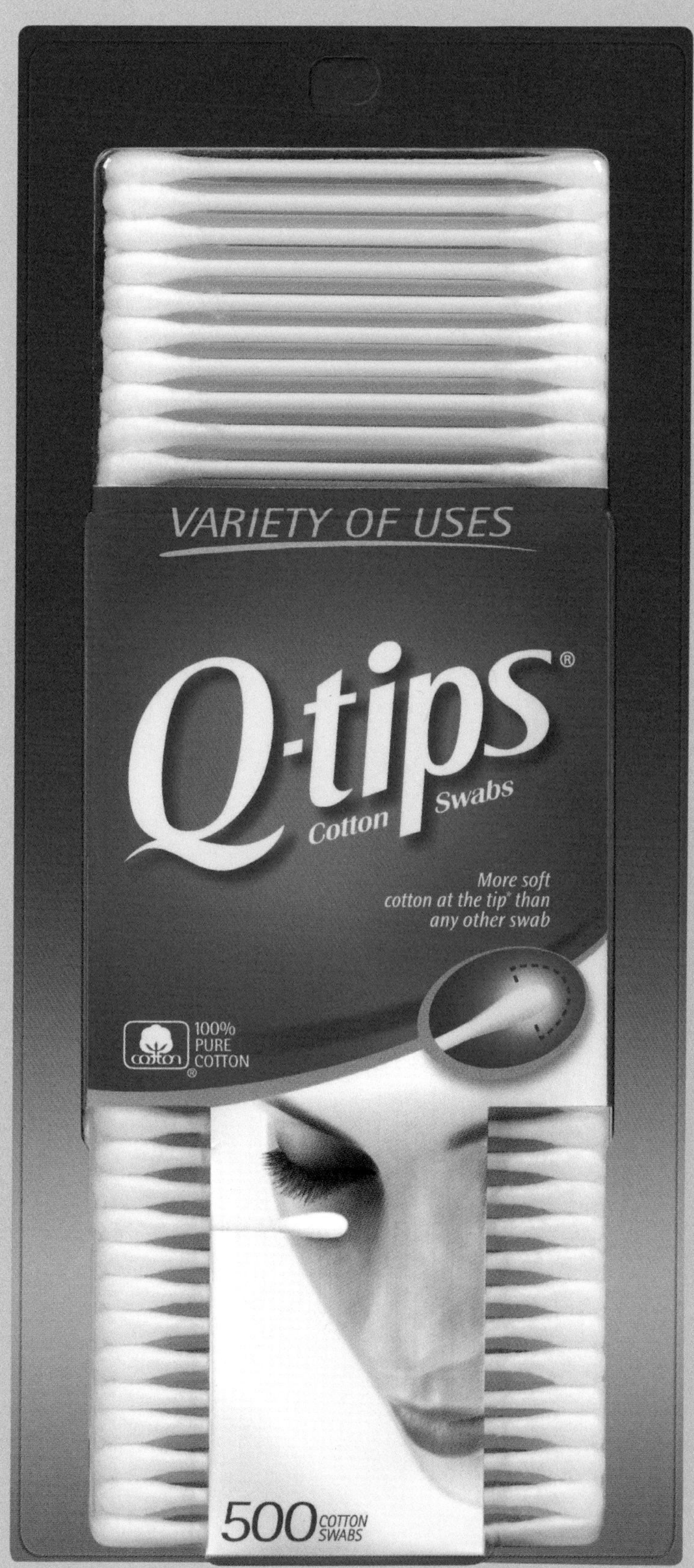
VARIETY OF USES
Q-tips®
Cotton Swabs
More soft
cotton at the tip® than
any other swab
100%
PURE
COTTON
500 COTTON SWABS

Radio City Music Hall

Home to the world-famous dance troupe the Rockettes, Radio City Music Hall in New York has been the largest indoor theater in the world since it opened its doors on December 27, 1932. At the time of the stock market crash in 1929, John D. Rockefeller Jr. held a $91 million, 24-year lease on a piece of midtown property. With the failing economy and grim business outlook, Rockefeller decided to build an entire complex of buildings of superior design and architecture to attract commercial tenants. The project would stand as a symbol of optimism and hope at a time when it was desperately needed.

A commercial partner was found in the Radio Corporation of America, a young company whose NBC radio programs were attracting huge audiences and whose RKO studios were producing and distributing motion pictures that served as a welcome diversion in hard times. Rockefeller and RCA were joined by the talented S. L. "Roxy" Rothafel, a theatrical genius who combined vaudeville, movies, and glamorous décor to revive struggling theaters across America. Together Rockefeller, RCA, and Roxy realized the dream of creating a theater unlike any that existed. It was the first completed project in the complex and was dubbed "Radio City" by RCA head David Sarnoff.

The building design was and still is a sight to behold. Donald Deskey, a relatively unknown interior designer, won the competition to design the interior spaces. He designed more than 30 separate spaces, each with its own motif, choosing elegance and grandeur over excess and glitz. Art was an integral part of the design, and fine artists were hired to create murals, wall coverings, and sculptures, textile designers to develop draperies and carpets, and craftsmen to make ceramics, wood panels, and chandeliers.

Radio City Music Hall features a marquee that is a full city block long. Its auditorium measures 160 feet from back to stage, and the ceiling is 84 feet high. There are no columns to obstruct views. The Great Stage is framed by a huge proscenium arch that measures 60 feet high and 100 feet wide. The shimmering gold stage curtain is the largest in the world. The "Mighty Wurlitzer" organ, built especially for the theater, has pipes that range from a few inches to 32 feet and are housed in 11 separate rooms.

The phenomenal space is the perfect showcase for movie premieres, with its huge screen and comfortable seating. Since 1933, more than 700 movies have opened at Radio City, including the original *King Kong, National Velvet, White Christmas, Breakfast at Tiffany's, Mary Poppins,* and *The Lion King.* A run at Radio City virtually guaranteed a movie's success nationally, and film stars often made an appearance on a film's opening day. Today, Radio City still premieres select films, but is best known as the leading hall for pop concerts, stage shows, and special attractions—most famously the Radio City Christmas Spectacular, a show that draws more than a million visitors every holiday season and has been a sellout since its debut in 1933.

Vital Statistics

Established 1932

Founders John D. Rockefeller Jr., Radio Corporation of America and S. L. "Roxy" Rothafiel

Parent Company Cablevision Systems Corporation

RADIO CITY
MUSIC HALL
RADIO CITY
MUSIC HALL
RADIO CITY Music Hall RADIO CITY
MAY 9 MOODY BLUES
LANG & LYLE LOVETT 6/21 JILL SCOTT TWO NIGHTS OF SOUL 6/13-14
DON'T BLOCK THE BOX
FINE + 2 POINTS
ACADEMY

Ragú

Any Italian home cook knows that an important barometer of prowess is the cook's *ragout*, a hearty tomato spaghetti sauce. Though the ingredients are simple, a good cook can make a distinctive sauce by paying attention to detail and hovering over the stove. That time-consuming process was made much simpler in 1937 with the introduction of the Ragú brand of spaghetti sauce by Giovanni and Assunta Cantisano. Homemakers at the time were still interested in eating well but were no longer willing to spend hours slaving over every meal. The Cantisanos brought their homemade recipe with them when they moved from Italy to America. They initially sold homemade sauce out of the trunk of their car, and eventually opened the first Ragú plant in their backyard in Rochester, New York.

The convenience offered by Ragú sauce in a jar was a welcome relief. That same year other convenience foods, including macaroni and cheese, made their debut, and for the first time, "grocery carts" became widely used in stores.

Ethnic food was less well known and available than it is today, and Ragú's early advertising successfully broadened the market in the United States for Italian food. Slogans such as "That's Italian," and "Ragú brings the Italian out in you" persuaded American cooks to incorporate spaghetti into their weekly dinner menus. The original recipe for Ragú has come a long way since then, with varieties including smooth Old World Style sauces, Chunky sauces that have more ingredients and bolder flavors, Cheesy Creations!, Pizza Quick sauces, Pizza Sauce, and a line of organic and lower-calorie pasta sauces. Ragú Old World style sauces use all-natural ingredients; it takes about nine billion tomatoes to make one year's worth of Ragú pasta sauce.

In 1971, Ragú was the very first jarred pasta sauce sold nationally. Ragú was the leading U.S. maker of pasta sauce by 1980, with a 50 percent market share, and today still holds the number-one position. It was bought by the Lipton and Bestfoods companies before being bought by Unilever in 2000. Ragú continues to develop new varieties of sauce and introduced the first mainstream organic pasta sauce (Ragú Organic) in 2005. The recipe for Ragú Old World Style sauce sold in stores today is almost identical to the original recipe created by the Contisano family 70 years ago.

Vital Statistics

Parent Company Unilever U.S.

Formulated by Giovanni and Assunta Contisano

CERTIFIED ORGANIC
ORGANIC
RAGÚ
smooth and flavorful
Traditional
USDA
ORGANIC

Ralph Lauren Home

Polo Ralph Lauren is a global lifestyle brand representing the best in American design, encompassing such celebrated brands as Ralph Lauren, Polo by Ralph Lauren, Ralph Lauren Purple Label, Black Label, and Blue Label. The company produces distinctive apparel, accessories, fragrances and home furnishings true to Ralph Lauren's vision, and the Home division in particular epitomizes Lauren's bold American aesthetic.

RALPH LAUREN

In the late 1960s, Ralph Lauren was working as a clothing salesman in New York City. He had no design experience, but he did have a good eye and a finely honed sense of classic American style. Still only in his mid-20s, Lauren persuaded clothier Beau Brummel to manufacture his new line of neckwear—ties that were wider and brighter than those on the market at the time. These ties launched the "wide-tie revolution" and marked the beginning of the Polo label.

Within a year, Lauren had brought his brother Jerry into the business and with $50,000 in backing from a Manhattan clothing manufacturer, the brothers founded Polo Fashions and released their first menswear collection. The expansion continued rapidly, and shirt, suit, and sportswear lines were soon introduced. In 1970, only three years after founding Polo, Lauren received the Coty Award for menswear. Two years later he launched a complete line of womenswear to much acclaim and with sales figures topping $10 million.

During the 1980s, the company expanded to include fragrances, eyewear, shoes, accessories, housewares, and a range of other products that encapsulated Lauren's elegant yet sporty style. 1983 saw the debut of Ralph Lauren Home, marking the first time a fashion designer launched an entire home collection. *House & Garden* called the collection, which numbered more than 2,500 items and included furniture, flatware, bedding, towels, area rugs, and wallcoverings, "the most complete of its kind conceived by a fashion designer." Lauren himself said of the home collection, "This was a vision of how I would love to live. I wasn't just creating a sheet—I was creating a complete home, which could reflect the kind of world people wanted to live in."

In subsequent years, Ralph Lauren Home has grown to include linens, floorcovering, lighting, a tabletop collection, home accessories, and expertly crafted furniture, and in 1995 introduced Ralph Lauren Paint.

Ralph Lauren is the quintessential American designer, and his company is a true arbiter of timeless style. He has received numerous awards, both to honor him as a leader in his field and in recognition of his philanthropic efforts. He has worked in practically every conceivable design arena and consequently has redefined the way Americans dress and decorate their homes. Today the Ralph Lauren brand is recognized all over the world and continues to inspire each new generation.

Vital Statistics
Parent Company Polo Ralph Lauren Corporation
Founder/Inventor Ralph Lauren
Employees 12,762
Annual Sales $3,746.3 million (2005)

Rawlings Sporting Goods Company

Rawlings is as American as baseball, probably because it is best known as a leading marketer and manufacturer of baseball equipment. An innovator in the world of sports, Rawlings makes the official baseball and helmet of Major League Baseball and the official ball of the National Collegiate Athletic Association baseball championships.

In 1887, brothers Alfred and George Rawlings opened a retail sporting goods store in St. Louis, Missouri. With a catalogue offering a wide variety of items that included fishing tackle, guns, and general sporting goods, the company soon folded, and in 1898, the Rawlings brothers got into manufacturing with a funding partner.

In 1902, Rawlings Manufacturing Co. introduced the first shoulder pads for football players—a fiber-and-felt model called Whitley's Armor Clothing. Rawlings designed the first all-weather football, and in 1906, the company began supplying uniforms to the St. Louis Cardinals. A year later, Rawlings first provided baseballs to a professional league. From its shaky beginnings, Rawlings quickly proved itself a pioneer in the sporting goods arena. In 1919, Cardinals pitcher Bill Doak designed the first modern baseball glove when he separated the thumb and forefinger with some rawhide to form a deep pocket in the glove. Doak went to Rawlings with the idea, and Rawlings manufactured the glove, making it a best seller for more than 25 years. In 1922, Rawlings hired Harry "Glove Doctor" Latina, who is responsible for various models, including the Deep Well Pocket (1930), Trapper (1940), and V-Anchored Web (1950) as well as about 30 patents for a variety of glove features.

After a brief alliance with Spalding, Rawlings was sold in 1963 to a group of investors, making it the only privately owned sporting goods manufacturer in the United States, and by 1967, it had annual sales of more than $20 million, with four manufacturing plants in Missouri and two in Puerto Rico. The company was sold to Automatic Sprinkler Corp. of America, which was renamed A-T-O Inc. in 1969. As a division under the name of Rawlings Sporting Goods, it also made golf and tennis equipment, and within one year, Rawlings had become the largest manufacturer of hockey equipment in the United States.

By 1970, 12 major-league baseball teams were wearing Rawlings-made uniforms and the American Basketball Association was using Rawlings' red, white, and blue ball. That same year, Rawlings teamed up with Adirondack to supply the Major League with bats, and in 1976, Rawlings won the contract as the exclusive supplier of baseballs to the American and National leagues. This contract amounted to 30,000 dozen baseballs a year, not including special balls for All-Star games and the World Series, and Rawlings is still supplying hand-stitched baseballs to the Major Leagues. Though it has had a colorful history supplying equipment for a variety of sports, Rawlings will always mean high quality and innovation in baseball.

Owned by sporting goods maker K2 Corp. since 2003, Rawlings Sporting Goods makes and distributes equipment and protective gear for baseball, softball, football, basketball, and volleyball. Rawlings sells through mass merchandisers, sporting goods retailers, and online. The company also licenses its name for a wide variety of merchandise, including clothing, shoes, and toys.

Vital Statistics

Established 1887

Founders Alfred and George Rawlings

Classic Product baseball

Headquarters St. Louis, Missouri

Annual Sales $174 million (2002)

Ray-Ban

Remember Tom Cruise in *Risky Business*? Then you know Ray-Bans–the epitome of cool for 70 years and the world's best-selling brand of sunglasses. Ray-Bans have long been known for their quality, style, and exceptional value. Today, the company is owned by Luxottica Group, the global leader in eyewear, with nearly 5,700 optical and sun retail stores in North America, Asia-Pacific, China, and Europe. In addition to a global wholesale network that touches 130 countries, the Group manages leading retail brands such as Sunglass Hut globally, LensCrafters and Pearle Vision in North America, OPSM and Laubman & Pank in the Asia-Pacific region.

The original aviator-style Anti-Glare sunglasses were created by Ray-Ban in 1936 for the U.S. Air Force and were an immediate success. As a result, the Ray-Ban trademark was registered in 1937. The scientific and technological innovations of the 1940s were powerful factors in Ray-Ban's growth, as the company's continued close collaboration with the Air Force encouraged research and testing on new materials. Gradient mirror lenses, now a sunglass staple, were developed during this period.

The 1950s were a decade of profound change, as consumers were beginning to perceive eyewear as a fashion accessory and no longer as just objects to be worn for practical reasons. In 1952 Ray-Ban launched the Wayfarer, that in 1961 was used during the shooting of the celebrated Audrey Hepburn film *Breakfast at Tiffany's*. The Wayfarer continued its Hollywood career outfitting Dan Aykroyd and John Belushi in *The Blues Brothers* (1980) and Tom Cruise in *Risky Business* (1983).

In 1999, Italian company Luxottica Group bought Ray-Ban from Bausch & Lomb together with other brands including Arnette and REVO. At that time, Ray-Ban shades sold for as little as $29 and were overdistributed. Manufacturing was scattered across the globe from Rochester, New York, to China and Ireland. Luxottica executives took the drastic step of cutting down production for six months to purge the market of low quality frames. Production was switched to Agordo (Italy) and the company immediately ramped up manufacturing for numerous existing Ray-Ban models, including Predator (made famous in the movie *Men in Black*), Shooters, and Caravan. In 2003, two new Ray-Ban lines were introduced: ophthalmic and Junior sun (for children between the ages of 8 and 12) followed in 2005 by Ray-Ban Junior optical.

Today Ray-Ban continues to symbolize a unique, inimitable style, skillfully proposed in a wide range of models that have been gracing the faces of millions around the world since 1937. Carefully selected materials, distinctive design, and attention to detail set Ray-Ban apart as the brand whose ever-popular, iconic models like Aviator and Wayfarer continue to write the history of eyewear. For countless reasons, Ray-Ban is not only the most iconic brand in eyewear globally, but also the best-selling sunglasses worldwide with about 12 million pieces sold in 2006.

Vital Statistics
Parent Company Luxottica Group S.p.A.
Classic Product Wayfarer sunglasses

Ray-Ban
Ray-Ban

Red Bull

Red Bull energy drink is a staple for today's youth market and in many ways a symbol of modern times. The non-alcoholic energy drink is ubiquitous in delis and nightclubs alike, and has become the drink of choice for many athletes, long-distance drivers, celebrities, law students, and even the occasional weary middle-aged adult in need of a jolt. Red Bull contains an amino acid called taurine, B-complex vitamins, caffeine, and carbohydrates—ingredients combined deliberately to give the body a nearly instant burst of energy.

Red Bull was founded by an Austrian man named Dietrich Mateschitz. In 1982, as his travels led him to Thailand, he discovered "tonic drinks" which were already very popular in Asia. While sitting at a hotel bar in Hong Kong, he was inspired to market those drinks outside Asia. One drink in particular—Krating Daeng, Thai for "Asian water buffalo"—seemed especially effective. In 1984, Mateschitz founded Red Bull GmbH in Austria as a partner with Chaleo Yoovidhya, the man who owned the company producing the beverages in Thailand. Mateschitz owned 49 percent of the company. It took three years, but in 1987, Red Bull hit the market, selling more than a million cans in Austria during that first year. When the partners decided to enter the Western market, they adapted the formula accordingly, adding carbonation and dropping several ingredients.

Red Bull billed itself as able to increase concentration and stamina, and the product took off internationally. In 1997, Red Bull reached American shores, starting small in California, Oregon, Texas, and Colorado. Red Bull was sold worldwide in narrow, 8.3-ounce cans for $2 each, and quickly established a niche in the market as an alternative soft drink choice. Red Bull appealed to the growing extreme sports movement, for one, and began sponsoring snowboarding, skiing, mountain biking, surfing, and skateboarding events. The media reported that Red Bull appeared neon green under nightclub lights, and bartenders started using it as a mixer with vodka and other types of alcohol. By the turn of the millennium, Red Bull was available in more than 50 countries.

Red Bull is much more than a sports drink—it is an energy drink intended to vitalize the body and mind. It has spawned many imitators, but none have come close to creating Red Bull's amazing buzz. Red Bull owns 80 percent of the energy-drink market in more than 130 countries all over the world. More than 3 billion cans were sold in 2006.

Vital Statistics
Product Launch 1987
Founder Dietrich Mateschitz
Employees 3,903
Annual Sales $2.7 billion (2006)

Lightly Carbonated.
Serve chilled.
Bull
With Taurine. Vitalizes body and mind.
8.3 FL OZ (250 ML)

Redken

Acquired by L'Oréal in 1993, Redken 5th Avenue NYC is a people-oriented, high-energy brand that continues to be an inspiration to the salon professional community and consumers alike. Taking its inspiration from the spirit, energy, and fashion on the streets and runways of the city it calls home, Redken delivers a unique mix of groundbreaking products, inspiring education for salon professionals and creativity with an urban edge.

The company was founded in 1960 by entrepreneur Paula Kent. Paula was highly sensitive to the products used by hairdressers and make-up artists so she worked with her friend and hairdresser Jheri Redding (thus the name "REDKEN") to formulate gentle yet high-performance haircare products. Redken was the first manufacturer to apply proteins and moisture to dramatically improve weakened and sensitized hair and restore strength and shine. From the beginning, the brand's philosophy has centered on intensive education for hairdressers about the chemistry of hair and skin.

More than 40 years later, the company's foundation is still based on extensive scientific knowledge and the belief in, and support of, the expertise of the salon professional. Redken is committed to help every salon professional "learn better, earn better and live better" and supports this goal not only with innovative products, but also with a strong, award-winning education program. The Redken Exchange, the industry's leading resource for learning, and Redken Symposium, the largest single-manufacturer educational event in the industry, offer stylists programs that develop their skills in the areas of design and color, business training, personal development, and wealth building.

The company's product portfolio includes a full line of haircare solutions addressing specific hair needs; styling products that create and control any style; a range of haircolor options that offer long-lasting, professional results; and a complete collection of men's grooming products.

Vital Statistics

Parent Company L'Oréal USA

Product Launch 1960

Headquarters New York, New York

REDKEN
5TH AVENUE NYC
Extreme
Shampoo
fortifier for distressed hair
lipids, proteins
10.1 FL OZ 300 ml
REDKEN
5TH AVENUE NYC
All Soft
Shampoo
softness for dry/brittle hair
avocado oil
10.1 FL OZ 300 ml
REDKEN
5TH AVENUE NYC
Body Full
Shampoo
anti gravity volume
for normal/fine hair
carbo-polymers
10.1 FL OZ 300 ml
UVB filter/vitamin C

Right Guard

People have been trying to control body odor ever since anyone can remember, starting with the use of heavily scented colognes and perfumes designed to mask the smell. The advent of regular bathing helped matters somewhat. But then scientists realized it's not sweat that smells; it's the bacteria growing in the damp, warm conditions of underarms that cause odors. They developed deodorants, which kill odor-causing bacteria, and they also made antiperspirants, which inhibit the activity of sweat glands, thereby reducing the ability of bacteria to grow. The first antiperspirant was patented in the United States in the late 1880s, but it was a waxy cream that was messy to apply. Other application methods, including pads, roll-ons, and powders, often left sticky hands and telltale residue in the armpit.

Today Right Guard comes in various forms, including invisible solid, deodorant solid, gel, aerosol, Clear Stick and Cool Spray. Right Guard has always been a leader in product innovation, which most recently includes the Clear Stick, PowerStripe, and Cool Spray technologies. In 2002, Right Guard launched the proprietary PowerStripe technology, which adds a powerful stripe of extra odor protection in both the invisible solid and deodorant solid sticks. In 2004, Right Guard launched Cool Spray, a revolutionary aerosol variant with a nozzle that sprays upward rather than to one side. Furthermore, Right Guard also owns the technology that produces the only truly clear solid stick in the market. Not to be confused with a gel, the Clear Stick goes on clear like a gel, but comes in the solid form that consumers have grown to love.

Right Guard connects with its consumers through TV, print, radio, online, and in-store advertising, as well as targeted sponsorships including the X Games and Dew Action Sports Tour, where Right Guard is the title sponsor of the Right Guard Open, one of the Tour's five stops.

The Dial Corporation bought Right Guard from Gillette, a Procter & Gamble subsidiary, in 2006.

Vital Statistics
Parent Company The Dial Corporation
Headquarters Scottsdale, Arizona

No Gel is
STRONGER!*
*vs. wetness
RIGHT GUARD
SPORT
FRESH
CLEAR GEL
ANTI-PERSPIRANT DEODORANT
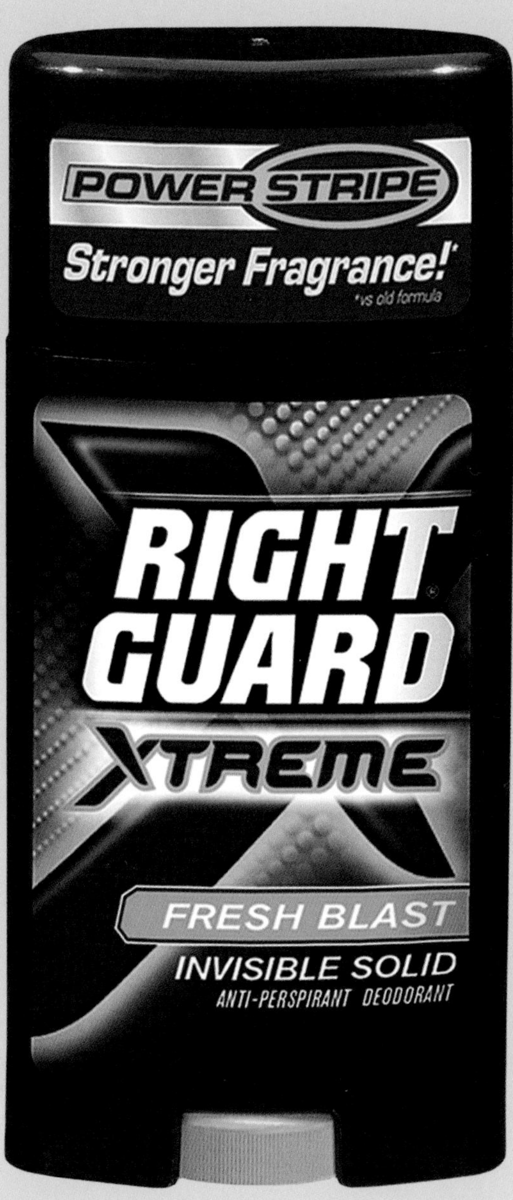
POWER STRIPE
Stronger Fragrance!*
*vs old formula
RIGHT GUARD
XTREME
FRESH BLAST
INVISIBLE SOLID
ANTI-PERSPIRANT DEODORANT

Ritz

Crisp, buttery, with fetching scalloped edges, Ritz crackers—in the distinctive red box—have been an American favorite for generations. First introduced to the United States in the 1930s, Ritz quickly became popular in Europe and Australia; apparently in Europe for some years Ritz crackers were presented to young women by their dates in lieu of traditional chocolates or flowers. Whether enjoyed alone or with various toppings as part of a cheese tray, Ritz crackers remain a classic favorite around the world.

Ritz's origins are more than 200 years old. In 1801, a retired sea captain named John Bent set out to make a tastier version of hardtack for a more general palate. His family took on the baking tasks while Bent traveled around selling his crackers from a wagon. In 1805, with Bent's approval, a company called the Kentucky Biscuit Works finessed the recipe, making the product lighter and flakier. In 1898, Bent joined forces with Kentucky Biscuit Works and dozens of other bakeries nationwide and formed the National Biscuit Company—to become Nabisco (now a part of Kraft Foods) in 1971. Company bakers continued to tinker with the cracker recipe, eventually eliminating the yeast and increasing the butter content.

During the great Depression, edible luxuries became scarce in all but the richest of households. One staple, however, that people refused to give up were crackers, and in 1934, the Ritz cracker was born. Named after the word *ritzy,* which symbolized perfection, elegance, and glamour, the Ritz was an instant classic. Its round shape, serrated edges, and buttery richness won legions of fans, leading to mass production beginning in Philadelphia later that same year. In 1935, Ritz crackers began to be nationally distributed, advertised as a "taste of affordable luxury." The company sold five billion units that year, which came out to an awe-inspiring 40 crackers for every American. The National Biscuit Company, the only American baking manufacturer with the capability of producing and distributing from coast to coast, kept the price of a box of Ritz crackers low: 19 cents. The *Queen Mary* never left shore without a large supply of Ritz crackers on board, and New York's Waldorf=Astoria placed them on their menu.

Today, Ritz sells almost 20 billion crackers every year. The crackers look and taste the same as they have since 1934. Variations such as Ritz Bits Sandwiches, miniature-sized Ritz cracker sandwiches, are available with cheese, peanut butter, s'mores, and peanut butter and jelly fillings. Toasted Ritz Chips and an elongated version called Ritz Sticks are also popular. Classic Ritz, however, is America's best-selling cracker and one of the country's top food brands overall. Recipes such as the notorious Mock Apple Pie are still popular with home cooks, and low-salt and whole-wheat crackers will ensure the brand's continued success.

Vital Statistics
Parent Company Kraft Foods
Product Launch 1934

NABISCO
GREAT WITH
KRAFT
CHEESE
See Recipes on Back
RITZ
CRACKERS
3 STAY FRESH PACKS
NET WT 12 OZ (340g)
Nutrition Facts
kraftfoods.com

Rock and Roll Hall of Fame

The only museum of its kind, the Rock and Roll Hall of Fame and Museum celebrates the music of the great American art form of rock and roll. Legends ranging from Chuck Berry to the Byrds to the B-52s are all represented, whether it's in the Museum's permanent collection of thousands of artifacts, its list of 500 Songs that Shaped Rock and Roll, or a place in the Hall of Fame, where inductees' signatures glow in laser-etched glass. Interactive exhibits, films, and video displays are part of the permanent programming, but the facility also hosts concerts, educational programs ranging from Toddler Rock to American Music Masters, and special events including the Hall of Fame Series. Since it opened in 1995 in Cleveland, Ohio, more than six million visitors have made the pilgrimage.

The Museum is housed in a daring piece of architecture designed by world-renowned architect I.M. Pei to embody the energy and dynamism of rock and roll music. Radiating out from a 167-foot tower, two geometric theater spaces are cantilevered over the shoreline of Lake Erie. A ground-level triangular glass tent functions as the main lobby.

Inside, the exhibits display artifacts from John Lennon's report card to Jim Morrison's Cub Scout uniform, and text panels educate as well as entertain. The Museum's permanent collection spans more than 100 years and includes Les Paul's guitar as well as Madonna's gold bustier. The curators' goal is to represent a broad panorama of artists and appeal to a variety of interests and tastes.

Acquiring such memorabilia is no easy task, however, and it hinges on the generosity of the stars and their relatives and friends. The Museum's first major acquisition came from John Lennon's widow, Yoko Ono. Recently the Museum displayed an impressive collection of the Ramones' memorabilia. Curators are careful to stay true to artifacts, collecting only items that represent something meaningful in the artist's life.

Excitement hits a fever pitch every year when the inductees into the Rock and Roll Hall of Fame are announced. Performers aren't eligible for nomination until 25 years after their first record is released. Nominees are voted on by a group of more than 500 rock experts around the world, and five to seven performers are selected every year. Recent inductees include R.E.M., Van Halen, and the Ronettes.

Next on the horizon is a new library and archive for students and scholars conducting serious research on the history of rock and roll. Housed in nearby Cuyahoga Community College's Center for American Music and Recording Arts, the archive will contain personal papers, contracts, and manuscripts from notables such as the *Rolling Stone* journalist Ben Fong-Torres, producer Jerry Wexler, and the musician Curtis Mayfield.

Vital Statistics
Established 1995
Location Cleveland, Ohio
Employees 100
Annual Sales $12.3 million (2005)
Annual Economic Impact $107 million

THE AMAZING JOURNEY

Rolling Stone

In April 2006, *Rolling Stone,* the nation's leading popular culture magazine, rolled out its thousandth issue. The twice-monthly publication has been a cultural icon for four decades, keeping its more than 12 million readers up to date in music, entertainment, politics, movies, and technology. Jann Wenner, its countercultural editor and founder, hasn't slowed down over the years. He remains at the helm of Wenner Media, a magazine empire that includes the iconic *Rolling Stone,* as well as *Men's Journal, Us Weekly,* and a book imprint.

It all began in 1967, when 21-year-old Wenner dropped out of the University of California at Berkeley to start a counterculture magazine with $7,500 of borrowed seed capital. Named after a Muddy Waters song with the line "a rolling stone gathers no moss," Rolling Stone's mission was to explore the attitudes, politics, and lifestyle of the 1960s that were embodied by popular music. The magazine got off to a slow start when all but 5,000 copies of its initial press run of 40,000 were returned, but Wenner persevered by hiring remarkably interesting writers, featuring incisive interviews, and offering incentives such as a free roach clip (for smoking marijuana) with every new subscription. By 1973, the magazine gained a reputation for excellent reporting from the *New York Times* and other established sources, and sales began to increase.

Rolling Stone's biggest boost came from "gonzo journalist" Hunter S. Thompson, who started writing for the magazine in 1970 with an article titled "Freak Power in the Rockies" that described his bid for sheriff of Pitkin County, Colorado. *Rolling Stone* sold out every time it published an installment of Thompson's most famous work, *Fear and Loathing in Las Vegas,* a chronicle of the presidential campaigns of Richard Nixon and George McGovern. Although Thompson's articles referred to musicians such as Lou Reed, he never wrote about music, and his work helped *Rolling Stone* extend its reputation beyond the music scene to politics and literature. Tom Wolfe, Truman Capote, and P. J. O'Rourke also published stories in *Rolling Stone,* as did celebrity journalists such as Cameron Crowe, whose autobiography of his career at the magazine became the basis for the Hollywood movie *Almost Famous.* The magazine also became famous for publishing some of the most well-known photographs in recent history. Annie Leibovitz, *Rolling Stone*'s staff photographer throughout the 1970s and early 1980s, published some of her best work for the magazine. Her portrait of a naked John Lennon clinging to a fully clothed Yoko Ono, taken the morning before Lennon's death, graced the front cover of *Rolling Stone* on January 22, 1981.

Today, *Rolling Stone* remains the leading music-oriented magazine in the United States, with a broad demographic that spans from teens to baby boomers. The cover of the thousandth issue featured a three-dimensional Sgt. Pepper–like lineup of star musicians and is reported to be the most expensive in magazine history. Wenner plans for *Rolling Stone* to target a younger demographic in the years to come by focusing more on emerging actors, artists, and writers.

Vital Statistics
Parent Company Wenner Media
Established 1967
Founder Jann Wenner
Headquarters New York, New York
Circulation 1.5 million

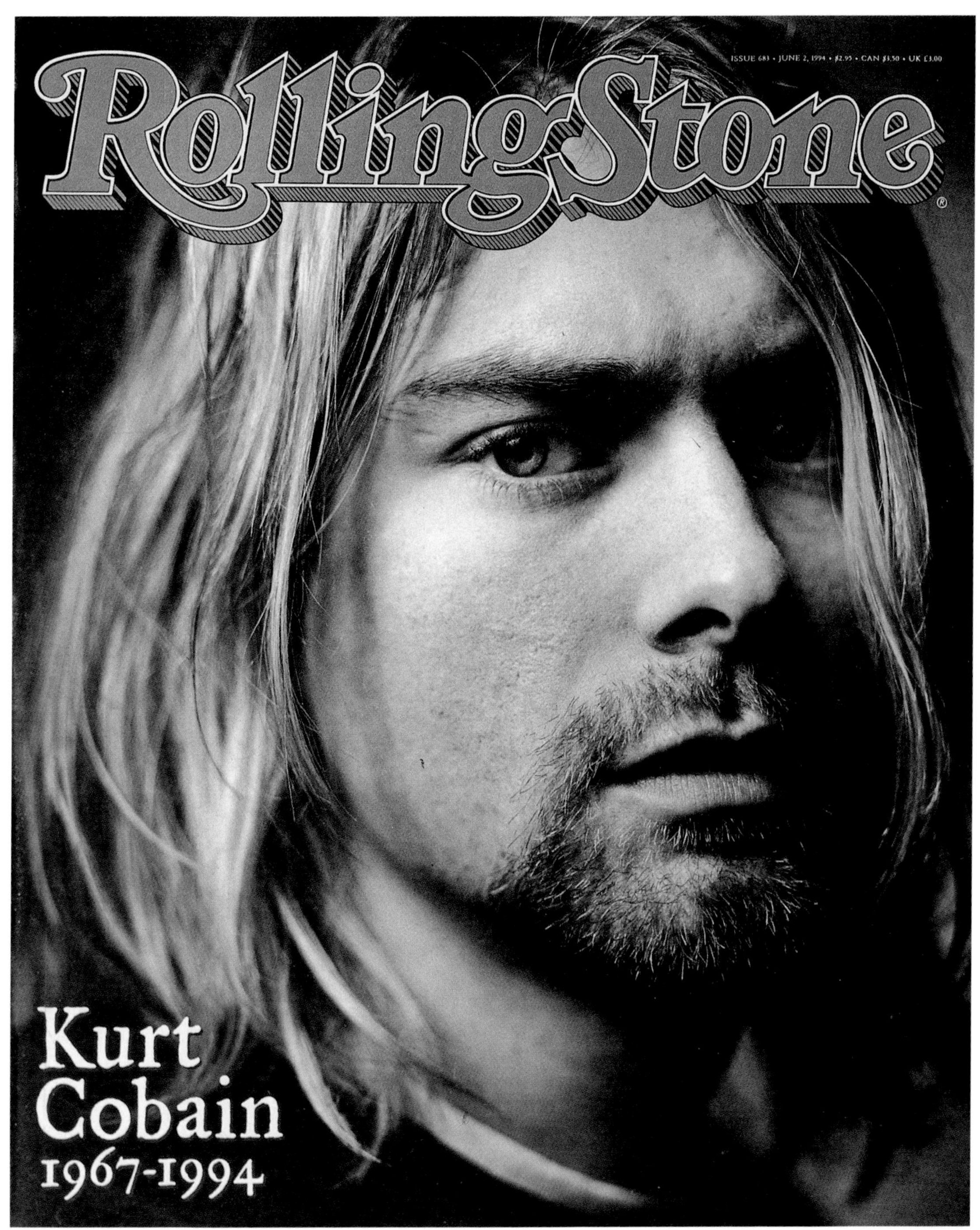
ISSUE 683 • JUNE 2, 1994 • $2.95 • CAN $3.50 • UK £3.00
RollingStone
Kurt
Cobain
1967-1994

Samsonite Corporation

Jesse Shwayder, founder of the Shwayder Trunk Manufacturing Company in Denver, Colorado, had one simple goal: to produce and sell an uncommonly well-made trunk that would stand up to the most rigorous travel. Shwayder started with trunks and inexpensive hand luggage, marketed in the western United States. Around this time, he had a photograph taken that would become the company's trademark. The photograph showed Shwayder, his father, and three of his brothers, representing nearly 1,000 pounds, standing on a plank supported by a Shwayder carrying case. During the depression, the company name changed to Shwayder Brothers.

Just before the United States entered World War II, Jesse Shwayder introduced a new style of luggage—the Samsonite Streamlite. Stressing strength and durability, it is named for Samson, the biblical giant who was one of Shwayder's heroes. Streamlite luggage was tapered in shape and made by covering a wooden frame with vulcanized fiber upon which a rawhide effect was lithographed. This was the first time someone could purchase a suitcase that looked like leather but sold for a comparatively low price. Lithographing vulcanized fiber was difficult, however, and getting consistent print quality was almost impossible, making it hard for sets to actually match. The company switched fibers, thereby making matched sets possible.

The advent of the jet age in 1955 prompted Shwayder and other executives to think of new styles to accommodate the future needs and tastes of the public. Streamlite was still popular, but Shwayder Brothers wanted to add a new line of luggage more suitable for modern travel. They created Ultralite, a lightweight piece of luggage made of magnesium using the Streamlite design. It was the first luggage to eliminate wooden box construction. In 1958, they introduced Silhouette, a modern shape to accompany the new material, creating the most advanced luggage made at the time. Locks, hardware, and fittings were all part of the design, and the hardware was recessed, to protect it from the wear and tear of travel.

With more accessible air travel, millions of people took to the skies for both business and pleasure. Samsonite was there to outfit the traveling executive with the Samsonite Classic Attaché, an item that became an iconic must-have for businesspeople in the 1960s. The Samsonite name was known around the world with the help of wide distribution, so in 1965, the name changed from Shwayder Brothers, Inc. to Samsonite Corporation. The growing company decided to create an abstract image to reflect its expansion, and in 1973, a symbol made its first appearance. Recognized as a symbol of quality and superb design, it graces millions of pieces of luggage worldwide.

Sold in more than 100 countries with annual sales of $967 million, Samsonite continues to grow and innovate. It has expanded into areas including a Black Label clothing division, accessories, and footwear, and has forged design collaborations with Philippe Starck, Matthew Williamson, Marc Newsom, and Alexander McQueen. Although the way we travel is constantly changing, Samsonite is always there to provide the luggage.

Vital Statistics
Established 1910
Founder Jesse Shwayder
Annual Sales $1,070.4 (2007)
Headquarters Denver, Colorado

Samuel Adams

When Jim Koch—Cincinnati native, graduate of Harvard's Law and Business schools, and descendant of five generations of brewers—abandoned his career as a management consultant in 1984, it was not for a vague career crisis. Aware of the inroads imported beers were making, he decided to embrace his destiny. With $100,000 of his own and $140,000 from friends and family, he launched The Boston Beer Company with his great-great-grandfather's recipe.

Koch named his first beer for the famous revolutionary thinker Samuel Adams. Made according to a strict German beer purity law, the lager contained only four ingredients: malted barley, yeast, hops, and water. Koch brewed his beer at the Pittsburgh Brewing Company. He brought in a partner, his former secretary Rhonda Kallman, and together they sold beer door-to-door, educating bartenders and consumers about what made this beer special. By the time the first batch was out of the aging tanks, 25 restaurants and bars in downtown Boston were eager to sell it. Initially unable to find a distributor, Koch rented a truck and delivered the beer himself. By the end of 1985, Samuel Adams was available in Massachusetts, Connecticut, and West Germany.

The following year, an agreement was made to serve Samuel Adams at the White House, aboard Air Force One, in the presidential box at the Kennedy Center, and at Camp David. Koch also developed radio commercials intended to educate the consumer about what makes a great quality beer.

In 1988, the company built a small brewery in Boston, and production reached 36,000 barrels per year. Expansion continued in New York City and the west coast. In 1990, the company opened a Samuel Adams Brew House—a casual pub with good food and Boston Lager on tap—with a Philadelphia restaurateur.

By 1994, Jim Koch had started to wonder how rich, complex, and strong beer could be, so he produced Triple Bock. In 2007 the company is slated to introduce its third "vintage" of Utopias, the strongest beer ever brewed, weighing in at an unparalleled 25.6% alcohol by volume. In blind tastings by food and wine professionals, Utopias was preferred over a fine French vintage Cognac and a vintage port.

Samuel Adams was voted "The Best Beer in America," in June 1985, just six weeks after the beer was first introduced. Over the years, the company continued to test its beers against the world's best, and in 1994 the company won more awards at the World Beer Championship than any other brand.

In its initial public offering in 1995, the company sold 3.1 million shares; they printed a special offer on six-packs so that loyal Samuel Adams drinkers could participate. Today, the company has the industry's leading program of seasonal styles as well as a "Brewmaster's Collection" of classic beer styles including Samuel Adams Double Bock and Cream Stout. The renowned chef David Burke recently teamed up with the company to create recipes featuring Samuel Adams beers and to create beer and food pairing dinners around the country.

In 2001, Koch stepped aside as President and CEO to focus on the Company's beer and brewing and its culture and employee training. He retained the position of Chairman. Martin Roper is now President and CEO. The Boston Beer Company introduced Sam Adams Light, with fewer calories than its regular beers, in 2002, and its success helped bring revenues to a record high level.

Vital Statistics

Parent Company The Boston Beer Company, Inc.

Established 1984

Founder James Koch

Employees 390 (2005)

Annual Sales $285.4 million (2006)

Sara Lee

"Nobody doesn't like Sara Lee" has worked beautifully as this company's slogan for a reason: it's true. Sara Lee frozen desserts have been delighting families for generations. Although today the company is a conglomerate in ownership of many significant American companies, Sara Lee is still the country's number-one name in home-style family desserts.

In 1935, a Chicago man named Charles Lubin and his brother-in-law bought an existing chain of bakeries called Community Bake Shops. Over the next 14 years, they expanded the chain from three to seven stores. By 1949, Lubin was running the businesses on his own and decided to introduce his own products. The first was a cheesecake, named after his daughter, Sara Lee. Lubin then changed the name of his business to the Kitchens of Sara Lee. In 1951, Lubin expanded his product line to include a carefully tested and long-perfected All Butter Pound Cake and All Butter Pecan Coffee Cake, which became near-instant hits with customers. A year later, a man from Texas fell in love with Lubin's baked goods and asked if he could have some shipped home. Knowing his fresh baked goods didn't freeze well and would get stale if shipped as they were, he came up with a line of frozen products that lived up to his meticulous standards for quality and taste, developing a method of freezing that soon became the industry standard. He also developed the first foil baking pans, which could be used for baking, freezing, and distributing his products. This revolutionized the food industry and made Sara Lee a household name.

By 1955, Lubin could deliver frozen baked goods to 48 states. In 1956, attracted by its innovative techniques and high-quality goods, one of the country's largest, most successful corporations—Consolidated Foods—acquired Kitchens of Sara Lee, with the aim of taking it even further. Lubin remained on board as CEO. Two years later, spurred on by rapid growth, Lubin oversaw the construction of a massive new facility in Deerfield, Illinois, with top-of-the-line equipment and capabilities. The new plant, which began operations in 1964, featured computerized systems, testing labs and bakeries, and modern warehousing, all designed to keep Sara Lee at the peak of its success and bring it into the future with equal glory. By 1965, it was considered to be the largest, most successful bakery in the world. Lubin felt sufficiently accomplished to retire that year. In 1968, the now-famous jingle debuted, and in the 1970s, Sara Lee went international. In 1976, Sara Lee made the country's bicentennial birthday cake, which was four stories high and sat in a place of honor in Philadelphia's Freedom Hall.

In 1985, Consolidated Foods Corporation decided, because of Sara Lee's overwhelming popularity, to change its name to Sara Lee Corporation, in spite of its many profitable, unrelated businesses. In 2001, Sara Lee purchased the country's second-most-successful bakery, the Earthgrains Company, giving it an even larger share of the national and international markets. And Sara Lee herself? She is a philanthropist, devoted to supporting girls and women in science. Her father would be proud.

Vital Statistics
Classic Product All Butter Pound Cake
Product Launch 1949
Employees 109,000 (2006)
Annual Sales $15,944 million (2006)

Premium
Sara Lee
Thaw in microwave
10
Seconds
Nutrition Facts
16 OZ (1LB)
453g
Family Size
Moist and Delicious!
All Butter Pound Cake
Keep Frozen

Saturn

Saturn has become synonymous with affordability and a friendly, approachable style—many car buffs who can't afford the luxury autos of their dreams are more than satisfied with General Motors' Saturn. The company's hallmarks are customer service and user-friendliness; it is safe to say that Saturn has transformed the way Americans buy cars. And if parent company GM has anything to say about it, Saturn will continue to run rings around the competition.

The year was 1982, the concept was simple: to create an affordable car with affable looks and a company that really focused on its customers. Alex C. Mair, at the time the vice president of GM's advanced engineering staff, held a meeting with fellow engineers Joe Joseph and Tom Ankeny. He proposed they join forces to create a new small car and suggested the code name *Saturn* for the secret project. The following year, General Motors Chairman Roger B. Smith and President F. James McDonald made their announcement about Saturn's impending arrival. In 1984, the prototype was complete and tinkering began. It took until 1985 for General Motors engineers to begin operations and introduce Saturn to the world. The company announced a surprising haggle-free policy, intended to stabilize prices. In 1989, Saturn engineer Rim Milunas and his team developed a traction control system that was soon patented for all Saturn automatic cars with antilock breaks. By 1990, Saturn was winning awards; *Popular Science* magazine named the car one of "The Year's 100 Greatest Achievements in Science and Technology." In 1992, Saturn shipped its first exported cars to Taiwan, bringing Saturn halfway around the world. More than 200,000 cars were sold that year, although experts advised that 300,000 would be necessary to remain profitable into the future. In 1995, the company revealed that it had sold 1,000,000 Saturn cars to date. In 1997, Saturn announced plans to build a larger car. Two years later, Cynthia M. Trudell was appointed Saturn chairwoman and president and became the first female leader of a major automobile company. General Motors invested $1.5 billion in Saturn for the development of new cars and the necessary expansion of the plants. In 2002, Saturn replaced its S series with the new Ion and unveiled its first SUV, the Vue. The stylish Sky followed, in 2005.

Saturn began as a sort of experiment on the part of General Motors to build a company and a brand based on customer service. Avoiding hard sales, price haggling, and superficial and pricey flourishes meant customer satisfaction to a degree that surprised even GM executives. Today, Saturn manufactures a range of automobiles, compact and midsize, including the Ion Quad coupe, Ion sedan, Vue compact SUV, Relay minivan, and Sky roadster. Other models are in the works, from Aura, a midsize sedan, to Outlook, a crossover SUV, and a Vue hybrid, sure to generate waiting lists of environmentally-conscious Saturn fans.

Opposite: 2007 Saturn Ion Red Line's Competition Package features unique Forged Wheels with a Gunmetal Finish.

Vital Statistics
Established 1982
Employees 9,600
Annual Sales $3,901 million (2005)

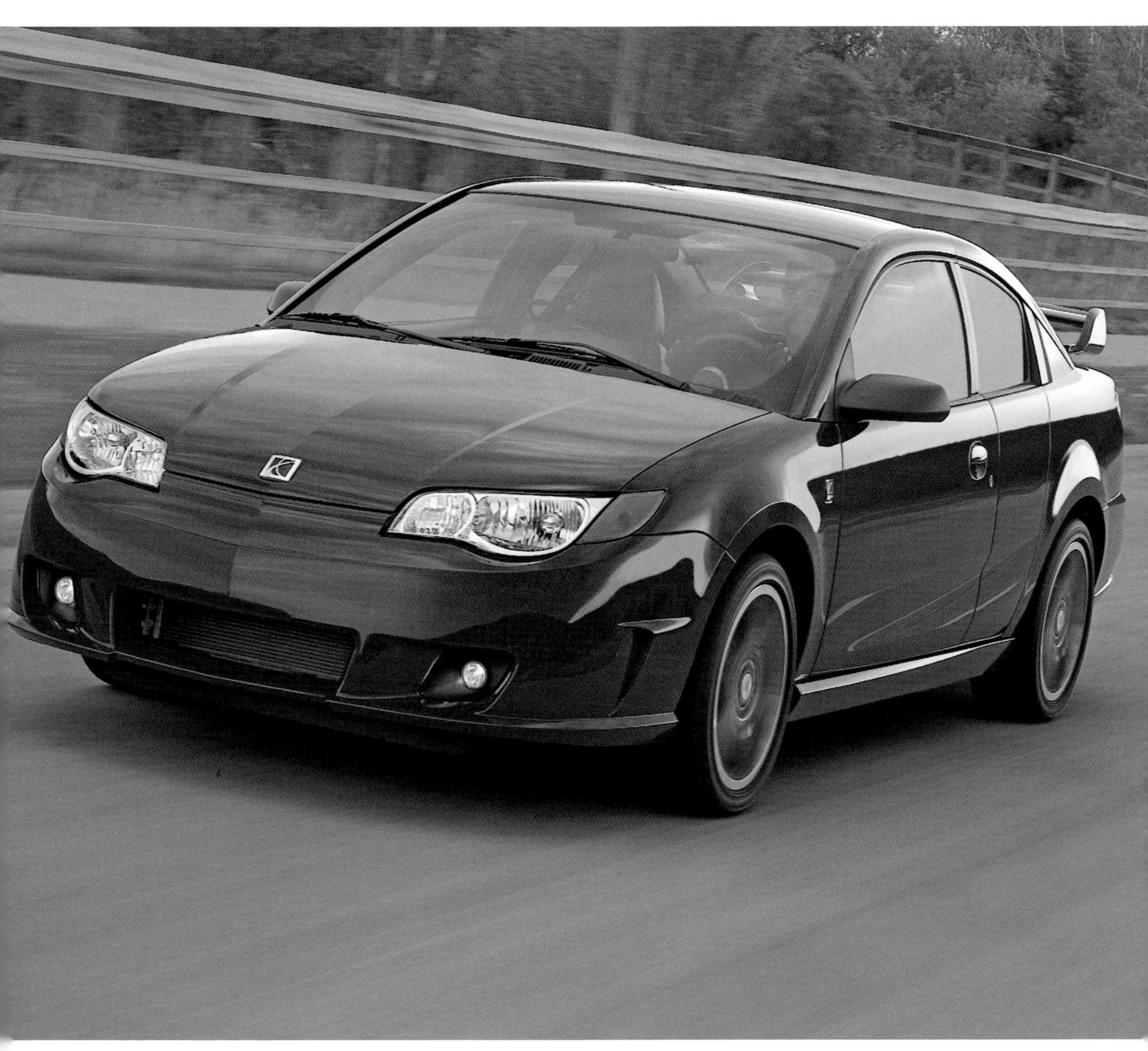

Scotch Tape

Scotch tape emerged during a golden era of innovation at the 3M Company. Under the leadership of Richard Carlton, Dick Drew, and Francis Okie, 3M, which was originally established as a mining concern, became a development lab for a host of new products. In 1923, Richard (Dick) Drew, a young engineering student, joined 3M, known officially as Minnesota Mining and Manufacturing Company from its founding in 1902 until 2002. The company, which made a point of sending sales representatives directly to shops that used their products, had sent him on calls to auto body shops to sell 3M's newest product, waterproof sandpaper. Drew saw that the shops struggled with the process—with glue and paper—used to paint cars in two tones. He promised that 3M would find a solution to prevent the colors from running together. Two years later, Drew invented a successful masking tape—the first of many tapes to come. Building on the success of this innovative product, 3M began to develop different applications for the new technology.

Scotch®

The brand name came about when Drew was testing his first masking tape and a customer, an auto body shop painter, was frustrated with a sample because it contained adhesive only around its edges. Using a pejorative term of the era to imply cheapness, he exclaimed, "Take this tape back to those Scotch bosses of yours and tell them to put more adhesive on it!" The name, and also the new, improved version of the product, stuck firmly.

In 1930, Dick Drew found a way to coat adhesive on cellophane, a DuPont invention, creating a transparent tape. Most products during the Great Depression were failures, but this was a period when consumers had to scrimp and save. Scotch transparent tape helped mend and repair and prolong the usefulness of items. It was good for 3M and its employees, too. Because the tape was so popular, 3M was one of the few companies that didn't have to lay people off during this difficult period.

During World War II, 3M ran advertisements apologizing to homemakers for the scarcity of tape and explaining that all available supplies had been diverted to the war effort. The company even came up with a hundred more kinds of tape designed specifically for use during the war.

3M became a publicly-traded company in 1946, and has seen great activity on the NYSE ever since. 3M's product line includes some of the most recognizable household products, from Post-it Notes, Scotchgard fabric protector, and Scotch-Brite scouring pads to many high-tech products. 3M's global presence includes 67,000 employees serving customers in more than 200 countries around the world.

Today, 3M makes more than 400 varieties of adhesive tape sold under the Scotch brand name and other trademarks. Scotch transparent tape, created more than 75 years ago, is still the most widely known and used. Transparent tape can be found in virtually every home, school, and office in America. And the Scotch brand has been extended beyond tapes to a wide range of product categories.

Vital Statistics

Parent Company 3M Company

Introduced 1930

Company Founders Lucius P. Ordway and John Ober

Sealy Posturepedic

Sealy Corporation, the world's largest bedding manufacturer, got its name from the small town of Sealy, Texas. It was the home of Daniel Haynes, a cotton-gin builder, who began making cotton-filled mattresses for his friends and neighbors in 1881. In 1889, he received a patent for the invention of a machine that compressed cotton for use in mattresses. The "Mattress from Sealy" became so popular that he sold patent rights to people in other markets who also began making the product.

In 1906, Haynes sold all of his patents and knowledge to a Texas company that changed the name to Sealy. At the same time, a young advertising executive named Earl Edwards launched Sealy on its way to national recognition. Edwards placed Sealy mattress ads in the *Saturday Evening Post* and *Ladies' Home Journal.* He made sure Sealy registered its name, developed a trademark, and gave the company the slogan "Sleeping on a Sealy is Like Sleeping on a Cloud."

Edwards sought licensees to enable more production facilities in various locations in an effort to promote expansion. By 1920, Sealy had 28 licensed plants and was the first mattress company to establish a licensing program. In 1950, Sealy began working with orthopedic surgeons to develop a mattress focused on the importance of orthopedically-correct support and long-lasting comfort. Led by Dr. Robert G. Addison, Sealy developed a new innerspring system that would provide consumers with proper spinal alignment, leading to the introduction of the first Sealy Posturepedic. In the 1960s, Sealy commissioned the first major research study to define the Sealy Posturepedic consumer, and in 1967, Sealy Posturepedic commercials ran during prime time on national television–a first for the mattress industry. In the 1970s, Sealy Posturepedic bedding became high-tech with programmed coils for increased support. At the same time, Sealy box springs became known as foundations, due to the development of a torsion bar module. In the late 1980s, Sealy introduced the PostureTech Coil, now used in all Sealy Posturepedic innerspring mattresses. It is highlighted by a patented sensory feature that senses and cushions movement, then responds with increasing support.

Today, Sealy Posturepedic continues to lead the industry in innovation in the area of overall orthopedic health and well-being. Sealy established and works with the Orthopedic Advisory Board, which includes top surgeons and clinicians from several of the nation's leading medical centers and universities. Sealy and the Orthopedic Advisory Board work together to ensure the science of sleep evolves and continues to provide more restful, restorative sleep. In addition to marketing its brand, Sealy is a world-class manufacturing organization that operates 31 plants worldwide. It is unlike many of its competitors because, in addition to mattress assembly, Sealy owns and operates a component-manufacturing subsidiary, enabling it to manufacture many of the important component parts that are used inside the mattress. Continued strong focus on product developments and innovation has helped Sealy secure its place at the top, making it the largest bedding manufacturer in the world.

As of April 2006, Sealy began trading publicly on the New York Stock Exchange under the ticker symbol ZZ. Its products are sold domestically through more than 7,000 retail outlets, including furniture stores, national mass merchandisers, specialty sleep shops, department stores and warehouse clubs. The company manufactures and markets a broad range of mattresses and foundations under the Sealy, Sealy Posturepedic, Stearns & Foster, and Bassett brands.

Vital Statistics

Company Name Sealy Corporation

Classic Product Sealy Posturepedic mattress

Established 1906

Founder Earl Edwards

Annual Sales $1,582 million (2006)

Seventh Generation Inc.

What started out as a small mail-order catalogue business in Burlington, Vermont, has turned into the nation's leading marketer of nontoxic, environmentally safe household and personal care products. Renew America was a small environmental organization with a small mail-order catalogue containing products designed to conserve energy. In 1988, lacking the money it needed to prosper, Renew America offered its wonderful little catalogue to a group of people with whom it had previously worked in Burlington. Those people happily accepted it and became Seventh Generation.

The name *Seventh Generation* was chosen to reflect the company, the catalogue, and the mission that guided it. At the suggestion of a Native American employee, the company gained inspiration and a name from the Six Nations Iroquois Confederacy, which says that "in every deliberation we must consider the impact of our decisions on the next seven generations."

Within months of the acquisition, the catalogue was packed with new items such as energy-saving lightbulbs, bathroom tissue made from unbleached, recycled paper, and nontoxic cleaning products. In addition to the catalogue, Seventh Generation started selling products to natural food stores and co-ops. As the company continued to grow, it became apparent that the staff was not able to keep up with the two distinct businesses they were running. So in 1995, Seventh Generation sold the catalogue to a Boulder, Colorado, company called Gaiam, which changed the name to Harmony. That allowed Seventh Generation to focus on providing safe household products to stores from coast to coast.

Working under the knowledge that natural products are better for people and the environment, the company offers a full line of nontoxic household products that are designed to work as well as their traditional counterparts. All Seventh Generation products are made of renewable, biodegradable, nontoxic, phosphate-free ingredients that are as gentle on the earth as they are on the people who use them. The company is constantly conducting research to develop and test new products as well as retest existing products to see how they can be improved.

A driving force in the company is its commitment and adherence to true corporate responsibility. Seventh Generation believes and operates under the imperative that it is necessary to view the company through a larger lens to recognize how its products affect the world. Through this guiding principle, it is able to offer products that are safe, effective, and environmentally friendly.

Vital Statistics
Established 1988
Founder Jeffrey Hollender
Sales $60 million (2005)

Sharpie

Sanford, maker of Sharpie brand markers, is one of many household brands offered by Newell Rubbermaid, a global marketer of consumer and commercial products with sales of approximately $6 billion. Newell acquired Sanford Corporation in 1992, entering the office products business which it has since expanded to include an impressive line of brands including Paper Mate, Rolodex, EXPO, Waterman, and more. Sanford got its start back in 1857, when William H. Sanford Jr. and Frederick W. Redington founded the Sanford Manufacturing Company in Worcester, Massachusetts. The company focused on the producing and selling of ink and glue. In 1866, the company expanded and moved west to Chicago.

Sharpie®

In 1964, Sanford Ink decided to focus on an emerging marker business and introduced the Sharpie marker. The Sharpie Fine Point black marker became the first pen-style permanent marker, able to write on almost any surface, including plastic, stone, and wood. Johnny Carson was one of Sharpie's first celebrity endorsers.

In 1979, Sanford introduced the Sharpie Extra Fine Point marker, which offered a new style tip and was available in four colors. The Sharpie Ultra Fine Point was introduced in 1989 featuring a slim barrel, a metal pocket clip, and a precise tip that produces clean lines. This model became the first marker to truly write like a pen.

Throughout the 1990s, the popularity of the Sharpie marker continued to escalate partly because of the $5 billion memorabilia market. Celebrities, sports figures, and fans alike use Sharpie markers on everything that can possibly be signed, from posters to baseballs to jerseys.

In the late 1990s, the Sharpie family of markers again expanded, adding five new Sharpie markers over a six-year period and offering a variety of new colors such as Berry and Turquoise. Accent Highlighters are also part of the Sharpie family of markers. New products continue to be added to the ever-growing product line, and new colors have brought the Sharpie palette up to 39 as of 2007.

Successful advertising and marketing campaigns have certainly added to Sharpie's vast popularity. Sharpie moved into sports marketing by sponsoring PGA golfers Arnold Palmer, David Toms, Chad Campbell, and Gary Player, and became the title sponsor of NASCAR's most popular event, the Sharpie 500. It also sponsors NASCAR's Dale Earnhardt Jr.

A truly memorable moment in Sharpie history came in 2002, when Terrell Owens scored a touchdown and had his Sharpie marker readily accessible so he could sign the football. That notorious end zone celebration provided Sharpie with approximately $5 million in publicity. This prompted Sharpie to create Autographs for Education in 2002, a program where Sharpie teams up with athletes and celebrities to support community-based educational organizations. The program continues today at Sharpie.com.

Sanford makes more than 6,000 products ranging from markers and pens to office organization products and professional art products.

Vital Statistics

Parent Company	Newell Rubbermaid
Classic Product	pens and markers
Product Launch	1964

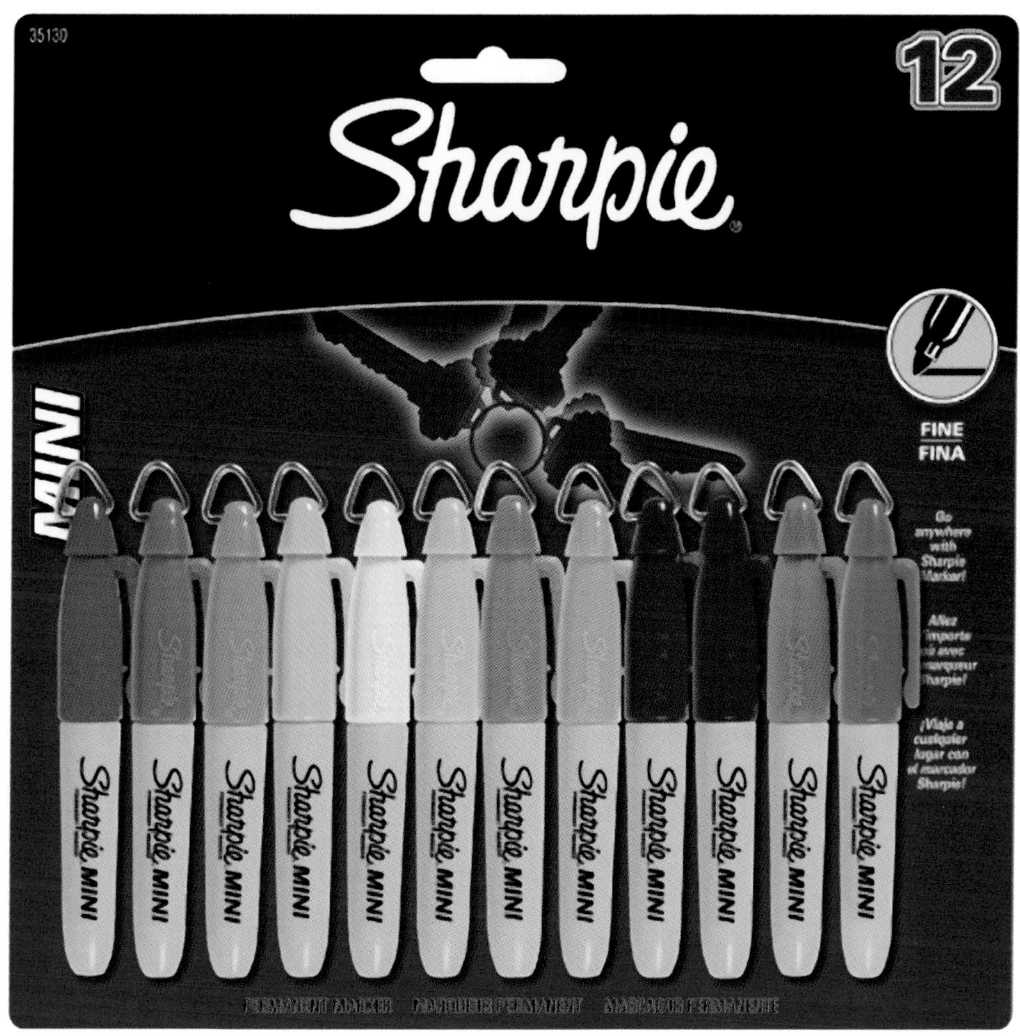

Singer Sewing Co.

Since 1851, the brand name Singer has been synonymous with sewing. The Singer brand has introduced the world to products for every level of sewing and produced the world's first zigzag and electronic machines, as well as the world's most advanced home sewing and embroidery machine. From home décor and clothing construction to embroidery and quilting, the Singer trademark is the number-one in sewing products, and has been for more than an awe-inspiring century and a half.

In 1850, after examining the most popular sewing machine of the time, Isaac Merritt Singer decided it was poorly designed. He commented that if he were to design a sewing machine, "Instead of the shuttle going around in a circle, I would have it move to and fro in a straight line. In place of the needle bar pushing a curved needle horizontally, I would have a straight needle and make it work up and down." After 11 days (and $40), Singer completed his invention: the world's first practical sewing machine. It had a straight eye-pointed needle and transverse shuttle, an overhanging arm, a table to support the cloth, a presser foot to hold the material against the upward stroke of the needle, and a roughened feed wheel extending through a slot in the table. Motion was communicated to the needle arm and shuttle by means of gears. It also had a treadle similar to that of a spinning wheel instead of a hand crank to generate power. A year later, Singer was granted a patent, launching one of the most successful business empires in America.

Throughout its history, the sewing machine has garnered admiration from figures as disparate as Gandhi, who declared it "one of the few useful things ever invented," and the Wright brothers, who used a Singer machine to sew on the wings of the world's first airplane. In 1856 Singer introduced the home sewing machine to the general market for the price of $125—unaffordable to all but the wealthiest, as the average family income for that year was about $500. However, Singer's business partner, Edward Clark, conceived of a system that was also to transform the American retail landscape: the installment plan. The sewing machine was so desired that consumers signed on to the plan, making Singer a fast millionaire and granting many women an opportunity to make a living they would not have had otherwise. The Singer sewing machine was the first home appliance so admired that it was awarded a first prize at the World's Fair in Paris its first year on the market. The Singer Building in Manhattan, built in 1906, was the world's first skyscraper. In 1968, it became the tallest building to be demolished, to make way for the World Trade Center complex. In 1975, the Singer brand produced the world's first electronic sewing machine, the Athena 2000, and three years later the Touchtronic 2001, the world's first computer-controlled machine. In recent years, the Singer brand again made history with the world's most advanced home sewing and embroidery machine: the Quantum XL-5000, with state-of-the-art features such as a fully automated re-threading system and wind-in-place bobbin-winding system.

In 2001, the company that now bears his name celebrated the 150th anniversary of Isaac Singer's patent on the first home sewing machine and, therefore, the official beginning of the Singer brand. Fortunately for home sewers everywhere, the Singer brand has maintained its commitment to the quality, reliability, innovation, and service that was so important to the inventor himself. Today's machines range from basic $150 models to computerized units that start at $3,000. Singer products are sold in more than 190 countries, through about 1,300 Singer-authorized retail outlets, 58,000 independent dealers and mass merchandisers, and a door-to-door sales force of more than 12,000 agents.

Vital Statistics

Parent Company	Singer Sewing Co./SVP Worldwide (Bermuda)
Established	1851
Founder/Inventor	Isaac Merritt Singer
Employees	12,222

Six Flags

For those seeking the fun of fast rides, waterslides, live shows, and other family entertainment, Six Flags theme parks are the destination of choice. The world's largest regional theme park company, Six Flags operates 20 locations in North America and boasts an average annual visitor rate of more than 27 million guests. The company aims to give families a complete one-stop entertainment experience that in addition to thrill rides includes children's areas, parades, concerts, restaurants, games, and merchandise outlets. Because of licensing agreements with Warner Brothers and DC Comics, the likes of Bugs Bunny, Wonder Woman, and Batman are some of the characters often seen roaming the parks. There's so much to do at a Six Flags park that it's easy to spend an entire day there and still have the kids beg for more.

The first Six Flags park was the creation of Angus Wynne, who wanted to build regional theme parks within driving distance of families throughout the country, making them convenient and affordable. Wynne opened Six Flags Over Texas in 1961, on a patch of prairie between Dallas and Fort Worth. He chose the name *Six Flags* because the flags of six countries or nations had flown over Texas during the state's history: the United States, the Confederate States of America, Mexico, Spain, France, and the Republic of Texas. He expanded on the concept by creating themed areas inside the park representing the cultures of the six flags. Guests could experience the life of a cowboy or a southern belle, or what it was like to live in Spain or France.

Wynne took another bold step when he decided to charge customers one price for everything instead of the usual practice at that time, which was to charge by the ride. The cost to get into Six Flags Over Texas in 1961 was $2.95, and soon other parks around the country were following Wynne's lead. The first Six Flags park was a success, and Six Flags Over Georgia opened in 1968, followed by Six Flags Over Mid-America, near St. Louis, in 1971.

Six Flags has 160 roller coasters. The biggest is Kingda Ka, which opened in 2005 at Six Flags Great Adventure in New Jersey for the tallest and fastest roller coaster in the world. The hydraulic launch rocket coaster blasts occupants horizontally and reaches 128 miles per hour in less than four seconds. It then climbs 456 feet up a 90-degree tower and plummets straight down the other side.

Vital Statistics
Opening date 1961
Headquarters New York, New York
Employees 34,000 (seasonal)
Annual Sales $1089.7 million (2005)

Slim-Fast Foods Company

The introduction of Slim-Fast meal-replacement drinks rocked the diet world. Today, the company—bought by Unilever in 2000 for about $2.6 billion—sells its meal-replacement shakes, powders, meal bars, and snack bars in the United States, Europe, Asia, and Latin America.

Slim-Fast was created in 1977 by S. Daniel Abraham, a salesman who had left the U.S. Army at the age of 21 to work for his uncle's small, New York–based drug company. He founded the Thompson Medical Company and, in 1956, created his first diet product: Slim-Mint gum. By 1960, he had added a line of diet pills called Figure-Aid. In 1976, however, his forays into weight-loss aids finally took off with Dexatrim, a diet pill containing the appetite suppressant phenylpropanolamine (PPA). Dexatrim soon became the best-selling diet pill on the market, and Thompson Medical reached over $50 million in sales by the end of the decade. In 1977, Thompson Medical introduced a more natural way to lose weight: Slim-Fast, a revolutionary powder that, when mixed with low-fat milk, looked and tasted like a milk shake. Slim-Fast was marketed as a meal replacement for breakfast and lunch, followed by a healthful, whole-food dinner. In the late 1970s, liquid diets were challenged by the FDA for their safety and taken off the market. Abraham used science to demonstrate the safety and effectiveness of Slim-Fast and was allowed to reintroduce the product. Abraham made a public offering of four million shares of Thompson Medical stock in 1979, generating significant income to advertise and promote Slim-Fast. The re-admittance of Slim-Fast helped Thompson Medical achieve sales of approximately $197 million in 1984. In late 1987, Abraham took the company private once again. A year later, he had acquired 33 percent of the stock, a controlling interest that he maintained into the mid-2000s. In 1988, Abraham decided on an advertising campaign that was to become the company's most successful of all time. Abraham hired Los Angeles Dodgers manager Tommy Lasorda and offered to contribute $20,000 to his favorite charity if he would stick to the Slim-Fast diet plan. Lasorda quickly lost 30 pounds and became a national favorite, spurring sales. In 1990, Abraham made Slim-Fast its own company, remaining chairman and majority stockholder.

Slim-Fast Nutritional Foods International, Inc. launched a new diet product, Jump Start, in 1997, which claimed consumers could lose five pounds in five days and carried the popular tagline "Give us a week, we'll take off the weight." In April 2000, Slim-Fast was bought by industry giant Unilever, which changed the name to Slim-Fast Foods Co. and continued to innovate the popular product and maintain its strong scientific standing. The entire product line was renovated in 2004 to contain an average of 50% less sugar than the original while providing the same great taste and balanced nutrition. And in 2006, the flagship meal replacement Optima shakes were reformulated using proprietary, novel food technology to help them control hunger for up to 4 hours, keeping dieters more satisfied and better able to manage between-meal hunger.

Today, Slim-Fast is the industry leader in meal replacement shakes and bars, with well over 30 peer-reviewed, published studies supporting the efficacy of the Slim-Fast plan, and is recognized by nutrition professionals and leading health authorities as an effective and successful weight management strategy.

Vital Statistics
Parent Company Unilever U.S.
Inventor S. Daniel Abraham

Slim·Fast
Optima®
Controls Hunger Longer
MEAL ON-THE-GO™
190 CALORIES
Rich Chocolate
Royale

Slinky

What began as a simple accident has turned into one of the most popular toys ever created. In 1943, Richard James, a naval engineer, was working on an experiment with tension springs when one of the springs dropped and bounced across the floor. Noticing the movement of the coil, James thought there might be something to it that would make a perfect children's toy. He went home to his wife, Betty, who thought he was on to something, and spent the next two years working on it before coming up with the popular toy. Betty consulted the dictionary to find just the right word to describe the movement of the new invention. She came up with ***slinky,*** a Swedish word meaning "stealthy, sleek, and sinuous." The Slinky, as we know it, was born.

The Slinky debuted during the 1945 Christmas season at Gimbel's department store in Philadelphia. Richard and Betty demonstrated the Slinky's ability to "walk," and although they weren't quite sure how successful their invention would be, all 400 Slinkys were purchased within 90 minutes. As sales increased, Richard James designed machinery to roll and coil the wire needed to make each Slinky, which was initially manufactured by an outside firm. James patented the wire composition and manufacturing process that he created and set up James Industries, Inc. in a Philadelphia suburb.

In 1948, a smaller version, Slinky Jr., was added to the product line and was followed in the 1950s by Slinky Train and Slinky Dog, which were designed by a homemaker from Seattle who submitted the ideas to the firm. The company went through a rough period, and in 1960, Richard James announced he was leaving his wife and family to move to Bolivia. Betty took over the company and shortly thereafter, moved her family and the company to her hometown of Hollidaysburg, Pennsylvania, to be near family and friends. Betty soon turned the business around with the help of its famous television advertising campaign and the catchy "It's Slinky" jingle. Sales increased dramatically, and the Slinky ads with the memorable tune continued to run for years.

Slinky has changed very little in the half century since it was created. Using about 63 feet of steel wire to create each Slinky, the popular toy has been used in some innovative ways over the years. In Vietnam, U.S. soldiers employed it as an antenna; it has been used for keeping leaves out of gutters and as a therapy tool for coordination. Betty James sold the company in 1998 to Poof Products a manufacturer of foam toys. Since it was created, more than 300 million Slinkys have been sold worldwide, and they are still manufactured in Hollidaysburg, Pennsylvania, on the original equipment designed and created by Richard James.

Vital Statistics

Parent Company Poof Products

Established 1945

Founder Richard James

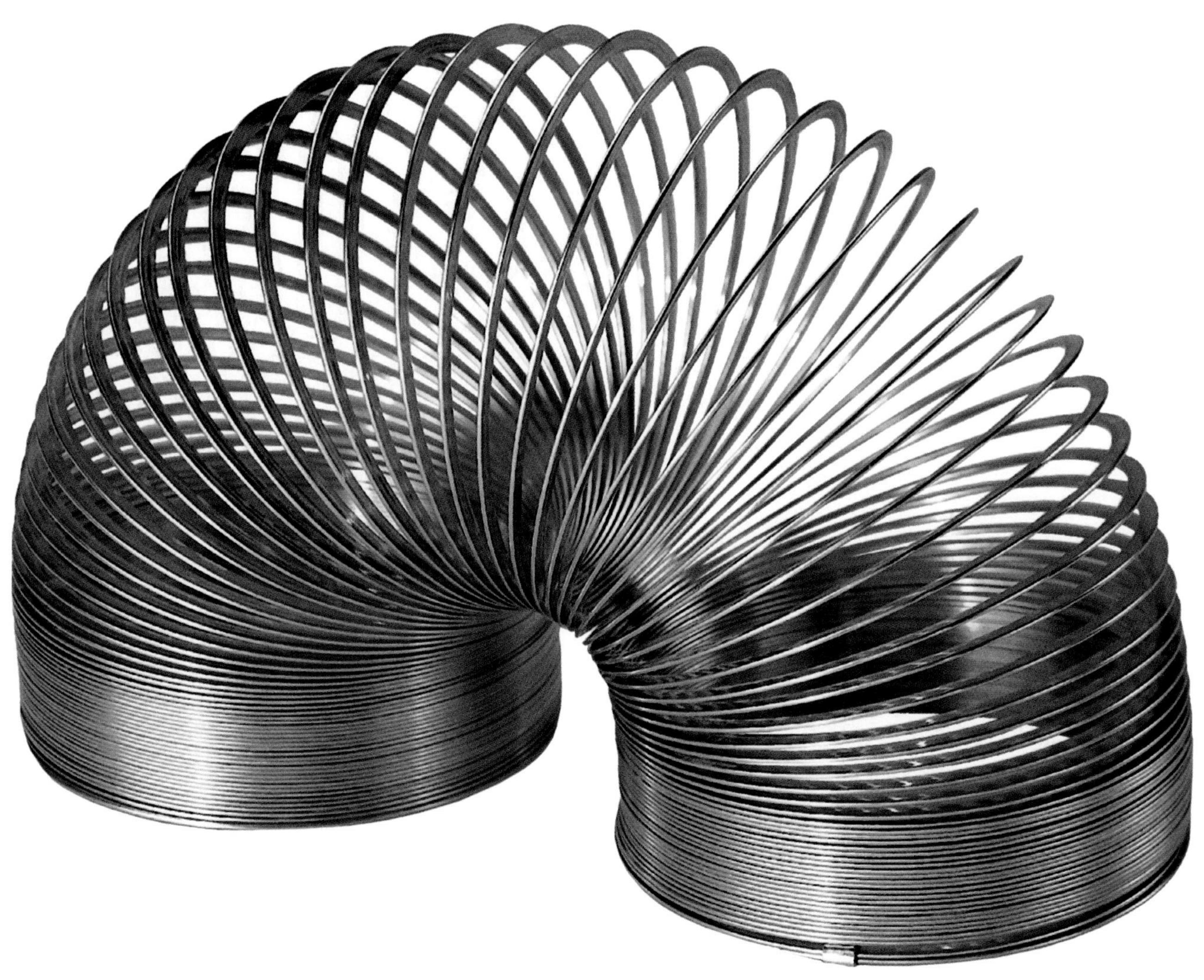

Smucker's

In 1897, Jerome Monroe Smucker, a Mennonite businessman, opened a cider mill in Orrville, Ohio. Cider sales were seasonal, so Smucker added a year-round product, apple butter, which he sold out of the back of a horse-drawn wagon. On every crock of apple butter he hand-signed his name—Smucker. The Smucker brand meant homegrown quality, a reputation perpetuated by one of the most famous slogans in advertising history: "With a name like Smucker's, it has to be good."

The J. M. Smucker Company incorporated in 1921, the same year it introduced its famous line of jams, jellies, and preserves. By 1928, the company was selling so much jam that the Pennsylvania Railroad had to build a new loading facility at the Smucker plant. In 1938, J. M. Smucker's eldest son, Willard, pioneered a packaging makeover from crockery to traditional-looking glass jars, and sales surged over the $1 million mark. By the time Jerome Monroe Smucker passed away in 1949, he had seen his company enjoy five decades of near-continuous growth.

Today, the J. M. Smucker Co. is America's top producer and marketer of jams, jellies, and preserves, and, recently, peanut butter. Recognizing that peanut butter complements jelly in the iconic PB & J sandwich, Smucker bought Jif, America's best-selling peanut butter brand, in 2002. Soon thereafter, Smucker's launched its Uncrustables line of crustless, ready-made frozen peanut butter and jelly sandwiches.

Smucker headquarters remain in tiny Orrville, Ohio, and the company continues to be family owned and operated. The co-chief executives, Timothy and Richard Smucker, great-grandsons of J.M., have been working at the company since they were teenagers. The brothers are notoriously modest and self-effacing. Not only do they decline requests to appear in Smucker commercials, but they are also reluctant to conduct interviews or even publish their photos in the company's annual report.

Observant Christian Scientists, Timothy and Richard Smucker say religion and family values guide them to make good business decisions. The Smucker brothers refuse to advertise the company's products on hit television shows because they find the content offensive. They believe that advertising targeted at children is manipulative, so they pitch their commercials to parents. Within the company, the brothers foster a consensus-oriented approach that helps employees feel valued. Since 1998, the J. M Smucker Co. has been ranked among the top 25 in *Fortune* magazine's annual "100 Best Companies to Work For" survey.

In recent years Wall Street has paid close attention to the J. M. Smucker Co., particularly after its $880 million acquisition of Procter & Gamble's Jif and Crisco brands and, in 2004, after its $840 million acquisition of International Multifoods Corp.'s Pillsbury and Hungry Jack brands. The company plans to focus on expanding its core areas of fruit-based foods, peanut butter, oils, and sweeteners.

Vital Statistics
Founder Jerome Monroe Smucker
Established 1897
Employees 3,500 (2006)
Annual Sales $2,154.7 million (2006)

Snap-on, Inc.

Prior to 1919, auto mechanics relied on one-piece socket wrenches. That year, Joe Johnson, manager of Wisconsin-based American Grinder Manufacturing Co.'s new socket wrench division proposed the concept of interchangeable sockets. After their proposed project was rejected by the company, he and coworker William A. Seidemann independently fabricated a set of five handles and ten sockets where the sockets would "snap on" to the interchangeable handles.

With the help of two salesmen, the partners generated more than 500 orders for the innovative new item. Propelled by the success of their new product, Johnson and Seidemann formed the Snap-on Wrench Co. in 1920. In search of a way to effectively sell their product, they ran an ad in the Chicago papers, attracting sales representative Stanton Palmer. Palmer would take the tool set directly to customers and demonstrate its use, which became the cornerstone of the company's marketing success. To divide the increasing load, Palmer partnered with another salesman, Newton Tarble. The sales method proved so successful that they created a formal distribution company, Motor Tool Specialty Co., to become the sole sales agent for Snap-on Wrench. This allowed Johnson and Seidemann to concentrate on tool production to keep up with growing customer demands.

By 1922, 12 sales branches had opened and new tools were added to the product line. In 1923, the first company catalogue was published, featuring nearly 50 items, including a special socket with an oval-shaped opening designed for fitting the spindle nut and adjusting cone on the Model T Ford front bearings. With requests from mechanics for other kinds of hand tools, Motor Tool added a line of open-end wrenches and a series of chisels and punches. These tools were first made by other firms for Motor Tool and sold under the name Blue Point. The popularity of these tools resulted in the formation of Blue-Point Tool Co., which operated under the same management as Motor Tool Specialty Co.

By 1929, Snap-on had 26 sales branches, nearly 300 salesmen, and a site in Kenosha selected for the headquarters of the growing firm. In 1930, to reflect its merger with Blue-Point Tool Co., Snap-on Wrench Co. became Snap-on Tools, Inc.

During World War II, Snap-on was a preferred source of hand tools for military use. Military needs led to tool shortages for civilian customers, so, in an effort to maintain goodwill with their customers, Snap-on released available stock to its sales force. As a result, salesmen's cars became their stockrooms, and by 1945, all salesmen were carrying stock and making immediate deliveries to customers. In so doing, the company pioneered the mobile tool distribution method of delivery to professional mechanics.

Snap-on continued cultivating its reputation as the foremost supplier of well-crafted products and superior customer service. In the 1980s, Snap-on became the major supplier of tools to NASA for the space shuttles. In 1990s, Snap-on made several acquisitions that expended its customer base to include franchise service centers and national chains, vehicle manufacturers, and industry. Today, the company markets its products in more than 100 countries. With more than 700 active and pending patents in the United States alone, Snap-on has led the way in innovative design for products for industrial, automotive, and aerospace use and remains one of the largest marketers in the tool manufacturing industry.

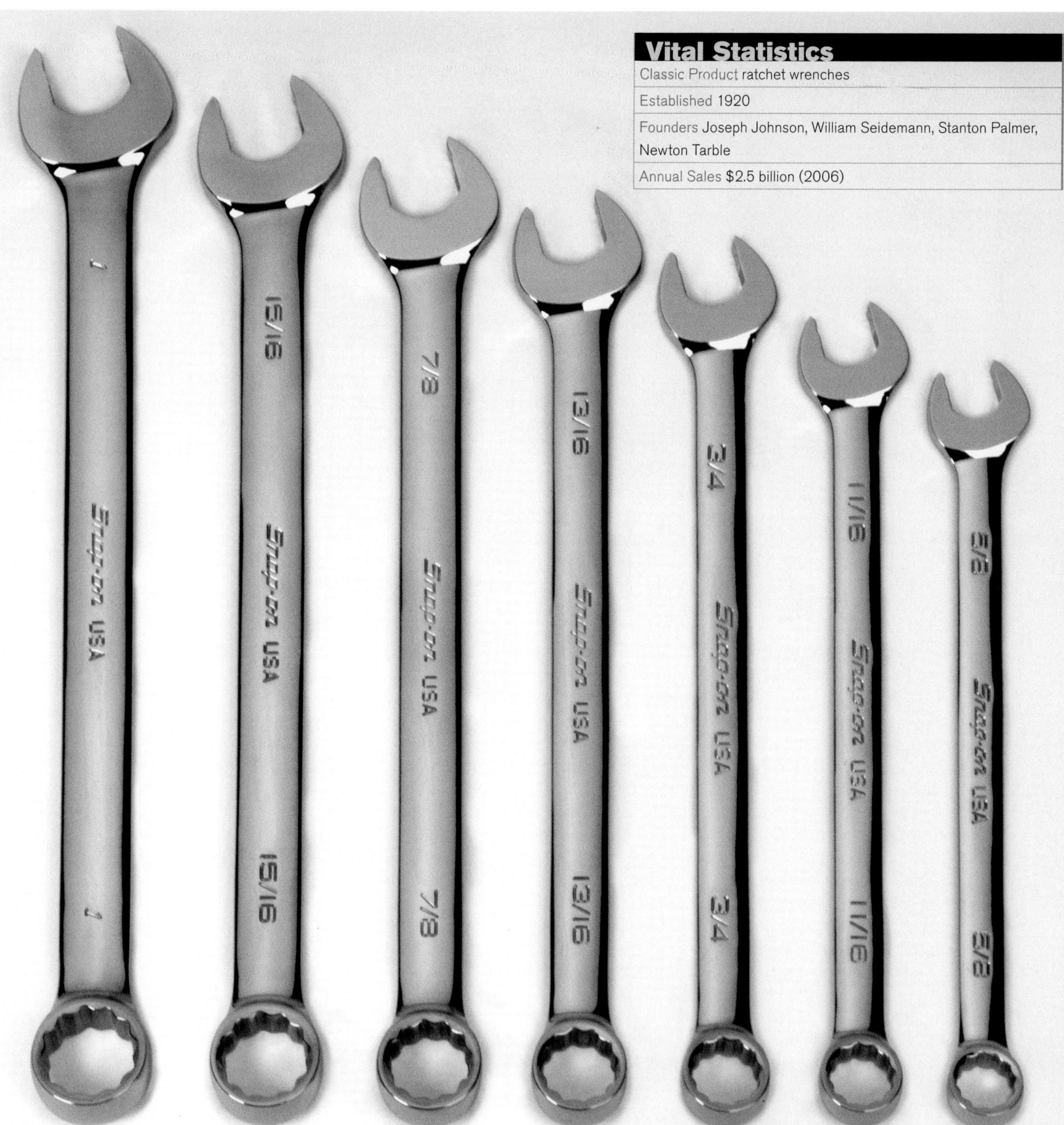

Vital Statistics

Classic Product ratchet wrenches

Established 1920

Founders Joseph Johnson, William Seidemann, Stanton Palmer, Newton Tarble

Annual Sales $2.5 billion (2006)

Snapple

Snapple Beverage Group is responsible for one of America's favorite bottled beverages—Snapple iced tea—as well as dozens of tasty variations. The company is the number one retailer of single-serving iced tea drinks and the second largest seller of fruit drinks in the country. Snapple began as a part-time business in the natural foods industry but didn't really take off until the 1980s, when the company gained its current reputation for great taste and clever advertising. Sales started to double yearly, and the national trend toward healthy, all-natural products ensured Snapple's ongoing success.

In 1972, Arnold Greenberg, Hyman Greenberg, and their boyhood friend Leonard Marsh were running a health food store on Manhattan's Lower East Side when they founded Unadulterated Food Products Inc. to sell their homemade fruit juices to other local health food stores. In 1978, Unadulterated Foods began marketing carbonated apple juice, which they called "Snapple," after buying the name for $500. After just a month, the company had sold a shocking 500 cases of the juice, and soon distributors were calling with requests. In 1979, as a result of increasing demand, the company hired its first salesman and began seeking out franchised distributors; a year later it expanded the Snapple line to include other all natural juices, adding natural sodas in 1982. Although at $1 a bottle the drinks were high priced, they became more and more popular in the northeast throughout the early '80s. Each new variety of Snapple took from six months to a year to develop, as alterations were made in taste, color, and name. The company strove for memorable names that were not too gimmicky—one famously rejected example is "Guava Nagilah."

Snapple's future changed forever, however, only when the creative partners decided they needed a special summertime drink and dreamed up their first iced tea. Unlike previous renditions, Snapple's tea was preservative-free; the company had spent three years working with a tea vendor and a bottler to perfect a method in which the tea was bottled while hot. In 1988, Snapple introduced a lemon-flavored iced tea made with the new process. Sales exploded, and by the end of 1988, Unadulterated Foods' sales had increased by 60 percent over the previous 12 months. Unadulterated Foods expanded the Snapple line to include 53 different flavors, and, in the first six months of 1989, the company's revenues increased by 600 percent. In order to continue expansion, the founders reached an agreement with a Boston-based investment banking firm, the Thomas H. Lee Company, forming the Snapple Holding Corporation in Delaware. In 1992, to counteract challenges from Coke and Pepsi in the iced tea arena, Snapple began running a new line of advertisements featuring its now trademark "Made from the Best Stuff on Earth" line. Snapple announced that it would sell stock to the public for the first time in December 1992. In preparation for the stock offering, Snapple Holding merged into its subsidiary, becoming the Snapple Beverage Corporation. By July 1994, Snapple had solidified its position as the fastest growing beverage company in the world. In 2000, Snapple was sold to Cadbury Schweppes and negotiated a five-year, multimillion-dollar marketing deal to sell its beverages in New York City in 2004.

Today, Snapple retains its small company quirkiness with the support of parent company Cadbury Schweppes. Cadbury Schweppes has incorporated Nantucket Nectars' operations into the Snapple embrace, and Snapple products are available in the United States and about 80 other countries worldwide.

Vital Statistics
Parent Company Cadbury Schweppes
Product Launch 1979
Employees 500
Annual Sales $854 million

S.O.S

They come to the rescue when you need help with a stubborn pot or pan, but S.O.S pads didn't get their name from the Morse code signal of distress. S.O.S pads were invented in 1917 by Ed Cox, who lived in San Francisco, California. Cox was selling aluminum pots door-to-door, trying to make a living. The pots were hard to clean, because back then aluminum pots weren't anodized. Anodization is the process that adds a protective layer to a metal surface. Unanodized aluminum reacts to acidic and salty foods by becoming cloudy and dark, and homemakers complained that they couldn't get their new pans looking shiny again.

Knowing that a good salesman listens to his customers, Cox decided to try to solve the problem by developing a scrub pad. In his kitchen, he dipped steel wool into soapy water. When it dried, he dipped again and again, until the steel wool couldn't hold any more soap. The pads proved very effective at cleaning pans, and he began giving out a free soap pad to every customer. Soon, his customers were waving off his attempts to sell pans but begging for soap pads. His product was so successful that he began manufacturing it.

He still needed a name, though. His wife came up with the idea to call the pads S.O.S, which stands for "Save Our Saucepans." To obtain a trademark for the name, the period after the last *S* was dropped so as not to infringe on the Morse code symbol.

The brand, owned by The Clorox Company, also includes a tougher, heavier pad that is designed for commercial use. Clorox bought S.O.S from Miles Inc., a unit of Bayer A.G. in Pittsburgh, Pennsylvania, in 1994.

Vital Statistics

Parent Company The Clorox Company

Product Launch 1917

Headquarters Oakland, California

CLEANS FASTER
LIMPIA MÁS RÁPIDO
S.O.S®
STEEL WOOL SOAP PADS ESPONJAS DE ACERO CON JABÓN 10

Soy Boy

Like many natural foods aficionados, friends Norman Holland and Andrew Schecter feel strongly that the food they eat should be grown and processed in environmentally friendly and socially aware ways. The two friends put their money where their mouths were in 1976 when they founded a business making an organic tofu they called SoyBoy. They wanted to eat right, but they also wanted to build a business that would create positive changes in society. So they got $7,000 in loans from friends and ran their new business, Northern Soy, according to their principles.

Back then, many Americans considered soybeans "hippie food." But soon, medical research began to show that eating soy-based foods was good for your health. Because soy foods are lower in calories, total fat, and saturated fat than comparable meat products, and have zero cholesterol, they may reduce the risk of heart disease, obesity, and cancer. Even mainstream media like *Time* magazine and the *Washington Post* ran stories about the benefits of soy, and sales and consumption of soy products skyrocketed. Books such as *The Simple Soybean* and *Your Health, Tofu Cookery,* and *The Book of Tofu* helped spread the word. And in 1999, the Food and Drug Administration approved a health claim for soy food labels that says that diets including 25 grams of soy protein a day may reduce the risk of heart disease.

Northern Soy is still in its birthplace in Rochester, New York, and Holland and Schecter, both still vegetarians, continue to run the day-to-day operations. The manufacturing process has changed considerably since the early days, now employing microprocessor-controlled machinery instead of manual labor. But the ingredients for SoyBoy Tofu—organic soybeans, water, and natural coagulants—are still the same. Every year, a USDA-accredited certifying agency inspects the production facility to ensure that all SoyBoy products meet organic standards and contain no artificial ingredients, chemical pesticides, fertilizers, or herbicides. Nor are ingredients that are bioengineered or irradiated used for making SoyBoy products.

Northern Soy is the only tofu maker in North America that uses a natural calcium chloride nigari as a coagulant, which the company claims makes their tofu higher in protein and calcium. Because tofu is more than 75 percent water, they've also installed a custom-designed, natural activated-charcoal water purification system to kill bacteria and filter out pollutants. For those who don't want to cook, Northern Soy also makes a line of tofu products that are ready to eat. There's Tofu Lin, marinated with traditional Asian flavorings, Italian Tofu, Caribbean Tofu, and Smoked Tofu. Perhaps the most familiar way to get introduced to tofu is SoyBoy's line of Tofu-filled ravioli.

Vital Statistics
Parent Company Northern Soy, Inc.
Product Launch 1977
Headquarters Rochester, New York
Employees 30

SOYBOY®
ORGANIC TOFU
FIRM
NO GMOS
USDA ORGANIC
KEEP REFRIGERATED

NET WT. 16 OZ • 454G

ALL NATURAL INGREDIENTS: Filtered water, organically-grown (non-GMO) soybeans, natural coagulants (calcium chloride [nigari], calcium sulphate).

NATURAL SOY ISOFLAVONES

visit soyboy.com

345 Paul Road, Rochester, NY 14624

ORGANIC CERTIFIED BY QAI **K**

Nutrition Facts

Serving Size 3 oz. (84g)
Servings Per Container about 5

Amount per Serving	
Calories 90 Calories from Fat 45	
	% Daily Value*
Total Fat 5g	8%
Saturated Fat 0.5g	3%
Sodium 5mg	0%
Total Carbohydrate 1g	0%
Protein 10g	

Calcium 10% • Iron 10%

Not a significant source of trans fat, cholesterol, dietary fiber, sugars, Vitamin A, or Vitamin C

*Percent Daily Values (DV) are based on a 2,000 calorie diet.

Spalding

Spalding is one of the oldest sporting goods brands in America. Known for its high quality and innovation, it is the world's largest basketball equipment supplier and a leading producer and marketer of basketballs, backboards, footballs, soccerballs, volleyballs, and softballs under the Dudley brand. Spalding is the official basketball of the National Basketball Association and the Women's National Basketball Association and is also the official backboard of the NBA and National Collegiate Athletic Association. Spalding also makes the official volleyball of the King of the Beach Volleyball tour and is the official football of the Arena Football League.

A. G. Spalding, founder of the company, won 241 of 301 games he pitched for the Boston Red Stockings and the Chicago White Stockings. He pitched every game with a ball he developed himself, and when he retired in 1876, the future Hall of Famer went into the sporting goods business full time. For the next 100 years, Spalding's baseball would remain the official ball of the Major Leagues. From the first baseball, Spalding went on to many other famous firsts in the sports world. In 1887, the company developed and manufactured the first football made of finest-quality foot leather and rawhide lacing. In 1891, Dr. James Naismith invented the game of basketball, which was originally played with a soccer ball, and asked Spalding to develop the first basketball. Shortly thereafter, Spalding was asked to develop and manufacture the first volleyball.

Spalding made headlines in the world of golf in 1930 with the technological advancement featured in the Kro-Flite, the first wound balata ball with a liquid center. This achievement in golf ball engineering raised the bar in distance and control in the game of golf. Spalding continued to lead the way in the sporting goods industry with improvements and advancements on sports equipment that the company made famous. In 1972, Spalding manufactured the first synthetic leather basketball and later developed the first composite leather cover materials in 1992, making the basketball more durable while providing greater feel and control than traditional leather.

Spalding's long line of firsts and innovation has continued into the 21st century. In 2001, Spalding introduced an Integrated MicroPump known as INFUSION technology for self-inflating balls (a built-in pump), The introduction of INFUSION led to a more than 50 percent increase in basketball sales in the first year while growing the sporting goods category by 12 percent. Five years after INFUSION, Spalding introduced NEVER FLAT, the first-ever ball with proprietary pressure retention technologies designed to hold air up to 10 times longer than traditional basketballs. NEVER FLAT, guaranteed to stay fully inflated for at least one year—with no additional air needed during that period, is the #1 selling basketball in the marketplace today.

Russell is a sportswear company that covers every step of the manufacturing process from weaving raw fibers into fabric, to dying, cutting, and sewing it into T-shirts, sweatpants, and sweatshirts that it sells through retailers and outlets. The Russell Athletic division supplies uniforms for baseball's Minor League, the U.S. Olympics, and Little League Baseball. Russell expanded its reach in the sporting goods world to include hard goods with the acquisition of Spalding Sports Worldwide in 2003. A division of Russell Corporation, the Spalding Group consists of three business units: Spalding, Huffy Sports, and American Athletic—together making it the largest basketball equipment supplier in the world.

Vital Statistics
Classic Products basketball, football, baseball, volleyball
Established 1876
Founder Albert Goodwill Spalding
Headquarters Springfeld, Massachusetts

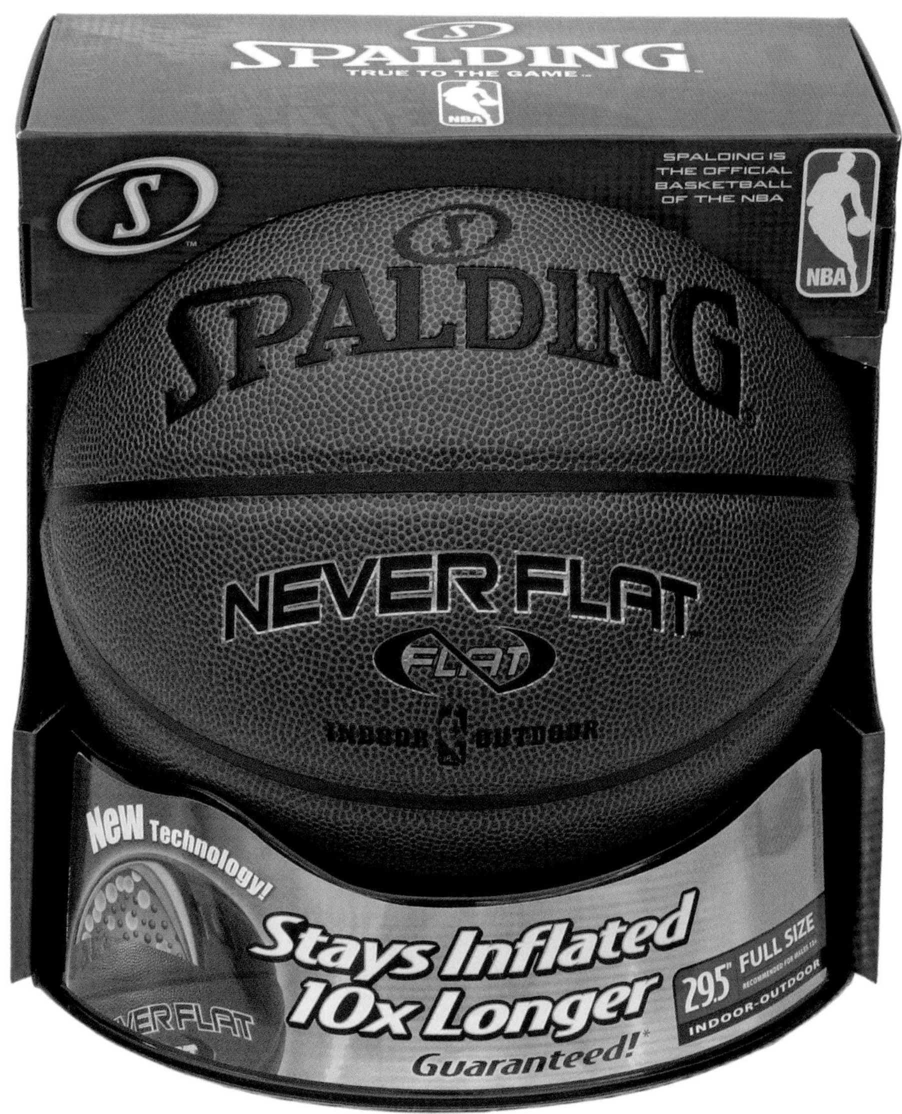

Starbucks

Starbucks isn't merely a coffeehouse. It's also a gathering place and a study hall. It's a brand of coffee ice cream, bottled drink, and liqueur. It's a music retailer that's also getting into the movie and book business. It's a daily ritual for millions of people around the world. And—with more than 11,000 locations in more than 30 countries with plans to grow to 30,000 worldwide—it's a global phenomenon.

Starbucks, the worldwide leader in the retail coffee business, was founded in 1971 by coffee aficionados Gordon Bowker, Jerry Baldwin, and Zev Siegl, who opened the first shop in Seattle's Pike Place Market. They named their business Starbucks after the first mate in *Moby Dick* and distinguished it with a logo of a two-tailed siren. By 1982, Starbucks had expanded to six stores and a business as a coffee supplier to restaurants. The three founders hired entrepreneur Howard Schultz to help run the company. In 1987, Schultz bought Starbucks and quickly opened dozens of new locations on the West Coast. In 1992, the company went public and began to spread across the country—into department stores and bookstores, on street corners, and at hotels, airports, and kiosks.

Starbucks introduced Americans to high-quality coffee made with rich, roasted Arabica beans similar to that served in Italian cafés. Standards are so high that employees at the Starbucks roasting plant aren't qualified to roast a batch of beans until they undergo a yearlong training program. In 2000, to bolster its corporate image, Starbucks announced that it would buy a percentage of its beans from "fair trade" farmers who receive several times the market price. Employees, including the "baristas" who make the drinks, are offered full benefits even if they work only part-time.

Most of Starbucks' revenue comes not from cups of coffee or espresso, but from the Frappuccino—a contraction of *frappé* and *cappuccino*—introduced in 1995. Many liken the Frappuccino to old-time drugstore shakes, but targeted to adults. A creamy, iced beverage, normally topped with whipped cream and chocolate drizzle, the Frappuccino is available in more than 25 flavors, including Coffee, Espresso, Mocha, and Java Chip, and noncoffee flavors such as Strawberries & Cream, Bananas & Cream, Vanilla Bean, Double Chocolate Chip, and Tazo Chai. Regarded by many as a treat, more Frapuccinos are ordered on Saturdays than any other day of the week. Bottled Frappuccino is available in grocery stores and amounts to more than 80 percent of the U.S. market for ready-to-drink coffee. In 2004, responding to concerns that the Frappuccino had more calories than a Big Mac, Starbucks rolled out a line whose versions were lower in fat and calories. In 2006, Starbucks launched Frappuccinos made with pomegranate and tangerine juice.

Starbucks regularly experiments with its menu by offering seasonal drinks and, in select stores, breakfast items. Lunch is also available at 60 percent of company-owned stores in the United States. In 2006, Starbucks announced it was seeking movies and books to promote along with the music it already sells in its stores. The unquenchable taste for Frappuccinos and coffees—and, now, Starbucks-promoted music, movies, and books—is driving the chain toward accomplishing its 30,000-outlet goal.

Vital Statistics

Founders Gordon Bowker, Jerry Baldwin, and Zev Siegl

Established 1971

Headquarters Seattle, Washington

Classic Product Frappuccino

Annual Sales $7.8 billion (2006)

Steinway

Without a doubt, the most recognizable piano in the world is the Steinway Concert Grand. More than 98 percent of the concert piano performances throughout the world performed on Steinway grand pianos.

Founded in 1853 in a Manhattan loft by Heinrich Steinweg (Henry Steinway), a master cabinetmaker from Germany, Steinway & Sons has a rich history. Trained in the classic European tradition, using skills that were passed down from master to apprentice over several generations, Henry Steinway built his first piano back home in his kitchen in Germany. With his five sons, Steinway spent the next 40 years developing the modern piano, gaining national recognition for innovative designs and exceptional craftsmanship. The company received international acclaim in 1867 at the Paris Exhibition, where Steinway received the Grand Gold Medal of Honor for excellence in manufacturing and engineering. Not only was it a great personal achievement, but it was the first time an American company had ever received this award.

In 1866, Steinway & Sons opened Steinway Hall, which soon became New York City's artistic and cultural center. In the 1870s, the Steinways moved their plant from Manhattan to Astoria, Queens, creating a community around the factory with housing, a library, a post office, and a kindergarten. Shortly after, in 1875, a London showroom opened, and in 1880, the Steinways opened a second factory and a retail operation in Hamburg, Germany.

Steinway continues to operate in the fine European tradition passed down from its founder. Each instrument is meticulously crafted one at a time, with a grand piano taking up to one year to create. From the selection of the woods, to its transformation into components that range from massive to minute, to the delicate balance of blending technology with craft to create each unique instrument, great care is taken to ensure the high quality and superior workmanship of a Steinway piano.

Steinway is the instrument of choice at some of the most noted music schools around the world, and more than 90 percent of the world's active concert pianists (more than 1,300) have the title Steinway Artist. That means the artist owns a Steinway and chooses to perform exclusively on Steinway pianos.

Through acquisitions over the years, Steinway has become known for more than just pianos. Steinway Musical Instruments designs, manufactures, and markets high-quality musical instruments throughout the world. With a network of dealers, Steinway sells less expensive pianos, and its Conn-Selmer subsidiary is the number-one maker of band and orchestral instruments in the United States. These include Bach trumpets and trombones and Ludwig drums. The products of Steinway Musical Instruments are sold worldwide to professional, amateur, and student musicians as well as orchestras and educational institutions.

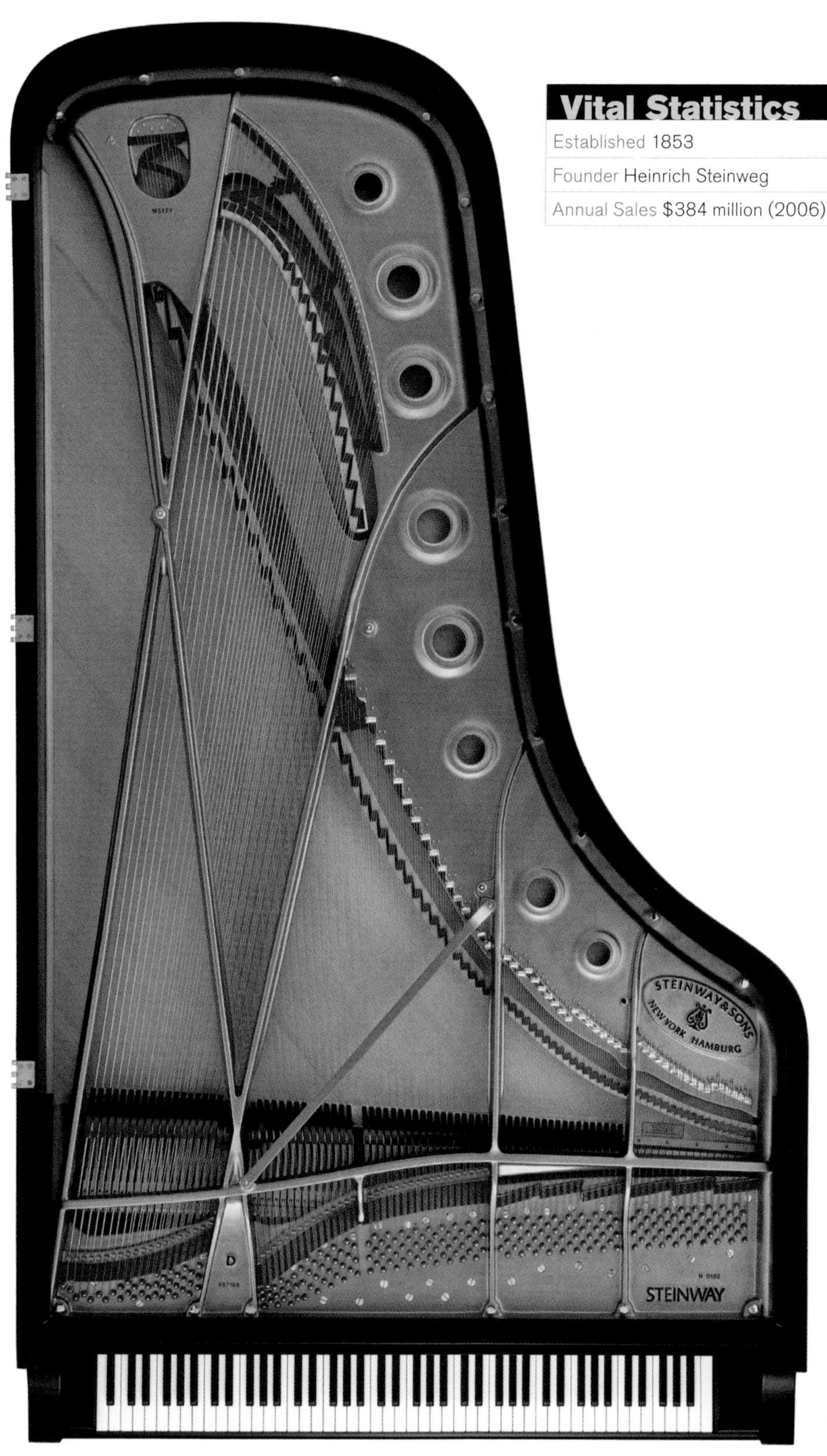

Vital Statistics

Established 1853

Founder Heinrich Steinweg

Annual Sales $384 million (2006)

Stonyfield Farm

Stonyfield Farm is a company whose product unequivocally reflects its values. It is committed to keeping artificial ingredients out of food, and its critically acclaimed yogurts use only all natural and organic ingredients, eschewing preservatives and artificial flavors, colors, and sweeteners.

The products are made with premium milk provided by farmers who refuse to use synthetic bovine growth hormone, and all organic ingredients are produced without antibiotics, synthetic growth hormones, or toxic pesticides and fertilizers.

Stonyfield Farm was founded in Wilton, New Hampshire, in 1983 as an organic farming school—a project to help revitalize the struggling New England dairy industry and support family farms. Chairman and founder Samuel Kaymen, one of the country's early authorities on organic and biodynamic agriculture, and President/CEO Gary Hirshberg, an environmental activist, windmill maker, author, and noted entrepreneur, launched their venture with seven Jersey cows and a yogurt recipe. Kaymen, who grew up on welfare in Brooklyn, and Hirshberg, who had been running an environmental think tank, borrowed $35,000 and at first did most of the work themselves, including milking the cows, taking sales calls, and hand-delivering their products. By 1989, the company had grown to such an extent that a move was necessary—to the specially designed Yogurt Works facility in Londonderry, New Hampshire, where their headquarters remain. A year later, Stonyfield Farm was No. 113 on INC 500's 1990 List of Fastest Growing Companies in the USA. In 2001, after careful deliberation, Stonyfield entered into a partnership with Groupe Danone. Today, Stonyfield Farm boasts more than $250 million in annual sales, and many more than seven cows are required to generate sufficient milk.

Stonyfield Farm takes pride in its social and environmental conscientiousness, as well as the healthful properties of its products. Its packaging emphasizes the importance of recycling and supporting family farmers, and the company donates 10 percent of its profits each year to efforts that help protect or restore the Earth. Through recycling, Stonyfield Farm ensures that tons of materials will never end up in a landfill or incinerator. And in a typical quirk, hundreds of thousands of people have "adopted" a dairy cow through a program that provides participants with a photograph of a real cow that produces milk for Stonyfield Farm, the cow's biography, and seasonal updates from "their" cow. All Stonyfield Farm yogurts, smoothies, and cultured soy products contain six live active cultures, and the company is the only American brand with *L. reuteri,* which helps promote good digestive health and inhibits the activity of harmful bacteria.

Stonyfield Farm sells natural and organic yogurts, yogurt smoothies, cultured soy, organic ice cream and frozen yogurt, and milk. A generation of parents is introducing children to yogurt with organic Yo Baby yogurts in flavors such as banana and pear. And although Samuel Kaymen is now retired, Hirshberg is still at the helm of the company the pair co-founded almost a quarter-century ago with a 50-gallon batch of whole-milk plain yogurt, still one of the company's best sellers.

Vital Statistics
Parent Company Groupe Danone
Classic Product yogurt
Established 1983
Founder Samuel Kaymen
Annual Sales $250 million (2005)

Stonyfield Farm
ALL NATURAL
fat free
STRAWBERRY CHEESECAKE
FLAVORED
smooth & creamy
Stonyfield Farm
ALL NATURAL
NEW FLAVOR!
fat free
KEY LIME
smooth & creamy
Stonyfield Farm
ALL NATURAL
NEW FLAVOR!
fat free
BLACKBERRY
smooth & creamy

Swingline

There's a good chance you've used your stapler today—probably several times. In fact, it's probably such a "staple" on your desk that you rarely give it any consideration. Although stapling machines in some form have been around since the 1700s, when one was designed for France's King Louis XV, the classic Swingline first appeared in the late 1930s. Swingline revolutionized stapling by creating a stapler that opened on top, allowing office workers to drop in a strip of 210 staples, and continues to lead innovation through ergonomic designs and improved functionality. Chances are the stapler on your desk or a stapler you used today is a Swingline.

Swingline®

In 1925, Jack Linsky founded the Parrot Speed Fastener Company and opened a manufacturing facility in Long Island City, N.Y., in 1931. He invented the stapler that opened on top and the strip of staples glued together for easy loading. The name for his invention came from his wife, who dubbed his tool "Swingline" for the swinging top.

In 1939, the company's name was changed to Speed Products, and then, in 1956, Swingline. In 1987, Swingline was acquired by ACCO, the former American Clip Company. ACCO Brands, Inc. markets a wide variety of office supplies, ranging from paper clips and staplers to personal organizers, computer peripherals and binders, with operations in 60 locations around the globe.

The original #4 stapler (pictured in back) brought innovation to the workplace by opening to tack posters and swing open for top loading of 210 count strips of the famous S.F.#4 staple. The innovation continued, leading to a 1970 launch of the industry standard 747 stapler. This is the model most widely used in today's offices, schools, and homes. A Swingline stapler made a dramatic appearance in 1999's cult classic *Office Space*, when an employee was devastated that his beloved red Swingline stapler was stolen from his desk, and set fire to the office building as revenge. Swingline's Rio Red Stapler (pictured center), introduced as a collector's edition in response to the movie, features durable die-cast, all-metal construction and staples up to 20 sheets of paper with ease.

Through intensive consumer research, Swingline continues to identify ways to improve the stapling experience. This has led to the introduction of ergonomically designed Optima staplers (pictured front) featuring increased sheet capacity and guaranteed jam-free stapling. The Swingline family also includes a full line of electric staplers, staples, punches, and paper trimmers. Improving productivity and efficiency is paramount in making users' lives easier. Proprietary technology, design, and exceptional performance make Swingline one of the most well-recognized brands in office products in the world, with over two-thirds brand preference in the marketplace.

In 2003, ACCO Brands Corporation celebrated its 100th anniversary, and a year later posted sales of more than $1 billion. ACCO's acquisition of the Swingline company was a major factor in its rise to the top. Swingline staplers and punches have revolutionized the way people record, store, and organize information in offices, schools, and workspaces, thanks to the widespread popularity of these ubiquitous tools.

Vital Statistics

Parent Company ACCO Brands Corporation

Headquarters Lincolnshire, Illinois

Classic Product Swingline top-load stapler

Founder/Inventor Jack Linsky

Employees 7,770

Tabasco Sauce

In the 1850s, Edmund McIlhenny, a New Orleans banker, received a gift of dried hot pepper seeds from a traveler who had recently been in Central America. McIlhenny planted the seeds in his garden on Avery Island, harvested the peppers, and concocted a recipe for a hot pepper sauce made with vinegar and local salt and aged in white-oak barrels. The sauce became so popular among his friends and family that in 1868, he decided to open a hot sauce business called the McIlhenny Company. He named the sauce after the variety of pepper, ***Tabasco,*** a word that most scholars say is a Central American Indian word for "land where the soil is hot and humid." McIlhenny packaged the Tabasco sauce in empty cologne bottles and sold them to wholesalers throughout the United States. In 1870, he patented Tabasco sauce and began to export it to Europe.

In the 1930s, Tabasco sauce became a key ingredient in a new hit drink, the Bloody Mary. Conceived a decade earlier as a vodka and tomato sauce cocktail, the drink was transformed in a New York City bar when a creative bartender added Tabasco sauce as well as Worcestershire sauce, lemon, lime, horseradish, and black pepper. Americans began to discover how Tabasco sauce could spice up almost every type of food: eggs, steaks, stews, salads, fried potatoes, and soups. The sauce became a standard table condiment.

Tabasco sauce has made its mark on world history. During the Vietnam War, General Walter McIlhenny, Edmund McIlhenny's grandson, distributed Tabasco sauce accompanied by a cookbook that instructed soldiers in how to zest up wartime rations by making recipes such as Combat Canapés and Breast of Chicken Under Bullets. The McIlhenny Company later issued another Tabasco cookbook, and the spicy red pepper sauce is now de rigueur in military cuisine. Accounts from the front lines of Afghanistan and Iraq describe how the ubiquitous Tabasco bottles are used as Christmas decorations and chess pieces. Tabasco sauce is also used at the front lines of space to liven up the bland food rationed to astronauts on NASA shuttle missions and at the International Space Station.

Today, the McIlhenney Company remains family owned and operated and manufactures more than 700,000 bottles of Tabasco sauce daily at its original site on Avery Island, Louisiana. Many of the red peppers used in Tabasco sauce are still grown on the island, where they are picked at the peak of their ripeness by workers using a ***baton rouge,*** or red stick, as a color matching guide. Although it faces competition from more than 100 varieties of other hot sauces on the market, Tabasco sauce remains the leading hot pepper sauce in the world. The company has introduced new condiment varieties under the Tabasco brand and plans to introduce more in the years to come. Recent offerings include pepper jelly, soy sauce, steak sauce, and new flavors of Tabasco sauce, including chipotle, garlic, and sweet and spicy.

Vital Statistics
Classic Product Tabasco hot pepper sauce
Established 1868
Founder Edmund McIlhenny
Main Production Site Avery Island, Louisiana
Distribution 700,000 bottles daily

TABASCO
BRAND PEPPER SAUCE
MADE IN U.S.A.
McILHENNY CO.
AVERY ISLAND
LA.
TABASCO
BRAND
PEPPER SAUCE

Taco Bell

Thinking outside the bun has turned out to be a very lucrative way of doing business. With a menu of tacos, burritos, nachos, quesadillas, and specialty items, Taco Bell is the number-one Mexican quick-service restaurant chain in the country, with more than 5,800 locations, plus 240 outside the United States.

Its beginnings date back to 1948 in San Bernardino, California, when Glen Bell, right out of the Marine Corps, had his eye on a new business venture. Bell wanted to bring back the recreational activities that had faded into the background during World War II, but though his head thought about miniature golf, his wallet pointed him toward a hot dog stand. Bell learned the restaurant business with Bell's Drive-In, which served hamburgers and hot dogs, and is believed to be the first stand-alone, take-out food operation in the United States. He sold it in 1952.

His second location included a variety of food. Since he was not the only vendor in town, Bell became interested in alternative menu items, and being a fan of Mexican food, recognized the difficulties of ordering tacos as a take-out item from a full-service restaurant. Bell's plan for experimenting with tacos was to set up a hot dog stand in a Mexican neighborhood so that if the tacos were successful, his competitors would attribute his success to the location rather than the items on the menu.

Success at the taco window convinced Bell that it was time to dedicate one solely to tacos. After co-owning three Taco-Tias, he partnered with four players from the LA Rams—who also happened to be taco fans—on the El Taco enterprise. Following this extremely profitable venture, Bell focused on opening his own operation, Taco Bell, in Downey, California in 1962.

The spirit of invention that led Glen Bell to his taco stand continues to thrive in Taco Bell's offering today. One new wildfire success has been the Crunchwrap Supreme, which is essentially a Taco Supreme wrapped up in a tortilla for improved portability. It wraps a classic Taco Bell taste inside a tortilla, creating a unique hexagon shape, sealed on all sides to prevent spills. It is Taco Bell's most successful product introduction since the introduction of the taco to its menu in 1962.

Serving more than 35 million customers each week, Taco Bell operates freestanding restaurants and quick-serve kiosks. These smaller Taco Bell Express outlets offer an abbreviated version of the menu, serving customers in airports, malls, hotels, and other locations. Taco Bell is also used under license by Kraft Foods, providing a line of Taco Bell items sold in supermarkets across the country, including taco shells, salsa, and other Mexican food items as well as all-in-one meal kits.

More than 80 percent of the Taco Bell restaurants are franchised or licensed; the remaining restaurants are company restaurants. Taco Bell is a subsidiary of Yum! Brands, Inc., the world's largest restaurant company.

Vital Statistics
Parent Company Yum! Brands Inc.
Established 1962
Founder Glen Bell
Annual Sales $1.8 Billion (2006)

TACO BELL

Target

For many, there could be no better evidence that Target transcends demographics than when the discount chain sponsored an entire issue of the highbrow *New Yorker* magazine. The August 22, 2005 release was covered from front to back with hip, stylized work from graphic illustrators who incorporated the Target bull's-eye into their designs. The red-and-white logo is so easily identifiable that readers knew Target was behind the scenes without even a mention of the store or any its products.

Pronounced "Tar-zhay" by some fans, in jest, to sound French, Target sets itself apart from its big-box discount store competitors. The difference is that its brand and merchandise appeal to the style-conscious consumer–the type of person who might otherwise shop at upscale stores for clothes and housewares. The chain collaborates with high-profile designers and fashion icons to launch exclusive lines such as Smith & Hawken outdoor dining sets, Isaac Mizrahi outfits, and Michael Graves housewares.

Target's roots date back to 1902, when businessman George Dayton opened Goodfellows–a single department store–in the heart of downtown Minneapolis, Minnesota. In 1903, the store's name changed to the Dayton Dry Goods Store, which became the Dayton Company, then the Dayton Hudson Corporation.

The first Target store opened in 1962 in Roseville, Minnesota, and became a chain. By 1975, Target stores had become the Dayton Hudson Corporation's greatest source of revenue, and in 2000, acknowledging the position of its Target stores division, the retailer changed its name to Target Corporation.

Target cemented its position as a leader in the movement for high-end design at low prices with the 1999 debut of its first line of designer products for the home by noted architect Michael Graves. The Michael Graves Design Collection featured 200 items, including the now-famous toaster and whistle teakettle, and brought to life the retailer's brand promise of "Expect More. Pay Less."

Identifying a successful formula, Target's partnership with Graves continues to this day as the retailer collaborates with a wide array of design partners. Mossimo Giannulli, Sonia Kashuk, Thomas O'Brien, and the rising stars of GO International, to name a few, have helped the retailer continue to make good on its philosophy of keeping smart, innovative design well within reach, while building plenty of buzz and excitement along the way.

In addition to its "democratization of design," Target is often recognized for its role as a corporate philanthropic leader. Since opening its first store, the retailer has demonstrated a commitment to the communities in which it does business. Today, Target gives back $3 million a week to strengthen families and communities across the nation, with a focus on education, the arts, social services, and other vital community partnerships.

Today, Target is the second-largest general merchandise discount retailer, with more than 1,500 Target and SuperTarget stores across the country. The company's momentum and its trademark bull's-eye continue to move forward with current plans to have 2,000 stores by the year 2011.

Vital Statistics

Employees	338,000
Headquarters	Minneapolis, Minnesota
Annual Sales	$59.5 billion (2006)

Texas Instruments

Texas Instruments Inc. is one of the world's largest manufacturers of semiconductors, and the company's graphing calculator has revolutionized math education. Texas Instruments is also a leading producer of analog chips and digital signal processors, found in devices such as DVD players and computer modems, and more than 50 percent of wireless phones function thanks to Texas Instruments. The company is also known for its digital light processing products.

In 1930, two men—Clarence "Doc" Karcher and Eugene McDermott—founded a company called Geophysical Service, Inc. (GSI) in Newark, New Jersey. The partners were interested in developing a new technology for finding oil and gas called reflective seismology. Four years later, the company moved to Dallas and began producing electronics for the military. Throughout World War II, GSI made submarine detectors for the navy and continued to grow. In 1951—thanks to its location—the company changed its name to Texas Instruments and began making transistors. The Regency Radio, the first portable transistor radio, appeared in 1954, along with the world's first commercial silicon transistor. The devices attracted a lot of attention, including that of IBM president Thomas Watson, who started using Texas Instruments as a supplier to his company in the late 1950s. Texas Instruments opened its first international plant in England in 1957, a year before employee and engineer Jack Kilby invented the integrated circuit—Kilby later won the Nobel Prize in physics for this in 2000.

Texas Instruments remained on the cutting edge throughout subsequent decades, inventing electronic handheld calculators in 1967 and single-chip microcomputers in 1971. Other inventions included digital watches, home computers, and educational toys such as Speak & Spell, which was the first Texas Instruments product to contain a digital signal processor. In 1990, Texas Instruments produced its first graphing calculator: the TI-81. The company had worked closely with educators to arrive at the perfect product. The TI-81 was an instant smash, and subsequent models improved upon the original with internal USB ports, preloaded applications, and technologically sophisticated display panels. The latest, the TI-Nspire family, is compatible with previous products and includes computer software to meet the needs of various classrooms.

Texas Instruments is a classic American company and one of the country's leaders in the electronics industry. As one of the nation's first companies to manufacture transistors and the first to introduce the first semiconductor integrated circuit, Texas Instruments' history provides a veritable parallel to the development of the electronics field in general over the course of the 20th century. Although in recent decades the company has had its share of ups and downs, its decision to focus on high-tech computer components and its revolutionary line of educational technology will serve Texas Instruments well in the years to come.

Vital Statistics
Classic Product learning technology
Employees 35,207
Annual Sales $14,255 million (2006)

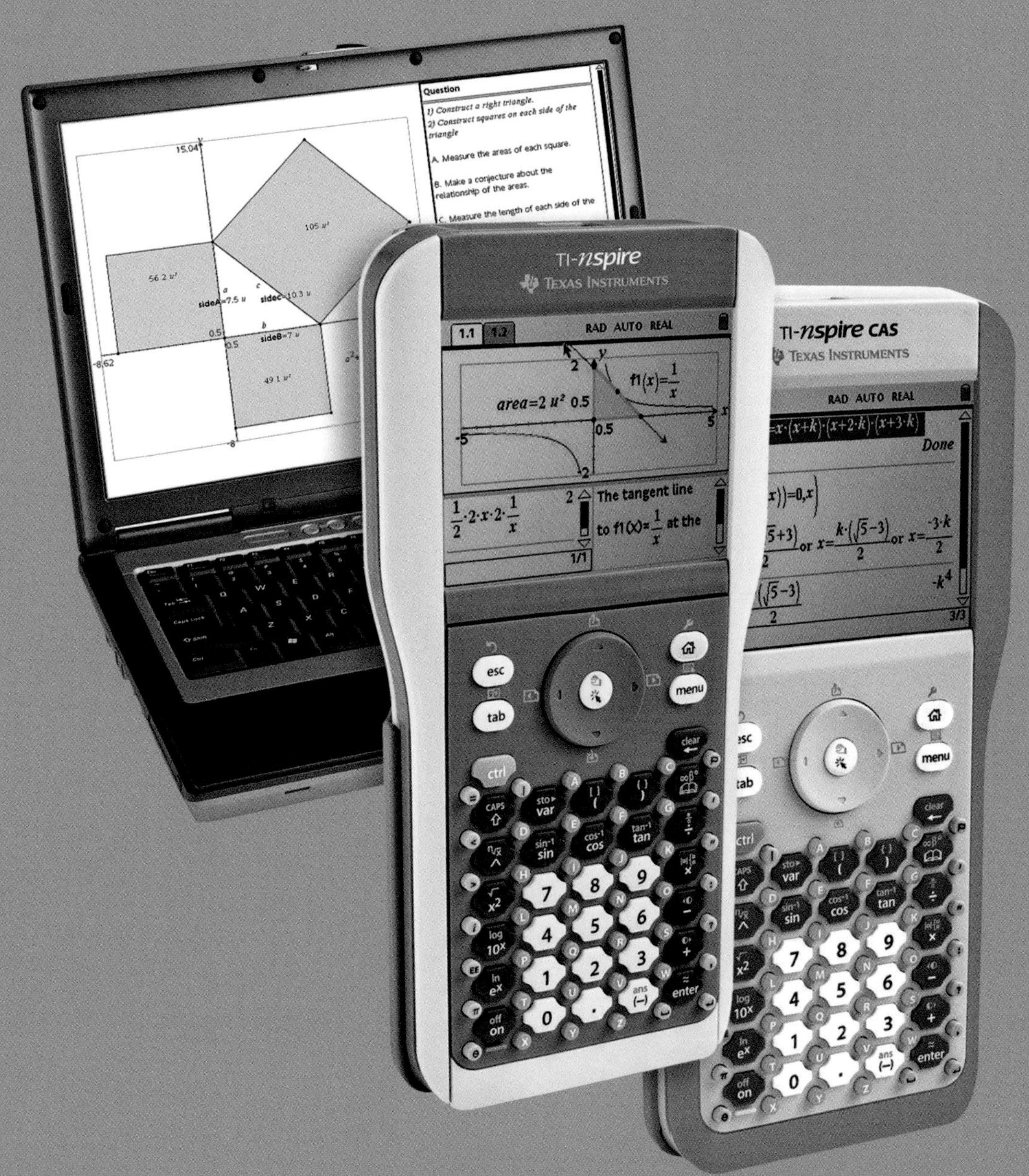
Question
1) Construct a right triangle.
2) Construct squares on each side of the triangle
A. Measure the areas of each square.
B. Make a conjecture about the relationship of the areas.
TI-nspire
TEXAS INSTRUMENTS
RAD AUTO REAL
The tangent line
TI-nspire CAS
TEXAS INSTRUMENTS
RAD AUTO REAL
Done

TGI Friday's Restaurants

T.G.I. Friday's Restaurants have become synonymous with end-of-the-work-day leisure time—enjoying a strawberry daiquiri, loaded potato skins, Jack Daniel's Grill and fun times with friends or family. The global restaurant chain includes both company-owned and franchised restaurants catering to working 21–49-year-olds in urban and suburban areas alike, and provides great tasting food and beverage in a fun, exciting, and friendly atmosphere.

In 1965, successful salesman Alan Stillman opened the first T.G.I. Friday's restaurant on Manhattan's Upper East Side. He designed the restaurant as a "pickup" joint—a fun, safe, vibrant place for single, professional men and women to meet and relax at the end of the day. The concept took off right away, and some credit it largely for the singles bar scene that transformed the American social landscape throughout the 1970s and 1980s. First-year revenues for the bar and eatery were more than $1 million.

By 1984, there were 105 T.G.I. Friday's restaurants, and the following year the chain went international, opening branches in Birmingham, England, and then London's Covent Garden district, with a restaurant that soon became the highest-dollar-volume store in the chain. By 1989, there were restaurants in Asia. By 1993, there were 243 Friday's restaurants in the United States and 20 more restaurants abroad. The company began to invest in national network media, including radio, billboards, local and national print, and coast-to-coast exposure through network television ads.

The T.G.I. Friday's brand has always been an innovator and a leader in the casual dining industry. The brand was the first to open an American casual dining restaurant in Moscow, Russia, in 1997. In 2003, T.G.I. Friday's restaurants was the first national casual dining restaurant chain to partner with Atkins Nutritional Approach to offer low-carb menu items, part of the chain's efforts to meet changing, modern needs. In 2005, it became the first American casual dining chain to reach the milestone 40th anniversary. In 2007 T.G.I. Friday's restaurants became the first American casual dining chain to offer guests a choice when it comes to dining out—smaller portions at a smaller price, all day, every day.

Innovators must continue to innovate. That's what the T.G.I. Friday's brand did in 2002 when it launched an entire brand revitalization. Company executives realized that the competitive landscape had dramatically changed, and the T.G.I. Friday's brand was losing its competitive edge. The decision was made to update the concept while still respecting the brand's heritage and value in order to appeal to younger guests and recapture the attention of lost customers. The revitalization was more than just paint and wallpaper. It was an entire rejuvenation of the brand that included redesigning restaurant exteriors and interiors, updating music format and uniforms, introducing a new menu layout and menu selections, enhancing the training program and modernizing technology. Friday's restaurants had a new, sleeker, more modern look—chrome fixtures, no kitsch—and customers, more enamored than ever of their frozen drinks and chicken wings, responded.

Today, with restaurants in 47 states and more than 56 countries, T.G.I. Friday's restaurants are equally popular with families and singles around the globe, winning awards and recognition for best place to work, best late-night restaurant, best happy hour, best burgers, best kids' menu, best appetizers, and more.

Vital Statistics

Classic Product Jack Daniel's Grill

Established 1965

Founder Alan Stillman

Employees 59,000 (U.S.); 86,000 (Worldwide)

Annual Systemwide Sales $2.7 billion

DESIGNATED
SMOKING AREA

Tiffany & Co.

Recognized the world over by its trademark Tiffany Blue Box, Tiffany & Co. leads the way when it comes to providing fine jewelry and other luxury goods. Its humble beginnings date back to 1837, when Charles Lewis Tiffany and John F. Young opened Tiffany & Young with $1,000 from Tiffany's father.

TIFFANY & CO.

The store, on Broadway in downtown Manhattan, sold stationery and a variety of goods. Unlike other stores at the time, Tiffany featured marked prices that were strictly adhered to, thus eliminating the customary haggling over pricing. Tiffany also insisted on cash payment rather than extending credit or accepting barter.

In 1845, the company began selling fine jewelry and published its first mail-order catalogue. In the late 1840s, it added silverware, timepieces, perfumes, and other luxury items, and with the acquisition of the operations of silversmith John Moore in 1851, Tiffany & Young added the design and manufacturing of silver to its business. Its standard for sterling silver was later adopted as the U.S. standard. Tiffany bought out his partners two years later and renamed the company Tiffany & Co.

Although popular with European royalty, Tiffany found its primary clientele in the rapidly growing sector of wealthy Americans, among them such prominent names as Astor and Morgan. In 1878, it acquired the Tiffany Diamond, one of the world's largest yellow diamonds, weighing 128.54 carats, and by 1887, the company had more than $40 million worth of precious stones in its vault.

Charles Lewis Tiffany was regarded as the "King of Diamonds," so it is no surprise that Tiffany & Co. introduced the engagement ring as we know it. The six-pronged "Tiffany Setting" lifts the diamond above the band and into the light, whereby each facet catches the light and reflects it, creating the magnificent sparkle of a truly exceptional diamond. Tiffany died in 1902, and his eldest living son, Louis Comfort Tiffany, joined the firm as artistic director. Louis designed jewelry and stained glass and remains, to this day, one of the most celebrated glass designers and a favorite among collectors.

In 1940, the company moved to its present landmark Fifth Avenue location. The flagship store is recognizable from its starring role in the 1961 movie adaptation of Truman Capote's novella ***Breakfast at Tiffany's,*** starring Audrey Hepburn. Acclaimed for its exceptional style and design in fine jewelry, Tiffany & Co. also puts its famous stamp on china and tableware, crystal, fragrances, personal accessories, sterling silver, watches and clocks, and writing instruments. Artistic collaborators over the years have included Elsa Peretti, Paloma Picasso, and Frank Gehry. With projected annual sales of $2.648 billion, Tiffany sells exclusively through more than 150 Tiffany & Co. stores and boutiques worldwide, its Web site, and its catalogues.

Opposite: The six-prong Tiffany Setting was introduced in 1886 and remains one of the world's most popular engagement ring styles. This innovative setting holds the diamond away from the band with six platinum prongs, permitting a more complete return of light through the diamond and maximizing its natural brilliance. This dazzling engagement ring, with sleek platinum Tiffany Band, is the ultimate symbol of love and Tiffany craftsmanship.

Photo credit: Stephen Lewis

Vital Statistics

Company Name	Tiffany & Co.
Established	1837
Founder	Charles Lewis Tiffany
Classic Product	solitaire diamond engagement ring
Annual Sales	$2.648 billion (projected for 2007)

Timberland

Although Timberland became famous by making hiking boots, millions of nonhiking men, women, and children around the world can be found sporting the company's footwear, apparel, and accessories. Today, Timberland has more than 220 stores in Asia, Canada, Europe, Latin America, the Middle East, and the United States and is still controlled by the Swartz family, who founded it more than 50 years ago.

In 1918, Nathan Swartz began work as an apprentice stitcher at a small shoe company in Boston. He learned the trade from the ground up, and in 1952 bought half an interest in the Abington Shoe Company. Three years later, he bought the remaining interest and invited his sons to join the company. Together, they made shoes for leading manufacturers for nearly 10 years. In the 1960s, the Swartz family originated its first truly waterproof leather boots by using revolutionary injection-molding technology that fused soles to uppers without stitching. Nathan retired in 1968, and his sons—after moving the company to New Hampshire—persuaded Goodyear to make a synthetic rubber sole that could be bonded to leather, leading to the creation of their signature product in 1973: the Timberland boot. At the advice of the Boston advertising firm Marvin & Leonard they placed ads in the *New Yorker* to appeal to upscale buyers, Consequently, Timberland boots took off at highbrow retailers such as Bergdorf Goodman, Lord & Taylor, and Saks Fifth Avenue. The company produced 5,000 pairs in 1974.

By 1975, production had jumped to 25,000 and sales neared the million-dollar mark. By the late 1970s, the company was producing 400,000 pairs of Timberland boots a year. In 1978, the newly christened Timberland Company introduced its first casual shoes for men. A distributor of Italian goods in 1979 ordered 3,000 pairs of boots to be sold in boutiques throughout Italy, where the boots reached cult status. Timberland opened its first store in 1986 and went public a year later. In 1989, sales topped $156 million, of which exports represented 30 percent. In 1991, Nathan's grandson, 31-year-old Jeffrey Swartz, was named Timberland's chief operating officer. Sales swelled to $637.6 million by the end of 1994, and Timberland products were sold in 50 countries, 12 retail stores, and more than 225 department store "concept" shops worldwide.

One indicator of Timberland's ubiquity in the marketplace came in the 1990s when the rapper known as the Notorious B.I.G. released a song in which he mentioned his "Tims." Suddenly Timberlands were the go-to boots for both a generation of urban, trendsetting teenagers and twentysomethings and a generation of outdoor enthusiasts. In 1998, Jeffrey Swartz became the company's CEO. Under Jeffrey's leadership, Timberland introduced the Mountain Athletics product line (since discontinued) Timberland PRO series, which was designed for tradespeople such as construction and factory workers.

Timberland continues to garner respect from the business world for its commitment to civic causes. The company is a major national founding sponsor of City Year, a national youth corps, and the originator of the Path of Service program, which gives employees 40 hours of paid time off for community service. Nathan Swartz would be proud of his grandson's ongoing focus on quality products and corporate consciousness.

Vital Statistics

Classic Product hiking boots

Founder Nathan Swartz

Employees 5,650

Annual Sales $1,568 million (2006)

Timex

Timex, the biggest watch company in the world, is a descendant of several 19th-century clockmakers in Connecticut's Naugatuck Valley. The first, the Waterbury Clock Company, was established in 1854 as a maker of inexpensive mantel clocks. In the 1880s, its sister company, the Waterbury Watch Company, and the Robert H. Ingersoll & Brothers firm opened and established themselves in the wristwatch market. Ingersoll, a brilliant marketer, sold 40 million units of the Yankee "dollar" watch. The watch industry consolidated after the stock market crash of 1929, and Waterbury launched the world-famous Mickey Mouse watch under the Ingersoll brand at the Chicago World's Fair.

In the 1950s, the Waterbury Watch Company, renamed U.S. Time Company, introduced a new best-selling watch called the Timex. The Timex was touted as a good-looking and nearly indestructible wristwatch created with the best of wartime technologies. Ads for the Timex featured the wristwatch strapped around Mickey Mantle's bat, a deep-sea diver's arm, an ice cube tray, a lobster's claw, and a turtle's back. U.S. Time invited customers to suggest new torture tests for the famous watch, which had sold more than 12 million units by the mid-1950s. The Timex slogan—"It takes a licking and keeps on ticking"—may be one of Madison Avenue's most well-known, and the brand became the best-selling watch in the world.

In the 1970s, after selling its 500 millionth Timex watch, U.S. Time renamed itself the Timex Corporation. Digital watches soon entered the market, and in 1986, Timex introduced the Ironman Triathalon watch. The Ironman, created by athletes and industrial designers, blew away its inexpensive competition from Asia. Like the original Timex, the Ironman was marketed as a rugged timepiece designed and engineered for serious athletic competition. The sleek metal and plastic watch quickly became the world's most popular sports watch.

In the decades that followed, Timex offered new varieties of the Ironman Triathalon. In 1992, it developed Indiglo dial illumination, a technology made famous by a survivor of the first World Trade Center bombing who used his Timex to guide his colleagues down a darkened stairwell. In 1994, Timex, in collaboration with Microsoft, outfitted watches with a Data Link personal organizer system. In 2000, Timex was the first to incorporate global positioning systems and heart rate monitors. A GPS-enabled Ironman watch was designed to tell users how far they go and how long it takes them to get to their destinations.

In 2006, Timex updated its slogan to "Keep On Ticking." The company continues to add new models to the Ironman Triathalon line, including, in 2006, the OVA (Optimal Viewing Angle) series, which allows wearers to see the display without twisting their arms and breaking their form. In addition, Timex launched its TX series, a collection of watches that combines old-world craftsmanship with hi-tech materials to create a new category of timepieces dubbed TechnoLuxury.

Vital Statistics
Classic Product Ironman Triathalon
Established 1854 (as Waterbury Clock Company)
Employees 5,500
Annual Sales $800 million (2003)
Annual Production 30 million watches per year

TIMEX
WED
15
14
13
PERPETUAL
CALENDAR
INDIGLO
WR 100M

Tinkertoy

The original creative children's toy, the Tinkertoy construction set, was the result of a friendship between two men who just weren't having any fun. Charles Pajeau and Robert Pettit met while commuting on the train from Evanston, Illinois, to Chicago. Pajeau, a stone mason, and Pettit, a trader at the Chicago Board of Trade, forged a friendship based on their mutual dislike of their chosen professions. They two men vowed to make a change and created a partnership.

Pajeau came up with the idea for the Tinkertoy construction set after observing children playing with empty spools of thread and pencils. He noticed that the children would spend hours at a time playing with simple household items using just creativity and ingenuity. He also noted the interest that children took in taking things apart and putting them back together, creating whatever came into their minds. With this basic premise in mind, Pajeau and Pettit set out to create a toy construction set made of spools and sticks.

Pajeau had the idea of drilling eight holes around the perimeter of the spools and one through the center. This piece would serve as the cornerstone and, when combined with sticks of varying lengths, form a construction system based on the Pythagorean principle of the progressive right angle. A triangle composed of sticks and spools could become the sides of an even bigger triangle, thereby enabling the construction of a three-dimensional object with endless possibilities.

They were sure it would be a hit and quickly began to manufacture and market the toy. They called their company The Toy Tinkers of Evanston, Illinois, and called their first product Tinkertoy because it inspired children to tinker to create objects. Introduced to the public in 1914, their toy garnered little interest, a result of a slow economy and too much product in the toy industry. To generate interest, the men set up Tinkertoy Ferris wheels around the Chicago area. Propelled by electric fans to keep the wheels in motion, their displays were a big success—creating demand that far exceeded the supply.

The following year, Pajeau went to New York to sell the product to major toy buyers. Having just come off a tough toy season in 1914, toy buyers in New York were hesitant to give Tinkertoy a chance. So Pajeau did what he knew would work. Just like in Chicago, he set up fan-powered construction displays, in Grand Central Station and at Broadway and 34th Street. They were a big hit with consumers and with toy buyers as well. Once again, he was taking more orders that he could accommodate, forcing the company to move to larger facilities to meet the demand.

Over the years, the Toy Tinkers of Evanston, Illinois, sold their Tinkertoy construction sets and grew their business by expanding the product line to include other toys such as dolls, rattles, table games, and pull toys. Although economy fluctuations and hardship occasionally threatened, they always managed to survive—all the while offering the Tinkertoy construction set that started it all.

Tinkertoys has been owned by Hasbro, one of the world's largest toy companies, since 1986.

Vital Statistics
Parent Company Hasbro, Inc.
Established 1914
Founders Charles Pajeau and Robert Pettit

Tommy Hilfiger

Tommy Hilfiger has achieved unique success: his clothes are coveted by trendsetting kids and suburban shoppers alike. Celebrities, from music stars to actors to athletes, all wear Tommy, and today his reach encompasses men's and women's sportswear, denim, athletic garb, children's clothes, swimwear, and accessories, all designed, made, and marketed by his company. Tommy Hilfiger bedding, fragrances, home furnishings, cosmetics, and belts are available to consumers thanks to licensing deals, and all Tommy products can be found at leading department stores and over 600 freestanding Tommy Hilfiger stores and outlets.

TOMMY HILFIGER

As a teenager in upstate New York, Tommy Hilfiger would drive into New York City to buy stylish clothes, then return home to sell them from the trunk of his car. As a high school senior, in 1969, he opened his own store—a harbinger of things to come. By the mid-1970s, Hilfiger had a chain of seven stores called The People's Place, for which he designed clothing himself. After a stint designing jeans for Jordache, he launched his first menswear collection in 1984, backed by mogul Mohan Murjani, a backer of Gloria Vanderbilt as well. By 1985, Hilfiger was being touted in ad campaigns as one of the "four great American designers for men," along with Ralph Lauren, Perry Ellis, and Calvin Klein. In 1989, with the help of new partners, Hilfiger created Tommy Hilfiger the company, which went public in 1992. Hilfiger launched the Tommy Hilfiger Corporate Foundation in 1995 to enrich the physical and intellectual well being of youth, with a major emphasis on education and cultural programs that impact a diverse population. Hilfiger became actively involved in a number of charities and causes, including the Washington D.C. Martin Luther King Jr. National Memorial Project Foundation and the Anti-Defamation League. He has also served on the board of directors for The Fresh Air Fund, a New York-based group that has been sending underprivileged children to summer camp since 1877, and the Race to Erase Multiple Sclerosis since 1994.

In 1994, Snoop Dog hosted *Saturday Night Live* and wore a rugby shirt with a Tommy Hilfiger logo for his monologue. Other celebrities and performers followed suit, including Beyonce, Sheryl Crow, Lenny Kravitz, Jessica Simpson, David Bowie, and the Rolling Stones, some dressing entirely in Tommy for public appearances. A year later, Tommy Hilfiger licensed the company Pepe Jeans USA to manufacture and distribute its women's wear and denim lines. Both quickly became successful, and the first Tommy Hilfiger store opened in 1997 in Beverly Hills, followed by another store in London. Hilfiger began producing men's and women's athletic and dress shoes, as well as women's hosiery and home furnishings. In 1998, Tommy Hilfiger was able to purchase Pepe Jeans, giving the Company control over the women's line as well as his Canadian licensee, Tommy Hilfiger Canada. Thus Tommy, his chairman, his director, and his CEO held almost 20 percent of the company stock. By 2001, Tommy Hilfiger had purchased its European licensee and the following year, launched a designer-priced line, attracting a slightly older and more sophisticated clientele. In the same year, Tommy Hilfiger was named chairman of the company that bears his name. The company was purchased by Apax Partners in 2006 for $1.6 billion. Since the sale of the company, the Tommy Hilfiger Group has capitalized on its premium positioning in the global marketplace.

Today, Tommy Hilfiger Group, which also owns the Karl Lagerfeld brand, is constantly improving and developing the product, and is considered a purveyor of quintessential American sportswear. Tommy has become an adjective in some circles, describing a certain youthful, vibrant, casual American look expressed by the designer's clothing.

Vital Statistics

Parent Company Apax Partners

Product Launch 1985

Employees 5,400

totes Isotoner

With all the gear you need for a rainy day, from automatic open-and-close umbrellas to rubber boots, totes has it covered—right down to the slippers to step into when you come in out of the rain. From the first pair of boots to the full ensemble, totes Isotoner continues to create stylish, high-quality, durable weather accessories for the whole family.

totes

The world's largest marketer of umbrellas, rubber rain boots, rainwear, gloves, and weather-related accessories started back in 1923 with a company called the SoLo Marx Company in a small suburb of Cincinnati, Ohio. In 1942, the plant was moved to Loveland, Ohio, where the first totes rubber rain boots were made. Called *totes* because of their portability, the totes rain boots became one of the company's most popular products.

With a new owner, Chicago businessman Brad Phillips, in 1961, the name was changed to totes, Incorporated, to reflect its popular brand. By 1969, Phillips held the first patent for a working folding umbrella, and in 1970, totes introduced the first folding umbrella in the United States. It was an instant hit. Throughout the 1970s, totes introduced many new products, including rainwear, rain scarves, hats, and slipper socks. The company continued to expand, and in 1985, it introduced Chromatics, a line of weather products aimed at supermarkets and drugstores.

In 1997, totes paired up with Isotoner, a company that created a sensation in the early 1970s with its nylon and leather "Isotoner" women's gloves. Combining *isometric* and *toning* to reflect the massaging properties and the stretch in the gloves, the gloves were a big success. That success led to additional products, including men's gloves and slippers. But totes Isotoner isn't just for foul weather—it is one of the largest retailers of sunglasses and sunglass accessories in the United States.

The totes Isotoner merger was a natural match, bringing together two of the most recognizable brands in the business to outfit the customer from head to fingers to toes.

Vital Statistics
Parent Company totes Isotoner Corporation
Established 1923
Annual Sales $51.7 million (2005)

Travelocity.com

The Roaming Gnome has seen it all, and the Web site that made him famous, Travelocity.com, is a powerhouse in the travel category. Travelocity was launched in 1996 by Sabre Interactive, at that time a division of AMR Corporation. Originally a development project for Sabre, Travelocity was built by a technology team of 30 people with the help of consultants, engineers, and other Sabre employees. Terrell Jones, the chief information officer of Sabre, was put in charge of the online booking system that would become Travelocity.com.

Initially, many people at Sabre saw Travelocity as a research and development project to test new technology, and did not expect to see it grow. Therefore, it was hard to persuade employees from other divisions to move to Travelocity. Those who did choose to leave their traditional travel careers were surprised to find just how big this new venture would become.

When Travelocity was being developed, the Internet was just starting to gain momentum, and Jones had a feeling that once people started using the online booking system, they would see its value and come back for more. By the time Travelocity was launched, the team had 10 years of online travel reservation experience with Sabre's first online reservation system, easySABRE. This early system enabled customers (travel agents) to book directly with American Airlines with the use of a modem. With that knowledge and the vision of a new way to conduct travel business, Travelocity was coming alive.

The construction of the original home page was a collaboration between the marketing and development teams at Travelocity and an advertising agency. The design plan for the launch was to have four large buttons that would direct the online customer: Air Reservations, Destination Information, Chats and Forums, and Merchandise Mall. A few weeks before the launch, sales and marketing personnel persuaded management to add some marketing text to each button and have banner advertising at the bottom of the page. Although advertising sales was a foreign concept to Sabre, it was permitted and eventually became a significant revenue driver.

In just a few years, a new business model that once offered only airline reservations has evolved into the place to go for anything travel-related, from flight information to hotel rooms to vacation packages and car rentals. From product innovation to customer feedback, all have played a major role in the success of this revolutionary online business.

Vital Statistics
Established 1996
Headquarters Southlake, Texas
Annual Sales $1.1 billion (2006)

Tropicana Orange Juice

If you drink orange juice, you are familiar with Tropicana, the company that has dominated the orange juice market for half a century. When Italian immigrant Anthony Rossi started a fruit packaging business in Florida in 1947, he had an idea that was to change American breakfasts forever. In 1954, with the help of a team of engineers, he perfected his flash pasteurization process for orange juice and began shipping chilled jars of fruit and fresh juice to hotels and restaurants east of the Mississippi in refrigerated trucks.

One of his first customers was the elegant Waldorf-Astoria hotel in New York, which soon had a standing order for 1,000 gallons of juice and jars of fruit each week. Once people got a taste of fresh-squeezed Floridian orange juice, Tropicana took off like wildfire. Rossi came up with increasingly savvy methods of transporting his juice as quickly as possible, including the S.S. *Tropicana,* a tanker ship, and the "Great White" Tropicana Train, both of which helped the company reach its iconic status. At peak capacity, the S.S. *Tropicana* carried 1.5 million gallons of orange juice from Florida to New York each week. The Tropicana Trains, made up entirely of refrigerated Tropicana railcars, are about a mile long and travel more than 35 million miles each year. Tropicana became the first company to sell bottled Florida orange juice overseas, when it received its first international order from France at a European food industry trade fair in 1965.

In 1969, Tropicana stock was first sold and the company earned a spot on the New York Stock Exchange, to Rossi's delight. Rossi called the development "a real milestone in our history." Tropicana began making its own boxes in 1972, which helped reduce dependency on suppliers. Over the course of the decade, Tropicana became one of the most respected companies in America, because of its efficient distribution, control over its own packaging, focus on quality, and steadily expanding market, into the Bahamas, Bermuda, and the West Indies, as well as Europe. *Forbes, Fortune,* and *Business Week* profiled Tropicana, and major corporations took serious interest in acquiring it. Rossi finally decided he was ready to retire and surrendered the presidency of his beloved company and tremendous success story in 1977. In 1978, Beatrice acquired Tropicana Products, Inc. from Rossi, providing the financial resources to develop new products, such as Tropicana Home-Style juice with pulp. In 1988, the Seagram Company Ltd. acquired Tropicana, which launched dozens of successful new beverages, including the Twister line, targeted at the youth market. Eight years later, Tropicana announced an agreement with the Tampa Bay Devil Rays to name its home stadium Tropicana Field. In 1998, Tropicana was acquired by PepsiCo, Inc., which owns it today, for $3.3 billion.

Tropicana is the leading marketer of orange juice in the United States. The company boasts a 44 percent share of the chilled juice market and as much as two-thirds of American not-from-concentrate sales. Its main brands include the flagship Tropicana Pure Premium (among the top five best-selling food brands in American supermarkets), Tropicana Twister, and Tropicana Smoothies.

Vital Statistics
Parent Company PepsiCo, Inc.
Classic Product Tropicana Pure Premium
Founder Anthony Rossi
Established 1947
Number of Employees 2,000

Tropicana
PURE PREMIUM
NO PULP
ORIGINAL
Tropicana
PURE PREMIUM
100%
PURE & NATURAL
ORANGE JUICE
PASTEURIZED
SMART CHOICES MADE EASY
NEVER FROM CONCENTRATE
64 FL OZ (2 QT) 1.89L

Tupperware

The Tupperware party is as American as apple pie, and it all started back in 1938, when Earl Tupper, an inventor with a high school education, left his job at DuPont to start his own company. He took with him an unwanted chunk of polyethylene, a by-product of the oil refining process. Tupper created his own refining process, and in 1942 created a clear, lightweight, unbreakable, odorless, nontoxic plastic that he called Poly-T.

Tupper continued to do contract work for DuPont during the war, making parts for gas masks and Navy signal lamps. He founded Tupperware in 1946 and began manufacturing food storage and serving containers with Poly-T. The following year, inspired by the lid on a paint can, Tupper created the Tupperware seal, which creates a virtually airtight partial vacuum. The Tupperware food storage container was born and was soon on the shelves of department and hardware stores.

Annual sales were hard to come by, because consumers were unfamiliar with the new material and didn't know how to work the seal. Sales eventually took off in the late 1940s when a few direct sellers of Stanley Home Products added Tupperware to their demonstrations. Salespeople explained the benefits of the plastic and demonstrated how to operate the seal. Additionally, Stanley did not sell their products door-to-door, but at home parties. This particular sales method was especially well suited to Tupperware because homemakers felt they were getting advice from other homemakers who actually used the products.

In 1951, Tupper created the subsidiary Tupperware Home Parties, Inc., and devoted his company to the home sales model. The home party system used a team of independent consultants who earned a flat percentage on the goods they sold and won incentives. By 1954, Tupperware had recruited 9,000 independent consultants—most of them women. Sales went through the roof, and, with no advertising, Tupperware was a household name by the late 1950s.

Tupperware parties enabled women by letting them schedule parties around responsibilities at home, and they were able to earn extra cash and get together with friends and neighbors at the same time.

Although Tupperware is well known for its plastic food storage containers, the company expanded into utensils and stovetop cookware, small appliances, baby products, and beauty items. Tupperware is one of the largest direct sellers in the world, represented in more than 100 countries with specially designed product lines to reflect the needs of the consumers. Since its inception, Tupperware has grown and evolved according to consumer needs, constantly reflecting the ever-changing global household.

Vital Statistics
Company Name Tupperware Brands Corporation
Classic Product Classic Sheer storage container
Established 1946
Founder Earl Tupper
Annual Sales $1,743 million (2006)

Tupperware®
Tupperware
Tupperware
Tupperware

UPS

Founded in 1907 as a messenger company by teenager Jim Casey with a mere $100, UPS has grown into a $47.5 billion corporation. Today, UPS is one of the most recognized and admired brands in the world, the world's largest package delivery company, and a leading provider of specialized transportation and logistics services in more than 200 countries and territories worldwide.

Jim Casey combined forces with competitor Evert McCabe in 1913 and started Merchants Parcel Delivery with an initial fleet consisting of one car and a few motorcycles. The company took off largely because of Casey's principles of customer courtesy, reliability, around-the-clock service, and low rates, which still guide UPS today.

In 1919, the company expanded into Los Angeles and became United Parcel Service. The color brown was chosen for the trucks for its stately appearance, in part because it was reminiscent of Pullman railroad cars. In the 1920s, UPS delivered for most of the major department stores in cities along the West coast. By 1930, the company had expanded to the East coast and moved its headquarters to New York City. By the mid-1940s, UPS was shipping more than 100 million packages a year to cities all over the country. The growth of the suburbs in the 1950s, however, proved to be a challenge. Americans were beginning to favor large new shopping centers and drove cars with big trunks for transporting their purchases. Jim Casey and his partners decided to redirect the company by acquiring "common carrier" rights to deliver packages between all customers, both private and commercial, putting UPS in direct competition with the U.S. Postal Service and in a position of requesting expanded operating authority from the Interstate Commerce Commission (ICC).

In 1953, UPS began common carrier operations in the few cities where it could do so without the authority of state commerce commissions and the ICC. It also began air operations with two-day service to major cities on the coasts. Until 1975, UPS fought to obtain authorization to ship freely among all 48 contiguous states, when they were finally granted authority. As a result, UPS became the first package delivery company to serve every address in the 48 states. By 1978, air service was available in every state, including Alaska and Hawaii. The demand for air parcel delivery increased in the 1980s and UPS launched an airline with its own jet cargo fleet.

By 1985, UPS Next Day Air service was available in all 48 contiguous states, Hawaii, and Puerto Rico. That same year, UPS added international air package and document services, linking the United States and six European countries. In 1991, the handheld Delivery Information Acquisition Device (DIAD)—today carried by every UPS driver—was deployed to immediately record and upload delivery information to the UPS network and allow drivers to stay in constant contact with their package centers. In 1992, UPS began electronically tracking all ground packages. By 1993, UPS was delivering 11.5 million packages and documents a day for more than one million regular customers. In 1994, UPS.com went live, and in 1995, UPS added functionality to its Web site that allowed customers to track packages while in transport. The resulting popularity of online package tracking exceeded all expectations. In 1999, UPS went public through what was then the largest IPO in U.S. history and its stock began trading on the New York Stock Exchange.

Since going public, UPS has acquired more than 30 other companies and now offers logistics, supply chain, heavy freight, and financial services in addition to retail services through The UPS Store. UPS is the world's largest package delivery company in terms of revenue and volume, delivering packages each business day for 1.8 million shipping customers to 6.1 million consignees. The company's delivery operations use a fleet of about 92,000 motor vehicles and more than 600 aircraft.

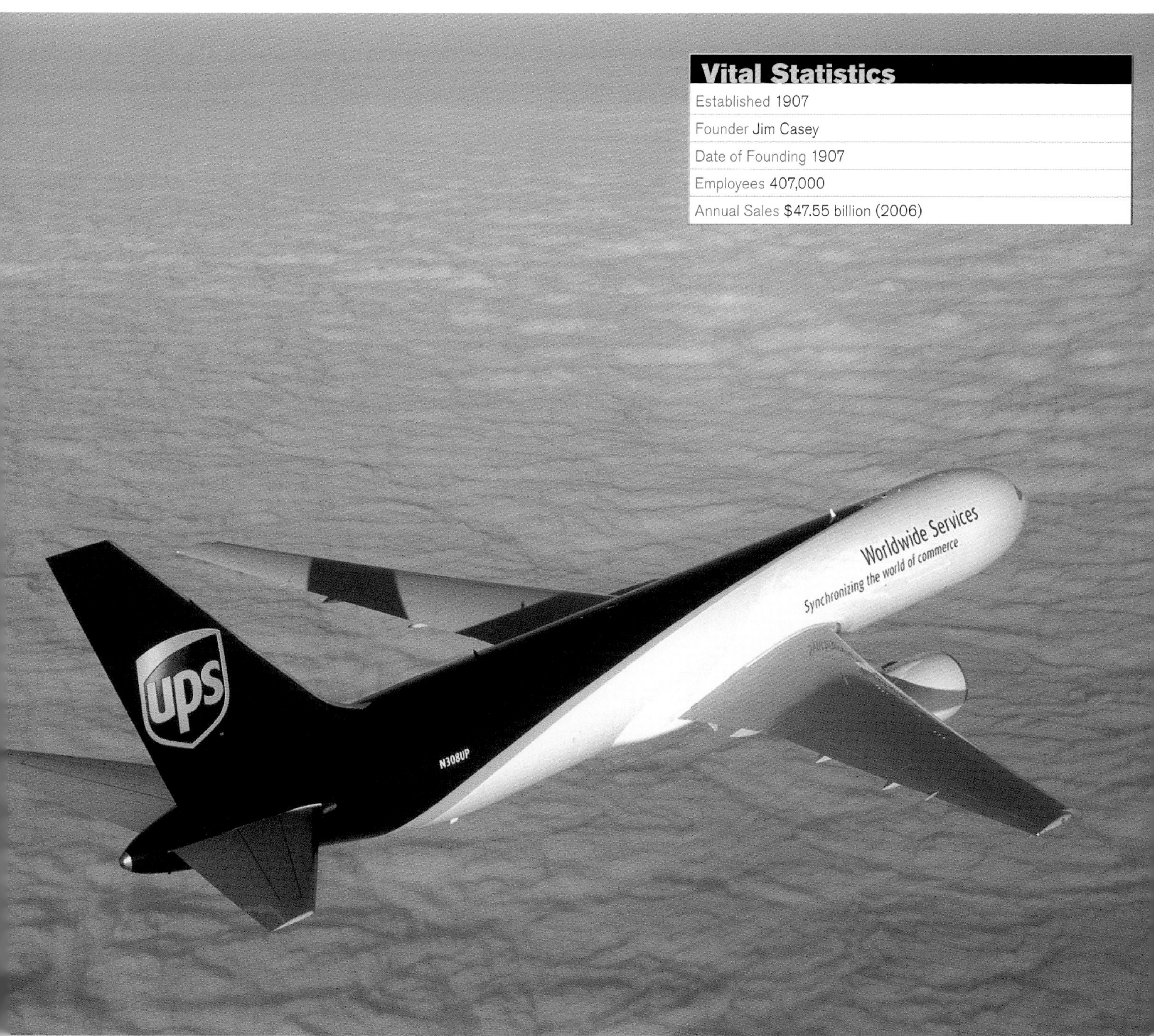

Vital Statistics

Vital Statistics
Established 1907
Founder Jim Casey
Date of Founding 1907
Employees 407,000
Annual Sales $47.55 billion (2006)

Vail Resorts, Inc.

Known as a pristine winter wonderland populated by celebrities and ski buffs alike, Vail Mountain is one of the most visited ski resorts in North America. What started as a dream back in 1957, when Peter Seibert and Earl Eaton first climbed what would become Vail Mountain, became a reality in December 1962 when Vail Mountain opened for skiing with two chairlifts, one gondola, and a lift ticket with a price tag of $5. Its inaugural season clocked 55,000 skiers.

Vail—its properties are not just for skiing. With three distinct businesses that include mountain, lodging, and real estate, Vail Resorts owns and manages five mountain resorts in the U.S.; owns or manages more than 4,100 hotel and condominium rooms; and operates six resort golf courses and a summer lodging resort in Grand Teton National Park.

With a focus on quality and impeccable guest service, Vail Resorts aims to find exciting ways to create the best vacation experience for its guests regardless of the season and offers a full range of activities year-round, including golf, tennis, fishing, rafting, horseback riding, hiking and mountain biking. And they must be doing a great job—summer resort revenues tripled between 2002 and 2005. Vail Resorts focuses on continually expanding and improving its existing resorts with new and diverse activities and unparalleled service to ensure its guests of a vacation worthy of world-class resorts.

Vail Resorts operates four mountain resorts in Colorado—Vail, Mountain, Beaver Creek, Breckenridge Mountain Resort and Keystone Resort—and Heavenly Mountain Resort in Lake Tahoe. Heavenly Mountain Resort is the leading winter resort at Lake Tahoe and in Northern California. Grand Teton Lodge Company in Wyoming operates three resorts in Grand Teton National Park.

Also part of the Vail Resorts portfolio is RockResorts, the famous luxury hotel brand. RockResorts owns or manages casually elegant resort properties throughout the Unites States, including ones in Vail, Colorado; Santa Fe, New Mexico; and Jackson Hole, Wyoming.

Vail has always been synonymous with sunshine and skiing and has been considered an ideal winter destination for as long as Vail Mountain has been providing a lift. Vail Resorts offers the perfect luxury resorts in a wide range of settings to satisfy the most discerning guest any time of the year.

Vital Statistics
Parent Company Vail Resorts, Inc.
Established 1962
Founders Pete Seibert and Earl Eaton
Annual Sales $839 million (2005)

Victoria's Secret

Victoria's Secret began as a small California-based company of six lingerie boutique stores and a quarterly catalogue. In 1982 the company was acquired by Limited Brands' founder Leslie H. Wexner, whose vision turned the Victoria's Secret brand into a household name. Over the past 25 years, under Wexner's leadership, Victoria's Secret has evolved into an internationally recognized brand and a $5 billion business.

VICTORIA'S SECRET

Victoria's Secret is the world's leading specialty retailer of lingerie and beauty products, with modern, fashion-inspired collections, prestige fragrances and cosmetics, celebrated supermodels, and world-famous runway shows. With more than 1,000 lingerie and beauty stores, a catalogue, and VictoriasSecret.com at their disposal, customers can shop the brand anywhere, anytime, from any place.

Victoria's Secret revolutionized the market by changing the customer mindset from "buying underwear" to shopping for lingerie for different wearing occasions, different moods, and different needs. It took center stage in the 1990s when it started employing supermodels for its catalogues and advertising campaigns, with names such as Tyra Banks, Heidi Klum, and Gisele Bundchen becoming linked with the lingerie and beauty products of Victoria's Secret. The brand made history in 1999 when a commercial during the Super Bowl for the first live webcast of the Victoria's Secret Fashion Show drove millions to VictoriasSecret.com. The show and webcast made fashion, advertising, and Internet history with an audience of a billion people in more than 100 countries.

Today, the Victoria's Secret brand—sexy, sophisticated, and forever young—keeps customers coming back for more by creating a unique customer experience. It has taken lingerie shopping out of the back corner of the department store and made lingerie cool and accessible. It continues to innovate and create new, successful categories. In 2002, Victoria's Secret launched Victoria's Secret PINK, a collection of loungewear and sleepwear designed for young women that in two years surpassed $700 million in sales.

Victoria's Secret is the largest subsidiary of Limited Brands (formerly The Limited, Inc).

Vital Statistics

Parent Company Limited Brands

Established 1979 by original founder Roy Raymond

Headquarters Columbus, Ohio

Sales $5 billion (2007)

Viking Range Corporation

Known for bringing commercial-style kitchen appliances into the home, Viking Range makes it a pleasure to go into the kitchen. From the first Viking range to the creation of an entire way of life, Viking's constant innovation and creativity in the design and manufacturing of all its products has made it one of the most desirable brands in the world.

Viking came into being as a result of a search that left Fred Carl with no other option. Carl, a fourth-generation builder, came up empty-handed when looking for a range for his own home. Carl and his wife, Margaret, were looking for a range with commercial looks as well as performance. But commercial ranges were impractical and unsafe for the home, so Carl decided to design one himself. After long hours at the sketchpad, he finally came up with a design that harnessed the power of a commercial range but was realistic for home use.

The first Viking ranges were shipped in 1987, and customer response was overwhelming for both Carl and his manufacturer. Viking quickly opened its own plant in Greenwood, Mississippi, and realized that there was opportunity to provide professional quality and design in every part of the kitchen. With this expansion came the focus on being innovative and creative through design and production while streamlining efficiency. The Viking way of business also became a way of life, and the way the company works is reflected in its products. Viking operates three manufacturing plants and a distribution center using state-of-the-art machinery and production techniques, employing more than 1,000 people locally and playing a key role in the community.

Viking manufactures high-end, professional-grade appliances, including ovens, refrigerators, freezers, outdoor grills as well as entire outdoor kitchens, dishwashers, disposals, wine cellars—you name it—not to mention the range that started it all. Viking products are sold through a network of domestic and international distributors who sell to high-end dealers and builders in the United States and around the world. More recently, Viking has branched out to provide its legendary quality and excellence to include small appliances, cutlery, and cookware. Its culinary products are available in upscale gourmet shops and through the Viking Culinary Arts Centers.

Viking is continually expanding and exploring ways to introduce new and innovative products to make the kitchen a wonderful place to be.

Vital Statistics
Established 1984
Founder Fred Carl
Annual Sales $111.1 million

VIKING
VIKING

W Hotels

W Hotels combine elegant, ultramodern style with state-of-the-art technology and incomparable service for the business traveler who wants the intimacy of a boutique hotel and the amenities and service of a major business hotel. By redefining the upscale hotel experience, W Hotels has become the most successful new hotel brand in the industry.

The concept began with the recognition that there were customers seeking a balance in their lives between substance and style that extended to their business travel destinations. With a focus on style, design, and service, W Hotels sought to create a haven for business travelers by providing an ultramodern living space that is refreshing and accessible with the comfort of exceptional amenities and service. Keeping that in mind, W Hotels created innovative, custom-designed spaces with original art, spa services, state-of-the-art fitness facilities with personal trainers, and anything else a customer could possibly want, all provided by an exceptional staff. Each room is an effortless blend of modern convenience, comfort, and design—fully equipped with the technology to provide a virtual office. Rooms are thoughtfully stocked with everything from custom-designed furniture to down comforters to Bliss bath products, to ensure all the creature comforts of being at home with the service and attention of a luxury hotel.

The first W Hotel was an instant hit when it opened its doors in 1998 on Lexington Avenue and 49th Street in New York. Its success quickly prompted the development of several more W Hotels in Sydney, Australia, Los Angeles, and Honolulu. All hotels feature signature restaurants and bar areas that attract hotel guests as well as hip locals. W Hotels successfully collaborated with renowned chef Drew Nieporent for the restaurant at the first W Hotel and subsequent others in New York and Seattle. Further partnerships with other famous chefs followed in several W Hotels, fostering the W Hotel approach of creating a gathering place with wonderful atmosphere akin to the grand hotels of the early 1900s.

The W Hotels chain, is part of Starwood Hotels & Resorts, one of the world's largest hotel and leisure companies with more than 845 properties in approximately 100 countries. Starwood's hotel empire includes luxury hotels such as Four Points, Sheraton, St. Regis, and Westin. Through its Luxury Collection, Starwood operates more than 50 high-end hotels and resorts. The W Hotels brand includes 21 hotels in the United States, Australia, Mexico, and Canada, with several more on the horizon.

Vital Statistics
Parent Company Starwood Hotels & Resorts Worldwide
Established 1991
Founder Barry Sternlicht

Walgreen Co.

Walgreens epitomizes American style: quality over quantity and steady growth over aggressive acquisition. It is the number-one drugstore in the nation in sales, with nearly 5,300 stores in every mainland state (by 2007) and Puerto Rico. Prescription drugs account for nearly 64 percent of sales; the rest comes from over-the-counter medications, cosmetics, and groceries. More than two-thirds of Walgreens stores offer drive-through pharmacies, and almost all offer one-hour photo processing.

In 1901, pharmacist Charles R. Walgreen borrowed $2,000 from his father and bought the Chicago drugstore where he had been employed. Eight years later, he bought a second drugstore; by 1915, there were five Walgreens drugstores in Chicago. Walgreen made many innovations to the drugstore concept, most notably the addition of soda fountains and, in particular, the malted milk shake. On one hot summer day in 1922, soda fountain clerk Pop Coulson added a generous scoop of vanilla ice cream to a malted, creating the immortal favorite. The creation was soon adopted by fountain managers in every Walgreens store.

Wanting quality control, Walgreen also began making his own line of drug products, which he could offer at lower prices than his competitors. By 1920, there were 20 Walgreens stores in Chicago, promoted with another Walgreens first: a company-owned-and-operated airplane. In 1927, the firm was listed on the New York Stock Exchange, and two years later—on the verge of the Great Depression—Walgreens' 397 stores in 87 cities had sales of almost $50 million. Although average sales per store dropped between the generally difficult years of 1931 and 1935, individual store earnings went up, thanks to a concerted emphasis on efficiency. Walgreens opened its first self-service store in 1952, and then 22 more in the following year. Over the next decade, Walgreens replaced its smaller, older stores with modern self-service branches, and sales grew by more than 90 percent. By 1960, Walgreens had 451 stores, half of which were self-service. Sadly, by the 1960s, the age of teenagers sipping milk shakes through a straw was drawing to a close, and the company began phasing out its unprofitable soda fountains. Walgreens continued to modernize and expand carefully through the 1980s, opening its 1,000th store in 1984. Developments in the 1990s included the incredibly efficient Healthcare Plus subsidiary to provide prescriptions by mail, the Pharmacy Direct Network to manage prescription drug programs for group health plans, the opening of a 2,000th store, and entrance into new markets, including Las Vegas and Dallas. In 1998, the founder's grandson Charles Walgreen III, stepped down as CEO, ending an era.

Walgreens pioneered many modern store and pharmacy features; many have become standards in the industry, including computerized pharmacies connected nationwide, point-of-sale scanning, and freestanding stores with drive-through pharmacies. It is certain that Charles Walgreen would be proud of the drugstore chain he created, which retains its focus on old-fashioned quality while keeping one foot firmly in the future.

Vital Statistics
Classic Product retail prescriptions
Established 1901
Founder Charles R. Walgreen
Employees 179,000
Annual Sales $47,409 million (2006)

PHARMACY
Walgreens
HOUR PHOTO
24
HOURS

Weber

Weber-Stephen Products Co., based in Palatine, Illinois, is the country's number-one manufacturer of charcoal and gas grills, shaping the way America cooks outdoors. In 1952, founder George Stephen designed the original and still best-selling Weber kettle, with a lid that made grilling possible regardless of weather conditions. The company, which began as Weber Brothers Metal Works, has been family owned for more than a century. Weber also has the strongest consumer outreach program in the industry with its all-year, round-the-clock call-in line and Web site with grilling tips, techniques, and recipes.

George Stephen was a steak lover who grew frustrated with his hard-to-control home grill in Mount Prospect, Illinois. He decided he needed a model that would keep wind and rain from interfering with the grilling process while sealing in desirable smoky flavor. Stephen was part owner of Weber Brothers Metal Works, a Chicago custom-order sheet metal shop that produced, among other products, half spheres that were welded together to make buoys for Lake Michigan. At work, he cut a metal buoy in half and made a dome-shaped grill with a rounded lid—creating the original Weber kettle grill, which quickly gained a loyal following. George's Barbecue Kettle, as the refined product was first called, was priced around $50 at a time when braziers cost just $7, yet it sold so well that by 1958, Stephen had bought out Weber Brothers and dropped all other metalworking projects in favor of building nothing but his outdoor grill. In the 1960s and 1970s, Weber became a nationally known brand with distribution in retail stores throughout the country.

In 1985, to meet growing demand for gas grills, Weber introduced a revolutionary line called Genesis that offered consumers precise heat control without flare-ups, transforming the market. In 1989, the company opened the first Weber Grill Restaurant, in Wheeling, Illinois. Weber restaurants specialize in 22-ounce steaks, classic American barbecue, and award-winning hamburgers, all cooked over Weber kettle grills. In March 2004, Weber-Stephen Products Co. acquired some assets of the Ducane company and began redesigning and distributing Ducane grills in the United States and Canada. Almost 20 percent of Weber's current business is grill accessories, which number in the hundreds and include an extra-wide spatula designed to help turn fish, racks for holding ribs, potatoes, or corn on the cob, and a canister that can substitute for a beer can in the increasingly popular grill specialty Beer Can Chicken.

Weber's full line of gas and charcoal grills are assembled and packaged in Palatine and Huntley, Illinois, and are sold in home centers, hardware stores, department stores, patio stores, and other retail outlets in the United States, Canada, and 39 other countries worldwide. Internationally, Weber products are distributed through two channels—Weber Stephen-Products Co. subsidiaries or importers. Stephen was always proud of the fact that Weber was a family business, and today 10 of his 12 children—and two of his grandchildren—have important roles within the company.

Vital Statistics

Company name Weber-Stephen Products Co.

Classic Product kettle grill

Established 1893

Founder/Inventor George Stephen

Employees 1,050 (2005)

Annual Sales $167 million (2005)

WebMD

WebMD is one of the most recognized and trusted providers of health information services, allowing consumers, employees, physicians, and health plan members to make informed healthcare decisions. Do people want to get medical information online? The proof is in the pudding: In the fourth quarter of 2006, over 35 million users visited the WebMD Health Network every month.

WebMD provides a number of significant services to its users in the areas of communication, decision-making, and health care information. The company aims to give consumers the ability to take control of their own health by ensuring that accurate, current information is readily available. The immediacy of the information has changed the way people manage their health. WebMD offers preventive information as well, with the goal of helping users prevent illness in the future. It gives physicians and other medical professionals the ability to obtain clinical reference materials instantly, keep up to date in terms of their information and current treatment options, interact with peers in the field, and earn education credits. And finally, WebMD helps employers and health plans to easily give their employees and plan members access to online health and benefits tools that enable them to make informed, smart choices. The content of WebMD Health is focused on articles about health and wellness from a variety of media sources, as well as decision-support services geared toward those needing to make important decisions about risks, providers, and options for treatment. Whether a consumer is suffering from a particular disease or condition and wishes to find detailed facts, or wants to analyze symptoms, store personalized information for later reference, find a doctor or specialist, or sign up for interactive online courses or communities, WebMD Health is the place to go. Another public portal owned by the company is Medscape.

Medscape and WebMD's network of professional medical sites are geared toward doctors and other health care professionals. Medscape allows them to stay current in their practice with the help of daily news bulletins, conference coverage, commentary by experts, columns, and even continuing medical education. Medscape also publishes an online journal called Medscape General Medicine, the original open access peer-reviewed general medical journal. WebMD also provides the industry's leading physician e-detailing services through its Medsite unit.

WebMD provides private online health and benefit management portals for both employers and health plans, in order to enable their employees and plan members to make informed benefit, treatment and provider decisions. They integrate the information provided by individuals with medical, pharmacy, and other claims data to give them the most comprehensive health profile possible.

WebMD Publishing Services provides content in a traditional paper format. Offline publications include *The Little Blue Book*, a directory of physicians, and *WebMD* the magazine, which can be found in most doctors' waiting rooms.

WebMD is majority-owned (84.5%) by Emdeon, which provides business, technology, and information solutions that transform both the financial and clinical aspects of healthcare delivery. WebMD became a separately traded company in September 2005 (Nasdaq: WBMD) and incorporated that same year as WebMD Health Corp. Its headquarters are in New York City, where it plans to continue giving the most people possible the very best information it can provide.

Vital Statistics

Parent Company	Emdeon
Product Launch	1997
Employees	720
Annual Sales	$253.9 million (2006)

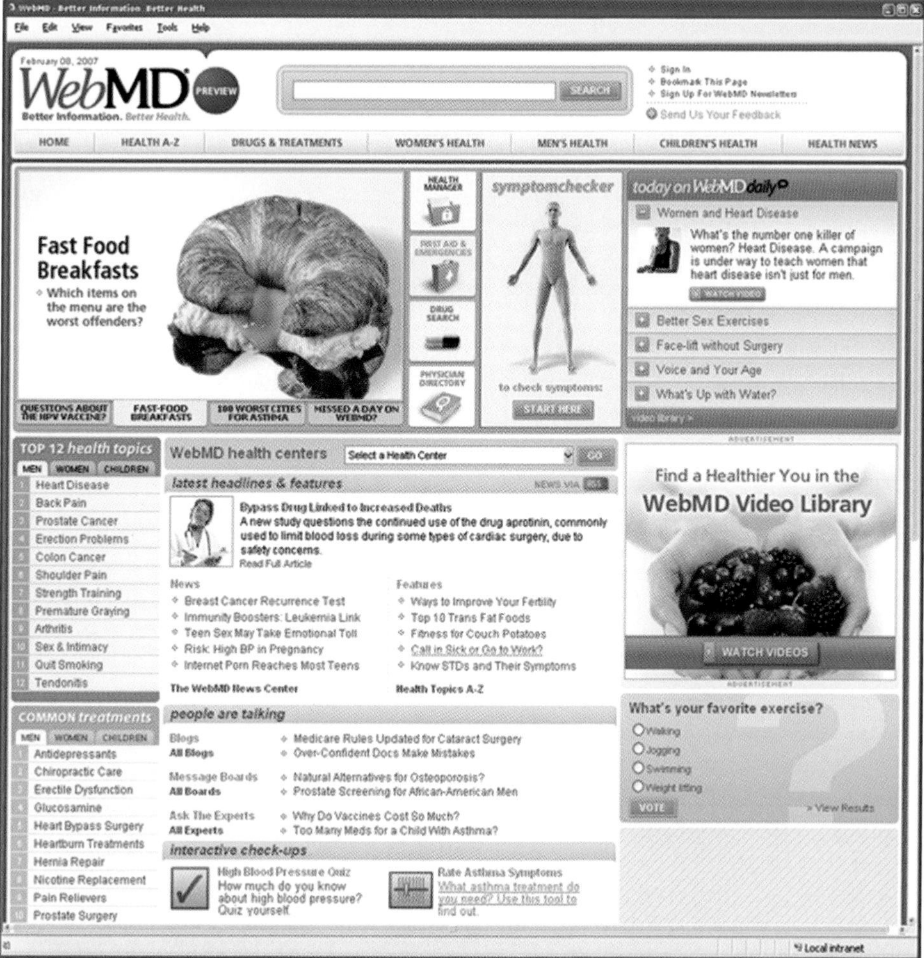

Wham-O Inc.

With products ranging from classic American toys to off-the-wall novelty items, Wham-O started back in 1948 when two college buddies, Richard Knerr and Arthur "Spud" Melin, were looking for a simple product to start a small company. The same year, they introduced the company's flagship product, a slingshot, and that was the start of the wild and wacky path of Wham-O. The company takes its name from the sound made from the missile of a slingshot hitting its mark. The partners were always experimenting, looking for potential new items to try out and launch.

The story of the Frisbee, one of Wham-O's most popular products, starts in 1955 when a building inspector named Fred Morrison refined a plastic flying disc that he sold to Wham-O. Introduced to consumers in 1957 as the Pluto Platter—a nod to America's obsession with UFOs at the time—it was modified and renamed the Frisbee disc in 1958, and has since become an American icon.

Knerr and Melin were always open to new and strange ideas, experimenting with the toys themselves and trying them out on potential customers. They had heard of Australian children using a bamboo ring for exercise and immediately produced the Hula-Hoop. In 1958, they promoted it on Southern California playgrounds, doing demonstrations and giving the hoops to children to get them to learn and play. This dedication and commitment paid off: the Hula-Hoop turned into the greatest fad ever, with 25 million sold in four months.

In 1966, chemist Norman Stingley accidentally created a plastic product that bounced uncontrollably. He offered it to Melin and Knerr, and it became the famous Super Ball. The popular item was followed by Super Gold Ball, Super Baseball, and Super Dice, and although competitors tried to capitalize on the Super Ball craze, only the original would do. The 1960s saw the sale of more than 20 million Super Ball products.

Wham-O has always been innovative and daring, creating a toy for every occasion. The Slip 'n Slide waterslide, introduced in 1961, has long been a warm-weather favorite for children all over the world. In 1962, when the limbo was all the rage, Wham-O sold a limbo party kit, complete with a record and instructions on how to do the dance. Other world-renowned Wham-O toys include Silly String (1972) and the Hacky Sack footbag, which spurred a "foot fad" and an internationally recognized sport.

Known for its simple, ageless creations, Wham-O has always been committed to providing high-quality, imaginative recreational products that are fun and affordable, which has made it one of the world's leading toy makers. With more than 70 popular items, Wham-O's toys have been keeping kids and adults around the world happy for more than 50 years.

Vital Statistics
Classic Product Frisbee
Established 1948
Founders Rich Knerr and Arthur "Spud" Melin

INFINITY
ORIGINAL
FRISBEE®DISC

Whirlpool Corporation

Whirlpool Corporation began as the Upton Machine Company, founded in 1911 by Louis, Frederick, and Emory Upton. to manufacture electric, motor-driven wringer washers. Their first order, for 100 washing machines, came from Federal Electric. When a gear in the transmission failed—in every single machine—Lou Upton replaced the defective parts with a new gear at no expense to the customer. Because of Upton's business ethics, Federal Electric doubled its original order to 200 washing machines.

A few years later, Sears, Roebuck and Co. began marketing two Upton-manufactured washers under the name Allen. Their relationship worked out so well that Sears was selling the washers faster than the Upton Machine Co. could manufacture them.

After World War I, sales through the Sears catalogue grew rapidly. To avoid dependence upon Sears, Upton launched a washer under its own brand name in the early 1920s. Subsequently, Sears' expansion into retailing, and Upton's selection as the sole supplier of washing machines to Sears forced the company to find a way to increase production and distribution efficiency. To accommodate this need, the Upton Machine Co. merged with the Nineteen Hundred Washer Company in 1929.

During World War II, the company converted its facilities to wartime production, manufacturing a piece of the P-40 Kittyhawk fighter wing. The company also produced airplane propellers, mortars, and a specialized tank steering device. In the 1940s, the company also developed an automatic, spinner-type washer. The Nineteen Hundred Corporation launched a complete line of Whirlpool home laundry appliances, including wringer and automatic clothes washers, electric and automatic dryers, and irons. The company became the world's first to introduce the top-loading automatic washer, which is still a classic today. In 1950, the company changed its name to Whirlpool Corporation.

The prosperity and increased consumerism of the 1950s propelled sales, but Whirlpool recognized the need to expand their product line beyond laundry equipment. The increased consumerism also created pressure on appliance manufacturers to provide better quality and service. In 1955, the company added refrigerators, followed quickly by air conditioners and cooking range products. In 1958, Whirlpool acquired an equity stake in the Brazilian appliance market, which would prove beneficial for later expansion into rapidly growing markets outside the United States.

Driven by customer loyalty, product innovation, and corporate responsibility, Whirlpool continues to successfully design, develop, and manufacture new products. In 2001, the Duet Laundry Family was introduced—a merger of design, performance, and efficiency—becoming the best-selling front-loading washer and dryer in the country. With nearly 70 manufacturing and technology research centers around the world, Whirlpool is the world's leading manufacturer and marketer of home appliances.

Vital Statistics
Company Name Whirlpool Corporation
Classic Product Duet Front Loading Washer & Dryer
Established 1911
Founders Louis, Frederick, and Emory Upton
Annual Sales $18 billion

Whole Foods Market

Whole Foods Market has changed the way Americans shop in a time when people care more than ever about the origins and quality of the food they eat. Whole Foods Market stores sell foods that are free of artificial flavors, colors, preservatives, sweeteners, and hydrogenated fats; the body care products are never tested on animals. The company operates almost 200 stores and counting in 30 states, the nation's capital, Canada, and the United Kingdom. Whole Foods Market has four lines of private-label products, including the extremely popular Whole Kids line, featuring organic products for kids. Whole Foods Market is the world's most successful natural foods store.

Whole Foods Market has its origins in Austin, Texas, where in 1978, a man named John Mackey partnered with, friend Renee Lawson Hardy, borrowed $10,000 from his dad and opened a store called Safer Way Natural Foods. Two years later, Safer Way merged with another local Austin market called Clarksville Natural Grocery and called the new store Whole Foods. The first Whole Foods was 11,000 square feet and took off immediately with health-conscious Austin residents. Mackey began to expand, opening additional stores in Texas: another in Austin in 1982, Houston in 1984, and Dallas in 1986. In the late 1980s Whole Foods Market moved into Louisiana and California. In 1992, Whole Foods Market introduced its first private-label products with the Whole Foods line. The company needed funds to continue expansion and went public that same year, raising $23 million. Whole Foods Market began eyeing health food stores all over the country with acquisitiveness. It purchased New England's beloved Bread & Circus chain in 1992, California's Mrs. Gooch's Natural Foods Market in 1993, and East Coast and Chicago chain Fresh Fields in 1996. A year later, the company could boast more than $1 billion in sales with almost 70 stores nationwide. In 2002, Whole Foods opened its first Canadian branch in downtown Toronto, a year before Mackey—whose company had grown exponentially in 22 years—was named Entrepreneur of the Year by Ernst & Young. In 2004, Whole Foods opened its largest store ever: a 59,000-square-foot showcase in the new Time Warner Center in New York City. The store attracts shoppers, tourists, and gawkers alike, as well as those drawn in by the 248-seat café, gourmet cheese section, and full-scale bakery, sushi bar, juice bar, and in-house florist. Most recently, Whole Foods Market has gone international, acquiring the British organic chain Fresh & Wild in 2005.

Whole Foods Market has virtually created a new world in retail, a world devoted to sustainable seafood, organic agriculture, and local and international products that meet stringent quality standards, minimally processed foods, and foods free from artificial additives, colorings, sweeteners, and preservatives. The company believes it has an obligation to help the planet and does more to support organic farming than almost any other institution worldwide. Locally, Whole Foods Market gives back to the communities in which it makes its homes, as well as to the employees who keep it running so smoothly. More than 5 percent of net profits each year are donated to nonprofit organizations.

Vital Statistics
Established 1980
Employees 42,000
Annual Sales $5.6 billion (2006)

SEAFOOD
Cod Fillets
Wild Halibut
IN SEASON
King Salmon Fillets
Grape Tomatoes
$2.99
Baby Roma Tomatoes
$2.99
Honey Tangerines
$1.99
Pummelo Grapefruit
$2.99

Williams-Sonoma, Inc.

Williams-Sonoma, Inc., is a nationwide specialty retailer of high-quality products for the home. These products, representing six distinct merchandise strategies—Williams-Sonoma, Pottery Barn, Pottery Barn Kids, PBteen, West Elm, and Williams-Sonoma Home—are marketed through 582 stores, seven mail-order catalogues, and six e-commerce Web sites.

WILLIAMS-SONOMA

Williams-Sonoma, Inc., is a shopping destination for home cooks and decorators, offering the highest-quality merchandise that is beautifully arranged in the stores. Through its catalogs, e-commerce Web sites, and retail stores, Williams-Sonoma has become virtually synonymous with kitchenware and home furnishings. The company's six distinct merchandise strategies are marketed through 582 stores in the United States and Canada. In addition, Williams-Sonoma distributes seven catalogs, including the most recent addition, Williams-Sonoma Home, and operates six e-commerce Web sites and an online bridal registry.

The first store had humble beginnings. After Chuck Williams served in the Air Force during World War II, he moved to the small town of Sonoma, California. There, he worked as a contractor building homes until a trip to France in the early 1950s changed his life. A passionate cook, Williams discovered a remarkable array of cookware in Paris that he had never seen in the United States, including omelette pans and soufflé molds.

In 1956, Williams bought a building in Sonoma, where he opened a store and stocked the shelves with the professional-quality cooking equipment he had discovered abroad. Two years later, he moved his store to San Francisco. The store's popularity grew in the 1960s, part of the culinary renaissance that was changing the way Americans thought about and cooked food. Professional chefs such as Julia Child and James Beard were extremely influential with home cooks, who were developing an interest in international cuisine and rediscovering the kitchen as the center of the home. In 1972, Williams-Sonoma introduced its first mail-order catalog.

In 1978, Williams sold the company to Howard Lester, who currently holds the position of Chairman and CEO. Lester was excited to build on Williams' concept and took Williams-Sonoma, Inc., public in 1983. In 1986, the company acquired Pottery Barn, which quickly evolved into the leading home furnishings retailer in the country. Today, there are more than 190 stores, a direct-mail business, and successful e-commerce site. The success of the brand led to the launch of Pottery Barn Kids in 1999, Pottery Barn Bed + Bath in 2000, and PBteen in 2003.

One of the latest brands to emerge is West Elm, which made its appearance as a catalogue in 2002, followed by a Web site and the first store the next year. Fresh and modern, the West Elm brand draws in design-savvy customers with stylish, high-quality furniture and accessories for every room in the home. With an extensive range of prices, the brand has earned a reputation for affordable style. Expanding on the style and quality represented by the Williams-Sonoma portfolio of brands, Williams-Sonoma Home came on the scene in 2004 with its home furnishings of casual elegance and exceptional craftsmanship.

For more than 50 years, Williams-Sonoma has been shaping how people think about and cook food. Today, the company has expanded its leadership to include every room of the home: from the kitchen to the living room, bedroom, bathroom, and even the home office. Despite its growth, Williams-Sonoma, Inc., has continued to focus on the core values that have distinguished the company since its start: quality, design, and customer service.

Vital Statistics
Classic Product housewares
Established 1956
Founder Chuck Williams
Employees 37,200 (2006)
Annual Sales $3,538.9 million

Wilson Sporting Goods Co.

Even before the lively "Wilson" costarred with Tom Hanks in *Cast Away* and won the Broadcast Film Critics Association award for "Best Inanimate Object", Wilson Sporting Goods Co. had been a symbol of excellence and quality in the world of sports for more than 90 years. The Chicago-based manufacturer of sporting goods started in 1914, as Ashland Manufacturing, a subsidiary of the Wilson & Co. meat company. It was renamed the Thomas E. Wilson Company until the name was changed to the current Wilson Sporting Goods Co. in 1931. By the mid-1930s, the Chicago plant employed about 800 people to accommodate the company's growth, and by the middle of the century, Wilson had become the leading manufacturer of sporting goods in the United States. Wilson headquarters moved from Chicago to the suburb of River Grove in 1957.

Wilson.

Long established in the tennis world, Wilson has helped develop the most dedicated and talented players in the world, winning more than 400 total Grand Slam Titles. Wilson has the distinguished honor of making the official ball of the U.S. Open for 29 years. According to *Sports Marketing Survey*, Wilson is the number-one racquet brand.

In the world of golf, Wilson introduced the sand wedge in 1933. The R-90, as it was called, was designed by Gene Sarazen and created after a plane ride inspired him to create a clubhead that would glide smoothly through sand. Wilson sold 50,000 of them that year, thereby creating the most popular sand wedge in golf. Sarazen was the first golfer to become a member of the Wilson Advisory Board in 1922, and maintained a 75-year relationship with Wilson, the longest-running sports contract in history.

Although Wilson has always been a mainstay in the tennis arena, it covers the sports world by providing equipment and apparel for golf, racquet sports (badminton, racquetball, squash, and tennis), and team sports (baseball, basketball, football, softball, soccer, and volleyball). Wilson Sporting Goods Co. has been a top leader, with accolades and endorsements across the various sports that it equips.

Wilson Sporting Goods Co. has been owned by Finland-based Amer Sports since 1989.

Vital Statistics
Classic Products: tennis balls; tennis racquets
Established 1914
Founder Thomas E. Wilson

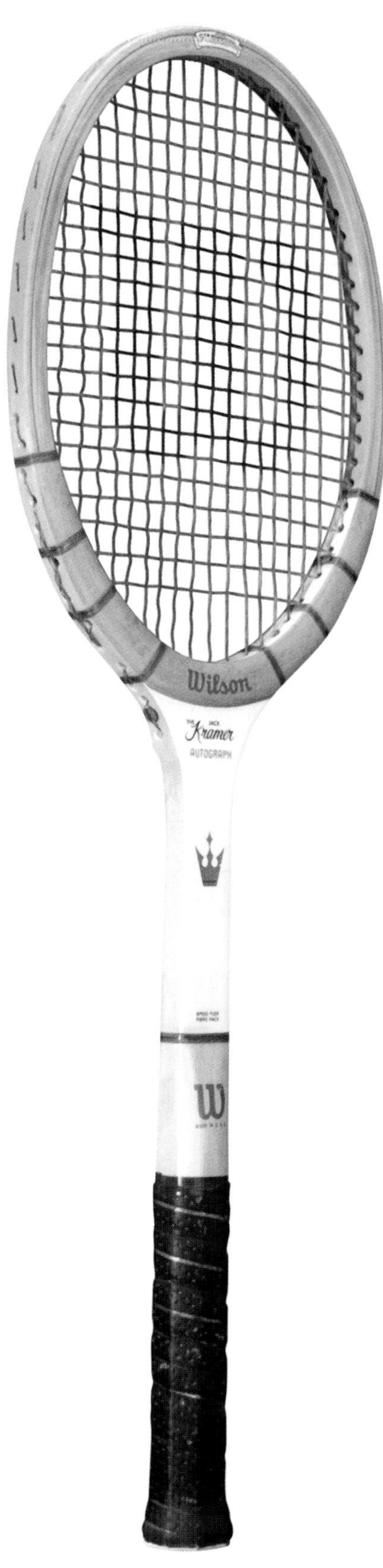
Wilson
THE JACK
Kramer
AUTOGRAPH

Wonder Bread

The year was 1921, and Taggart Baking Company of Indianapolis was gearing up to introduce a new one-and-a-half pound loaf of bread. But first the new product needed a name and identity. Vice President Elmer Cline was charged with merchandising development for the new bread loaf. While taking in the International Balloon Race at the Indianapolis Speedway, Cline was captivated by the scene of hundreds of balloons floating through the Midwestern sky. To Elmer, the image signified a sense of "wonder," and Wonder bread was born. Since that time, the colorful red, blue, and yellow balloons have been the cornerstone of Wonder bread's logo and package.

In 1925, Continental Baking Company bought Taggart Baking Company, and Wonder bread became a national brand. Then in 1930, Wonder bread became the first major brand to distribute what may be the greatest innovation in the baking world: *sliced* bread. "Wonder-Cut" bread became a hit, boosted in part by the publicity it received as sponsor of the Chicago World's Fair in 1933 and the New York World's Fair in 1939.

In the 1940s, Wonder bread became an important part of a government sponsored program to enrich bread with vitamins and minerals as a way of combating certain diseases. Known as the "quiet miracle," the enrichment program nearly eliminated the diseases beriberi and pellagra. Around this time, Wonder bread also launched its signature "build strong bodies" ad campaign and introduced a revolutionary new way of baking that eliminated holes in bread, and Wonder bread became the best-selling bread in the country.

In 1995, Interstate Bakeries Corporation of Kansas City, Missouri, acquired Continental Baking Company and became one of the largest producers of wholesale bread and cake in the United States. Wonder bread continues to evolve to address the needs of consumers looking for added nutrition, including the addition of more whole grain options in recent years.

Vital Statistics
Established 1921 (by Taggart Baking Company)
Parent Company Interstate Brands Corporation
Distribution United States
Headquarters St. Louis, Missouri

wonder
CLASSIC
Excellent Source of Calcium!
NET WT. 20 OZ. (1LB. 4 OZ.) 567g CALCIUM FORTIFIED ENRICHED BREAD
Excellent Source of Calcium!
wonder
CLASSIC
wonder

Woolite

When it comes to washing precious items of clothing, nothing comes close to Woolite, the standard-bearer for generations of home launderers. Woolite Original Fabric Wash is the product Americans have come to love, although today—owned by behemoth Reckitt Benckiser, Inc.—Woolite manufactures a wide range of fabric washers that won't cause changes in shape or fading and even protect from color-bleeding effects. These products leave out harsh ingredients that can damage clothes, to keep them looking new longer. That is why Woolite is the country's top name in fine fabric care.

Although many people entrust their fine washables—from silk to wool to cashmere—to dry cleaning shops, it takes only one ruined sweater to realize that the process can be lethal to delicate fabrics. This is where Woolite comes in. With a minimum of effort, a capful of Woolite will help protect those favorite garments from common damages ranging from stretching and shrinking to fading and color bleeding. Woolite can be used in washing machines as well, and is equally effective by hand and in the spinner. Woolite comes in a variety of packaging, from smaller bottles intended for convenient hand washing to new larger 50- and 75-ounce containers suitable for the laundry room and larger batches of clothing to be tackled. Woolite has a Web site, Woolite.com, which provides guidelines for use and expert tips and suggestions available to consumers around the clock. The site also features fashion trends straight off the runway, cognizant of the fact that those who own and wear designer clothes need to wash them and might be seeking inspiration. There is also an interactive feature providing information on how to use the washing machine to treat beloved clothing with the help of Woolite.

Today, most clothing is machine washable, even items reserved for special occasions. With the assistance of the country's classic washing liquid—and the modern convenience of the washing machine—those who desire to do so can care for the vast majority of their clothing without leaving home. The Woolite collection includes other products as well, from Woolite Dark Laundry to the newest addition, Woolite For All Colors, which not only prevents fading, but also allows consumers to wash all colored clothes in one single load, without further sorting and bleeding effects.

With the help of Reckitt Benckiser, Woolite is poised to remain a household staple well into the 21st century. In fact, because of the recent addition of the larger laundry room-sized packaging, it is likely that Woolite's presence is increasing nationwide. Although Reckitt Benckiser is the world's number-one producer of household cleaning products, and can lay claim to beloved products such as Lysol, Electrasol, and French's Mustard, Woolite is one of the company's proudest brands. What won't Woolite do? It won't shrink, discolor, stretch, fade, or damage your clothing in any way. Now available all over the world, and online to boot, Woolite—around for more than half a century and counting—is more than ready for the cleanest of futures.

Vital Statistics

Parent Company Reckitt Benckiser Inc.

MACHINE USE
Clothes look like new!
FABRIC WASH
Woolite®
ORIGINAL

Wm. Wrigley Jr. Company

Launched more than 110 years ago, the Wm. Wrigley Jr. Company is the largest chewing-gum manufacturer in the world, producing almost half of the chewing gum sold in the United States and Europe. Its most famous brands, including Juicy Fruit, Doublemint, Big Red, and Wrigley's Spearmint, have enviable name recognition and durability, and the company's other brands, including Extra and Winterfresh, have firmly established themselves in niche markets.

Remarkably, fourth-generation William Wrigley Jr. is the company's current president and CEO, continuing to build on his family's tradition of constant innovation. In 1891, at the age of 29, the first William Wrigley Jr. moved to Chicago to set up a midwestern branch of his father's soap business. To spur sales, he offered a customer incentive of free baking soda with a soap purchase. He soon discovered that baking soda was a more popular product than soap, so he left the soap business for the baking soda business. Shortly thereafter, he began offering free chewing gum as a customer incentive, and within two years his business took another ironic turn.

Wrigley had seen chewing gum as a young soap peddler and suggested to their supplier that it try making gum with chicle, a coagulated latex extract from tropical sapodilla trees used in the manufacture of rubber. The process worked, and in 1893, Wrigley's Spearmint was created, along with Juicy Fruit later that year. Both brands were sold in a package featuring a design that endures today. In 1898, Wrigley merged with Zeno Manufacturing to form Wm. Wrigley Jr. & Co. Struggling with advertising, he trained his salesmen to "Tell 'em quick and tell 'em often," and by 1910, sales had increased to more than $3 million and Wrigley's Spearmint was the best-selling gum in America. In 1914, Wrigley added a peppermint flavor, Doublemint, which was marketed as "double strength," "double good," and "double distilled," and which led to the world-renowned Doublemint Twins, one of the most successful and long-lasting advertising campaigns ever created. In 1916, Wrigley was rich enough to buy a share in the Chicago Cubs baseball team and then buy out his partners' interests. Before he died in 1932, he also bought Santa Catalina Island and turned it into a wildly popular tourist destination. His only son, Philip K. Wrigley, became the company's president after his death.

Gum production was scaled back during World War II, but sales were climbing again by the 1960s, when Wrigley launched a successful campaign aimed at ending social prejudice against gum chewing, which had risen in the conservative 1950s. Freedent and Big Red appeared in the 1970s, and Philip's son William became president of the company in 1977, reaching out to kids with brands such as Hubba Bubba. The company spent the 1990s focused on growing international markets but introduced Winterfresh in 1994 in another successful attempt to jump-start American sales. Fourth-generation William Wrigley Jr. became CEO in 2001.

Today, Bill Wrigley is known to the industry as a savvy risk-taker and Chicago's famous Wrigley building is a distinctive fixture of city's skyline. Wrigley is a regular on the Forbes 400 list, with a $3.4 billion fortune, and controls 74 percent of the company's voting stock.

Vital Statistics

Classic Product	Doublemint Gum
Established	1891
Founder	William Wrigley Jr.
Employees	14,300 (2005)
Annual Sales	$4,686 million (2006)

Xbox

When 19-year-old Harvard dropout Bill Gates founded Microsoft in 1975 with his friend Paul Allen, he probably did not envision the effect his company was to have on the lives of millions of video game addicts at the turn of the century. Today, Gates runs the world's leading software company, used in homes and offices everywhere, and Microsoft is responsible for giving the world the Xbox, which has become a buzzword for teenage boys and other gaming aficionados. Although Xbox is young, its future seems limitless as the company gears up to challenge its competition. As far as Gates is concerned, Xbox is a key to securing the next generation of Microsoft users.

The Xbox made its auspicious debut at a fitting location: the November 2001 issue of *Wired* magazine, a favorite with gamers. Xbox had been in the works for a few years, having been developed by a team of designers, including Seamus Blackley. Blackley was a physicist as well as a game developer, in whom Gates held great confidence. In fact, Gates had been teasing the media since 1999 that a gaming/multimedia device poised to conquer the world of digital entertainment was soon to be released. Finally, in 2000, it was confirmed: Microsoft issued a formal press release announcing its "Xbox project." Video games were perceived, and rightly so, as a growing threat to PCs, which had game offerings but nothing that could compare to the variety and graphics and equipment of the specialty devices. As always, Gates was also preoccupied with diversifying Microsoft products and expanding beyond software, which had long been its focus and largest earner. When it appeared in stores, the initial Xbox was a marvel. It featured a technologically sophisticated GeForce 3 equivalent graphics processor, a built-in Ethernet adapter, and Dolby Digital 5.1 sound. It allowed users to play hundreds of games designed explicitly for Microsoft, but also enabled them to watch movies and listen to music. The games encompassed every genre, from action and adventure to racing, sports, and fantasy. Some of the most popular titles were—and remain—Halo, Halo 2, Full Spectrum Warrior, Dead or Alive, DOOM 3, and Fable. Some franchised hits include Grand Theft Auto, Need for Speed, and sports titles such as Madden NFL 2005. Most recently, Xbox Live has revolutionized the gaming world, allowing users to compete against gamers worldwide. With Xbox Live, consumers can download new content in their own homes and "chat" about strategies, failures, and successes.

Xbox is ready to take on the world with new developments such as the DVD Movie Playback Kit, which transforms an Xbox into a home entertainment center, and a built-in hard drive that allows users to store and play back songs. Pleasing anxious parents, Xbox is the only gaming device available with adult controls, so that parents can limit violent or otherwise inappropriate content for children. And Microsoft, as always, is keeping up with the trends of the culture, with games showcasing Harry Potter and Shrek for its youngest fans.

Vital Statistics
Parent Company Microsoft Game Studios
Product Launch 2001
Founder Bill Gates

X Games

When you're seeking a thrill but want to stay safe at home on your sofa, tune in to the X Games. X Games, a multisport event that focuses on action sports such as skateboarding, snowboarding, surfing, motocross, BMX, and rally car racing, is aired twice a year in the winter and summer by ESPN and ABC. First broadcast in 1995, the event was considered countercultural and its participants extreme and outrageous. Now, as these sports have become increasingly popular and mainstream, the X Games are being watched by young and old alike.

X Games competitors vie for gold, silver, and bronze medals in the categories of BMX, Moto X, skateboarding, surfing, rally car racing, skiing, snowboarding, and snowmobiling. These sports have been called extreme sports, or action sports, because they feature speed, height, risk, a high level of physical exertion, stunts, or all of the above. They also tend to be individual rather than team sports.

Usually dominated by young athletes, extreme sports play an increasingly important role in the development of youth culture, including clothing, video games, and music. The X Games, though primarily a sporting event, takes on the atmosphere of a festival, with live music and plenty of opportunities to interact with the athletes.

The status of the X Games has made it the place of choice for athletes who want to showcase a never-before-seen stunt or attempt to break a record. In fact, regardless of whether they actually execute the trick, athletes are cheered wildly simply for attempting something new. Creativity and boldness are the most revered traits in an X Games competitor.

Tony Hawk landed the 900, a midair 900-degree spin on a skateboard that had never before been done, at X Games Five in 1999. Not only does the trick require remarkable skill, but Hawk showed unbelievable perseverance. It took him 12 tries to land it, well past the time allowed in the rules. But as one announcer said, "We make up the rules as we go along. Let's give him another try." None of the other contestants protested, and Hawk won the Best Trick competition easily.

ESPN, Inc. pioneered the concept of the X Games, and advertisers quickly saw the potential to reach young viewers. As a result, both competitors and organizers are reaping the benefits. The network, which began as an alternative to standard sports news broadcasts and newspapers, is now the leading cable sports broadcaster with seven domestic networks. It reaches 89 million U.S. homes and is broadcast in another 190 countries. Originally called the Entertainment and Sports Programming Network, it was formed in 1979 and acquired in 1984 by the American Broadcasting Company, which is now part of the Walt Disney Company. The franchise includes a Web site and theme restaurants.

Vital Statistics
First X Games 1995
First Winter X Games 1997
Athletes per Event over 250
Employees 2,600

ESPN
HOME DEPOT
TOYOTA DEALERS
Coca-Cola
73
2

Yankee Candle

The Yankee Candle Company, Inc. is the nation's leading designer, manufacturer, wholesaler, and retailer of premium scented candles, as well as a designer and marketer or proprietary candle accessories, home fragrance products, and scented home care items.

The year was 1969, and 16-year-old Michael Kittredge decided to make his mother a candle for Christmas. He melted some crayons and poured the mixture into a milk carton, pulling the wick from an ordinary taper he found in the house. When a neighbor stopped by and admired his handiwork, Kittredge sold it to them and crafted a replacement for his mother. After that initial sale, Kittredge began selling candles to friends, then to local gift shops, making his candles in his parents' garage in South Hadley, Massachusetts. In 1974, he set up shop in a former paper mill. By 1983, Yankee Candle had more than 30 employees and moved to a larger space in South Deerfield, Massachusetts. Yankee Candle continued to grow, with 150 employees and 40,000 square feet of factory space by 1987, as well as distribution throughout the United States and Canada. The early 1990s saw expansion of the Yankee Candle stores, with 20 opening along the Eastern Seaboard in 1995 alone. That same year, a restaurant—candlelit, of course—was added to the company's flagship store, along with a car museum to appeal to noncandle lovers brought along for the ride. In 1996, Kittredge stepped down to chairman, and Michael Parry became the company's president; Parry was made CEO in 1998, the year an investment firm called Forstmann Little & Co. purchased 90 percent of Yankee Candle for $400 million. With the new influx of funds, Yankee Candle was able to expand even more, modernizing its warehouses and starting distribution in European markets. In 1999, Yankee Candle went public and opened dozens of new stores. Parry retired as CEO and was succeeded in 2001 by Craig Rydin, who became chairman of the board in 2003, when Kittredge resigned, retaining the title of chairman emeritus.

The Yankee Candle name is the most highly recognized brand of any premium scented candle manufacturer. The company's hundreds of products come in numerous varieties, including Housewarmer Jar Candles, Samplers Votive Candles, Tarts Wax Potpourri, Scented Tea Lights, and Electric Home Fragrancers. Their scents include fruit fragrances such as Berry Bramble and Vanilla Lime, food fragrances such as Apple Cider and White Chocolate Mint, floral fragrances like Lavender and Sweet Honeysuckle, fresh fragrances like Aloe Vera and Willow Breeze, and festive fragrances like Christmas Cookie and Sparkling Pine. Recent additions to their product line include a reed diffuser and a moving musical windmill wax potpourri burner. Yankee Candle also makes Car Gel and Car Jar air fresheners, specially blended with odor eliminating agents to combat annoying odors n cars and at home.

Yankee has a 36 year history of offering distinctive products and marketing them as affordable luxuries and consumable gifts. The Company sells its candles through a North American wholesale customer network of approximately 17,250 store locations, a growing base of Company owned and operated retail stores (385 located in 42 states as of July 1, 2006), direct mail catalogs, its Web site, yankeecandle.com, international distributors, and to a European wholesale customer network of approximately 2,340 store locations (through its distribution center located in Bristol, England).

Vital Statistics
Founder Michael Kittredge
Employees 3,100
Annual Sales $601.2 million (2005)

YANKEE CANDLE
COUNTRY LINEN
housewarmer candle
YANKEE CANDLE
COUNTRY LINEN
housewarmer candle
our strongest scented candle
YANKEE CANDLE
housewarmer
electric home fragrancer
COUNTRY LINEN
Adjustable fragrance strength

Zatarain's

Of all America's great food cities, New Orleans is possibly the most celebrated and beloved, and most Americans have tasted some of its regional specialties even if they have never actually visited the Big Easy itself. For more than a century, Zatarain's has been helping people all over the country savor the distinctive taste of New Orleans, from rice and pasta dishes to seasoning blends and spices designed to allow home cooks to re-create the magic themselves.

In 1889, a New Orleans man named Emile A. Zatarain got himself a product trademark and began to make a local favorite beverage: root beer. When the root beer proved popular, Zatarain added mustards, pickled vegetables, and various extracts to his repertoire. These products led to the development of Zatarain's classic spice combinations, affording home cooks nationwide the ability to make authentic New Orleans dishes in their own kitchens. In 1963, Zatarain and his family sold the business, which relocated to Gretna, Louisiana. The company continued to expand, and the product line grew to contain rice dinner mixes, pasta dinner mixes, breadings, seasoning and spices, seafood boils, stuffing mixes, and more. Zatarain's has helped build brand recognition by maintaining an extremely active presence in greater New Orleans. The company supports a number of organizations, events, and programs in the city, including the New Orleans Jazz & Heritage Festival. Zatarain's sponsors the festival's Cajun Cabin and Food Heritage Stage, where local chefs prepare Cajun and Creole dishes for the crowd. The festival greets half a million visitors annually. Zatarain's also sponsors the French Quarter Fest's Cajun & Zydeco Music Stage, which showcases local musicians and music from jazz to classical, Cajun to zydeco, rhythm and blues to gospel, and more. Zatarain's gets involved with the more than 60 food and beverage booths to further satisfy the music fans who flock to the scene. And finally, Zatarain's is a significant supporter of New Orleans' minor-league baseball team, the New Orleans Zephyrs.

Today, Zatarain's operates under the auspices of powerful parent company McCormick & Company, Inc., which purchased it from Citigroup Venture Capital and other investors for $180 million in 2003. McCormick has high hopes for its acquisition, which was a natural fit because of McCormick's pledge to give consumers the very best in flavors for food. Zatarain's was and remains America's number-one national brand when it comes to New Orleans–style cooking and prepared foods. Each year, company sales grow and surpass the numbers from the previous year. Zatarain's headquarters have stayed put just outside New Orleans, where the company can keep a metaphorical finger on the pulse of the city that created it more than 100 years ago. McCormick's has no intention of moving Zatarain's from its birthplace, although it does aspire to bring jambalaya and gumbo to an even greater number of cooks around the world. Zatarain's is also continuing its tradition of doing good, with its massive contributions to the Hurricane Katrina relief efforts. The company donated more than 100,000 prepared meals for those in need and gave much-appreciated financial support to its area employees.

Vital Statistics
Parent Company McCormick & Company, Inc.
Product Launch 1889
Employees 8,000

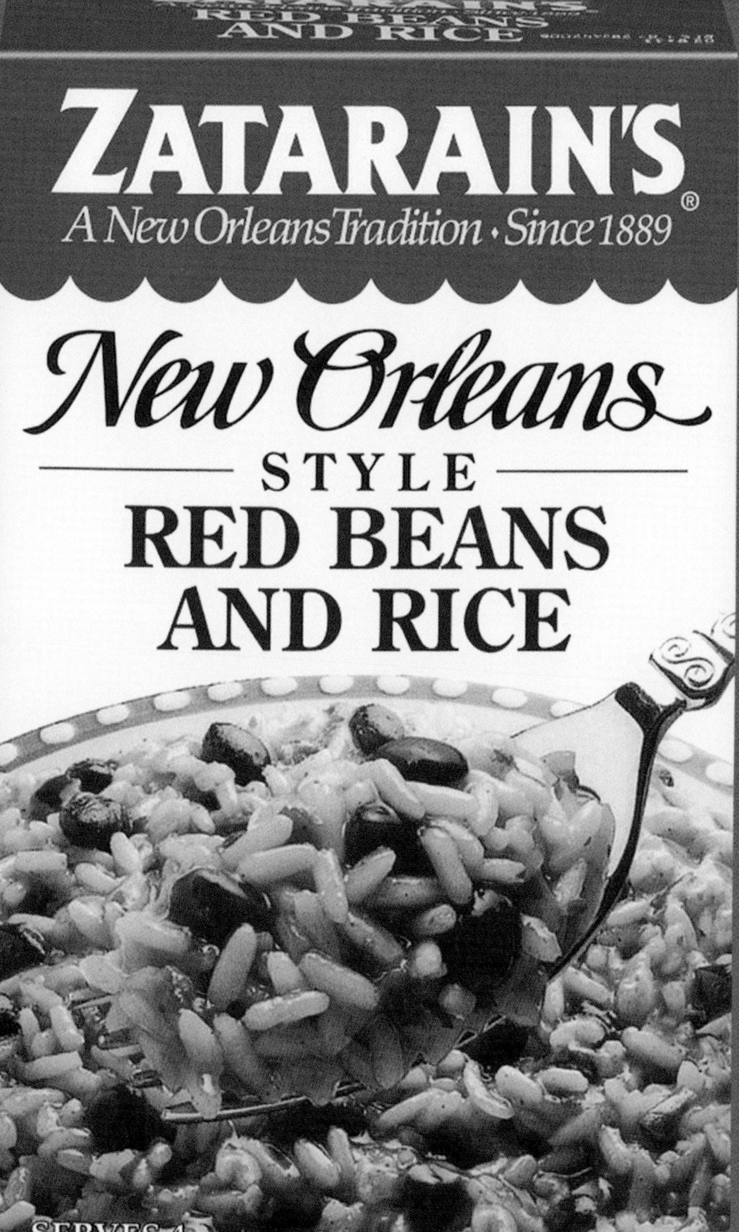
RED BEANS
AND RICE
ZATARAIN'S
A New Orleans Tradition • Since 1889®
New Orleans
STYLE
RED BEANS
AND RICE
SERVES 4
SERVING SUGGESTION
NET WT. 8 OZ.(227g)

Index

7-Eleven
2711 North Haskell Avenue
Dallas, TX 75204
214-828-7011
www.7-eleven.com

Ace Hardware
2200 Kensington Court
Oak Brook, IL 60523
630-990-6600
www.acehardware.com

Adobe Systems Incorporated
345 Park Avenue
San Jose, CA 95110
408-536-6000
www.adobe.com

Advil
Wyeth
5 Giralda Farms
Madison, NJ 07940
973-660-5000
www.advil.com

Airstream, Inc.
419 West Pike Street
Jackson Center, OH 45334
937-596-6111
www.airstream.com

Alka-Seltzer
Bayer Corporation
100 Bayer Road
Pittsburgh, PA 15205-9741
412-777-2000
www.alkaseltzer.com

American Girl, Inc.
8400 Fairway Place
Middleton, WI 53562
608-836-4848
www.americangirl.com

American Express Company
World Financial Center
200 Vesey Street
New York, NY 10285
212-640-2000
www.home.americanexpress.com

Andersen Corporation
100 4th Avenue North
Bayport, MN 55003
651-264-5150
www.andersenwindows.com

Annie's Homegrown, Inc.
564 Gateway Drive
Napa, CA 94558
707-254-3700
www.annies.com

Arm & Hammer
Church & Dwight Co., Inc.
469 North Harrison Street
Princeton, NJ 08543
609-683-5900
www.armandhammer.com

Aveda
The Esteé Lauder Companies Inc.
767 5th Avenue
New York, NY 10153
212-572-4200
www.aveda.com

Avery Dennison Corporation
150 North Orange Grove Boulevard
Pasadena, CA 91103
626-304-2000
www.avery.com

Band-Aid
Johnson & Johnson
1 Johnson & Johnson Plaza
New Brunswick, NJ 08933
732-524-0400
www.band-aid.com

Ben & Jerry's Homemade
30 Community Drive
South Burlington, VT 05403
802-846-1500
www.benandjerrys.com

Benjamin Moore & Co.
51 Chestnut Ridge Road
Montvale, NJ 07645
201-573-9600
www.benjaminmoore.com

Best Buy Co., Inc.
7601 Penn Avenue South
Richfield, MN 55423
612-291-1000
www.bestbuy.com

Betty Crocker
General Mills, Inc.
One General Mills Boulevard
Minneapolis, MN 55426
763-764-7600
www.bettycrocker.com

Birdhouse Skateboards
Blitz Distribution
15272 Jason Circle
Huntington Beach, CA 92649
714-379-0020
www.birdhouseskateboards.com

The Black & Decker Corporation
701 East Joppa Road
Towson, MD 21286
410-716-3900
www.blackanddecker.com

Bounce
The Procter & Gamble Company
1 Procter and Gamble Plaza
Cincinatti, OH 45202
513-83-1100
www.pg.com

Brooks Brothers
346 Madison Avenue
New York, NY 10017
212-682-8800
www.brooksbrothers.com

W. Atlee Burpee & Company
300 Park Avenue
Warminster, PA 18974
215-674-4900
www.burpee.com

Butterball
ConAgra Foods, Inc.
1 ConAgra Drive
Omaha, NE 68102
402-95-4000
www.butterball.com

Cadillac
General Motors Corporation
300 Renaissance Center
Detroit, MI 48265
313-556-5000
www.cadillac.com

Callaway Golf Company
2180 Rutherford Road
Carlsbad, CA 92008
760-931-1771
www.callawaygolf.com

Calphalon
Ampoint Industrial Park
3rd & D Street
Perrysburg, OH 43551
419-666-8700
www.calphalon.com

Campbell Soup Company
1 Campbell Plaza
Camden, NJ 08103
856-342-4800
www.campbellsoup.com

Cannondale Bicycle Corporation
16 Trowbridge Drive
Bethel, CT 06801
203-749-7000
www.cannondale.com

Carnival Corporation
3655 NW 87th Avenue
Miami, FL 33178
305-599-2600
www.carnivalcruise.com

Carrier Corporation
1 Carrier Place
Farmington, CT 06034
860-674-3000
www.carrier.com

Century 21 Real Estate LLC
1 Campus Drive
Parsippany, NJ 07054
877-221-2765
www.century21.com

Champion Spark Plugs USA
Federal-Mogul Corporation
26555 Northwestern Highway
Southfield, MI 48034
248-354-7700
www.federalmogul.com

Chapstick
Wyeth
5 Giralda Farms
Madison, NJ 07940
973-660-5500
www.chapstick.com

Charmin
The Procter & Gamble Company
1 Procter & Gamble Plaza
Cincinatti, OH 45202
513-983-1100
www.charmin.com

Chef Boyardee
Conagra Foods, Inc.
1 ConAgra Drive
Omaha, NE 68102
402-595-4000
www.chefboyardee.com

Chevrolet
30007 Van Dyke Avenue
Warren, MI 48093
810-492-8841
www.chevrolet.com

Chicken of the Sea
Tri-Union Seafoods, LLC
9330 Scranton Road, Suite 500
San Diego, CA 92121
858-558-9662
www.chickenofthesea.com

Citibank
399 Park Avenue
New York, NY 10022
212-627-3999
www.citibank.com

Claritin
Schering-Plough Corporation
2000 Galloping Hill Road
Kenilworth, NJ 07033
908-298-4000
www.claritin.com

Claussen
Kraft Foods North America
3 Lakes Drive
Northfield, IL 60093
847-646-2000
www.kraftfoods.com/cla

Coach, Inc.
516 West 34th Street
New York, NY 10001
212-594-1850
www.coach.com

The Coca-Cola Company
1 Coca-Cola Plaza
Atlanta, GA 30313
404-676-2121
www.cocacola.com

The Coleman Company, Inc.
3600 North Hydraulic
Wichita, KS 67219
316-832-2700
www.coleman.com

Colgate-Palmolive Company
300 Park Avenue
New York, NY 10022
212-310-2000
www.colgate.com

Conair Corporation
150 Milford Road
East Windsor, NJ 08520
609-426-1300
www.conair.com

Converse Inc.
1 High Street
North Andover, MA 01845
978-983-3300
www.converse.com

Coppertone
Schering-Plough Corporation
2000 Galloping Hill Road
Kenilworth, NJ 07033
908-298-4000
www.coppertone.com

CorningWare
WKI Holdings Company, Inc.
11911 Freedom Drive, Suite 600
Reston, VA 20190
703-456-4700
www.corningware.com

Costco Wholesale Corporation
999 Lake Drive
Issaquah, WA 98027
425-313-8100
www.costco.com

Crane & Co.
30 South Street
Dalton, MA 01226
413-684-2600
www.crane.com

A. T. Cross Company
1 Albion Road
Lincoln, RI 02865
401-333-1200
www.cross.com

Dawn
The Procter & Gamble Company
1 Procter and Gamble Plaza
Cincinatti, OH 45202
513-983-1100
www.dawn-dish.com

Dell Inc.
One Dell Way
Round Rock, TX 78682
512-338-4400
www.dell.com

Diane von Furstenberg
389 West 12th Street
New York, NY 10014
212-741-6607
www.dvf.com

Diaper Genie
Playtex Products, Inc.
300 Nyala Farms Road
Westport, CT 06880
203-341-4000
www.diapergenie.com

Dixie
Georgia-Pacific Corporation
133 Peachtree Street NE
Atlanta, GA 30303
404-652-4000
www.dixie.com

Dole Food Company, Inc.
1 Dole Drive
Westlake Village, CA 91362
818-879-6600
www.dole.com

Domino's Pizza, Inc.
30 Frank Lloyd Wright Drive
Ann Arbor, MI 48106
734-930-3030
www.dominos.com

Dove
Unilever Cosmetics International
700 Sylvan Avenue
Englewood Cliffs, NJ 07632
201-894-4000
www.dove.com

Dr. Bronner's Magic Soaps
751 North Citracado Parkway
Escondido, CA 92029
www.drbronner.com

Drano
S.C. Johnson & Son, Inc.
1525 Howe Street
Racine, WI 53403
262-260-2000
www.drano.com

Electronic Arts Inc.
209 Redwood Shores Parkway
Redwood City, CA 94065
650-628-1500
www.ea.com

Energizer Holdings, Inc.
533 Maryville University Drive
Street Louis, MO 63141
314-985-2000
www.energizer.com

e.p.t.
Johnson & Johnson
1 Johnson & Johnson Plaza
New Brunswick, NJ 08933
732-524-0400
www.pfizerch.com

Ethan Allen Interiors, Inc.
Ethan Allen Drive
Danbury, CT 06811
203-743-8000
www.ethanallen.com

The Evercare Company
3440 Preston Ridge Road
Suite 650
Alpharetta, GA 30005
770-570-5000
www.helmac.com

Exxon-Mobil Corporation
5959 Las Colinas Boulevard
Irving, TX 75039
972-444-1000
www.exxonmobil.com

Febreze
The Procter & Gamble Company
1 Procter & Gamble Plaza
Cincinatti, OH 45202
513-983-1100
www.febreze.com

Fidelity Investments
82 Devonshire Street
Boston, MA 02109
617-563-7000
www.fidelity.com

Fiesta
The Homer Laughlin China Company
672 Fiesta Drive
Newell, WV 26050
304-387-1300
ww.hlchina.com

Folger's
The Procter & Gamble Company
1 Proctor & Gamble Plaza
Cincinatti, OH 45202
513-983-1100
www.folgers.com

Ford Motor Company
1 American Road
Dearborn, MI 48126
313-322-3000
www.ford.com

French's
Reckitt Benckiser, Inc.
399 Interpace Parkway
Parsippany, NJ 07054
973-404-2600
www.frenchsmustard.com

Frigidaire
Electrolux Home Products—North America
250 Bobby Jones Expressway
Augusta, GA 30907
706-651-1751
www.frigidaire.com

E. & J. Gallo Winery
600 Yosemite Boulevard
Modesto, CA 95354
209-341-3111
www.gallo.com

The Gap, Inc.
2 Folsom Street
San Francisco, CA 94105
650-952-4400
www.gap.com

The Gatorade Company
555 West Monroe Street
Chicago, IL 60661
312-222-7111
www.gatorade.com

General Electric Company
3135 Easton Turnpike
Fairfield, CT 06828-0001
203-373-2211
www.ge.com

Government Employees Insurance Company (GEICO)
5260 Western Avenue
Chevy Chase, MD 20815
301-986-3000
www.geico.com

George Foreman
Salton, Inc.
1955 West Field Court
Lake Forest, IL 60045
847-803-4600
www.saltoninc.com

Gerber Products Company
200 Kimball Drive
Parsippany, NJ 07054
973-503-8000
www.gerber.com

Gibson Guitar Corp.
309 Plus Park Boulevard
Nashville, TN 37217
615-871-4500
www.gibson.com

Global Gillette
Prudential Tower Building
Boston, MA 02199
617-421-7000
www.gillette.com

Glaceau
Energy Brands Inc.
1720 Whitestone Expressway
Whitestone, NY 11357
718-746-0087
www.glaceau.com

Gold's Gym International, Inc.
125 East John Carpenter Freeway, Suite 1300
Irving, TX 75062
214-574-4653
www.goldsgym.com

Goldfish
Pepperidge Farm, Inc.
595 Westport Avenue
Norwalk, CT 06851
203-846-7000
www.pfgoldfish.com

The Goodyear Tire & Rubber Company
1144 East Market Street
Akron, OH 44316
330-796-2121
www.goodyear.com

Google Inc.
1600 Amphitheatre Parkway
Mountain View, CA 94043
650-253-0000
www.google.com

Goya Foods, Inc.
100 Seaview Drive
Secaucus, NJ 07096
201-348-4900
www.goya.com

Greyhound Lines, Inc.
P.O. Box 660689, MS 490
Dallas, TX 75266
972-789-7000
www.greyhound.com

H&R Block, Inc.
4400 Main Street
Kansas City, MO 64111
816-753-6900
www.hrblock.com

Hallmark Cards, Inc.
2501 McGee Street
Kansas City, MO 64108
816-274-5111
www.hallmark.com

Harley-Davidson, Inc.
3700 West Juneau Avenue
Milwaukee, WI 53208
414-342-4680
www.harley-davidson.com

Harrah's Entertainment, Inc.
One Harrah's Court
Las Vegas, NV 89119
702-407-6000
www.harrahs.com

Harvard University
University Hall
Cambridge, MA 02138
617-495-1000
www.harvard.edu

Home Box Office, Inc.
1100 Avenue of the Americas
New York, NY 10036
212-512-1000
www.hbo.com

H.J. Heinz Company
600 Grant Street
Pittsburgh, PA 15219
412-456-5700
www.heinz.com

Hellman's
Unilever United States, Inc.
700 Sylvan Avenue
Englewood Cliffs, NJ 07632
201-894-4000
www.mayo.com

The Hershey Company
100 Crystal A Drive
Hershey, PA 17033
717-534-6799
www.hersheys.com

Hertz Global Holdings, Inc.
225 Brae Boulevard
Park Ridge, NJ 07656
201-307-2000
www.hertz.com

Hewlett-Packard Company
3000 Hanover Street
Palo Alto, CA 94304
650-857-1501
www.hp.com

The Home Depot, Inc.
2455 Paces Ferry Road NW
Atlanta, GA 30339
770-433-8211
www.homedepot.com

The Hoover Company
TTI Floor Care North America
7005 Cochran Road
Glenwillow, Ohio 44139
330-499-9499
www.hoover.com

Igloo Products Corp.
777 Igloo Road
Katy, TX 77494
713-584-6900
www.igloocoolers.com

iPod
Apple Inc.
1 Infinite Loop
Cupertino, CA 95014
408-996-1010
www.apple.com

Iron Horse Ranch & Vineyards LLC
9786 Ross Station Road
Sebastopol, CA 95472
707-887-1507
www.ironhorsevineyards.com

J. Crew Group, Inc.
770 Broadway
New York, NY 10003
212-209-2500
www.jcrew.com

Jack Daniel's
Brown-Forman Corporation
850 Dixie Highway
Louisville, KY 40210
502-585-1100
www.jackdaniels.com

Jell-O
Kraft Foods North America
3 Lakes Drive
Northfield, IL 60093
847-646-2000
www.kraftfoods.com/jello

Jelly Belly Candy Company
One Jelly Belly Lane
Fairfield, CA 94533
707-428-2800
www.jellybelly.com

Jet Blue Airways Corporation
118-29 Queens Boulevard
Forest Hills, NY 11375
718-286-7900
www.jetblue.com

Johnson & Johnson
1 Johnson & Johnson Plaza
New Brunswick, NJ 08933
732-524-0400
www.jnj.com

K2 Inc.
5818 El Camino Real
Carlsbad, CA 92008
760-494-1000
www.k2skis.com

Kellogg Company
1 Kellogg Square
Battle Creek, MI 49016-3599
800-962-1413
www.kelloggs.com

Kenneth Cole Productions, Inc.
603 West 50th Street
New York, NY 10019
212-265-1500
www.kennethcole.com

Kiehl's Since 1851 LLC
L'Oréal USA, Inc.
575 5th Avenue
New York, NY 10017
212-818-1500
www.kiehls.com

Kleenex
Kimberly-Clark Corporation
351 Phelps Drive
Irving, TX 75038
972-281-1200
www.kleenex.com

Eastman Kodak Company
343 State Street
Rochester, NY 14650
800-698-3324
www.kodak.com

Kohler Co.
444 Highland Drive
Kohler, WI 53044
920-457-4441
ww.kohler.com

Kool-Aid
Kraft Foods North America
3 Lakes Drive
Northfield, IL 60093
847-646-2000
www.kraftfoods.com/koolaid

Krazy Glue
Elmer's Products, Inc.
1 Easton Oval
Columbus, OH 43219
614-985-2633
www.krazyglue.com

Lawn Boy
The Toro Company
8111 Lyndale Avenue South
Bloomington, MN 55420
952-888-8801
www.lawn-boy.com

Lay's
Frito-Lay, Inc.
7701 Legacy Drive
Plano, TX 75024
972-334-7000
www.lays.com

La-Z-Boy Incorporated
1284 North Telegraph Road
Monroe, MI 48162
734-242-1444
www.la-z-boy.com

Levi Strauss & Co.
1155 Battery Street
San Francisco, CA 94111
415-501-6000
www.levi.com

Life Saver
Wm. Wrigley Jr. Company
410 North Michigan Avenue
Chicago, IL 60611
312-644-2121
www.wrigley.com

Lillian Vernon Corporation
2600 International Parkway
Virginia Beach, VA 23452
757-427-7700
www.lillianvernon.com

Lipitor
Pfizer, Inc.
235 East 42nd Street
New York, NY 10017
212-573-2323
www.lipitor.com

Lipton
Unilever United States, Inc.
700 Sylvan Avenue
Englewood Cliffs, NJ 07632
201-894-4000
www.lipton.com

Listerine
Johnson & Johnson
1 Johnson & Johnson Plaza
New Brunswick, NJ 08933
732-524-0400
www.listerine.com

L.L. Bean, Inc.
15 Casco Street
Freeport, ME 04033
207-865-4761
www.llbean.com

M&M'S
Mars, Incorporated
6885 Elm Street
McLean, VA 22101
703-821-4900
www.m-ms.com

Macy's
Federated Department Stores, Inc.
7 West 7th Street
Cincinatti, OH 45202
513-579-7000
www.macys.com

Maidenform Brands, Inc.
154 Avenue E
Bayonne, NJ 07002
201-436-9200
www.maidenform.com

Manischewitz
R.A.B. Food Group, LLC
1 Harmon Plaza
Secaucus, NJ 07094
201-333-3700
www.manischewitz.com

MasterLock Company
137 West Forest Hill Avenue
Oak Creek, WI 53154
414-444-2800
www.masterlock.com

Match.com LP
8300 Douglas Avenue
Suite 800
Dallas, TX 75225
214-576-9352
www.match.com

Maytag Dairy Farms Inc
2282 East 8th Street North
Newton, IA 50208
641-792-1133
www.maytagdairyfarms.com

McCulloch Motors Inc
12802 Leffingwell Road
Santa Fe Springs, CA 90670
562-926-9699
www.mccullochpower.com

McDonald's Corporation
2111 McDonald's Drive
Oak Brook, IL 60523
630-623-3000
www.mcdonalds.com

MeadWestvaco Corporation
1 High Ridge Park
Stamford, CT 06905
203-461-7400
www.meadwestvaco.com

The Meow Mix Company
400 Plaza Drive
Secaucus, NJ 07094
201-520-4000
www.meowmix.com

Milk-Bone
Del Monte Foods Company
One Market @ The Landmark
San Francisco, CA 94105
415-247-3000
www.milkbone.com

Monopoly
Hasbro, Inc.
1027 Newport Avenue
Pawtucket, RI 02862
401-431-8697
www.monopoly.com

Monster Worldwide, Inc.
622 3rd Avenue, 39th Floor
New York, NY 10017
212-351-7000
www.monster.com

Morton International, Inc.
123 North Wacker Drive
Chicago, IL 60606
312-807-2000
www.mortonsalt.com

Motorola, Inc.
1303 East Algonquin Road
Schaumburg, IL 60196
847-576-5000
www.motorola.com

Mr. Clean
The Procter & Gamble Company
1 Proctor & Gamble Plaza
Cincinatti, OH 45202
513-983-1100
www.mrclean.com

Nalgene
Thermo Fisher Scientific
81 Wyman Street
Waltham, MA 02454-9046
781-622-1000
www.nalgene-outdoor.com

New York City Transit Authority
2 Broadway
New York, NY 10004
718-330-3000
www.mta.info/index.html

New York Yankees Partnership
Yankee Stadium
East 161st Street and River Avenue
Bronx, NY 10452
718-293-4300
www.yankees.mlb.com

Newman's Own, Inc.
246 Post Road East
Westport, CT 06880
203-222-0136
www.newmansown.com

Nickelodeon Networks
1515 Broadway, 42nd Floor
New York, NY 10036
212-258-7500
www.nickelodeon.com

Nicoderm CQ
GlaxoSmithKline PLC
1 Franklin Plaza
Philadelphia, PA 19101
215-751-4000
www.nicodermcq.com

The North Face, Inc.
2013 Farallon Drive
San Leandro, CA 94577
510-618-3500
www.thenorthface.com

Office Max Incorporated
263 Shuman Boulevard
Naperville, IL 60563
630-438-7800
www.officemax.com

Old Town Canoe Company (Inc)
35 Middle Street
Old Town, ME 04468-1449
207-827-5514
www.oldtowncanoe.com

Omaha Steaks, Inc.
11030 O Street
Omaha, NE 68137
402-597-3000
www.omahasteaks.com

Oneida Ltd.
163-181 Kenwood Avenue
Oneida, NY 13421
315-361-3000
www.oneida.com

Ore-Ida Foods
H.J. Heinz Company
357 6th Avenue
Pittsburgh, PA 15222
412-237-5700
www.oreida.com

Oreo
Kraft Foods North America
3 Lakes Drive
Northfield, IL 60093
847-646-2000
www.nabiscoworld.com/oreo

Oscar Mayer
Kraft Foods Global, Inc.
910 Mayer Avenue
Madison, WI 53704
608-241-3311
www.kraftfoods.com/om

OshKosh B'Gosh, Inc.
112 Otter Avenue
OshKosh, WI 54901
920-231-8800
www.oshkoshbgosh.com

Oster
Jarden Corporation
555 Theodore Fremd Avenue
Suite B-302
Rye, NY 10580
914-967-9400
www.oster.com

Pampers
The Procter & Gamble Company
1 Procter & Gamble Plaza
Cincinnati, OH 45202
513-983-1100
www.pampers.com

Parkay
ConAgra Foods, Inc.
1 ConAgra Drive
Omaha, NE 68102
402-595-4000
www.parkay.com

Patagonia
259 West Santa Clara Street
Ventura, CA 93001
805-643-8616
www.patagonia.com

Poland Spring
Nestlé Waters North America Inc.
777 West Putnam Avenue
Greenwich, CT 06830
203-531-4100
www.polandspring.com

Polaris Industries, Inc.
2100 Highway 55
Medina, MN 55340
763-542-0500
www.polarisindustries.com

Post-it
3M Company
3M Center
St. Paul, MN 55144
651-733-2204
www.3m.com

Prozac
Eli Lilly and Company
Lilly Corporate Center
Indianapolis, IN 46285
317-276-2000
www.prozac.com

Purell
GOJO Industries
One GOJO Plaza
Suite 500
Akron, OH 44311
800-321-9647
www.purell.com

Q-Tip
Unilever United States, Inc.
700 Sylvan Avenue
Englewood Cliffs, NJ 07632
201-894-4000
www.qtips.com

Radio City Music Hall
Madison Square Garden, L.P.
4 Pennsylvania Plaza
New York, NY 10001
212-465-6000
www.radiocity.com

Ragu
Unilever United States, Inc.
700 Sylvan Avenue
Englewood Cliffs, NJ 07632
201-894-4000
www.eat.com

Ralph Lauren Home
Polo Ralph Lauren Corporation
650 Madison Avenue
New York, NY 10022
212-318-7000
www.rlhome.polo.com

Rawlings Sporting Goods Company
510 Maryville University Drive
Suite 110
St. Louis, MO 63141
314-819-2800
www.rawlings.com

Ray-Ban
Luxottica Group
420 Fifth Avenue
New York, NY 10018
212-302-1200
www.ray-ban.com

Red Bull North America Inc.
1740 Stewart Street
Santa Monica, CA 90404
310-393-4647
www.redbullusa.com

Redken
L'Oréal USA, Inc.
575 5th Avenue
New York, NY 10017
212-818-1500
www.redken.com

Right Guard
The Dial Corporation
15501 North Dial Boulevard
Scottsdale, AZ 85260
480-754-3425
www.rightguard.com

Ritz
Kraft Foods North America
3 Lakes Drive
Northfield, IL 60093
847-646-2000
www.nabiscoworld.com/ritz

Rival Crock Pot
Jarden Corporation
555 Theodore Fremd Avenue, Suite B-302
Rye, NY 10580
914-967-9400
www.crockpot.com

Rock and Roll Hall of Fame
1 Key Plaza
Cleveland, OH 44114
216-781-7625
www.rockhall.com

Rolling Stone
Wenner Media LLC
1290 Avenue of the Americas, 2nd Floor
New York, NY 10104
212-484-1616
www.rollingstone.com

Samsonite Corporation
11200 East 45th Avenue
Denver, CO 80239
303-373-2000
www.samsonite.com

Samuel Adams
The Boston Beer Company, Inc.
1 Design Center Place
Suite 850
Boston, MA 02110
617-368-5000
www.samueladams.com

Sara Lee Corporation
3500 Lacey Road
Downers Grove, IL 60515-5424
630-598-8100
www.saralee.com

Saturn Corporation
100 Saturn Parkway
Spring Hill, TN 37174
931-486-5000
www.saturn.com

Scotch Tape
3M Company
3M Center
St. Paul, MN 55144
651-733-2204
www.3m.com

Sealy Corporation
One Office Parkway at Sealy Drive
Trinity, NC 27370
336-861-3500
www.sealy.com

Seventh Generation Inc.
60 Lake Street
Burlington, VT 05401
802-658-3773
www.seventhgeneration.com

Sharpie
Sanford, L.P.
2707 Butterfield Road
Oakbrook, IL 60523
708-547-6650
www.sharpie.com

Singer Sewing Company
1224 Heil Quaker Boulevard
La Vergne, TN 37086
615-213-0880
www.singerco.com

Six Flags, Inc.
122 East 42nd Street
New York, NY 10168
212-652-9403
www.sixflags.com

Slim-Fast Foods Company
Unilever United States, Inc.
700 Sylvan Avenue
Englewood Cliffs, NJ 07632
201-567-8000
www.slim-fast.com

Slinky
Poof-Slinky, Inc.
45400 Helm Street
Plymouth, MI 48170
734-454-9552
www.poof-slinky.com

The J. M. Smucker Company
1 Strawberry Lane
Orrvile, OH 44667
330-682-3000
www.smuckers.com

Snap-On Incorporated
2801 80th Street
Kenosha, WI 53143
262-656-5200
www.snapon.com

Snapple Beverage Corporation
900 King Street
Ryebrook, NY 10573
914-612-4000
www.snapple.com

S.O.S
The Clorox Corporation
1221 Broadway
Oakland, CA 94612
510-271-7000
www.thecloroxcompany.com

Soy Boy
Northern Soy, Inc.
345 Paul Road
Rochester, NY 14624
585-235-8970
www.soyboy.com

Spalding
150 Brookdale Drive
Springfield, MA 01104
800-772-5346
www.spalding.com

Starbucks Corporation
2401 Utah Avenue South
Seattle, WA 98134
206-447-1575
www.starbucks.com

Steinway Musical Instruments, Inc.
800 South Street, Suite 305
Waltham, MA 02453
781-894-9770
www.steinway.com

Stonyfield Farm, Inc.
10 Burton Drive
Londonderry, NH 03053
603-437-4040
www.stonyfield.com

Swingline
ACCO Brands Corporation
300 Tower Parkway
Lincolnshire, IL 60069
847-484-4800
www.swingline.com

Tabasco
McIlhenny Company
Highway 329
Avery Island, LA 70130-6037
337-365-8173
www.tabasco.com

Taco Bell
YUM! Brands, Inc.
1441 Gardiner Lane
Louisville, KY 40213
502-874-8300
www.tacobell.com

Target Corporation
1000 Nicollet Mall
Minneapolis, MN 55403
612-304-6073
www.target.com

Texas Instruments Incorporated
12500 TI Boulevard
Dallas, TX 75243
972-995-2011
www.ti.com

TGI Friday's
Carlson Restaurants Worldwide, Inc.
4201 Marsh Lane
Carrollton, TX 75007
972-662-5400
www.tgifridays.com

Tiffany & Co.
727 Fifth Avenue
New York, NY 10022
212-755-8000
www.tiffany.com

The Timberland Company
200 Domain Drive
Stratham, NH 03885
603-772-9500
www.timberland.com

Timex Corporation
555 Christian Road
Middlebury, CT 06762
203-346-5000
www.timex.com

Tinkertoy
Hasbro, Inc.
10027 Newport Avenue
Pawtucket, RI 02862
401-431-8697
www.hasbro.com/tinkertoy

Tommy Hilfiger U.S.A., Inc.
601 West 26th Street
New York, NY 10001
212-549-6000
www.tommy.com

totes Isotoner Corporation
9655 International Boulevard
Cincinatti, OH 45246
513-682-8200
www.totes-isotoner.com

Travelocity.com LP
3150 Sabre Drive
Southlake, TX 76092
682-605-1000
www.travelocity.com

Tropicana Products, Inc.
1001 13th Avenue East
Bradenton, FL 34208
941-747-4461
www.tropicana.com

Tupperware Brands Corporation
14901 South Orange Blossom Trail
Orlando, FL 32837
407-826-5050
www.tupperware.com

UPS
55 Glenlake Parkway NE
Atlanta, GA 30328
404-828-6000
www.ups.com

Vail Resorts
137 Benchmark Road
Avon, CO 81620
970-476-5601
www.vailresorts.com

Victoria's Secret Stores, Inc.
4 Limited Parkway East
Reynoldsburg, OH 43068
614-577-7000
www.victoriassecret.com

Viking Range Corporation
111 Front Street
Greenwood, MS 38930
662-455-1200
www.vikingrange.com

W Hotels
Starwood Hotels & Resorts Worldwide, Inc.
1111 Westchester Avenue
White Plains, NY 10604
914-640-8100
www.starwoodhotels.com

Walgreen Co.
200 Wilmot Road
Deerfield, IL 60015
847-940-2500
www.walgreens.com

Weber-Stephen Products Co.
200 East Daniels Road
Palatine, IL 60067
847-934-5700
www.weber.com

WebMD
Emdeon Corporation
669 River Drive
Center 2
Elmwood Park, NJ 07407-1361
201-703-3400
www.webmd.com

Wham-O Inc.
5903 Christie Avenue
Emeryville, CA 94608
510-596-4202
www.wham-o.com

Whirlpool Corporation
Administrative Center
2000 North M-63
Benton Harbor, MI 49022
269-923-5000
www.whirlpool.com

Whole Foods Market Inc.
550 Bowie Street
Austin, TX 78703
512-477-4455
www.wholefoodsmarket.com

Williams-Sonoma, Inc.
3250 Van Ness Avenue
San Francisco, CA 94109
415-421-7900
www.williams-sonoma.com

Wilson Sporting Goods Co.
8700 West Bryn Mawr Avenue
Chicago, IL 60631
773-714-6400
www.wilson.com

Wonder
Interstate Bakeries Corporation
12 East Armour Boulevard
Kansas City, MO 64111
816-502-4000
www.wonderbread.com

Woolite
Reckitt Benckiser Inc.
399 Interpace Parkway
Parsippany, NJ 07504
973-404-2600
www.woolite.com

Wm. Wrigley Jr. Company
410 North Michigan Avenue
Chicago, IL 60611
312-644-2121
www.wrigley.com

Xbox
Microsoft Corporation
1 Microsoft Way
Redmond, WA 98052
425-882-8080
www.xbox.com

X-Games
ESPN, Inc.
935 Middle Street
Bristol, CT 06010
860-766-2000
www.expn.go.com

The Yankee Candle Company, Inc.
16 Yankee Candle Way
South Deerfield, MA 01373
413-665-8306
www.yankeecandle.com

Zatarain's
McCormick & Company, Incorporated
18 Loveton Circle
Sparks, MD 21152
410-771-7301
www.zatarain.com